IFIP Advances in Information and Communication Technology 745

IFIP Advances in Information and Communication Technology

The IFIP AICT series publishes state-of-the-art results in the sciences and technologies of information and communication. The scope of the series includes: foundations of computer science; software theory and practice; education; computer applications in technology; communication systems; systems modeling and optimization; information systems; ICT and society; computer systems technology; security and protection in information processing systems; artificial intelligence; and human-computer interaction.

Edited volumes and proceedings of refereed international conferences in computer science and interdisciplinary fields are featured. These results often precede journal publication and represent the most current research.

The principal aim of the IFIP AICT series is to encourage education and the dissemination and exchange of information about all aspects of computing.

More information about this series at https://link.springer.com/bookseries/6102

Lili Nemec Zlatolas · Kai Rannenberg ·
Tatjana Welzer · Joaquin Garcia-Alfaro
Editors

ICT Systems Security and Privacy Protection

40th IFIP International Conference, SEC 2025
Maribor, Slovenia, May 21–23, 2025
Proceedings, Part I

Springer

Editors
Lili Nemec Zlatolas
University of Maribor
Maribor, Slovenia

Tatjana Welzer
University of Maribor
Maribor, Slovenia

Kai Rannenberg
Goethe University Frankfurt
Frankfurt, Germany

Joaquin Garcia-Alfaro
SAMOVAR, Télécom SudParis
Palaiseau, France

ISSN 1868-4238 ISSN 1868-422X (electronic)
IFIP Advances in Information and Communication Technology
ISBN 978-3-031-92881-9 ISBN 978-3-031-92882-6 (eBook)
https://doi.org/10.1007/978-3-031-92882-6

This Springer imprint is published by the registered company Springer Nature Switzerland AG
The registered company address is: Gewerbestrasse 11, 6330 Cham, Switzerland

Preface

We are honoured to present this collection of the best papers submitted to the 40th IFIP International Conference on ICT Systems Security and Privacy Protection, which took place in Maribor, Slovenia, May 21–23, 2025. IFIP SEC conferences are the flagship events of the International Federation for Information Processing (IFIP) Technical Committee 11 on Information Security and Privacy Protection in Information Processing Systems (TC-11). IFIP SEC 2025 was accompanied by two co-located events, the 17th World Conference on Information Security Education (WISE 2025) and the International Workshop on Network and Distributed Systems Security (WNDSS 2025).

The 2025 edition of the IFIP SEC proceedings includes 28 high-quality papers covering a wide range of research areas in the information security field. They were authored by researchers from 15 different countries.

The selection process was rigorous; out of 111 submissions we received, the papers were evaluated based on their significance, novelty, and technical quality. Two papers were desk-rejected. Of the 109 remaining papers, each paper received at least three, but most of them at least four reviews by the Program Committee. To prevent PC members from handling papers for which they had a close working relationship with the authors, conflict-of-interest guidelines were established. Following the review phase, a discussion phase took place. 21 papers were accepted and 9 papers on the borderline of acceptance or rejection underwent a shepherding process, which for 7 papers lead to acceptance and for 2 to rejection.

Finally, from the 111 submitted papers 28 were selected for presentation at the conference, leading to an acceptance rate of 25%. The PC consisted of 102 experts in the field of IT security and privacy, as well as 54 sub-reviewers, who helped with the reviews. The selection of papers was made through a single-blind peer review process. The authors of the not accepted papers were provided with feedback to assist them in the improvement of their future submissions. This volume of the conference proceedings contains the revised versions of the 28 papers that were selected. The final revised versions of the papers were not reviewed again, and the authors are responsible for their contents.

These proceedings also have a special part dedicated to the WNDSS workshop, which in an independent review process accepted seven papers from 16 submissions after a single-blind review process in which submissions received on average 3.8 reviews each.

We want to express our appreciation to all the contributors who helped to make IFIP SEC 2025 a success. There is a long list of people who volunteered their time and energy to put together the conference and who deserve acknowledgement. We want to thank the members of the Program Committee and the external reviewers, who devoted significant amounts of their time to evaluating all the submissions, especially the shepherds, who performed an additional round. Special thanks go to the keynote speakers, who accepted our invitation to present their latest work at the conference: Nastja Cepak from Creaplus,

Slovenia, Reinhard Posch from Graz University of Technology, Austria, and Jaideep Vaidya from Rutgers University, USA, the Kristian Beckman 2025 awardee.

Further individuals who deserve special thanks and without whom the current program and success of the conference would not have been possible include Paul Haskell-Dowland, IFIP TC-11 Chair, IFIP SEC 2025 organising chair Marko Hölbl, and the members of the Organizing Committee Saša Grašič, Luka Hrgarek, Marko Kompara, Maj Perovšek Tribušon, and Tomi Perša, all from the University of Maribor, Faculty of Electrical Engineering and Computer Science, and Nikolaos Pitropakis, IFIP SEC 2024 organising chair. They kept all things smooth and flowing.

Special recognition goes to Hotel City Maribor and the Maribor Convention Bureau, who were very accommodating. We also acknowledge the institutional support for IFIP SEC 2025, which came from the University of Maribor, Faculty of Electrical Engineering and Computer Science, Institute of Informatics. Without this support, it would not have been possible to organise the conference. Additionally, we extend our gratitude to the Springer team for managing the publication of the conference proceedings.

Last but certainly not least, we thank all the authors who submitted papers and all the conference's attendees. We hope you find the proceedings of IFIP SEC 2025 interesting, stimulating, and inspiring for your future research and application of research results.

April 2025

Lili Nemec Zlatolas
Kai Rannenberg
Tatjana Welzer

Organization

General Chair

Tatjana Welzer	University of Maribor, Slovenia

Program Committee Chairs

Lili Nemec Zlatolas	University of Maribor, Slovenia
Kai Rannenberg	Goethe University Frankfurt, Germany

Organizing Chair

Marko Hölbl	University of Maribor, Slovenia

Program Committee

Rose-Mharie Åhlfeldt	University of Skövde, Sweden
Alessandro Aldini	University of Urbino "Carlo Bo", Italy
Narges Arastouei	Goethe University Frankfurt, Germany
Claudio Agostino Ardagna	Università degli Studi di Milano, Italy
Vijay Atluri	Rutgers University, USA
Maria Bada	Queen Mary University London, UK
Marcus Belder	Department of Defence, Defence Science and Technology Group, Australia
Matt Bishop	University of California, Davis, USA
Tamara Bonaci	University of Washington, USA
Nora Boulahia-Cuppens	Polytechnique Montréal, Canada
Dagmar Brechlerova	Euromise Prague, Czech Republic
Henrich C. Pöhls	University of Passau, Germany
Umit Cali	University of York, UK
Barbara Carminati	University of Insubria, Italy
K. P. Chow	University of Hong Kong, China
Christos Chrysoulas	Heriot Watt University, UK
Nathan Clarke	University of Plymouth, UK

Miguel Correia	INESC-ID, Instituto Superior Técnico, Universidade de Lisboa, Portugal
Paolo D'Arco	University di Salerno, Italy
Sabrina De Capitani di Vimercati	Universita' degli Studi di Milano, Italy
Nicola Dragoni	Technical University of Denmark, Denmark
Isao Echizen	National Institute of Informatics, Japan
Carmen Fernández-Gago	University of Málaga, Spain
Elena Ferrari	University of Insubria, Italy
Simone Fischer-Hübner	Karlstad University, Sweden
Stephen Flowerday	University of Tulsa, USA
Sara Foresti	Università degli Studi di Milano, Italy
Steven Furnell	University of Nottingham, UK
Lynn Futcher	Nelson Mandela University, South Africa
Martin Gilje Jaatun	SINTEF Digital, Norway
Hélder Gomes	Escola Superior de Tecnologia e Gestão de Águeda, Universidade de Aveiro, Portugal
Anna Grocholewska-CzuryBo	Technical University of Poznań, Poland
Nils Gruschka	University of Oslo, Norway
Ville Haapakangas	Tampere University of Applied Sciences, Finland
Jonas Hallberg	Swedish Defence Research Agency, Sweden
Paul Haskell-Dowland	Edith Cowan University, Australia
Kirsi Helkala	Norwegian Defence Cyber Academy, Norway
Dominik Herrmann	University of Bamberg, Germany
Marko Hölbl	University of Maribor, Slovenia
Luka Hrgarek	University of Maribor, Slovenia
Xinyi Huang	Fujian Normal University, China
Dieter Hutter	DFKI GmbH, Germany
Pedro Inácio	Universidade da Beira Interior, Portugal
Lech Janczewski	University of Auckland, New Zealand
Jan Jürjens	Fraunhofer Institute for Software & Systems Engineering ISST and University of Koblenz-Landau, Germany
Georgios Kambourakis	University of the Aegean, Greece
Sokratis Katsikas	Norwegian University of Science and Technology, Norway
Stefan Katzenbeisser	University of Passau, Germany
Georgios Kavallieratos	University of Oslo, Norway
Dogan Kesdogan	Universität Regensburg, Germany
Dongseong Kim	University of Queensland, Australia
Kwangjo Kim	Korea Advanced Institute of Science and Technology, South Korea
Ella Kolkowska	Örebro University School of Business, Sweden

Marko Kompara	University of Maribor, Slovenia
Zbigniew Kotulski	Warsaw University of Technology, Poland
Stephan Krenn	AIT Austrian Institute of Technology GmbH, Austria
Lukasz Krzywiecki	Wrocław University of Science and Technology, Poland
Peeter Laud	Cybernetica AS, Estonia
Maryline Laurent	Télécom SudParis, Institut Polytechnique de Paris, France
Heejo Lee	Korea University, South Korea
Maciej Liskiewicz	University of Lübeck, Germany
Giovanni Livraga	University of Milan, Italy
Luigi Logrippo	Université du Québec en Outaouais, Canada
Javier Lopez	Universidad de Málaga, Spain
João Paulo Magalhaes	Polytechnic Institute of Porto, Portugal
Carol Marsh	Celestia, UK
Fabio Martinelli	Institute for High Performance Computing and Networking, Italy
Andrew McGettrick	University of Strathclyde, UK
Weizhi Meng	Lancaster University, UK
Haralambos Mouratidis	University of Essex, UK
Tim Muller	University of Nottingham, UK
Yuko Murayama	Tsuda College, Japan
Alexios Mylonas	Hertfordshire University, UK
Sergio Nunes	ISEG-Lisbon School of Economics and Management, Portugal
Melek Önen	EURECOM, France
Jacques Ophoff	Abertay University, UK
Brajendra Panda	University of Arkansas, USA
Sebastian Pape	Social Engineering Academy GmbH, Germany
Miguel Pardal	Universidade de Lisboa, Portugal
Günther Pernul	Universität Regensburg, Germany
Nikolaos Pitropakis	American College of Greece, Greece
Alen Rajšp	University of Maribor, Slovenia
Ching Bon Raymond Chan	Singapore Institute of Technology, Singapore
Carlos Rieder	isec ag, Switzerland
Juha Röning	University of Oulu, Finland
Elham Rostami	Örebro University, Sweden
Pierangela Samarati	Università degli Studi di Milano, Italy
Jürgen Schönwälder	Constructor University, Germany
Andrew Seely	Hillsborough Community College, USA
Jun Shao	Zhejiang Gongshang University, China

Carlton Shepherd	Newcastle University, UK
Paria Shirani	Ryerson University, Canada
Daniel Slamanig	Universität der Bundeswehr München, Germany
Adesina S. Sodiya	Federal University of Agriculture, Abeokuta, Nigeria
Eliana Stavrou	Open University of Cyprus, Cyprus
Chunhua Su	University of Aizu, Japan
Shamik Sural	Indian Institute of Technology Kharagpur, India
Gurvirender Tejay	Hofstra University, USA
Ding Wang	Nankai University, China
Vladimir Zadorozhny	University of Pittsburgh, USA
Yuexin Zhang	Fujian Normal University, China
André Zúquete	University of Aveiro, Portugal

Additional Reviewers

Aous Al Salek
Arafat Asim
Nicola Bena
Filippo Berto
Salva Daneshgadeh Cakmakci
D. Jonathan Sebastian Cardenas
Ferhat Ozgur Catak
Yijia Chang
Gaurav Choudhary
Giovanni Ciaramella
Pietro Colombo
Joana C. Costa
Lynne Coventry
Givemore Dube
Kamil Erdayandi
Randy Esser
Abulfaz Hajizada
Ugur Halden
Xiaohan Hao
James Higgs
Alberto Ibarrondo
Lejla Islami
Nika Jeršič
Hyunjae Kang
Dima Kashchuk
Dimitrios Kasimatis
Mengyan Li
Konstantinos Limniotis
Chao Lin
Evangelos Markakis
Francesco Mercaldo
Marcus Nohlberg
Tomasz Nowak
Maria Papaioannou
Luca Petrillo
Pedro Pinto
Rui Pinto
Ubaid Ur Rehman
Christian Rondanini
Tiago Roxo
Sarwar Sayeed
Mariusz Sepczuk
Bernardo Sequeiros
Lynsay Shepherd
Christos Smiliotopoulos
Gabriele Spini
Viktor Taneski
James Todd
Chengling Wang
Yamei Wang
Tatjana Welzer
Aljoscha Windhorst
Chenming Xu
Xianwu Zeng

Contents – Part I

Industrial and Critical Infrastructure Security

Contents – Part II

Privacy Protection

Advanced Strategies for Privacy Preserving Data Publishing to Improve Multi-class Classification

Tibo Laperre, Jenno Verdonck, Kevin De Boeck, Michiel Willocx(✉), and Vincent Naessens

DistriNet, KU Leuven, Ghent, Belgium
{tibo.laperre,jenno.verdonck,kevin.deboeck,michiel.willocx, vincent.naessens}@kuleuven.be

Abstract. Data anonymization has become an essential preprocessing step in many analytics, especially the ones that rely on machine learning. Retrieving external data sources can significantly improve the quality of machine learning models but the sensitive nature often hinders data exchange. On the other hand, anonymization tactics can substantially decrease their utility resulting in inferior machine learning models. This work assesses the quality of anonymized datasets for multi-class classification purposes. A hybrid anonymization pipeline is employed, combining masking and sampling. Deliberate sampling – achieved by balancing the target attribute – not only offers strong and quantifiable privacy guarantees but also improves the utility of released datasets. Our findings are supported by experiments that are executed on three distinct datasets, demonstrating the effectiveness of the approach.

Keywords: anonymity · sampling · masking · utility · machine learning

1 Introduction

The use of data has become indispensable in our modern society. Data-driven decision making empowers economic growth and increases competitiveness within companies by enhancing productivity and accelerating innovation [6]. Moreover, data fuels many research related to global challenges such as climate change [20], optimizing the handling of pandemics [2] and the development of new medicines [24]. Governments also heavily rely on data-driven insights to optimize our society. Examples are transportation [13], social security [7] and crime prevention [34]. Along with the increased importance of data in our society comes the need to share data. Nowadays, many data-driven collaborations are set up between governments and commercial stakeholders [14]. On the one hand, organizations can opt to enrich internal data with external sources, thereby

Published by Springer Nature Switzerland AG 2025
L. Nemec Zlatolas et al. (Eds.): SEC 2025, IFIP AICT 745, pp. 3–16, 2025.
https://doi.org/10.1007/978-3-031-92882-6_1

optimizing the prediction power of existing models. On the other hand, many businesses rely on external entities to analyze their data and to build prediction models. This is often due to the significant amount of knowledge and computing power that is required for those tasks. Lastly, companies can retrieve additional revenues by selling their data to interested stakeholders.

Personal data is part of many data sharing scenarios. The GDPR regulation stipulates the anonymization of such data before it can be released to other parties [12]. The anonymization phase then prevents that sensitive attributes or records in shared datasets can be linked to individuals. Note further that data anonymization can also be applied by organizations as part of their data retention strategy. Privacy regulation forbids companies to store personal data indefinitely. However, anonymized data can still be employed for building machine learning models over a larger time span.

This paper focuses on the anonymization of sensitive data for ML purposes and restricts the experiments to multi-class classification. More specifically, our research aims to increase the quality of machine learning models by embracing the learning purpose from the beginning (i.e. during dataset anonymization).

Contributions. This paper applies a hybrid anonymization pipeline to improve the quality of machine learning models that rely on sensitive datasets, with a major focus on multi-class classification. The pipeline combines generalization and intelligent sampling as essential building blocks. The latter is partially steered by the learning purpose. A vast set of experiments that are executed on three datasets with varying characteristics show the added value of embracing the learning purpose during anonymization. Furthermore, the experiments allow to extract guidelines to configure hybrid anononymization pipelines based on the learning purpose and dataset characteristics (like size, balance, nature ...).

The remainder of this work is structured as follows. Section 2 positions our paper to related work and outlines the hybrid anonymization pipeline employed in this research. Section 3 introduces the datasets used in our experiments. Section 4 describes the experimental setup. The results are presented and discussed in Sect. 5 and 6 respectively. This paper ends with conclusions.

2 Related Work and Preliminaries

Machine Learning Strategies. The main focus of this paper is building ML models for multi-class classification [30] purposes. Classification is a form of supervised learning [28], where labeled data is leveraged to train models to predict outcomes or classify inputs. Our work specifically focuses on micro data, containing demographic, economic or other characteristics of a large set of individuals.

When creating machine learning models, a dataset is typically split into a training set and a test set, allowing to assess the efficacy of the trained model by testing it with new inputs. To eliminate the effect of the random selection of a test and training set, multi-fold cross-validation [22] is often applied. This technique assesses multiple combinations of test and training sets, reducing the risk of overfitting or underfitting, thereby increasing the quality of the model. We employ this strategy for all experiments conducted in this work.

Another pitfall for training ML models is the use of unbalanced datasets. Many datasets are by nature unbalanced. Examples are datasets containing financial records for fraud detection, and medical records intended for diagnoses and anomaly detection. Training with unbalanced datasets often results in models that are inferior on minority classes. Hence, it is advised to balance data before model training [15,35]. Our work aims to balance the dataset during anonymization, thereby aiming to increase the quality of the resulting ML models while at the same time guaranteeing a threshold anonymity level for each record in the anonymized dataset. Numerous studies have already shown the growing interest in training ML models with sensitive data [8,29,32].

Data Anonymization Tactics. This work focuses on statistical methods for data anonymization [33]. These methods range from perturbative techniques such as noise addition [21] and micro aggregation [1] to non-perturbative techniques such as sampling and masking. Noise addition is often employed in the context of differential privacy [11], a well-known technique for sharing aggregate dataset values in a privacy-friendly manner. As our work focuses on the anonymization of complete datasets, techniques related to differential privacy are out of scope. The tactics applied in this work are masking and sampling.

Masking is applied to quasi-identifying attributes (QIDs) in a dataset. Examples are age, gender and ZIP code. Generalization strategies (like masking) result in transformed datasets that achieve a privacy level in accordance to a privacy model. The best known and most frequently used privacy model is k-anonymity [27], which states that all records should be indistinguishable from at least $k - 1$ other records (when only considering the QIDs). Groups of records with the same set of QIDs in a dataset instance are called equivalence classes (EQs). The k-anonymity privacy model provides protection against record linkage but fails to protect against attribute disclosure attacks [25]. Other privacy models such as l-diversity [19] and t-closeness [16] offer this protection but are often detrimental to the utility of the resulting anonymous dataset [3].

Sampling [5,17] removes records from the dataset. When this technique is applied in an intelligent way, a considerable amount of uncertainty can be introduced in the dataset, preventing an attacker of knowing whether a target individual is even in the dataset. Previous research has shown that sampling does not necessarily has a negative impact on data analytics. This has been demonstrated for both optimization [9] and machine learning [32] tasks.

Combining masking and sampling as a promising hybrid anonymization approach was introduced by Verdonck et al. in [32]. Sampling was introduced to guarantee uncertainty towards an attacker, hence, preventing leakage of sensitive attributes. That seminal work was validated in the restricted setting of binary classification and one dataset, resulting in preliminary guidelines and conclusions. We build further upon this work and validate it to three different use cases related to multi-class classification problems allowing to draw more fine-grained conclusions. Stratified and balanced sampling were used in previous experiments, and will also be applied in this work. The former ensures that records are cut from each equivalence class. The sampling rate then reflects the certainty a target is in the dataset. As records are cut from each equivalence class, individuals in the original dataset are no longer present in the sampled one with certainty resulting in plausible deniability for each individual. The latter provides the same certainty guarantees while at the same time balancing a target attribute in the dataset. That may be beneficial for later ML purposes. That work provided a best-effort tactic leading to some records still showing an undesirable amount of certainty, and a more strict one cutting the records that exceed the desired certainty limits.

3 Envisioned Scenarios

This paper focuses on scenarios involving multiple classes and a realistic set of quasi-identifiers. Note that a large number of QIDs has a negative impact on the anonymity-utility balance as it typically forces to apply larger generalizations. A large number of features is generally also not desirable from a machine learning perspective, as such conditions can decrease the model performance. This curse of dimensionality typically necessitates feature reduction strategies to be applied in a preprocessing step (as is also assumed for the rest of this paper).

To validate the robustness of our findings in a realistic context, we have selected three datasets that vary significantly with respect to several characteristics. These aspects include the size of the dataset, the predictive power of the models derived from these datasets, and the balance of class distributions within each dataset. Such diversity ensures a comprehensive examination of the impact of the hybrid anonymization pipeline on machine learning performance. Table 1 gives an overview of the characteristics of each dataset.

The *ACSIncome* dataset was acquired using the Folktables tool [10] and comprises of 1,664,500 records. This dataset is designed to predict individual income levels based on census data gathered by the American Census Bureau. It serves as a potential alternative to the extensively utilized ADULT dataset in machine learning research [4]. Unlike the ADULT dataset, which categorizes income into binary classes – either below or above $50,000 – the ACSIncome dataset allows for the customization of the income thresholds. For the purposes of this research, income has been categorized into three classes: incomes from 0 to $20,000 are considered as `poor`, from $20,000 to $100,000 as `medium`, and above $100,000 as `rich`. 14% of the dataset is comprised of the `rich` class.

The *Nursery* dataset [26], which comprises 12,960 records, originates from a hierarchical decision model initially devised for assessing applications to nursery schools. The primary objective of this dataset is to facilitate the prediction of the appropriateness of admitting a child into a specific nursery school. Given the well-defined structure of this dataset, the models trained on it exhibit high predictive accuracy. Consequently, this dataset represents an exemplary case of a dataset with very high predictive power. The dataset is notably imbalanced, as the minority class `very_recom` makes up less than 5% of the dataset.

The *Contraceptive Method Choice* (CMC) [18] dataset is a subset derived from the National Indonesian Survey on Contraceptive Prevalence conducted in 1987. It consists of 1,473 records, each representing a married woman who was not pregnant at the time of the interview. The objective of this dataset is to predict a woman's choice of contraceptive method, differentiating between `no use`, `long-term` methods, and `short-term` methods. It shows the least imbalance, with the minority class `long-term` constituting approximately 23% of the dataset. The CMC dataset is known for its notably poor predictive power. An overview of the three datasets is given in Table 1.

Table 1. Dataset characteristics

Dataset	#QID	#Records	#Classes	Minority Class Size	Predictive power
ACSIncome	8	1,664,500	3	14%	Good
Nursery	8	12,960	4	5%	Very good
CMC	7	1,473	3	23%	Poor

4 Methodological Approach

An overview of the methodological approach for this work is given in Fig. 1. To enhance the statistical significance of the results and ensure the correctness of our findings, 10-fold cross-validation is employed. Therefore, the first step of our setup divides the dataset in 10 folds, resulting in 10 experiments. Each experiment takes one fold as test set and the other 9 for training.

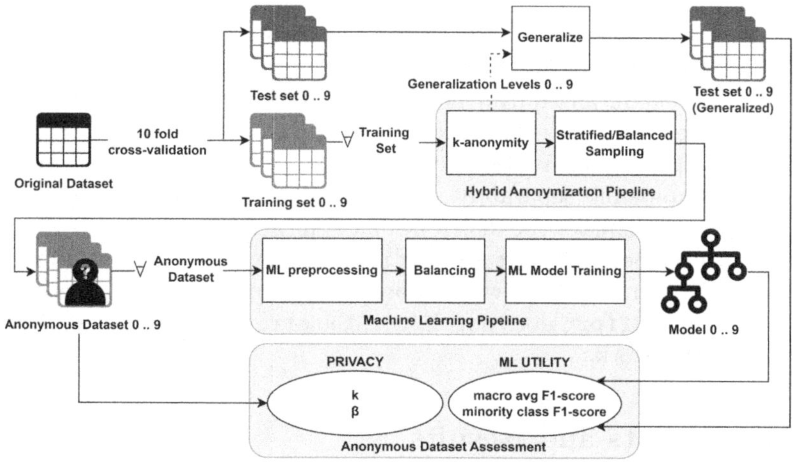

Fig. 1. Methodological approach

Anonymization Pipeline. A generalization step and a sampling step is applied to each training set. During generalization, the k-anonymity privacy model is applied for a predefined value of k. Note that the same generalizations need to be applied to the test set as the training set before the model can be evaluated. This is required because the test data must exhibit the same format as the data used in the model training step. During the sampling step, either the strict variant of stratified sampling (`ssample_S`) or balanced sampling (`bsample_S`) is executed with a predefined value of sampling rate β.

Machine Learning Pipeline. Prior to their use in machine learning algorithms, the anonymized training sets undergo a mandatory preprocessing step. Numerical attributes that are generalized into intervals are converted to their interval mean. Categorical attributes are ordinarily encoded, and attributes that are fully generalized are assigned a value of -1. To ensure balance, the ML pipeline evenso applies balancing techniques, specifically undersampling for the larger ACSIncome and Nursery datasets and oversampling for the smaller CMC dataset. Classification models are trained using the GradientBoostingClassifier from the scikit-learn Python library [23].

Assessing Anonymized Datasets. In our research, anonymized datasets are evaluated on both their machine learning utility and their privacy characteristics. ML utility is represented by the macro average F1-score and the F1-score of the minority class because these metrics assess the overall and minority class performance. The latter is often critical in real life use cases. To calculate the F1-score for a model, the test set is first generalized according to the generalization levels of the corresponding anonymous training set. By applying 10-fold cross-validation in our setup, every experiment results in 10 different ML models. In order to fairly quantify the overall machine learning utility, the results are presented as a combination of the mean and the range.

When applying the strict sample methods, the parameter β offers a guaranteed threshold privacy level, similar to k in k-anonymity and l in l-diversity. In such anonymous datasets, sampling rate β limits the maximum probability that a record is present in an equivalence class (EQ) to be not larger than β. This probability is referred to as the certainty metric. Consequently, there is no need to analyze the privacy characteristics of datasets processed through the hybrid anonymization pipeline separately, as these are fully defined by k and β. To clarify this, Fig. 2 displays the distribution of the certainty with a β-value of 0.5 applying both the `Best-Effort` and `Strict` strategy. The `Strict` strategy guarantees a hard upper threshold with respect to the certainty level of each record, whereas the `Best-Effort` does not. Hence, the `strict` strategy is applied in the remainder of this work.

5 Experiments and Results

This section presents the results of our experiments applying the setup discussed in the previous section. For every dataset, a number of values for k and β were

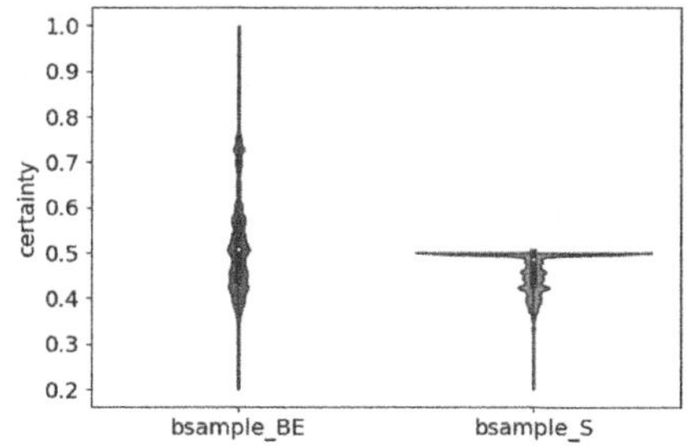

Fig. 2. Certainty for `bsample_BE` and `bsample_S` in the ACSIncome dataset

selected, namely 10, 20, 50 and 100 for k and 0.5, 0.1 and 0.01 for β. Our tests are executed for every combination of these parameters. Note that, for a fair comparison, a balancing step is executed in the machine learning pipeline regardless of the applied sampling strategy.

Due to the large amount of experiments conducted in this work, we are unable to include all results. Therefore, this section presents our main findings. An exhaustive overview of our experimental results along with the generalization hierarchies applied to the QIDs in our experiments can be found on Gitbub[1].

5.1 Comparison of Balanced Sampling and Stratified Sampling

This first set of experiments assesses the effect of balanced sampling compared to stratified sampling. Figure 3 presents the macro average F1-score and the F1-score for the minority class for a set of β and k values. To allow for a direct comparison, the `bsample_S` and `ssample_S` strategies are presented side by side.

The figure indicates that overall, the balanced sampling method scores slightly better in many cases. In large datasets, the difference between both approaches is negligible. However, smaller datasets do benefit from balancing in the anonymization pipeline, especially for smaller values of β. This can be attributed to the fact that the `bsample_S` strategy returns a more balanced dataset than the `ssample_S`, reducing the amount of deleted records during the machine learning pipeline's balancing step. This results in a larger anonymous dataset to train the classification model. The remainder of this section focuses on the `bsample_S` strategy. Therefore, the `ssample_S` results are ommitted from the remainder of our figures.

5.2 Effect of the Sample Rate

An important aspect of the hybrid anonymization pipeline that requires assessment is the effect of the sample rate on the utility of the anonymized dataset. For this, we refer back to Fig. 3.

---

[1] https://github.com/ku-leuven-msec/HybridPipeline-MulticlassML.

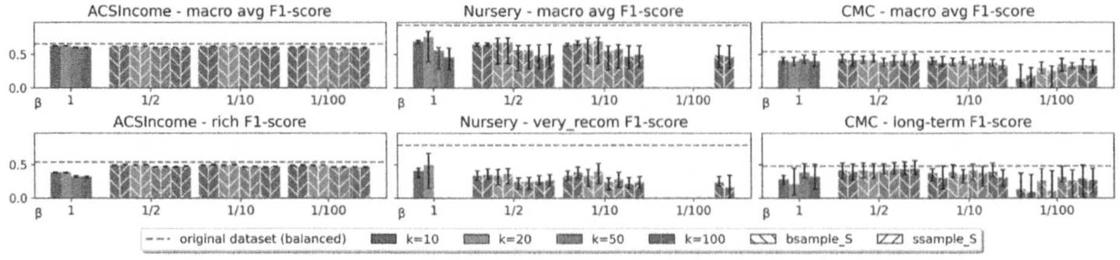

Fig. 3. ML utility for `bsample_S` and `ssample_S`

Moderate Sample Rate. When transitioning from no sampling ($\beta = 1$) to sampling with $\beta = 0.5$, the (macro average) F1-score of the minority class show no negative impact or even improve. This is the case for all three datasets and for every value of k. Therefore, it is advisable to always opt for sampling with a minimum β-value of 0.5, as this approach does not adversely affect the ML utility while providing a robust level of privacy. In some cases, a higher level of privacy protection might be desirable. To examine the effect of smaller sampling rates on ML utility, the remainder of this analysis focuses on $\beta = 0.1$ and $\beta = 0.01$.

Small Sample Rate. Before discussing the results for smaller sampling rates, it is important to address the relationship between parameters β and k. Due to the nature of the `Strict` variants, an EQ with a size smaller than $1/\beta$ cannot exist in the anonymous dataset after sampling without violating the certainty threshold. For such an EQ, $\lfloor \beta \cdot |EQ| \rfloor = 0$, resulting in it being removed entirely.

The k-anonymity privacy model imposes a lower limit on the size of an EQ. However, this does not mean that a sample rate of $\beta < 1/k$ results in removing all EQs. Due to uneven distributions within a dataset, many EQs are larger than k. This is illustrated by the EQ distributions of our datasets as shown in Fig. 4. Hence it is feasible to apply sample rates for which $\beta < 1/k$.

ACSIncome. For the ACSIncome dataset, both the mean macro average F1-scores and the mean rich F1-scores remain stable for the smaller β-values 0.1 and 0.01. In larger datasets, the likeliness increases that EQs exceed the minimal required size k. The distribution in Fig. 4 reveals numerous EQs with sizes larger than 100, making sampling with a β-value of 0.01 feasible while still leaving sufficient records to train a qualitative classification model.

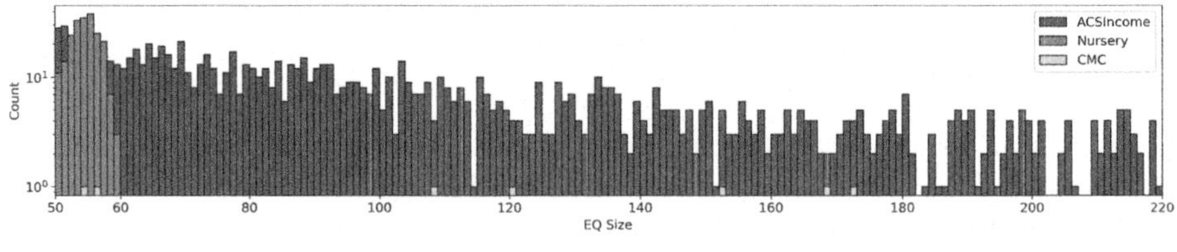

Fig. 4. EQ size distributions for $k = 50$, test fold $= 0$

Nursery. The macro average F1-scores remain consistent at a β-value of 0.1 for every value of k. The minority class, however, the F1-scores for the minority class significantly drop for $k = 10$, $k = 20$ and $k = 50$, and increase both in lower bound and mean at $k = 100$. At a β of 0.01, both F1-scores for all k-values equal zero except for $k = 100$. This can be explained by the EQ distribution for Nursery, which shows that at $k = 50$, no EQ is larger than 100. Therefore, using `bsample_S` with the parameters $k = 50$ and $\beta = 0.01$ results in 10 empty training sets. Evidently, these datasets are not suitable for anonymization.

CMC. Both F1-scores remain stable for each k at $\beta = 0.1$. For $\beta = 0.01$, the macro average F1-score significantly drops for each k-value. The reliability of the results for the F1-score of the minority class is questionable, with lower bounds standing at zero for all k-values, except for $k = 50$. This means that one or multiple training sets were unusable after anonymization. The EQ distribution of the CMC dataset shows that there are five EQs larger than 100 for $k = 50$. This means that the output dataset for $k = 50$, $\beta = 0.01$ consists of only five records. Clearly, this dataset is too small to conduct meaningful ML.

5.3 Variability of the F1-Scores Between the Training Sets

Our experiments are executed with a 10-fold cross-validation. For each combination of k and β, 10 distinct training sets are created and fed through the anonymization pipeline. Variation in the F1-scores are a result of both generalization (k-anonymity) and sampling, and largely depends on the nature of the data and the size of the anonymized training set after anonymization.

Figure 3 shows that for each dataset the range of the F1-scores remains stable when transitioning from $\beta = 1$ to $\beta = 0.5$. This indicates that the main source of variation is introduced during the k-anonymity process. Depending on the specific content of each training set, the k-anonymity algorithm may identify different optimal generalization levels for different training sets. This in turn could lead to differences in ML utility as key predictive attributes are generalized differently. The effect is clearly visible in the Nursery dataset. At k-values of 20, 50, and 100, respectively, 4, 4, and 5 different generalization levels were applied, explaining the larger ranges. This is in contrast to $k = 10$ where the range is small and all training sets use the same generalization levels.

A second cause of variation is the effect of a low β-value. Take, for example, the CMC dataset, where the variations remain stable when transitioning from $\beta = 1$ to $\beta = 0.5$, but significantly increase as β is further reduced to 0.01. At this lower β-value, the anonymous CMC dataset consists of merely five records, causing ML utility to be highly dependent on which exact records are retained. This dependency explains the increased variation seen with smaller β-values in small datasets. In larger datasets such as ACSIncome, this increase in variation is not observed, as the anonymous datasets remain large enough to be effective.

5.4 Effect of Dataset Size

Our previous results have demonstrated that there is a significant impact of the dataset size on the behavior of the hybrid anonymization pipeline. In order to accurately assess this effect, we create two new datasets by taking a small, random subset of the original large ACSIncome dataset with respectively 16,645 and 1,640 records. The ML utility for these datasets is shown in Fig. 5.

As established in the previous section, the most significant source of variation in these two new datasets is attributed to the k-anonymity process. Additionally, we observe that the variation increases as the size of the dataset decreases, regardless of the value of k and β. In both datasets, the F1-scores remain relatively stable when transitioning from $\beta = 1$ to $\beta = 0.5$ and show a marginal decrease when further reduced to $\beta = 0.1$. Similar to the CMC dataset, a β-value of 0.01 is too small for the ACSIncome dataset with 1,664 records, which results in unreliable F1-scores.

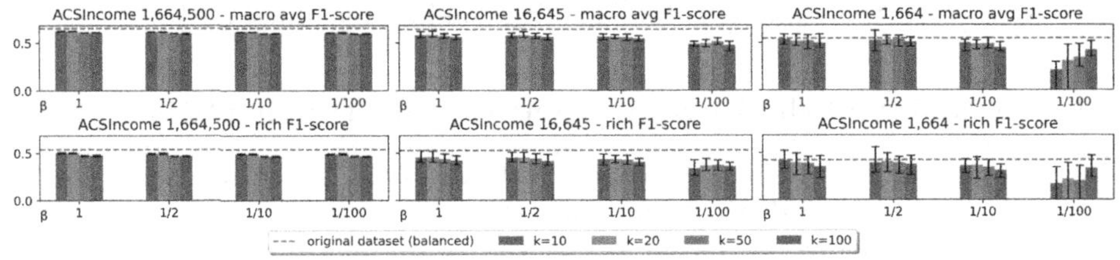

Fig. 5. ML utility for ACSIncome subsets (`bsample_S`)

6 Discussion

The results discussed in the previous section prove the viability of advanced sampling during anonymization to improve the privacy-utility balance for building multi-class classification models. This section extracts guidelines for creating hybrid anonymization pipelines, compares its properties to existing approaches and demonstrates its potential in the context of emerging data spaces.

Instantiating and Employing Hybrid Anonymization Pipelines. Depending on the characteristics of the dataset and the intended use case, different configurations of the hybrid anonymization pipeline should be considered.

Balanced Versus Stratified Sampling. When a dataset is used for classification, balanced (stratified) sampling is preferable compared to stratified sampling. Balanced sampling not only anonymizes the data implicitly up to a certain level but also succeeds to balance the target attribute. Since balancing is a well-known preprocessing step in machine learning for classification purposes, shifting this step to the anonymization phase is advantageous if the machine learning purposes are known in advance. However, when the intended use of the dataset remains open at the time of anonymization, opting for stratified sampling increases flexibility with respect to potential future use. Selecting the latter strategy can negatively impact the privacy-utility balance with respect to a specific machine learning scenario that is known in advance. However, our experiments have shown that stratified sampling remains a feasible tactic for classification purposes.

Selecting Feasible Privacy Parameters. Deliberate selection of privacy parameters can have a positive impact on the privacy-utility balance in many scenarios. This is shown by variations in sampling rate β and anonymity level k that are applied during the experiments on multiple datasets. A sampling rate β of 0.5 is shown to be acceptable for many datasets based on our experiments on three different ones with heterogeneous characteristics. The experiments show that this sampling rate does not diminish ML utility while effectively protecting against attribute disclosure attacks (even for the smaller ones). For larger datasets, such as the ACSIncome dataset, it can be preferable to employ a smaller sampling rate, while for smaller datasets, such as CMC, larger sampling rates might be favorable to build qualitative machine learning models. Our tests further show that in most cases, for a certain β value, increasing the k-value up to a certain extent does not negatively effect the efficacy of the classification model. Moreover, as our experiments have shown, larger k values even improve the quality of the anonymized dataset when small β values are applied in many scenarios.

Sampling Outperforms Tactics Striving for l-Diversity. The main goal of the hybrid anonymization pipeline is to prevent attribute disclosure without negatively impacting the utility of datasets. Both intelligent sampling and l-diversity are tactics that can be combined with k-anonymity to protect against attribute disclosure. Given the fundamental differences in approach between the two tactics, comparing them is by far not straightforward. There exists no trivial mapping between β-values and l-values to assess the privacy level.

To compare the effectiveness of both approaches, the three datasets were anonymized applying both strategies. In a first set of experiments, sampling was applied with low β-values (i.e. 0.1 and 0.01) resulting in a high privacy level. In a second set of experiments, l-diversity was applied with a low l-value (i.e. 2.0) resulting in a low privacy level. Our findings show that the anonymized datasets in the first set of experiments outperform the ones resulting from the second set for building classification models. This demonstrates that intelligent sampling is superior compared to tactics striving for l-diversity. A broad set of experiments with varying β and l values are depicted in Fig. 6. Note that these experiments rely on the entropy l-diversity variant.

For the ACSIncome dataset, the F1-scores are even slightly higher at $\beta = 0.01$ compared to $l = 2.0$ across all k-values. Moreover, the F1-scores are significantly higher compared to $l = 3.0$ for large k-values of 50 and 100. Note that we have shown earlier that a β-value of 0.01 is not feasible for both the Nursery and CMC dataset and yet not discussed further. In the Nursery dataset, l-diversity has much lower macro average F1-scores for every k-value. The dataset is highly imbalanced, which explains the low F1-scores. To comply with the l-diversity constraint, there must be sufficient diversity within each EQ. This means that EQs need to be filled with records from the minority class, of which there are few. Consequently, the dataset is more harshly generalized to achieve larger EQs, which makes it hard for a classification algorithm to make accurate predictions.

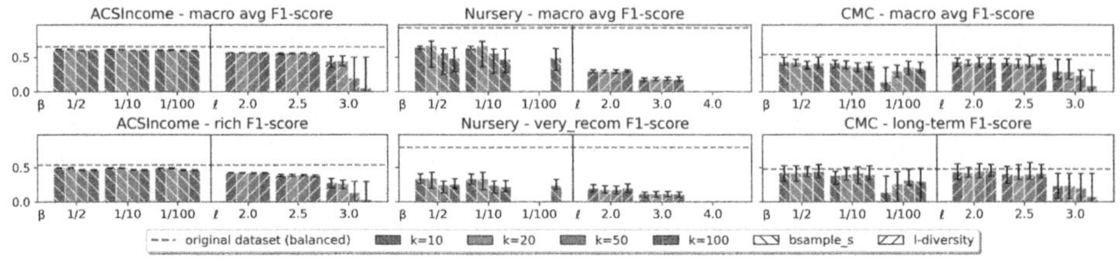

Fig. 6. Comparison of ML utility between `bsample_S` and l-diversity

Hybrid Anonymization Pipelines in the Context of Emerging Data Spaces. Data spaces are currently gaining a lot of traction [31]. The hybrid anonymization pipeline in this work can be a key building block within this emerging domain by enabling data owners to release information within these data spaces in a privacy-preserving manner. When a large set of data providers release a small anonymized sample of their dataset, the collective pool of data can be feasible for many analytic purposes while offering strong privacy guarantees. Mechanisms can even be added to hide the source of the individual records resulting in increased privacy towards data processors. Fusing data from multiple sources in combination with very small (and anonymized) samples per data source effectively prevents an attacker from ever linking records back to a specific individual.

7 Conclusion

This work performed a vast set of experiments on a hybrid anonymization pipeline consisting of advanced sampling tactics as a key building block and combined with generalization strategies to achieve k-anonymity. The experiments were executed on three different use cases relying on three benchmark datasets with varying characteristics with respect to size, distribution of target attributes and nature. They resulted in meaningful guidelines that can be applied when instantiating anonimization pipelines for machine learning purposes. First, balanced (stratified) sampling is superior compared to stratified sampling, especially for smaller datasets. Second, deliberate selection of privacy parameters can positively influence the privacy-utility balance. Third, sampling outperforms tactics striving for l-diversity with respect to the privacy-utility balance based on the experiments that were performed in this work. l-diversity introduces theoretic information loss by generalizing attribute values to larger intervals, whereas sampling does so by withholding records. However, although generalization of the experimental findings cannot be proven, practical information loss was each time higher when striving for l-diversity.

References

1. Abidi, B., Ben Yahia, S., Perera, C.: Hybrid microaggregation for privacy preserving data mining. J. Ambient. Intell. Humaniz. Comput. **11**(1), 23–38 (2020)
2. Ahmed, I., Ahmad, M., Jeon, G., Piccialli, F.: A framework for pandemic prediction using big data analytics. Big Data Res. **25**, 100190 (2021)
3. Almasi, M.M., Siddiqui, T.R., Mohammed, N., Hemmati, H.: The risk-utility tradeoff for data privacy models. In: 2016 8th IFIP International Conference on New Technologies, Mobility and Security (NTMS), pp. 1–5. IEEE (2016)
4. Becker, B., Kohavi, R.: Adult. UCI Machine Learning Repository (1996). https://doi.org/10.24432/C5XW20
5. Bild, R., Kuhn, K.A., Prasser, F.: SafePub: a truthful data anonymization algorithm with strong privacy guarantees. Proc. Priv. Enhanc. Technol. **2018**(1), 67–87 (2018). https://doi.org/10.1515/popets-2018-0004
6. Calzon, B.: The importance of data driven decision making for business. BI Blog | Data Visualization & Analytics Blog | datapine (2023)
7. Cao, L.: Social security and social welfare data mining: an overview. IEEE Trans. Syst. Man Cybern. Part C (Appl. Rev.) **42**(6), 837–853 (2012)
8. Carvalho, T., Moniz, N.: The compromise of data privacy in predictive performance. In: International Symposium on Intelligent Data Analysis, pp. 426–438. Springer (2021)
9. De Boeck, K., Verdonck, J., Willocx, M., Lapon, J., Naessens, V.: Dataset anonymization with purpose: a resource allocation use case. In: 2021 International Symposium on Computer Science and Intelligent Controls (ISCSIC), pp. 202–210. IEEE (2021)
10. Ding, F., Hardt, M., Miller, J., Schmidt, L.: Retiring adult: new datasets for fair machine learning. In: Advances in Neural Information Processing Systems, vol. 34 (2021)
11. Dwork, C.: Differential privacy. In: International colloquium on automata, languages, and programming, pp. 1–12. Springer (2006)
12. EUR-Lex: Regulation (EU) 2016/679 of the European Parliament and of the Council of 27 April 2016 (2016). https://eur-lex.europa.eu/eli/reg/2016/679/oj. Accessed 20 Oct 2022
13. Kaffash, S., Nguyen, A.T., Zhu, J.: Big data algorithms and applications in intelligent transportation system: a review and bibliometric analysis. Int. J. Prod. Econ. **231**, 107868 (2021)
14. Karkera, A., Kelkar, M., Mariani, J., Nuttall, Dr.K.: Bridging the data-sharing chasm | Deloitte. Deloitte Insights (2023)
15. Kim, M., Hwang, K.B.: An empirical evaluation of sampling methods for the classification of imbalanced data. PLoS ONE **17**(7), e0271260 (2022)
16. Li, N., Li, T., Venkatasubramanian, S.: T-closeness: privacy beyond k-anonymity and l-diversity. In: 2007 IEEE 23rd International Conference on Data Engineering, pp. 106–115. IEEE (2006)

17. Li, N., Qardaji, W., Su, D.: On sampling, anonymization, and differential privacy or, k-anonymization meets differential privacy. In: Proceedings of the 7th ACM Symposium on Information, Computer and Communications Security, pp. 32–33 (2012)
18. Lim, T.S.: Contraceptive method choice. UCI Machine Learning Repository (1997). https://doi.org/10.24432/C59W2D
19. Machanavajjhala, A., Kifer, D., Gehrke, J., Venkitasubramaniam, M.: l-diversity: privacy beyond k-anonymity. ACM Trans. Knowl. Discov. Data (TKDD) **1**(1), 3–es (2007)
20. Mastrola, M.: How AI can help combat climate change - Johns Hopkins Institute for assured autonomy. Johns Hopkins Institute for Assured Autonomy (2023)
21. Mivule, K.: Utilizing noise addition for data privacy, an overview. arXiv preprint arXiv:1309.3958 (2013)
22. Nti, I.K., Nyarko-Boateng, O., Aning, J., et al.: Performance of machine learning algorithms with different k values in k-fold cross-validation. Int. J. Inf. Technol. Comput. Sci. **13**(6), 61–71 (2021)
23. Pedregosa, F., et al.: Scikit-learn: machine learning in Python. J. Mach. Learn. Res. **12**, 2825–2830 (2011)
24. Qian, T., Zhu, S., Hoshida, Y.: Use of big data in drug development for precision medicine: an update. Expert Rev. Precis. Med. Drug Dev. **4**(3), 189–200 (2019)
25. Rajendran, K., Jayabalan, M., Rana, M.E.: A study on k-anonymity, l-diversity, and t-closeness techniques. IJCSNS **17**(12), 172 (2017)
26. Rajkovic, V.: Nursery. UCI Machine Learning Repository (1997). https://doi.org/10.24432/C5P88W
27. Samarati, P.: Protecting respondents identities in microdata release. IEEE Trans. Knowl. Data Eng. **13**(6), 1010–1027 (2001)
28. Sen, P.C., Hajra, M., Ghosh, M.: Supervised classification algorithms in machine learning: a survey and review. In: Emerging Technology in Modelling and Graphics: Proceedings of IEM Graph 2018, pp. 99–111. Springer (2020)
29. Slijepčević, D., Henzl, M., Klausner, L.D., Dam, T., Kieseberg, P., Zeppelzauer, M.: k-anonymity in practice: how generalisation and suppression affect machine learning classifiers. Comput. Secur. **111**, 102488 (2021)
30. Tanha, J., Abdi, Y., Samadi, N., Razzaghi, N., Asadpour, M.: Boosting methods for multi-class imbalanced data classification: an experimental review. J. Big Data **7**(1), 1–47 (2020). https://doi.org/10.1186/s40537-020-00349-y
31. The European Commission: A European strategy for data (2020). https://digital-strategy.ec.europa.eu/en/policies/strategy-data. Accessed 20 Jun 2024
32. Verdonck, J., De Boeck, K., Willocx, M., Lapon, J., Naessens, V.: A hybrid anonymization pipeline to improve the privacy-utility balance in sensitive datasets for ml purposes. In: Proceedings of the 18th International Conference on Availability, Reliability and Security, pp. 1–11 (2023)
33. Wagner, I., Eckhoff, D.: Technical privacy metrics: a systematic survey. ACM Comput. Surv. (CSUR) **51**(3), 1–38 (2018)
34. Xu, Z., Cheng, C., Sugumaran, V.: Big data analytics of crime prevention and control based on image processing upon cloud computing. J. Surveill. Secur. Saf. **1**, 16–33 (2020)
35. Zheng, W., Jin, M.: Effects of training data size and class imbalance on the performance of classifiers. In: Conference on Artificial Intelligence and Natural Language, pp. 3–17. Springer (2019)

COLIBRI: Optimizing Multi-party Secure Neural Network Inference Time for Transformers

Daphnee Chabal[1(✉)], Tim Muller[1], Eloise Zhang[1], Dolly Sapra[1], Cees de Laat[1], and Zoltán Ádám Mann[2]

[1] University of Amsterdam, Amsterdam, The Netherlands
d.n.m.s.chabal@uva.nl
[2] University of Halle-Wittenberg, Halle, Germany

Abstract. Secure Neural Network Inference (SNNI) protocols enable privacy-preserving inference by ensuring the confidentiality of inputs, model weights, and outputs. However, large neural networks, particularly Transformers, face significant challenges in SNNI due to high computational costs and slow execution, as these networks are typically optimized for accuracy rather than secure inference speed. We present COLIBRI, a novel approach that optimizes neural networks for efficient SNNI using Neural Architecture Search (NAS). Unlike prior methods, COLIBRI directly incorporates SNNI execution time as an optimization objective, leveraging a prediction model to estimate execution time without repeatedly running costly SNNI protocols during NAS. Our results on Cityscapes, a complex image segmentation task, show that COLIBRI reduces SNNI execution time by 26–33% while maintaining accuracy, marking a significant advancement in secure AI deployment.

Keywords: Secure Neural Network Inference · Privacy-Preserving AI · Neural Architecture Search · Transformers · Visual Segmentation · Secure Inference

1 Introduction

In many real-world Artificial Intelligence (AI) applications, multiple stakeholders are involved, leading to specific security and privacy requirements [1]. In this paper, we focus on the situation where a company – the *model holder* – trains a neural network and then offers inference with this neural network as a service. A *client* can provide an input to the neural network and request inference on this input. The client's input and inference output may contain sensitive information that must be protected from unauthorized access. Additionally, the weights of the neural network constitute the model owner's intellectual property and must also be protected. As illustrated in Fig. 1, Secure Neural Network Inference (SNNI) protocols enable inference, fulfilling all the aforementioned secrecy requirements.

Published by Springer Nature Switzerland AG 2025
L. Nemec Zlatolas et al. (Eds.): SEC 2025, IFIP AICT 745, pp. 17–31, 2025.
https://doi.org/10.1007/978-3-031-92882-6_2

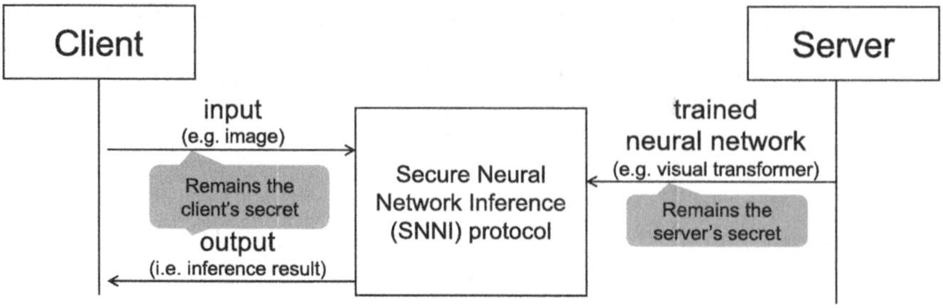

Fig. 1. Overview of the Secure Neural Network Inference (SNNI) process.

A significant challenge with SNNI is its high computation and communication demand [17]. SNNI requires complex cryptographic protocols that need substantial resources for the secure execution of even simple operations. Despite recent significant advancements making SNNI protocols more efficient [12], secure inference remains significantly slower than standard inference [10]. Another challenge is the increasing size and complexity of neural networks developed by the AI community to handle larger inputs and achieve higher accuracy [7].

A more subtle challenge is the mismatch between AI and SNNI objectives. For the AI community, achieving high accuracy is paramount, while keeping costs low is secondary. In SNNI, however, reducing secure inference time is critical, as excessive delays could render services impractical. Functions like SoftMax and ReLU, which minimally affect model size or standard inference time, are computationally expensive in secure execution [19].

This paper introduces COLIBRI, an innovative approach to creating transformer architectures with state-of-the-art accuracy and reduced SNNI execution time. COLIBRI uses neural architecture search (NAS), which automatically identifies the best neural architecture for a task by exploring candidate architectures. Previous NAS-based approaches to accelerate SNNI [13,19,21] optimized proxies such as the number of ReLU operations rather than explicitly targeting SNNI execution time. COLIBRI is the first approach to *optimize explicitly for SNNI execution time in a given hardware/software configuration.* This is important because bottlenecks in SNNI depend heavily on the hardware and software used (e.g. network bandwidth [15] and GPU availability [8]).

Relying on proxies for optimization can yield suboptimal results, while COLIBRI directly targets SNNI execution time for better outcomes. However, explicitly optimizing SNNI execution time during NAS is challenging due to the need to evaluate numerous neural architectures. Running the costly SNNI process for each candidate would result in prohibitive computational costs for NAS, requiring thousands of GPU days. To address this, COLIBRI employs a prediction model to estimate SNNI execution time for candidate architectures in a given setup, avoiding the need for actual SNNI execution during NAS.

We implemented COLIBRI using the HR-NAS search algorithm [5] for visual transformers and the CrypTen SNNI protocol [9]. Because the COLIBRI approach is orthogonal to how NAS algorithms and SNNI protocols work, COLIBRI is adaptable to different choices for implementation, making it versatile for various AI tasks. Our implementation achieves efficient SNNI for large transformers in visual segmentation tasks, which are more complex than simpler benchmarks (e.g., image classification [4,21]). Empirical results show that COLIBRI-generated visual transformers reduce SNNI execution time by 26–33% compared to baseline NAS approaches, while maintaining accuracy.

2 Preliminaries

Secure Neural Network Inference (SNNI) protocols enable collaborative AI inference without sharing confidential data, as shown in Fig. 1. Clients encrypt input data, while model holders protect the secrecy of trained weights, ensuring secure execution of the inference process. Only the client receives the output, with cryptographic guarantees provided by secure multi-party computation (MPC) or homomorphic encryption (HE) [12].

SNNI protocols simulate neural network operations using cryptographic functions, tailored to each layer type. Linear layers (e.g., fully connected or convolutional) are relatively efficient, while non-linear operations like SoftMax and ReLU are computationally intensive under MPC/HE [12]. Our implementation uses CrypTen [9], an MPC-based SNNI protocol, though COLIBRI is compatible with any SNNI protocol.

Neural Architecture Search (NAS) [16] automates the discovery of optimal neural network architectures by exploring a space of possible architectures. NAS evaluates performance metrics like accuracy and computational efficiency, to retain or prune architectures from the search space. NAS uses methods like evolutionary algorithms or gradient-based optimization to perform the search. Modern NAS approaches often use a *supernet* – a large, over-parameterized neural network that encompasses numerous potential architectures [2]. For example, in HR-NAS [5], the supernet consists of 51 search blocks, and each search block is composed of Search Units (SUs). A Search Unit (SU) represents possible architecture paths, such as mini-Transformers or convolution-based sequences. Pruning reduces each search block to at most one SU, while iteratively shrinking dimensions (e.g., matrix sizes, channels, tokens, strides) within SUs. Supernet training combines pruning and training, lowering computational costs. In HR-NAS, the size of search units is penalized, while their contribution to task accuracy is rewarded [5]. The process outputs a trained neural network.

Predicting SNNI time can be done with a prediction model, accounting for the SNNI protocol and hardware/software configuration [20]. The model uses formulas to predict execution time for various layer types. In an offline phase, parameters in the formulas are fine-tuned using measured SNNI execution times across layer types and sizes. This calibration captures how layer types and sizes influence execution time for the given configuration.

3 Our Approach

By combining NAS with SNNI and a prediction model for predicting SNNI execution time of candidate neural architectures, COLIBRI offers a first-of-its-kind

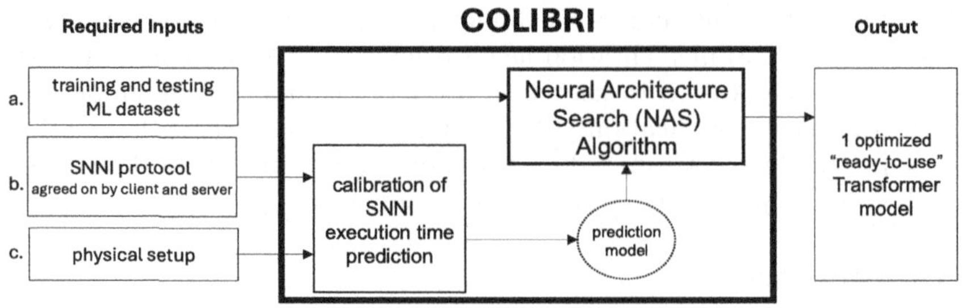

Fig. 2. Overview of the COLIBRI approach.

approach that directly minimizes predicted SNNI execution time in the given client/server setup during NAS, going beyond existing methods that merely aim at reducing the use of allegedly expensive operations like ReLU or SoftMax. As shown in Fig. 2, COLIBRI takes three inputs: (a) the training and testing datasets for an AI task to be performed by the neural network, (b) the chosen SNNI protocol that client and server will use for secure inference, and (c) the used client/server setup, including hardware and software. The output of COLIBRI is a trained Neural Network, optimized for high accuracy and low SNNI execution time in the given client-server setup, ready to be used for secure inference. COLIBRI is adaptable to various SNNI protocols, NAS algorithms, AI tasks, and Neural Network types. In our implementation, we used the CrypTen SNNI protocol [9] and the HR-NAS [5] search algorithm for visual transformers. A central part of COLIBRI is the prediction model that is used to predict SNNI execution time for a neural network in a given hardware/software setup.

3.1 SNNI Execution Time Prediction Model

The SNNI execution time prediction model helps the NAS algorithm optimize Neural Network architectures by minimizing SNNI execution time, avoiding the need to execute the costly SNNI protocol for all candidate architectures. This explicit optimization is a key advantage of COLIBRI over traditional NAS methods, which often rely on metrics like parameter count or FLOPs, poorly correlating with SNNI execution time. COLIBRI's prediction model builds on the analytical prediction approach from [20] (see Table 1). Typically, SNNI protocols execute the secure inference process layer by layer. Similarly, our prediction model predicts the SNNI execution time per layer, summing these to estimate the total SNNI execution time. The secure execution time T_i of layer i is calculated as:

$$T_i = c_1 \cdot S_{\text{in}} + c_2 \cdot S_{\text{par}} + c_3 \cdot N_{\text{op}} + c_4 \cdot S_{\text{out}} + c_5. \tag{1}$$

Here, S_{in}, S_{par}, and S_{out} are the input, parameter, and output sizes, respectively, of layer i, and N_{op} is the number of operations in non-secure inference with layer i. These parameters are estimated for different types of layers as presented in Table 1. The coefficients $c_1, \ldots, c_5$ capture how factors like input size

Table 1. Factors contributing to SNNI execution time for different layer types [20]. N_I/N_O: number of inputs/outputs; C_I/C_O: number of input/output channels; H_I/W_I: input height/width; H_O/W_O: output height/width; H_F/W_F filter height/width; N: number of neurons; C: number of channels; H/W: height/width of input and output

Layer type	S_{in}	S_{par}	N_{op}	S_{out}
Fully connected	N_I	$(N_I + 1)N_O$	$2N_IN_O + N_O$	N_O
Convolutional	$H_IW_IC_I$	$C_IH_FW_FC_O$	$2C_IH_FW_FH_OW_OC_O$	$H_OW_OC_O$
MaxPool/AveragePool	H_IW_IC	0	$H_FW_FH_OW_OC$	H_OW_OC
Batch normalization	HWC	$2C$	$2HWC$	HWC
ReLU	N	0	N	N

and parameter size affect a layer's secure execution time. These values depend on the SNNI protocol, layer type, and client/server hardware and network setup.

COLIBRI's prediction model consists of sub-models for each supported neural network layer type, following Eq. (1). The coefficients $c_1, \ldots, c_5$ and the calculations of S_{in}, S_{par}, S_{out}, and N_{op} vary by layer type, as summarized in Table 1. This model enables fast and accurate SNNI execution time predictions.

The prediction model used in COLIBRI can be calibrated for various SNNI protocols and different hardware and software properties of the client, the server, and the network connection between them. Here, the calibration is done by adjusting the coefficients $c_1, \ldots, c_5$ in each layer-type-specific sub-model. To achieve this, $c_1, \ldots, c_5$ are derived from a regression analysis of actual SNNI execution times, measured when running the specific SNNI protocol in the given client/server setup. The calibration phase involves creating neural networks with layers of different types and sizes and measuring the per-layer SNNI execution time by running the protocol in the specific client/server setup. The linear regression model is trained with non-negative coefficients (from Equation (1)) for each layer type to derive $c_1, \ldots, c_5$.

The simple structure of the prediction model ensures fast and accurate predictions, as validated in [20]. Trained on actual SNNI execution times, the model reliably captures protocol and setup impacts, enabling the NAS algorithm to make informed decisions about candidate architectures.

3.2 NAS Algorithm

Using the calibrated prediction model, NAS aims to produce a Neural Network optimized for high accuracy and low SNNI execution time. The NAS algorithm trains and prunes a supernet iteratively. Pruning is done incrementally, removing the least promising parts of the supernet. Typically, in NAS algorithms, the metrics that form the basis for pruning decisions are combined into a loss function. Thus, in COLIBRI, the output of the SNNI execution time prediction model is integrated into the loss function. In the following discussion, we describe the change required for a representative NAS algorithm, HR-NAS [5].

The original loss function of HR-NAS is:

$$\mathcal{L} = \mathcal{L}_{\text{task}} + \mathcal{L}_{\text{cost}} \tag{2}$$

where $\mathcal{L}_{\text{task}}$ represents the standard loss used in training for the specific machine learning task. The second term, $\mathcal{L}_{\text{cost}}$, is an L1 penalty term that captures the complexity of the neural network architecture. This penalty term aims to drive the overall complexity of the supernet to a minimum, and is defined as:

$$\mathcal{L}_{\text{cost}} = \lambda_{\text{FLOPs}} \cdot \sum_{i \in SU} \Delta_i \cdot |\alpha_i| \tag{3}$$

where SU is the set of search units in the supernet, and for every search unit i, Δ_i is its computational cost, while α_i is a trainable parameter, denoting the importance factor of search unit i in maintaining or enhancing the model's accuracy. λ_{FLOPs} is an empirically determined coefficient for the L1 penalty.

In HR-NAS, the computational cost for every search unit, denoted as Δ_i, is measured in FLOPs alongside a resource-aware term that quantifies the search unit's overall cost. Pruning search unit i during the NAS would reduce the computational cost of the model by Δ_i. This value can be determined based on the shape of the search unit (i.e., the shape of its designated input matrix, its number of channels and kernel sizes for convolutional units, and number of tokens for Transformer units) in addition to the resource-aware factor reflecting the search unit's computational demands. In COLIBRI, the $\mathcal{L}_{\text{cost}}$ penalty term is modified to integrate the predicted SNNI execution time, as follows:

$$\mathcal{L}_{\text{cost}}^{\text{COLIBRI}} = \lambda_{\text{sec}} \cdot \sum_{i \in SU} \Gamma_i \cdot |\alpha_i| \tag{4}$$

Here, Γ_i is the predicted SNNI execution time of search unit i, generated by the prediction model. While the α_i coefficient remains semantically the same as in the original penalty term, the λ_{FLOPs} coefficient is renamed to λ_{sec} to reflect the switch in the computational cost metric from non-secure inference cost in FLOPs to SNNI execution time in seconds. Compared to the loss of HR-NAS in (3), the loss of COLIBRI in (4) leads to different relative penalties for various search units. Operations such as ReLU that are expensive in secure inference have relatively higher values of Γ_i and thus a higher penalty in the loss.

The NAS algorithm in COLIBRI, utilizing the loss $\mathcal{L}_{\text{cost}}^{\text{COLIBRI}}$, is summarized as pseudocode in Algorithm 1. The process starts by initializing the supernet M_Θ, where Θ represents the trainable weights. The model is trained over E epochs. For each epoch, the loss function ($\mathcal{L}_{\text{task}} + \mathcal{L}_{\text{cost}}$) is computed (line 3), and the supernet is trained with this loss function (line 4). After each epoch, and for every Search Unit, the importance factor α_i is computed (line 7), while the prediction model is used to compute Γ_i (line 6). At every pre-defined pruning interval (pri) epochs, the least important search units with the smallest α_i are removed (line 10), while the remaining SU_i are pruned by an amount r_j (line 12). r_j is relative to the height and width of the input of a given search unit. The process repeats until the model is fully trained and optimized for fast SNNI execution. The final optimized model is returned by the algorithm (line 17).

Algorithm 1: COLIBRI Neural Architecture Search

Input :
- supernet M_{Θ} (where Θ are the trainable weights),
- set of search units SU,
- prediction model Pred_L,
- number E of epochs for training,
- pruning interval pri,
- relative pruning amount r (%).

Output: A trained model optimized for fast SNNI execution time.

epoch = 0;
while $epoch < E$ **do**
    M_{Θ}.train() ;
    foreach i *in* SU **do**
        Compute $\Gamma_i = \text{Pred}_L(i)$;
        Calculate α_i, the importance factor for i;
    end
    Calculate $\mathcal{L}_{\text{task}}$ and $\mathcal{L}_{\text{cost}}$ for one epoch;
    if $epoch\%pri == 0$ **then**
        Remove SU_i with $min(\alpha)$;
        foreach *remaining* j *in* SU **do**
            Prune j by amount r_j;
        end
    end
    epoch+ = 1;
end
return optimized M_{Θ}

After NAS finishes, the resulting Neural Network is deployed. Client and server can collaboratively execute the chosen SNNI protocol, achieving secure inference with high accuracy and low SNNI execution time, as optimized by COLIBRI. The neural network can be reused for secure inference multiple times.

4 Experiments

We evaluated COLIBRI using visual transformers on the Cityscapes dataset [3], which reflects the complexity of real-world AI tasks like high-resolution urban scene segmentation. By optimizing for accuracy and SNNI execution time, COLIBRI proves effective for real-world applications.

Furthermore, we used two Virtual Machines to simulate the two parties performing SNNI with COLIBRI's output model. The same setup was used to calibrate the prediction model and measure SNNI execution time. To ensure robustness, experiments were conducted in two setups, requiring separately calibrated prediction models, to compare COLIBRI and HR-NAS outputs. Setup 1 consisted of two identical virtual machines, each having 32 GB of RAM with 8 double-thread CPU cores; the machines communicated with 7 Gbps bandwidth

(10 ms ping time). Setup 2 consisted of two physical servers, each with 64 GB of RAM and 8 double-thread CPU cores, and 10 Gbps bandwidth (5ms ping time). Both Setup 1 and 2 machines ran the Debian 5.10 Linux OS and operated on 8 double-thread CPU cores. We implemented COLIBRI with CrypTen [9] 0.4.1, HR-NAS [5], and Python 3.9.2.

NAS training was conducted in a high-performance environment to handle the computational demands of training and hyperparameter tuning. Nodes with 1–2 GPUs (Tesla A40 or A10), 60–68 single-thread CPU cores, and 50 GB RAM were used. NAS training for every Transformer was set at epochs $E = 500$, with iterative supernet pruning set at $pri = 20$. For the λ coefficient in the loss function, we experimented with two different values. The first value, $\lambda_{\text{sec}} = 0.00014$, was empirically determined to correspond to the original λ_{FLOPS} used in HR-NAS [5]. The second value, $\lambda_{\text{sec}} = 0.00028$, was chosen because COLIBRI uses λ in units of seconds instead of FLOPs, which influences the effect of λ on the final loss term.

Prediction Model Calibration. To perform the calibration of the prediction model, three types of neural networks were created, each with different combinations of layers, resulting in a total of 30 neural networks, each consisting of 15 to 40 layers. Every layer has a random selection (from a predefined pool of viable options) of hyper-parameters, including kernel size, stride, padding, and number of input and output channels. All of these layers were converted to their secure counterpart for the CrypTen protocol [9]. SNNI execution time of each layer of these neural networks was measured when executing the protocol in Setup 1 and Setup 2 separately. To ensure reliable data collection, each neural network was assigned one of ten random seeds to initiate the protocol, while inference time on each neural network was measured 5 times. The accuracy of these neural networks was irrelevant for the prediction model, so training was omitted. The linear regression for predictions was created using the scikit-learn 1.5.2 module in Python and saved into usable files with joblib 1.4.2. To evaluate the regression model, Mean Absolute Scaled Error (MASE) and R^2 scores were used.

Comparison Methodology and Metrics. To evaluate the performance of COLIBRI, we compare the Transformers generated by COLIBRI with those produced by the original NAS algorithm, HR-NAS [5], under similar conditions. A key advantage of HR-NAS is its stable block structure; pruning affects only search units within blocks, not the blocks themselves. As a result, models generated by both HR-NAS and COLIBRI have the same number of search blocks and a similar number of layers, differing only in layer dimensions and function types. This allows a direct comparison of their effectiveness without the confounding factor of architecture depth. Transformers produced by COLIBRI and HR-NAS are compared based on three main characteristics: size (# of parameters), accuracy on the AI task, and SNNI execution time. For the task of image segmentation, accuracy is measured per input image with two metrics: mean Intersection over Union (mIoU) and mean Accuracy (mAcc).

Table 2. Evaluation of Prediction model in Setup 2.

Layer type	Average Real SNNI time (s)	Average Predicted SNNI time (s)	R^2	MASE
Fully Connected	0.26	0.26	0.99	0.02
Convolutional	0.79	0.79	0.99	0.05
MaxPool	15.47	15.54	0.99	0.03
AveragePool	0.002	0.002	0.81	0.41
Batch normalization	0.2	0.12	0.98	0.37
ReLU	7.03	6.86	0.97	0.08

5 Results

Prediction Model Validation. The regression models developed for each layer type demonstrated high predictive accuracy for SNNI execution times. Each regression model was trained using the measured execution times specific to the corresponding layer type (see Table 2).

The low MASE values across all layer types indicate minimal prediction errors relative to the actual execution times. Additionally, R^2 scores are consistently close to 1.0, highlighting the models' effectiveness in capturing the variance in the measured SNNI execution times. These results confirm that the predicted execution times closely align with the real SNNI execution times, validating the accuracy of our regression approach for modeling SNNI execution times across different layer types.

Table 2 shows that among all layer types, ReLU and MaxPool are more time-consuming to compute using SNNI. For ReLU, this is consistent with findings in [19]. MaxPool has been less tested in the context of SNNI work, which often excludes it in favor of convolutional, ReLU, and fully connected layers [12]. Our MaxPool measurements (and predictions) are, however, in line with [20]. Indeed, like ReLU, MaxPool is not trivially computed in a secure protocol as no information can be revealed on which value of a matrix is the maximum, thus requiring complex cryptographic primitives [18].

SNNI Execution Time. Given the particular complexity of the segmentation task and the size of the images in Cityscapes, SNNI with CrypTen on relevant visual transformers takes several minutes per image in our inference setup. To ensure that the evaluation does not take a prohibitively long time, we limited the evaluation to a randomly selected subset of the Cityscapes testing dataset. We opted for randomly selecting 5 images and running inference four times on each of them. This led to 20 results for each combination of technical setup and tested transformer, allowing us to investigate variance across different images as well as variance between different runs on the same image.

Our results showed that accuracy and SNNI execution time differed little between images and between different runs on the same image. The results are

Table 3. Results for the image segmentation dataset Cityscapes. Average over 20 inferences. Best SNNI execution times per setup are marked bold.

Approach	parameters	Performance on Cityscapes			
			SNNI time (s)	mIOU (%)	mAcc (%)
Setup 1					
HR-NAS [5]	1.2M	avg±std	888.14±10.29	70.36 ±2.89	79.18 ±5.96
		min	875.53	66.93	74.59
		max	905.39	73.83	90.18
COLIBRI $\lambda_{sec} = 0.00014$	1.4M	avg±std	829.04±6.84	73.26±4.15	80.61 ±5.93
		min	815.33	69.6	76.13
		max	839.26	81.04	92.29
COLIBRI $\lambda_{sec} = 0.00028$	1.3M	avg±std	**654.56±13.28**	73.58±4.34	80.88±5.55
		min	**640.57**	66.54	72.87
		max	**675.21**	79.86	89.57
Setup 2					
HR-NAS [5]	1.2M	avg±std	312.23±1.26	same as above	
		min	310.342		
		max	314.753		
COLIBRI $\lambda_{sec} = 0.00014$	0.9M	avg±std	292.96 ±1.1	69.24 ±3.52	76.72 ±6.48
		min	291.53	65.87	70.94
		max	294.91	76	89.39
COLIBRI $\lambda_{sec} = 0.00028$	0.9M	avg±std	**209.51±1**	71.53±4.57	75.46±4.63
		min	**207.76**	66.43	75.46
		max	**211.07**	78	87.94

shown in Fig. 3. Overall, our experiments show that COLIBRI-generated Transformers have consistently lower SNNI execution time than HR-NAS-generated Transformers. The average speedup of COLIBRI-generated Transformers over HR-NAS-generated Transformers is 33% in Setup 1 and 26% in Setup 2. A Mann-Whitney U test with $\alpha = 0.001$ confirmed that the difference in SNNI execution time between transformers generated by COLIBRI versus HR-NAS is *statistically significant*. Moreover, the COLIBRI-generated Transformer was faster than the HR-NAS-generated Transformer *on each image*.

The validity of COLIBRI was further demonstrated when looking at task accuracy. Here, we aimed at accuracy retention rather than accuracy drop. Figure 3 shows some variation between images, but a Mann-Whitney U test with $\alpha = 0.001$ confirmed that there is *no statistically significant difference* between COLIBRI-generated Transformers and HR-NAS-generated Transformers in terms of accuracy. This holds true for both of the considered accuracy metrics and for both of the considered technical setups. Thus, overall, we can state that COLIBRI leads to significantly faster transformers without affecting

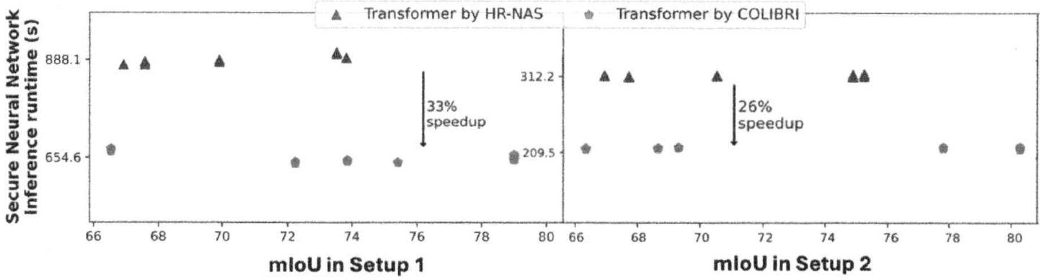

Fig. 3. Measured SNNI execution time and accuracy metric mIOU.

accuracy. Further details of the experimental results are given in Table 3. An interesting phenomenon that can be observed from this table is that for Setup 1, transformers created by COLIBRI are larger (i.e., have more parameters) than the transformer created by HR-NAS. Still, secure inference with the COLIBRI-generated transformers is faster than with the HR-NAS-generated transformer. This once again demonstrates that size is a poor predictor of SNNI execution time, and that COLIBRI's way of explicitly optimizing for SNNI execution time achieves the desired effect.

Overall, the experimental results demonstrate the efficacy of using COLIBRI over another NAS algorithm. This not only proves the feasibility of SNNI execution time prediction in NAS but also highlights the potential of this approach to produce Neural Networks optimized for secure inference.

6 Discussion

High SNNI Execution Time. Despite the speedup achieved by COLIBRI, SNNI execution time is about 10 min in Setup 1 and about 3 min in Setup 2. The appropriateness of this duration may vary depending on the specific use case. Notably, these times are achieved on a complex segmentation task with large images, exceeding the complexity of typical benchmarks used in SNNI evaluations. If desired, SNNI execution time can be mitigated in several ways: upgrading the technical setup (e.g., higher CPU capacity, increased bandwidth, reduced network latency) or using a faster SNNI protocol than CrypTen, such as [8], which offers improved efficiency.

Applying COLIBRI to Different Types of SNNI Protocols. COLIBRI is compatible with other and newer SNNI protocols, which may differ significantly from CrypTen. For instance, some involve more than two parties [6], protect against malicious adversaries [18], or separate input-independent operations into an offline preprocessing phase [8]. Investigating the speedups COLIBRI can achieve with such protocols would be an interesting avenue for future research.

Varying Technical Setups. COLIBRI fine-tunes neural network architectures for fast SNNI in a specific client/server setup, making it ideal for scenarios where the setup is consistent and used repeatedly. If the inference setup differs from the one used for calibrating COLIBRI's prediction model, the neural network will still function accurately and securely, but SNNI execution time may be suboptimal. One way to address this is to run COLIBRI multiple times, creating networks optimized for various setups. During inference, the network optimized for the setup closest to the current conditions can be used. Future research could focus on automating this process to enhance efficiency and effectiveness.

7 Related Work

Recent advances in Secure Neural Network Inference (SNNI) focused on improving computational efficiency by simplifying non-linear layers like SoftMax and ReLU, which are computational bottlenecks in secure protocols. Existing approaches primarily target two strategies: (1) reducing or removing these layers entirely to simplify inference [18], or (2) applying polynomial approximations to linearize them, thereby streamlining the underlying MPC protocol [10]. While effective, these methods focus narrowly on layer-specific optimizations and overlook broader architectural inefficiencies.

Some efforts have employed neural compression techniques, such as knowledge distillation and NAS, to reduce neural network complexity without compromising accuracy. These approaches have largely focused on Convolutional Neural Networks (CNNs) [14], with limited exploration of Transformers. For Transformers, methods like MPCFormer [10] and SecFormer [11] leverage knowledge distillation and approximate SoftMax layers, while MPCViT [19] and PriViT [4] reduce reliance on costly non-linear functions. SAL-ViT [21] employs NAS to optimize attention heads, but all these approaches lack a comprehensive strategy for minimizing overall SNNI execution time. Additionally, they often focus on simplified tasks or benchmarks, limiting real-world applicability.

COLIBRI introduces a novel direction by targeting a previously overlooked variable: predicted SNNI execution time during neural network design. Unlike

Table 4. Summary of approaches related to COLIBRI. KD: Knowledge Distillation

Approach	Compression technique	Optimization target	Supports complex segmentation	Low compute setup
MPCFormer [10]	KD	–	No	No
SecFormer [11]	KD	–	No	No
MPCVit [19]	NAS/KD	# of attention heads	No	Yes
PriViT [4]	KD	–	No	–
SAL-ViT [21]	NAS	Hybrid attention costs	No	Yes
COLIBRI	NAS	Predicted SNNI time	Yes	Yes

existing methods, COLIBRI integrates a calibrated prediction model directly into the NAS process, enabling optimization of architectures specifically for SNNI execution time. This approach is compatible with existing techniques for accelerating non-linear layers but shifts the focus to holistic architectural optimization. To maintain consistency, we employed HR-NAS [5], ensuring the number of SoftMax and ReLU layers remains constant by keeping the search unit structure fixed. Instead, COLIBRI prunes layer dimensions based on predicted SNNI execution time, providing targeted and flexible optimization.

COLIBRI's Contribution. While prior work has evaluated SNNI on relatively small tasks, COLIBRI addresses the challenges of complex, real-world applications. By optimizing speed and accuracy for tasks like image segmentation while accounting for hardware and network factors, COLIBRI sets a new benchmark for SNNI acceleration research. A comparison of COLIBRI with related methods is provided in Table 4.

We are the first to apply these techniques to visual transformers in complex image segmentation tasks, such as Cityscapes, surpassing the simpler benchmarks typically used for SNNI evaluation. COLIBRI's adaptability to various protocols and hardware setups represents a significant advancement in the field.

8 Conclusions

This paper has introduced COLIBRI, a novel approach for automatically creating neural networks – particularly Transformers – with high accuracy and low SNNI execution time. By integrating an SNNI execution time prediction model into NAS, COLIBRI enables the design of architectures explicitly optimized for fast secure inference without running the full SNNI protocol during NAS. This makes COLIBRI scalable and efficient for complex tasks.

Our work opens a new avenue of research into SNNI execution time prediction during NAS, emphasizing the importance of explicitly considering SNNI execution time when optimizing AI models. Departing from previous works that only targeted the number of allegedly expensive functions, such as ReLU, in their NAS strategy, COLIBRI enables the creation of Transformers optimized for a specific SNNI setup.

In the future, we aim to investigate COLIBRI performance with different underlying SNNI protocols and NAS algorithms, as well as with different physical setups. It can be beneficial to assess memory utilization and communication overhead within SNNI protocols to inform future modifications.

References

1. Chan, K.Y., et al.: Deep neural networks in the cloud: review, applications, challenges and research directions. Neurocomputing (2023)
2. Chitty-Venkata, K.T., Emani, M., Vishwanath, V., Somani, A.K.: Neural architecture search for transformers: a survey. IEEE Access **10** (2022)

3. Cordts, M., et al.: The Cityscapes dataset for semantic urban scene understanding. In: Proceedings of the IEEE Conference on CVPR (2016)
4. Dhyani, N., et al.: PriViT: vision transformers for fast private inference. arXiv preprint arXiv:2310.04604 (2023)
5. Ding, M., et al.: HR-NAS: searching efficient high-resolution neural architectures with lightweight transformers. In: Proceedings of the IEEE/CVF Conference on CVPR (2021)
6. Dong, Y., Xiaojun, C., Jing, W., Kaiyun, L., Wang, W.: Meteor: improved secure 3-party neural network inference with reducing online communication costs. In: Proceedings of the ACM Web Conference (2023)
7. Gholami, A., Yao, Z., Kim, S., Mahoney, M.W., Keutzer, K.: AI and memory wall. RiseLab Medium Post (2021)
8. Jawalkar, N., Gupta, K., Basu, A., Chandran, N., Gupta, D., Sharma, R.: Orca: FSS-based secure training and inference with GPUs. In: IEEE Symposium on Security and Privacy (SP). IEEE (2024)
9. Knott, B., Venkataraman, S., Hannun, A., Sengupta, S., Ibrahim, M., van der Maaten, L.: CrypTen: secure multi-party computation meets machine learning. In: Advances in Neural Information Processing Systems (NeurIPS), vol. 34 (2021)
10. Li, D., Shao, R., Wang, H., Guo, H., Xing, E.P., Zhang, H.: MPCFormer: fast, performant and private transformer inference with MPC. arXiv preprint arXiv:2211.01452 (2022)
11. Luo, J., et al.: SecFormer: fast and accurate privacy-preserving inference for transformer models via SMPC. arXiv preprint arXiv:2401.00793 (2024)
12. Mann, Z.Á., Weinert, C., Chabal, D., Bos, J.W.: Towards practical secure neural network inference: the journey so far and the road ahead. ACM Comput. Surv. **56**(5) (2023)
13. Mishra, P., Lehmkuhl, R., Srinivasan, A., Zheng, W., Popa, R.A.: Delphi: a cryptographic inference system for neural networks. In: 29th USENIX Security Symposium. USENIX Association (2020)
14. Peng, H., et al.: AutoReP: automatic ReLU replacement for fast private network inference. In: Proceedings of the IEEE/CVF International Conference on Computer Vision (ICCV) (2023)
15. Prins, J., Mann, Z.Á.: Secure neural network inference for edge intelligence: implications of bandwidth and energy constraints. In: IoT Edge Intelligence. Springer (2024)
16. Ren, P., et al.: A comprehensive survey of neural architecture search: challenges and solutions. ACM Comput. Surv. (CSUR) **54**(4) (2021)
17. de Vries, R., Mann, Z.Á.: Secure neural network inference as a service with resource-constrained clients. In: Proceedings of the IEEE/ACM 16th International Conference on Utility and Cloud Computing (UCC) (2023)
18. Wagh, S., Tople, S., Benhamouda, F., Kushilevitz, E., Mittal, P., Rabin, T.: FALCON: honest-majority maliciously secure framework for private deep learning. Proc. Priv. Enhanc. Technol. (2021)
19. Zeng, W., et al.: MPCViT: searching for accurate and efficient MPC-friendly vision transformer with heterogeneous attention. In: Proceedings of the IEEE/CVF International Conference on Computer Vision (2023)

20. Zhang, E., Mann, Z.Á.: Predicting the execution time of secure neural network inference. In: IFIP International Conference on ICT Systems Security and Privacy Protection. Springer (2024)
21. Zhang, Y., Chen, D., Kundu, S., Li, C., Beerel, P.A.: SAL-ViT: towards latency efficient private inference on ViT using selective attention search with a learnable softmax approximation. In: Proceedings of the IEEE/CVF International Conference on Computer Vision (2023)

SAAFL: Secure Aggregation for Label-Aware Federated Learning

Aftab Akram[1(✉)], Harry N. H. Pham[1], Melek Önen[1], and Clémentine Gritti[2]

[1] Department of Digital Security, EURECOM, 06410 Biot, France
{aftab.akram,huan.pham,melek.onen}@eurecom.fr
[2] CITI Lab, INSA Lyon – Inria, 69100 Villeurbanne, France
clementine.gritti@insa-lyon.fr

Abstract. Secure aggregation (SA) has emerged as a vital component of federated learning (FL), enabling collaborative training of a global machine learning model while safeguarding the privacy of clients' local datasets. Most existing SA protocols implement the privacy preserving-variant of federated averaging (FedAvg) as the aggregation technique and assume independent and identically distributed (IID) datasets across clients. This assumption makes FedAvg unsuitable for non-IID scenarios, where variations in client datasets lead to less effective global model. We propose SAAFL, a SA protocol specifically designed for non-IID settings and more specifically for the recently proposed federated label-aware aggregation (FedLA) protocol. SAAFL computes the weighted average of clients' inputs where weights depend on the label distributions and should remain confidential. SAAFL is resilient to client dropouts and supports client selection. Our experimental results show that it achieves comparable model accuracy with FedLA and remains efficient in terms of computation and communication.

Keywords: Federated Learning · Secure Aggregation · non-IID data

1 Introduction

Federated learning (FL) [13] has received significant interest across various stakeholders nowadays. In such a framework, machine learning models are trained with the collaboration of multiple clients: FL clients train models locally with their data and send them to a server, which aggregates them into a global model, ensuring that data samples never leave clients' premises. As for the aggregation operation, Federated Averaging (FedAvg) [13] is widely used in FL which consists of simply computing the average of all clients' inputs. Unfortunately, recent findings have shown that FedAvg falls short in achieving good model accuracy level when datasets are heterogeneous or non-identically distributed (non-IID) [15,19]. To address this, authors in [9] develop a Federated Label-Aware Aggregation (FedLA) protocol which assigns label-specific weights to improve the accuracy of

Published by Springer Nature Switzerland AG 2025
L. Nemec Zlatolas et al. (Eds.): SEC 2025, IFIP AICT 745, pp. 32–46, 2025.
https://doi.org/10.1007/978-3-031-92882-6_3

non-IID data aggregation. On the other hand, the literature has shown that sharing FL clients' inputs in plaintext can leak information about the training data [14,17] and there has a been a plethora of secure aggregation (SA) solutions [12] to thwart such attacks. Indeed, SA consists of computing an aggregated value without discovering individual inputs. While existing SA methods seem very promising when the aggregation operation consists of FedAvg, these methods, unfortunately, cannot be directly employed for FedLA. Relying on FedLA with non-IID data makes the SA process much more complex since the aggregation is not a simple sum anymore, and the assigned weights should remain confidential, too. Client dropouts also pose a significant challenge in the context of FedLA. While with FedAvg, dropouts were already addressed by reconstructing an encrypted zero-value, such a solution unfortunately falls short in the context of FedLA and may drop the accuracy of the model significantly.

In this paper, we propose a new FL protocol, named SAAFL[1], that is customized for FedLA. This solution ensures, through a new SA building block, a privacy-preserving clients' weighted model update aggregation along with secure clients' weight computations. Moreover, at each training round, SAAFL enables online clients to reconstruct dropped clients' contributions as specific weighted updates based on the previous round's model parameters.

Section 2 identifies the challenges for the design of SA customized for FedLA. In Sect. 3, the main SA building block is described. Section 4 describes the entire SAAFL protocol which is further studied in terms of performance in Sect. 5.

2 Towards Privacy-Preserving FedLA

In this section, we remind the FedLA algorithm and further identify the main challenges to design its privacy-preserving variant. We finally introduce our solution in high-level, explaining how each of these challenges are addressed.

2.1 FedLA Algorithm

As described in [9], FedLA is a FL framework designed to address non-IID data distributions. Compared to the standard FedAvg [13] method whereby the average of FL clients' model updates is computed, in FedLA the server computes a weighted average of these updates, whereby weights translate the distribution of classification labels among FL clients' datasets. Indeed, each client is assigned a so-called FedLA-weight that depends on the distribution of labels among data samples. More specifically, with n clients participating in the training of the FL model, and k labels represented in the entire dataset, let s_u be the number of samples held by client u, s_l be the total number of samples with label l across all clients, and $s_{u,l}$ be the number of samples with label l held by client u. To compute the overall FedLA-weight of each client, the process begins by determining the proportion of data that u owns with label l defined as: $w_{u,l} = \frac{s_{u,l}}{s_l}$. These

[1] SAAFL means simple in Urdu.

terms are further summed up across all labels to compute: $w_u = \sum_{l=1}^{k} w_{u,l}$. Finally, the FedLA-weight for each client u is determined as:

$$w_{FedLA,u} = \frac{w_u}{\sum_{u=1}^{n} w_u} \quad (1)$$

This FedLA-weight serves as the global model's averaging coefficient.[2]

2.2 Challenges When Integrating Secure Aggregation in FedLA

Similar to traditional FL, FedLA is vulnerable to membership inference attacks (MIA) if gradients are sent in the clear and, unfortunately, integrating SA into FedLA is not straightforward and raises new challenges. We describe them below after introducing the aligned threat model as in [11].

Threat Model: An untrusted FL server may collude with some clients, along with the possibility that honest clients unintentionally fail or drop out. These failures can occur at any stage, and the adversary (comprising the server and colluding clients) aims to extract private information about honest clients' individual inputs. Two adversarial settings are considered: in the *passive model*, the adversary follows the protocol correctly but tries to infer private information from the protocol transcript, while in the *active model*, the adversary manipulates messages to uncover private data. We consider attacks that alter the aggregated results or perform denial-of-service (DoS) attacks out of scope. Additionally, attacks, where adversaries impersonate clients, are not considered either, since these can be easily mitigated through the deployment of public key infrastructures (PKI).

FedLA-Weight Privacy (C_1)**:** Unlike the traditional FL approach whereby the aggregator only receives private model updates and executes SA, FedLA firstly requires the private computation of each client's FedLA-weights (which depend on some private inputs from other clients as well). As described in the previous section, these FedLA-weights should remain confidential to the server [21]. As a result, FedLA introduces a dual-layer privacy requirement: one for the private computation of each client's weight based on other clients' inputs and one for the computation of the global model (through a dedicated SA protocol).

Client Dropout in FedLA (C_2)**:** Another challenge that arises with secure FedLA as well as in the standard FL framework is client dropouts. In many real-world scenarios, clients may be intermittently unavailable due to network issues, device power limitations, or other reasons. When clients drop out, their model updates are not received, which can disrupt the training of the model. There already exist many solutions [2,3,8,10,11,18] that are resilient to client dropouts in privacy-preserving variants of FL frameworks. In these schemes, online clients mainly reconstruct the encryption of a zero-value for dropped

[2] The term $\sum_{u=1}^{n} w_u$ equals k in the dataset: $\sum_{u=1}^{n} w_u = \sum_{u=1}^{n}\sum_{l=1}^{k} w_{u,l} = \sum_{u=1}^{n}\sum_{l=1}^{k} \frac{s_{u,l}}{s_l} = \sum_{l=1}^{k}\sum_{u=1}^{n} \frac{s_{u,l}}{s_l} = \sum_{l=1}^{k} \frac{s_l}{s_l} = k$.

clients [2,3,11,18]. Unfortunately, these solutions fall short in the case of FedLA because clients' FedLA weights depend on the contributions of all the other clients including the dropped ones. Hence, the reconstruction of the encryption of a zero-value for dropped clients remains insufficient because this simple addition could skew the FedLA aggregation, leading to inaccurate model updates and degraded performance. Therefore, FedLA requires a new, dedicated fault-tolerant SA scheme that can somehow reconstruct proper FedLA weights that would remove the impact of dropped clients.

Client selection in SA for FedLA (C_3)**:** Another challenge in achieving privacy-preserving FedLA through the use of SA consists of addressing client selection at each round. Indeed, in SA, the aggregation key usually depends on all clients' individual keys, and at each FL round, SA should still be correct while non-selected clients' keys are not included. Since, in FedLA, the distribution of clients is assumed to be non-IID and this is reflected through the use of FedLA weights, these weights of non-selected clients also need to be omitted while still achieving SA correctly.

2.3 Our Solution - Overview

In this section, we explain our design goals to address each of the three challenges identified in the previous section are addressed in the newly proposed solution, named as SAAFL, that is further described in details in Sect. 4.

Privacy-Preserving FedLA-weight Computation (G_1)**:** As previously mentioned, the new solution should incorporate two privacy layers: one to compute each client's FedLA-weight $w_{FedLA,u}$ and one to compute global (aggregated) model parameters during the actual FL round. To compute $w_{FedLA,u}$ in a privacy-preserving manner, we propose that each client u protects the local label distribution $s_{u,l}$ through a standard SA framework and transfers it to the FL server. The server aggregates these received values from all clients to calculate the overall weight per label s_l, which is subsequently returned to each client. Clients can now individually determine their $w_{FedLA,u}$ weight relative to the global label distribution as described in Sect. 2.1, and this, without having access to other clients label weights $s_{v,l}$ in cleartext. These weights should be computed only once in the *Registration* step and require only one communication round. Once weights are determined, clients can proceed to the SA of the weighted model parameters.

Fault-Tolerant FedLA (G_2)**:** Regarding C_2, because the inputs of each client are not independent of each other due to $w_{FedLA,u}$, to address client dropouts, we propose a simple, yet effective, fault-tolerant SA solution based on a variant of the threshold Joye-Libert scheme proposed in [11]. In this new solution named **TJL-A**, each online client sends the difference between their current and previous round weighted inputs.

Once the server receives all inputs, the result will correspond to the aggregation of online clients' weighted parameters together with the previous model parameters multiplied by the remaining weight (corresponding to the dropped clients). Hence dropout clients' inputs become previous model's parameters that are properly weighted. In Sect. 5, we experimentally demonstrate the performance of this solution.

Handling Client Selection in SA for FedLA (G_3)**:** To address the impact of non-selected clients, we apply the same technique proposed in G_2 to handle dropout clients. Hence, non-selected clients are considered as dropouts.

In the sequel of the paper, we describe how SAAFL achieves these three design goals starting by describing the new **TJL-A** building block.

3 Building Blocks

In this section, we outline the key building blocks necessary for designing our solution SAAFL, including the newly proposed **TJL-A** aggregation solution.

Secret Sharing Over the Integers (ISS): ISS used to secret share clients' keying material and some contributions for dropped clients.

- $\{(u, [\Delta s]_u)\}_{u \in \mathcal{U}} \leftarrow$ **ISS.Share**$(s, t, \mathcal{U} = \{1, \ldots, n\})$: This algorithm splits secret $s \in [-I, I]$ into n shares $[\Delta s]_u$, assigning each share to a user $u \in \mathcal{U}$, with t being the reconstruction threshold and $\Delta = n!$. The algorithm creates a random polynomial $p(x)$ of degree $t-1$ where $p(0) = \Delta s$ and each share is $[\Delta s]_u = p(u)$.
- $s \leftarrow$ **ISS.Recon**$(\{(u, [\Delta s]_u)\}_{u \in \mathcal{U}'}, t)$: This algorithm reconstructs secret $s \in [-I, I]$ from at least t shares received from users in $\mathcal{U}' \subseteq \mathcal{U}$. Using the Lagrange interpolation, the secret is computed as:

$$s = \frac{\sum_{u \in \mathcal{U}'} \mu_u [\Delta s]_u}{\Delta^2}, \quad \text{such that } \mu_u = \frac{\Delta \cdot \prod_{v \in \mathcal{U}' \setminus \{u\}} v}{\prod_{v \in \mathcal{U}' \setminus \{u\}} (v - u)}.$$

  μ_u represents the Lagrange coefficient for user u.

Label-aware Threshold Joye-Libert Aggregation (TJL-A): We propose a new variant of the **TJL** scheme originally proposed in [11] that helps SAAFL take into account the FedLA weights of dropped clients during aggregation. The main difference between the newly proposed **TJL-A** scheme and **TJL** is that when FL clients drop, their inputs are not replaced with zero-values anymore. Indeed, the original **TJL** reconstructs the zero-value encrypted with the dropped clients' individual keys. As also shown in Fig. 3 in Sect. 5, in the context of a non-IID distribution of FL clients, aggregating a zero-value for dropped clients significantly impacts the accuracy of the actual model. Therefore, we propose to replace this zero-value with a previous round's model parameters weighted with a specific coefficient. This carefully selected value compensates for the missing contributions of the dropped clients more accurately and ensures the correctness of the aggregation at the same time. Furthermore, the initial contribution of each FL client becomes a weighted differences of their model parameters and the previous model parameters: $x_{u,\tau} = w_{FedLA,u}\theta_u^{\tau} - w_{FedLA,u}\theta^{(\tau-1)}$. Therefore, at the aggregation phase, the server will reconstruct a weighted average of online clients' inputs and previous model parameters for dropped clients.

Accordingly, the proposed **TJL-A** scheme consists of the following PPT algorithms:

- $(sk_0, \{sk_u\}_{u\in\mathcal{U}}, N, H, \sigma) \leftarrow$ **TJL-A.Setup**(λ) : Given security parameter λ, this algorithm outputs one secret key per client sk_u, the aggregator key $sk_0 = -\sum_{u\in\mathcal{U}} sk_u$ and the public parameters $pp = (N, H)$ such that $N = pq$ (p and q being large and equal-size prime numbers) and H is a cryptographic hash function $H : \mathbb{Z}_N \rightarrow \mathbb{Z}_{N^2}$. Additionally, it sets security parameter σ for **ISS**.
- $\{(v, [\Delta sk_u]_v)\}_{v\in\mathcal{U}} \leftarrow$ **TJL-A.SKShare**$(sk_u, t, \mathcal{U})$: This algorithm invokes **ISS.Share** with $sk_u \in [-2^b, 2^b]$, with b representing the bit-length of modulus N and outputs the output of **ISS**, namely the secret shares of sk_u for each user $v \in \mathcal{U}$.
- $Y_{u,\tau} \leftarrow$ **TJL-A.Protect**$(pp, sk_u, \tau, x_{u,\tau})$: This algorithm encrypts private input $x_{u,\tau}$ as described in Eq. 2 for round τ using sk_u and outputs ciphertext $Y_{u,\tau}$ using the original JL algorithm [7]:

$$Y_{u,\tau} = (1 + Nx_{u,\tau}) \cdot H(\tau)^{sk_u} \mod N^2 \tag{2}$$

- $[Y'_\tau]_u \leftarrow$ **TJL-A.ShareProtect**$(pp, \{[\Delta sk_v]_u\}_{v\in\mathcal{U}_{\text{off}}}, \tau, x'_{u,\tau})$: As opposed to the original **TJL.ShareProtect**, this algorithm protects $x'_{u,\tau}$ which is a non-zero value using the shares of the keys of dropped clients $\mathcal{U}_{\text{off}}$ and **ISS** parameters Δ and μ_u:

$$[Y'_\tau]_u = (1 + Nx'_{u,\tau})^{\Delta^2\mu_u^{-1}} \cdot H(\tau)^{\sum_{v\in\mathcal{U}_{\text{off}}}[\Delta sk_v]_u} \mod N^2 \tag{3}$$

- $Y'_\tau \leftarrow$ **TJL-A.ShareCombine**$(\{u, [Y'_\tau]_u\}_{u\in\mathcal{U}_{\text{on}}}, \tau)$: This algorithm calls **ISS.- Recon** and reconstructs the non-zero value that will be further used for the final aggregation. Hence, Y'_τ is computed as $\prod_{u\in\mathcal{U}_{\text{on}}}([Y'_\tau]_u)^{\mu_u} \mod N^2$, here $\mathcal{U}_{\text{on}}$ being the set of online clients, and we obtain:

$$Y'_\tau = \left(1 + N\sum_{u\in\mathcal{U}_{\text{on}}} x'_{u,\tau}\right)^{\Delta^2} \cdot H(\tau)^{\Delta^2\sum_{v\in\mathcal{U}_{\text{off}}} sk_v} \mod N^2 \tag{4}$$

- $x_\tau \leftarrow$ **TJL-A.Agg**$(pp, sk_0, \tau, \{Y_{u,\tau}\}_{u\in\mathcal{U}_{\text{on}}}, Y'_\tau)$: Given public parameters pp, aggregation key sk_0, the ciphertexts of online clients $u \in \mathcal{U}_{\text{on}}$, and the ciphertext of the non-zero value corresponding to dropped clients $v \in \mathcal{U}_{\text{off}}$, this algorithm first computes the aggregated ciphertext Y_τ for round τ as $Y_\tau = \left(\prod_{u\in\mathcal{U}_{\text{on}}}(Y_{u,\tau})\right)^{\Delta^2} \cdot Y'_\tau \mod N^2$ which corresponds to:

$$Y_\tau = \left[1 + N\Delta^2\left(\sum_{u\in\mathcal{U}_{\text{on}}} x_{u,\tau} + \sum_{u\in\mathcal{U}_{\text{on}}} x'_{u,\tau}\right)\right] \cdot H(\tau)^{\Delta^2\cdot\sum_{u\in\mathcal{U}} sk_u} \mod N^2 \tag{5}$$

Finally, to obtain the overall aggregate in cleartext, the algorithm computes:

$$V_\tau = H(\tau)^{\Delta^2\cdot sk_0} \cdot Y_\tau, \quad x_\tau = \frac{V_\tau - 1}{N\Delta^2} \mod N.$$

This recovers the sum of the inputs:

$$x_\mathcal{T} = \sum_{u \in \mathcal{U}_{\text{on}}} w_{FedLA,u} \theta_u^\mathcal{T} + \left(1 - \sum_{u \in \mathcal{U}_{\text{on}}} w_{FedLA,u}\right) \theta^{(\tau-1)} \tag{6}$$

4 SAAFL

In this section, we describe SAAFL, which uses **TJL-A** to compute each client's FedLA weight in a privacy-preserving manner, along with a traditional fault-tolerant SA scheme for aggregation. SAAFL also makes use of a pseudo-random generator (PRG), key agreement scheme (KA), authenticated encryption (AE), and the Shamir's secret sharing Scheme (SS) which due to space constraints are not described in the paper but the reader can refer to [11] as these are the same protocols. SAAFL consists of two phases: (1) *Setup Phase* whereby FL clients are registered and each party receives its keying material and (2) *training phase* whereby model parameters are aggregated and updated in several *FL Rounds.*

Setup Phase. The protocol starts with the *Setup Phase* which comprises three steps: *Registration, Key Setup* and *FedLA-weight Calculation.* Each of these steps is executed only once. At the *Registration* step, a trusted dealer (TD) generates the secret keys sk_u for each client and aggregation key sk_0 for the server along with relevant public parameters pp required by the clients and server. Each client generates public-private key pair over the pp using **KA.Gen** and registers itself by sending the public key to the server. At the *Key Setup* step, once each client receives the list of all registered clients together with their public keys, they establish pairwise keys with each of them and use **TJL-A.SKShare** to generate the shares of their individual **TJL-A** key sk_u. Finally, at the *FedLA-weight Calculation* step, each FL client u encrypts $s_{u,l}$ of data samples with label l with the **TJL-A** secret key sk_u (generated in the previous *Key Setup* step) and sends them to the FL server. The server performs their aggregation using **TJL-A.Agg** and sends s_l of samples with label l to all FL clients. Then, each client calculates its FedLA-weight $w_{FedLA,u}$ (see Eq. 1).

The Training Phase. The training phase consists of the execution of several *FL Rounds* until reaching a certain level of accuracy. Each *FL Rounds* consists of two steps: *Protection* and *Aggregation.* At the *Protection* step, all selected clients encrypt their inputs and send them to the server. Then, at the *Aggregation* step, clients interact with the server to account for the dropped and non-selected clients so that the server can perform the aggregation correctly and accurately. Each FL round begins with the selection of clients $\mathcal{U}^\tau \subseteq \mathcal{U}$ that will participate in the aggregation, and this is performed based on selection ratio k_τ as in the FedLA and ensures that all parties are aware of which clients will participate in the current *FL Rounds* τ in advance.

At the *Protection* step, after training the local models, each client generates a random seed $b_{u,\tau}$ to generate a blinding mask $B_{u,\tau}$ for masking its input $x_{u,\tau}$

and then encrypts it using **TJL-A.Protect**. These blinding masks are used in the same way as in [4,11] to protect the privacy of the clients' inputs in case the server receives the protected values of a given client (usually a straggler) twice using the same τ. Each client then secretly shares seed $b_{u,\tau}$ with other clients using **SS.Share** through the server and transmits its protected input $Y_{u,\tau}$ masked with $B_{u,\tau}$ to the server.

At the *Aggregation* step, the clients receive the list of encrypted shares of blinding mask seeds $b_{u,\tau}$ and deduce the list of online clients $\mathcal{U}_{\text{on}}^{\tau}$ from those shares. Online clients encrypt the relevant value $x'_{u,\tau}$ for non-selected and dropped clients $\mathcal{U} \setminus \mathcal{U}_{\text{on}}^{\tau}$ with **TJL-A.ShareProtect** and the key-shares of these clients. This is to ensure that the FedLA-weights of non-selected and dropped clients also appear in the final aggregation as discussed in Sect. 2.3. Then, each online client sends to the server the shares of the blinding mask seeds

SAAFL - Setup Phase

Registration: $|\mathcal{U}| = n$. $|\mathcal{L}| = k$.

- **Trusted Dealer (TD):**
  1. Run $pp^{\text{KA}} \leftarrow$ **KA.Param**(λ) and $(sk_0, \{sk_u\}_{u\in\mathcal{U}}, N, H, \sigma) \leftarrow$ **TJL-A.Setup**(λ).
  2. Set $pp = (pp^{\text{KA}}, N, H, \sigma, t, n, m, R, \mathbb{F})$ where m is the number of model parameters defined in $\mathbb{Z}_R$, t is the threshold and $\mathbb{F}$ is the field for the **SS** scheme.
  3. Send (pp, sk_u) to each client u and (pp, sk_0) to server.
- **Clients ($\forall u \in \mathcal{U}$):**
  1. Receive (pp, sk_u) from TD.
  2. $(c_u^{\text{PK}}, c_u^{\text{SK}}) \leftarrow$ **KA.Gen**(pp^{KA}): Generate a key pair and send c_u^{PK} to the server.
- **Server:**
  1. Receive (pp, sk_0) from TD and c_u^{PK} from each client $u \in \mathcal{U}$.
  2. Broadcast to all clients the list $\{u, c_u^{\text{PK}}\}_{u\in\mathcal{U}}$.

Key Setup:

- **Clients ($\forall u \in \mathcal{U}$):**
  1. Collect $\{v, c_v^{\text{PK}}\}_{v\in\mathcal{U}}$ of all registered clients.
  2. $\forall v \in \mathcal{U} \setminus \{u\}$, $c_{u,v} \leftarrow$ **KA.Agree**$(\text{pp}^{\text{KA}}, c_u^{\text{SK}}, c_v^{\text{PK}}, H)$: Establish pairwise shared keys.
  3. $\{(v, [sk_u]_v)\}_{v\in\mathcal{U}} \leftarrow$ **TJL-A.SKShare**$(sk_u, t, \mathcal{U})$: Generate t-out-of-n shares of sk_u.
  4. $\forall v \in \mathcal{U} \setminus \{u\}$, $\epsilon_{u,v} \leftarrow$ **AE.Enc**$(c_{u,v}, u \,\|\, v \,\|\, [sk_u]_v)$: Encrypt each share with $c_{u,v}$ and send $\{(u, v, \epsilon_{u,v})\}_{v\in\mathcal{U}}$ to server.
- **Server:**
  1. Collect and forward $\{(u, v, \epsilon_{u,v})\}_{v\in\mathcal{U}}$ to registered clients.

FedLA-weight Calculation:

- **Clients ($\forall u \in \mathcal{U}$):**
  1. $\forall l \in \mathcal{L}, W_{u,l} \leftarrow$ **TJL-A.Protect**$(pp, sk_u, \tau_0, s_{u,l})$: Protect the local label distribution $s_{u,l}$ and send $W_{u,l}$ to the server.
- **Server:**
  1. Collect all $W_{u,l}$ from clients.
  2. $\forall l \in \mathcal{L}, s_l \leftarrow$ **TJL-A.Agg**$(pp, sk_0, \tau_0, W_{u,l}, Y'_{\tau_0})$: Aggregate all $W_{u,l}$ to obtain the total number s_l of samples with label l. Here, $Y'_{\tau_0} = 1$.
- **Clients** ($\forall u \in \mathcal{U}$):
  1. Compute $w_{FedLA,u}$ (see Eq. 1 in Section 2.1).

Fig. 1. Detailed description of the *Setup Phase* of SAAFL

for other online clients and the share of the protected non-zero value $[Y'_\tau]_u$ for the non-selected and dropped clients. The server reconstructs the blinding masks using **SS.Recon** and **PRG** and combines the shares of the protected approximated value $[Y'_\tau]_u$ using **TJL-A.ShareCombine**. Finally, the server computes the masked sum c_τ of the weighted inputs of online clients $x_{u,\tau}$ and the approximated value $x'_{u,\tau}$ for non-selected and dropped clients with **TJL-A.Agg** and removes the clients' blinding masks to obtain the aggregated model x_τ for *FL Round* τ (Fig. 1).

Security Analysis: SAAFL must guarantee the privacy of the clients' inputs against the passive and active adversaries. We sketch the proofs following [11] (Fig. 2).

SAAFL - FL Round (τ)

<u>**Client Selection:**</u> Clients are selected based on the parameter k_τ and previous round model $\theta^{\tau-1}$. Let $\mathcal{U}^\tau \subseteq \mathcal{U}$ represent the set of selected clients in the current FL round τ.
<u>**Protection:**</u>

- **Clients** ($\forall u \in \mathcal{U}^\tau$):
  1. $b_{u,\tau} \xleftarrow{R} \mathbb{F}$: Sample a seed for **PRG**.
  2. $B_{u,\tau} \leftarrow$ **PRG**$(b_{u,\tau})$: Extend the seed using **PRG** to produce the blinding mask.
  3. $x_{u,\tau} \leftarrow w_{FedLA,u}\theta_u^\tau - w_{FedLA,u}\theta^{(\tau-1)}$: Compute client u's input.
  4. $Y_{u,\tau} \leftarrow$ **TJL-A.Protect**$(pp, sk_u, \tau, x_{u,\tau} + B_{u,\tau})$: Mask and protect the input $x_{u,\tau}$.
  5. $\{(v, [b_{u,\tau}]_v)\}_{v\in\mathcal{U}^\tau} \leftarrow$ **SS.Share**$(b_{u,\tau}, t, \mathcal{U}^\tau)$: Generate t-out-of-n shares of $b_{u,\tau}$.
  6. $\forall v \in \mathcal{U}^\tau \setminus \{u\}$, $e_{(u,v),\tau} \leftarrow$ **AE.Enc**$(c_{u,v}, u\|v\|[b_{u,\tau}]_v)$: Encrypt shares.
  7. If any of the above steps fails, abort. Otherwise, send $(\{e_{(u,v),\tau}\}_{v\in\mathcal{U}^\tau}, Y_{u,\tau})$ to the server.
- **Server:**
  1. Collect $(\{e_{(u,v),\tau}\}_{v\in\mathcal{U}^\tau}, Y_{u,\tau})$ from remaining clients.
  2. Define the set of online clients $\mathcal{U}_{\text{on}}^\tau \subseteq \mathcal{U}^\tau$ based on received tuples. If $|\mathcal{U}_{\text{on}}^\tau| < t$, then abort. Otherwise, send $\{(u, v, e_{(u,v),\tau})\}_{u,v\in\mathcal{U}_{\text{on}}^\tau}$ to online clients.

<u>**Aggregation:**</u>

- **Clients** ($\forall u \in \mathcal{U}_{\text{on}}^\tau$):
  1. Receive $\{(v, u, e_{(v,u),\tau})\}_{v\in\mathcal{U}_{\text{on}}^\tau}$ from the server and deduce $\mathcal{U}_{\text{on}}^\tau$.
  2. $\forall v \in \mathcal{U}_{\text{on}}^\tau \setminus \{u\}$, $v'\|u'\|[b_{v,\tau}]_u \leftarrow$ **AE.Dec**$(c_{u,v}, e_{(v,u),\tau})$: Decrypt secret shares. Assert that $v' = v$ and $u' = u$.
  3. $x'_{u,\tau} = \frac{1}{|\mathcal{U}_{\text{on}}^\tau|}\theta^{(\tau-1)}$: Compute the approximation for non-selected and dropped clients.
  4. $[Y'_\tau]_u \leftarrow$ **TJL-A.ShareProtect**(pp, $\{[\Delta sk_v]_u\}_{v\in\mathcal{U}\setminus\mathcal{U}_{\text{on}}^\tau}, \tau, x'_{u,\tau})$: Protect $x'_{u,\tau}$ with client u's key shares of non-selected and dropped clients.
  5. If any of above steps fails, abort. Otherwise, send $(\{[b_{v,\tau}]_u\}_{v\in\mathcal{U}_{\text{on}}^\tau}, [Y'_\tau]_u)$ to the server.
- **Server**
  1. Collect $(\{[b_{v,\tau}]_u\}_{v\in\mathcal{U}_{\text{on}}^\tau}, [Y'_\tau]_u)$ from online clients.
  2. $\forall u \in \mathcal{U}_{\text{on}}^\tau$, $b_{u,\tau} \leftarrow$ **SS.Recon**$(\{[b_{u,\tau}]_v\}_{v\in\mathcal{U}_{\text{on}}^\tau}, t)$: Reconstruct blinding mask seeds.
  3. $\forall u \in \mathcal{U}_{\text{on}}^\tau$, $B_{u,\tau} \leftarrow$ **PRG**$(b_{u,\tau})$: Reconstruct the blinding masks.
  4. $Y'_\tau \leftarrow$ **TJL-A.ShareCombine**$(\{[Y'_\tau]_u\}_{u\in\mathcal{U}_{\text{on}}^\tau}, t)$: Reconstruct the protected approximations.
  5. $c_\tau \leftarrow$ **TJL-A.Agg**(pp, $sk_0, \tau, \{Y_{u,\tau}\}_{u\in\mathcal{U}_{\text{on}}^\tau}, Y'_\tau)$: Aggregate all inputs from the online clients and all approximations from the dropped and non-selected clients.
  6. $x_\tau = c_\tau - \sum_{v\in\mathcal{U}_{\text{on}}^\tau} B_{u,\tau} = \sum_{u\in\mathcal{U}_{\text{on}}^\tau} x_{u,\tau} + \sum_{u\in\mathcal{U}_{\text{on}}^\tau} x'_{u,\tau}$: Calculate the final result by removing the blinding masks.

Fig. 2. Detailed description of the FL Round in SAAFL

Security in the Passive Model: In the honest-but-curious model, the server follows the protocol but colludes with up to $n - t$ clients. Let $\mathcal{U}_C$ represent the corrupted clients, and $\mathcal{C} = \mathcal{U}_C \cup \mathcal{S}$ where $\mathcal{S}$ is the server. The view of $\mathcal{C}$ is computationally indistinguishable from a simulated view if $|\mathcal{U}_C| = n - t < t$. Therefore, $t > n/2$, allowing recovery from up to $n/2 - 1$ client failures. This relies on the security of the underlying cryptographic primitives. KA ensures that entities in $\mathcal{C}$ cannot distinguish the honest clients' pairwise keys from random values. The **TJL-A** scheme ensures that protected inputs and honest clients' shares appear random if entities in $\mathcal{C}$ have fewer than t shares. SS (and ISS) guarantees that entities in $\mathcal{C}$ cannot distinguish the shares from random values if they have no more than $t - 1$ shares.

Security in the Active Model: In the active model, the server can manipulate its inputs. The server only distributes clients' public keys and encrypted shares, which it cannot alter due to the AE scheme. The server's power is limited to withholding shares, potentially misleading clients about which are online. Importantly, the server can provide different views to clients, convincing some to send a protected approximation Y'_τ for client u, while others send shares of the blinding mask $b_{u,\tau}$. If the server obtains both Y'_τ and $b_{u,\tau}$ for the same client u in round τ, it can unmask the input. Colluding with $n-t$ corrupted clients, the server can gain $n - t$ shares of Y'_τ and $b_{u,\tau}$. For the remaining t honest clients, it can manipulate half to send shares of Y'_τ and the other half shares of $b_{u,\tau}$, learning up to $n - t + t/2$ shares. Hence, $n - t + t/2 < t$, implying $t > 2n/3$, allowing recovery from up to $n/3 - 1$ client failures.

5 Performance Evaluation

Experimental Setup. We have implemented SAAFL[3] and to evaluate its performance, experiments are conducted on a machine equipped with an AMD EPYC 7272 processor, 128 GB of RAM, and 4 NVIDIA GeForce RTX 3090 graphics cards. The underlying cryptographic primitives consist of the same building blocks and libraries as in [11]. We use the EMNIST-balanced dataset [6] with $k = 47$ labels, each of which represented by 2400 samples. This is one of the two datasets utilized in [9] to evaluate the original FedLA. We also employ the same CNN model of [9] which consists of two convolutional layers, one dropout layer, and two linear layers. The model is configured with a batch size of 256 and a learning rate of 0.01.

To evaluate the accuracy of the resulting model, similar to [9], the EMNIST-balanced dataset is distributed among $n = |\mathcal{U}| = 10$ clients according to two parameters: the number of unique labels that each non-IID client has, denoted as $unique_c$ and $noniid_s$ which is the proportion of non-IID clients. We vary $unique_c$ across $\{1, 2, 3, 4, 6\}$ and $noniid_s$ across $\{0.1, 0.3, 0.5, 0.7\}$. Each IID client holds 2400 samples while each non-IID client holds all samples of the labels to which it is assigned: e.g., if $unique_c = 2$, each non-IID client holds $2 \times 2400 = 4800$

[3] The code is available in https://github.com/Aftab201/SAAFL.git.

samples. At each FL round, we define the selection ratio $k_\tau \in \{0.7, 0.8, 0.9\}$. Each setting is evaluated by running experiments over 100 FL rounds each with 10 local epochs. In our protocol, non-selected clients are treated as dropped. We set the **TJL-A** threshold to $t = 6$ and allow a maximum dropout rate f of 0.1, 0.2, or 0.3 when k_τ is 0.7, 0.8, or 0.9, respectively. We further evaluate the performance of SAAFL in terms of computation and communication while considering 100 users and $k_\tau = 0.8$, $f = 0.2$.

Experimental Results. First, we compare testing accuracy of SAAFL under a non-IID setting with that of FedAvg, original FedLA, and FedLA-FTSA [11] which executes **TJL** with dropout clients' inputs set to zero. We evaluate worst-case scenario for SA, i.e., a maximum dropout rate that each method can handle.

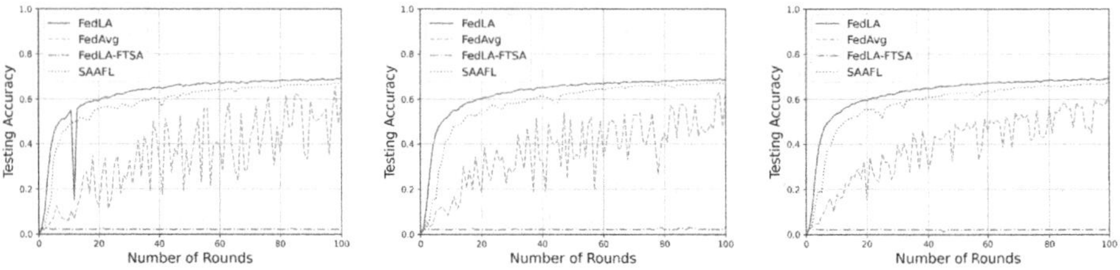

(a) $k_\tau = 0.7, f = 0.1$ (b) $k_\tau = 0.8, f = 0.2$ (c) $k_\tau = 0.9, f = 0.3$

Fig. 3. Testing accuracy for FedLA, FedAvg, FedLA-FTSA, and SAAFL with $unique_c = 1$, $noniid_s = 0.7$.

Since FedLA has been proved to have superior accuracy to FedAvg in data distribution in which the non-IID clients are the majority [9], we choose to discuss the results of the experiments in which $unique_c = 1$ and $noniid_s = 0.7$. As shown in Fig. 3 and as expected, FedAvg suffers more unstable performance than FedLA and SAAFL because of the highly non-IID data distribution. We also observe that FedLA-FTSA yields worst performance mainly because dropped clients' inputs are considered as zero and this does not help achieve aggregation correctness in FedLA. Meanwhile, SAAFL achieves almost as good accuracy level as FedLA thanks to the proposed **TJL-A** scheme which sets dropped clients' inputs as model parameters of the previous round weighted with specific coefficients. Furthermore, in Fig. 3a, FedLA has significant accuracy drop in one early round in which all selected clients have non-IID data distribution. This may happen when proportion of non-IID clients $noniid_s$ is equal to the selection ratio k_τ. On the contrary, SAAFL avoids this issue by adding to FedLA-weighted average $\sum_{u \in \mathcal{U}_{\text{on}}^{\tau}} w_{FedLA,u} \theta_u^{\tau}$ an approximated value $\left(1 - \sum_{u \in \mathcal{U}_{\text{on}}^{\tau}} w_{FedLA,u}\right) \theta^{(\tau-1)}$ that compensates for the impact of non-IID clients.

Furthermore, we also propose to integrate differentially private stochastic gradient descent (DP-SGD) [1] in the local training of each client using Opacus [20] in order to add another layer of privacy protection to protect against global membership inference attacks. We compare the performance of FedAvg and SAAFL. DP-SGD requires three extra parameters: the maximum gradient norm C, privacy budget per client per FL round (ϵ, δ). Fine-tuning of these parameters is required to balance the negative impact of DP to the performance and the privacy protection level. We choose optimized parameters $C = 7.0, \epsilon = 2.0, \delta = 10^{-5}$ for these experiments. Figure 4 shows the accuracy of the FedAvg and SAAFL when applying DP-SGD. While, due to the noise added to the models, both methods experience a performance decrease, compared to the results without DP-SGD, FedAvg has a more significant drop in testing accuracy than SAAFL does.

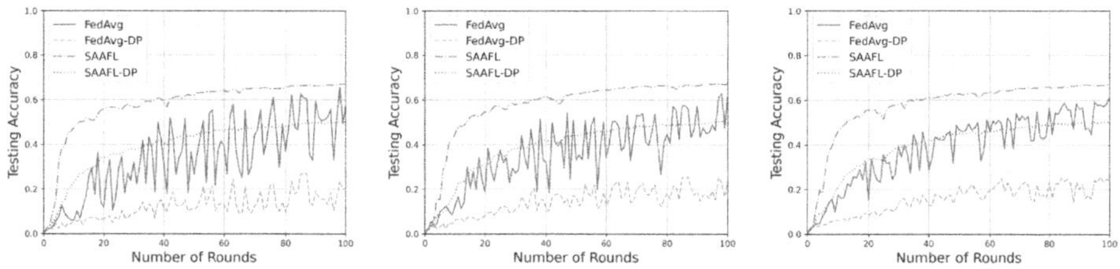

(a) $k_\tau = 0.7, f = 0.1$ (b) $k_\tau = 0.8, f = 0.2$ (c) $k_\tau = 0.9, f = 0.3$

Fig. 4. Testing accuracy for FedAvg, and SAAFL with DP-SGD ($C = 7.0, \epsilon = 2.0, \delta = 10^{-5}$) with $unique_c = 1$, $noniid_s = 7$.

We finally evaluate the performance of SAAFL in terms of computation time and communication cost. We set the number of clients to 100. As shown in Table 1, with $k_\tau = 0.8$, and $f = 0.2$, each client takes 249 ms to run the *Key Setup* whereas the server takes 1.55 ms. The calculation of *FedLA-weights*, takes 38 ms at the client and 1085 ms at the server. Finally, at each *FL Round*, each client takes 6463 ms for the SA of model updates and the server, 46475 ms. The data transfer at each client in *Key Setup*, *FedLA-weight Calculation*, and *FL Round* are measured as 14.27 KB, 14.64 KB, and 24.88 KB, respectively.

Table 1. Computation and Communication Cost of SAAFL with $n = 100$, $k_\tau = 0.8$, $f = 0.2$.

SAAFL	Server	Client	BW
Key Setup	1.55 ms	249 ms	14.27 KB
FedLA-weight Calculation	1085 ms	38 ms	14.64 KB
FL Round	46457 ms	6463 ms	24.88 KB

When compared with the solution in [11], SAAFL incurs the same complexity, namely: $O(n + m)$ for the client and $O(n^2 + nm)$ for the server both for communication and storage, and $O(n^2 + m)$ for the client and $O(n^2 + nm)$ for the server in terms of computation. (n and m being the number of clients and the number of model parameters, respectively).

6 Related Work

We study the related work according to the three challenges that we have identified in Sect. 2. Many SA schemes have been proposed for FL [12]: The majority of them unfortunately omit the case with non-IID clients (C_1) and use the standard FedAvg solution to obtain the aggregated model. Such solutions become ineffective in the non-IID case. Regarding client dropouts (C_2), existing solutions either (i) rely on online clients to reconstruct offline clients' inputs [4,11] or, (ii) define dedicated parties such as *decryptors* in [10], to ensure aggregation correctness, or (iii) consider online clients' inputs only and define aggregation keys on the fly [18] (this also seems to address client selection). SAAFL, relies on online clients but to achieve a good level of accuracy in the non-IID context, the reconstructed value for dropped clients is not zero but a customized one. Recently, [16] develops a FL scheme that uses a dedicated polynomial integer neural network to address both non-IID distribution and client dropouts. Regarding C_3, most of the existing solutions, including [16], assume that client selection has already happened and usually omit this important operation, whereas in SAAFL, non-selected clients are considered as dropouts too. Finally, the very recent work in [5] considers the use of DP mechanisms for non-IID clients. This work can be considered as independent as it does not implement SA. A combination of this work with SAAFL can be an interesting future work direction.

7 Conclusion and Future Work

We have developed a new privacy-preserving FL framework named SAAFL that is suitable to environments where clients datasets are non-IID and runs in two communication rounds, only. SAAFL is based on a customized SA protocol **TJL-A** where the dropped clients' shares depend on the previous round's parameters. Thanks to **TJL-A** and as shown by our experimental results, SAAFL exhibits an acceptable level of accuracy. Finally, the DP-SGD mechanism is used to add another protection level for global model parameters. For future work, we aim to address stronger threat models, ensuring the privacy and correctness of the aggregated value even in the presence of malicious users and/or aggregators.

Acknowledgments. This work has been partially supported by the TRAIN project number ANR-22-FAI1-0003, the 3IA Côte d'Azur programme reference number ANR-23-IACL-0001 and the project number ANR-23-CPJ1-0060-01.

References

1. Abadi, M., et al.: Deep learning with differential privacy. In: ACM SIGSAC Conference on Computer and Communications Security (ACM CCS) (2016)
2. Bell, J.H., Bonawitz, K.A., Gascón, A., Lepoint, T., Raykova, M.: Secure single-server aggregation with (poly)logarithmic overhead. In: ACM SIGSAC Conference on Computer and Communications Security (CCS) (2020)
3. Bonawitz, K., et al.: Towards federated learning at scale: system design (2019)
4. Bonawitz, K., et al.: Practical secure aggregation for privacy-preserving machine learning. In: ACM SIGSAC Conference on Computer and Communications Security (CCS) (2017)
5. Chen, L., Ding, X., Bao, Z., Zhou, P., Jin, H.: Differentially private federated learning on non-IID data: convergence analysis and adaptive optimization. IEEE Trans. Knowl. Data Eng. **36**, 4567–4581 (2024)
6. Cohen, G., Afshar, S., Tapson, J., Van Schaik, A.: EMNIST: extending MNIST to handwritten letters. In: International Joint Conference on Neural Networks (IJCNN) (2017)
7. Joye, M., Libert, B.: A scalable scheme for privacy-preserving aggregation of time-series data. In: International Conference on Financial Cryptography and Data Security (FC) (2013)
8. Kadhe, S., Rajaraman, N., Ramchandran, K.: FastShare: scalable secret sharing by leveraging locality. In: 2021 IEEE International Symposium on Information Theory (ISIT) (2021)
9. Khalil, A., et al.: Label-aware aggregation for improved federated learning. In: International Conference on Fog and Mobile Edge Computing (FMEC) (2023)
10. Ma, Y., Woods, J., Angel, S., Polychroniadou, A., Rabin, T.: Flamingo: multi-round single-server secure aggregation with applications to private federated learning. In: IEEE Symposium on Security and Privacy (SP) (2023)
11. Mansouri, M., Önen, M., Ben Jaballah, W.: Learning from failures: secure and fault-tolerant aggregation for federated learning. In: 38th Annual Computer Security Applications Conference (ACSAC) (2022)
12. Mansouri, M., Önen, M., Ben Jaballah, W., Conti, M.: SOK: secure aggregation based on cryptographic schemes for federated learning. In: Proceedings on Privacy Enhancing Technologies (PoPETS) (2023)
13. McMahan, B., Moore, E., Ramage, D., Hampson, S., Aguera y Arcas, B.: Communication-efficient learning of deep networks from decentralized data. In: International Conference on Artificial Intelligence and Statistics (AISTATS) (2017)
14. Nasr, M., Shokri, R., Houmansadr, A.: Comprehensive privacy analysis of deep learning: passive and active white-box inference attacks against centralized and federated learning. In: IEEE Symposium on Security and Privacy (SP) (2019)
15. Oza, P., Patel, V.M.: Federated learning-based active authentication on mobile devices. In: IEEE International Joint Conference on Biometrics (IJCB) (2021)
16. Shao, J., Sun, Y., Li, S., Zhang, J.: DReS-FL: dropout-resilient secure federated learning for non-IID clients via secret data sharing. In: 36th International Conference on Neural Information Processing Systems (NIPS) (2022)
17. Shokri, R., Stronati, M., Song, C., Shmatikov, V.: Membership inference attacks against machine learning models. In: IEEE Symposium on Security and Privacy (SP) (2017)
18. Taiello, R., Önen, M., Gritti, C., Lorenzi, M.: Let them drop: scalable and efficient federated learning solutions agnostic to client stragglers. In: International Conference on Availability, Reliability and Security (ARES) (2024)

19. Xiao, P., Cheng, S., Stankovic, V., Vukobratovic, D.: Averaging is probably not the optimum way of aggregating parameters in federated learning. Entropy **22**(3), 314 (2020)
20. Yousefpour, A., et al.: Opacus: user-friendly differential privacy library in PyTorch (2021)
21. Zari, O., Xu, C., Parra-Arnau, J., Ünsal, A., Önen, M.: Link inference attacks in vertical federated graph learning. In: 40th Annual Computer Security Applications Conference (ACSAC) (2024)

"We've Met Some Problems": Developers' Issues with Privacy-Preserving Computation Techniques on Stack Overflow

Patrick Kühtreiber(✉), Sabrina Heimermann, Sebastian Schillinger, and Delphine Reinhardt

Institute for Computer Science, University of Göttingen, Goldschmidtstr. 7, 37077 Göttingen, Germany

Abstract. Software developers must adhere to privacy regulations and apply privacy principles. However, developers may not be privacy experts and hence are likely to encounter issues when choosing, applying, and implementing the corresponding *Privacy-Preserving Computation* (PPC) techniques. As a result, these methods may be misunderstood or even not applied. In order to mitigate these issues, we must first identify and understand them in detail. To this end, we have conducted a study on the popular developer Q&A website Stack Overflow. Using manual coding, we have extracted themes and issues related to PPC techniques and discussed by developers. Additionally, we have analyzed and discussed use cases and how they align with current research. Our results confirm our assumption, showing (1) a lack of awareness and understanding, (2) complex or missing documentation, and (3) a lack of easy-to-use libraries. Based on our obtained results, we provide recommendations to educators and developers on how to address the identified issues.

Keywords: Stack Overflow · Privacy-preserving Computation · Qualitatitive Analysis

1 Introduction

In today's data driven world, most applications process users' personal data. Data breaches are not only harmful to users, but also costly in terms of both money and reputation [25,43]. Privacy regulations, such as the European *General Data Protection Regulation* (GDPR), aim at minimizing the individuals' risks caused by these data collections by, e.g., making it mandatory for any data-provessing application to comply with *Privacy-by-Design* (PbD) guidelines. However, the existing worldwide data protection regulations only include high-level guidelines. As a result, developers are responsible for choosing and applying the appropriate methods, even if they are not experts in privacy. This process

Published by Springer Nature Switzerland AG 2025
L. Nemec Zlatolas et al. (Eds.): SEC 2025, IFIP AICT 745, pp. 47–60, 2025.
https://doi.org/10.1007/978-3-031-92882-6_4

can be difficult for them. Indeed, no quantifiable metrics, established processes, or well-known tools for developers to comply with the PbD guidelines exist [26]. Therefore, *Privacy-Enhancing Technologies* (PETs) are underused in most companies [19]. Moreover, developers rarely receive any training regarding PETs, which leads to misconceptions [20,38,52]. Developers seek help by consulting colleagues [54], friends, or searching online [8,17]. Among existing online information sources, *Stack Overflow* (SO) is one of the main sources developers use to ask for advice from peers with over 100 million monthly visitors, ranging from data scientists to software developers [5,46]. Until now, SO has been used in research to identify topics and trends in areas such as mobile development [3,32] [51], non-functional requirements [3,61,62], and general privacy [48].

In comparison, we focus on *Privacy-Preserving Computation* (PPC) techniques that are designed to ensure the protection of personal data while keeping them useful for analysis. PPC techniques are a subset of PETs and are designed to help developers in improving privacy protection [18]. However, they are often not well understood and underused [11,12,27]. One reason behind these misconceptions and lower adoption is the lack of useful frameworks or libraries [2,19]. We further hypothesize that there is a gap between the practical use cases for PPC techniques and the research community's focus. By identifying these practical use cases, research efforts can better focus on solving real-world problems and, thus, increase the adoption rate of PPC techniques.

As basis for our analysis, we have looked into related works [2,28] and four worldwide leading and well-renowned institutions, namely the *European Union Agency for Cybersecurity* (ENISA) [10], *Information Systems Audit and Control Association* (ISACA) [34], the UN [50], and the *National Institute for Standards and Technology* (NIST) [49]. No unifying taxonomy of PPC techniques exists beyond these sources that provide an international view on the PPC landscape. As a result, we consider *Differential Privacy* (DP), *Homomorphic Encryption* (HE), and *Secure Multi-Party Computation* (SMPC), as these are the only techniques mentioned in all of the relevant sources.

By identifying developers' issues, our ultimate goal is to design solutions that help and guide them towards privacy-preserving software development. To this end, we first aim at answering the following research questions:

- **RQ1;** Which PPC technique raises the most questions as indicator of developers' interests or particular difficulties?
- **RQ2:** What are the concrete difficulties encountered with PPC techniques and what are their primary use cases?

By answering them, our contributions are as follows:

1. We increase the understanding of developers' issues with privacy-preserving software development and identify (1) lack of documentation, (2) false expectations, (3) high perceived complexity, (4) limited perceived utility, and (5) limited awareness as main obstacles.
2. We identify real-world use cases of the investigated PPC techniques and thereby point out where the gap between practice and research lies.

3. We provide recommendations on how the most discussed issues can be addressed. For example, programming education should include PPC techniques, such as DP, in order to mitigate misunderstandings.

The remainder of this paper is structured as follows: We discuss related work in Sect. 2 and present our methodology in Sect. 3. Next, we present our results in Sect. 4, before discussing them in Sect. 5, and make concluding remarks in Sect. 6.

2 Related Work

DP [16] is a statistical principle promising that nothing about an individual in a dataset can be learned that would not otherwise have been learned if they were not a part of the dataset. HE allows for computation on encrypted data [21]. However, no practical solution currently exists that does not introduce substantial overhead. SMPC allows multiple parties to collaboratively evaluate a function over secret data without revealing any data to each other [56].

Acar et al. were among the first who called for research on developers' struggles with implementing privacy-preserving techniques [1]. Moreover, developers' views on privacy do not necessarily overlap with users' views [45], which is why it is worthwhile to consider developers separately from users. Hadar et al. interviewed 27 developers and show that, besides other factors, developers' adoption of privacy frameworks depend on their usability throughout the whole software development life-cycle [22]. Similar results have been obtained by a study with 149 developers and found that useful techniques and interoperability with existing work are the most important factors in adopting privacy-enhancing methods [44]. Iwaya et al. evaluated developers' mindset while implementing privacy techniques and found, i.a., that established procedures and tools increase their adoption, thus, improving individuals' data privacy [24]. They did however not take concrete PPC techniques into account.

Using *Latent Dirichlet Allocation* (LDA), Yang et al. investigated and categorized security related posts on SO [55]. Tahaei et al. performed two analyses on SO: (1) applying LDA to privacy-related questions on SO [48] and (2) investigating SO questions of health app developers [47]. Diepenbrock et al. investigated developers' problems with privacy policies on SO and found the generation of privacy policies, compliance, and implementation of PETs to be the main issues [15]. Finally, May et al. evaluated security related posts on SO and concluded that configuration issues are the primary problems encountered by developers [35]. Instead of using SO, Li et al. investigated questions related to personal data on Reddit and found that developers mostly talk about privacy when they are compelled to implement it [31]. These works do however not focus on concrete PPC techniques. We argue that this focus is necessary to identify concrete problems, use cases, and misconceptions from developers with hands-on experience.

Agrawal et al. interviewed nine industry experts on their perception of the PPC techniques DP, HE, and SMPC and identified several usability challenges that need to be overcome before they will be adopted by developers [2]. Kühtreiber et al. investigated factors that contribute in PPC technique adoption and found that an increase in PPC technique awareness can contribute in developers using them in practice [28]. These works focus mainly on the same PPC techniques as we do; however, they do not analyze the content of SO posts in detail.

Therefore, previous work on analyzing developers' issues do not cover (1) the implementation struggles, (2) technical misconceptions, (3) degrees of interest, or (4) use cases of the PPC techniques. We cover all of these points in our study.

3 Methodology

To answer the research questions formulated in Sect. 1, we search for the PPC techniques through SO's search function using citation marks to guarantee that the whole term is searched for. For example, our search term for DP questions looked like this: '"differential privacy" is:question'. Note, that we also used different spellings, such as, e.g., "differentially private". To identify significant trends in the temporal evaluation, we calculate Mann-Kendall statistics [37]. Posts extracted manually through the search function were inductively and independently coded [9] by two authors. We used Cohen's kappa to calculate inter-rater reliability after the initial round of coding and resolved differences via discussions between the coders after the second round. We use the scale provided by Landis and Koch for the interpretation of the calculated kappa values [29]. We considered all posts from SO's inception in 2008 until October 2024. Additionally, we conduct a qualitative analysis to provide further evidence of our findings.

3.1 Ethical Considerations

We have conducted our study according to the ethical standards recommended for big data analysis [41]. We did not collect any potentially identifying information and restricted both the collection and analysis to the content of the post itself. The posts' processing and storage is done locally in our infrastructure.

4 Results

We first compare the number of posts and cover the temporal factor in Sect. 4.1, thus answering **RQ1**. We present our established themes and the extracted use cases in Sect. 4.2, answering **RQ2**.

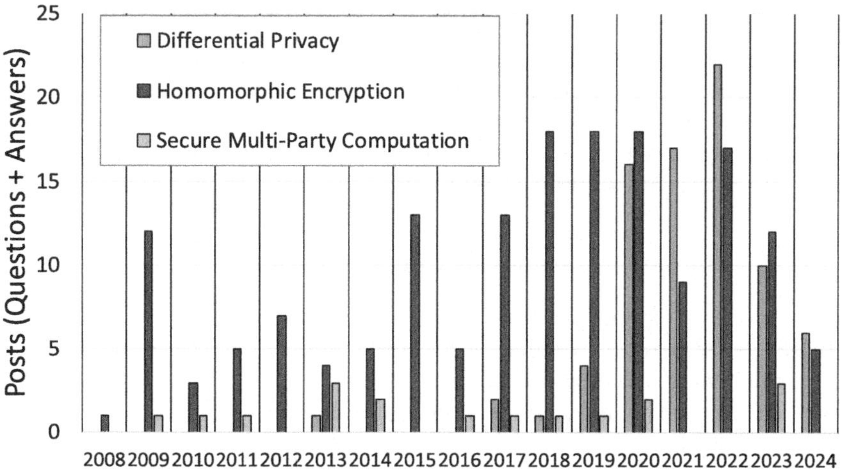

Fig. 1. While interest in HE and SMPC shows no substantial spikes or drops, the number of DP posts spiked between 2020 to 2022.

4.1 RQ1: Developers' Interest in PPC

Number of Posts. In this section and in Sect. 4.1, we deal with **RQ1**: *Which PPC technique raises the most questions as indicator of developers' interests or particular difficulties?*

Comparing the total number of questions and answers shows that HE (74Q+91A) is the most discussed PPC technique followed by DP (47Q + 28A) and SMPC (8Q+8A). The low number of SMPC posts is not surprising since it has a very specific use case. However, the increase in collaborative development increases the need to hide data from contributors, warranting future efforts to raise awareness about SMPC and to create more usable solutions.

Temporal Evaluation. The total number of posts regarding DP increased steadily over time with a peak in 2022, when DP libraries became more readily available (see Fig. 1). Mann-Kendall tests show that the increase in DP posts is a significant upwards trend ($\tau = .66, p = .003$). Most posts in the DP corpus mention *Federated Learning* (FL), driven by the availability of usable libraries, such as *Tensor Flow Federated* (TFF) which were also published around that time. In contrast, DP was introduced in academia in 2006 [16] and FL in 2017 [36].

Regarding HE, we observe varying interest since 2008. Comparing HE to DP, in 2021 HE ceased to be the most prominent PPC technique. This is likely caused by the limited availability of usable libraries. In research, HE is discussed since 1978 [42], but it took until 2009 before a fully HE scheme was proposed [21]. Mann-Kendall tests show that the increase in HE posts is also a significant upwards trend ($\tau = .41, p = .03$). One possible reason for the low number of SMPC posts is limited recognition. In research, a general model for SMPC was introduced in 1982 [56].

Summary and Answering RQ1. HE receives the most attention but, lately, DP-related posts increased in number compared to HE. We can attribute this result to (1) the readiness of the technology (especially regarding FL), (2) available libraries, and (3) timeliness of privacy-preserving *Machine Learning* (ML). It is noteworthy that total number of HE posts is still higher when compared to DP, but the difference diminishes with time and may be inverted in the future.

4.2 RQ2: Themes in Questions and Answers.

In this section, we explore the themes and use cases of the posts, thereby addressing **RQ2**: *What are the concrete difficulties encountered with PPC techniques and what are their primary use cases?*

We extract the themes via two rounds of inductive coding and the inter-rater reliability after the first round was substantial regarding DP questions (0.76), moderate regarding DP answers (.56) and HE answers (.59), and only fair regarding HE questions (.35). The reason for the poor reliability score regarding HE questions is different interpretations of the codes *Implementation* and *Application*. The coders discussed and settled these differences, however. Following these discussions, the coders reached full agreement.

Questions. All extracted topics and their share within the larger corpora are visualized in Fig. 2a. In the following, we go through each of these PPC techniques and present the results of our analysis.

Differential Privacy. Regarding the questions, 65% deal with ML. The relative majority has issues with TFF and Pytorch-DP (incl. Opacus), i.e., DP libraries that primarily target ML development. Not only is TFF the most popular technology mentioned, but it is also the main driver for the increasing number of posts dealing with DP, particularly for implementation-related questions dealing with, e.g., gradient problems and passing parameters to DP functions.

Developers are also concerned with theory. They ask whether DP is worth it, how and why noise is applied, and how the accuracy of the data is preserved. Moreover, issues arise regarding the adjustment of the privacy parameter ϵ which is context dependent. Hence, developers ask for guidance: "*[I]s there any way to guarantee/influence this so that the accuracy is still at a near-optimum at the point that the algorithm reaches the specified* ϵ".

DP is mostly used in combination with FL, which makes FL its primary use case and not, e.g., privacy-preserving data publishing, for which DP was initially intended. Moreover, questions regarding DP's theory and parameters highlight the lack of understanding which is not surprising since DP is a complex subject, which is not well understood by laypeople [27]. While developers are more tech-savvy than the average person, it is still necessary to teach these concepts thoroughly in programming curricula or continuous education offered in companies. This, in turn, improves the privacy climate within a company and, thus, also increases the adoption of privacy-preserving techniques [24].

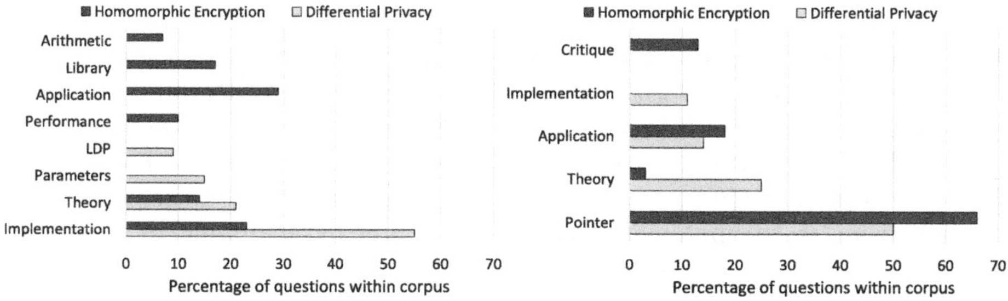

(a) Questions (b) Answers

Fig. 2. Posts regarding DP and HE often revolve around similar issues.

Homomorphic Encryption. A relative majority of the questions deal with finding or investigating potential applications for HE. The first question arose in 2008; however, in 2024, users are still asking if HE is applicable to their problem. Other questions deal with problems implementing or installing HE libraries. The most mentioned library is SEAL [40].

Most theory questions focus on basic understanding of the idea and details of HE. For example, an author asked: "*Homomorphic will understand the 'meaning' of encrypted text?*". The fact that fully HE is not yet available with an acceptable performance is also an issue. Authors also mention that the time it takes to compute HE results is too long in practice, as this person, using Microsoft SEAL, wrote: "*I [..] calculate the dot product of two ciphertext vectors. I found that when the size of the ciphertext vector is 600, it takes about 12 s. I don't know if there is a way to improve the efficiency of my code, or is this the upper limit of the calculation speed of homomorphic encryption?*". Developers also struggle with implementing arithmetic operations, such as division or subtraction: "*We've met some problems when we're trying to Implement fully homomorphic encryption [...]. We're wondering whether we have to build some new homomorphic method, division or comparison for instance, by using the binary operations or not?*"

Most questions revolve around using HE for what it is currently available: calculations with encrypted numbers. Other perceived use cases, or questions regarding use cases are dealing with privacy-preserving ML, comparing ciphertexts, or *Searchable Encryption* (SE) to name a few examples. Most of the applications are experimental and from developers who want to try HE using the already available libraries. As HE is not fully viable as of today, actual real-world use cases can not be expected.

To summarize, developers struggle with known issues such as poor performance and limited usability. Moreover, practical use cases are also often not clear. Therefore, research into usable and efficient HE solutions as well as raising awareness about HE's applicability can increase its future usage. These aspects can be emphasized in education for practitioners.

Secure Multi-party Computation. Due to the lack of posts we did not extract themes from SMPC. Questions are either theoretical, implementation specific, or focus on combining SMPC with blockchain technology. Given the limited number of posts, we must be careful to draw any general conclusions, but developers ask about SMPC with a diverse array of use cases in mind. Two posts mention that their use case for SMPC is sharing secrets in the blockchain. Other developers mention using it to implement privacy-preserving data mining, or to update ciphertexts based on changes to the plaintext.

Answers. As we did with the questions we now present the answers by PPC technique in the following (see Fig. 2b).

Differential Privacy. The majority of all PPC technique's answers fall into the category *Pointer*. This describes answers that point the person asking the question to the respective PPC technique. Regarding DP, posters link TFF-tutorials or scientific papers. In some cases, the concept was explained directly in the answer. One post also criticizes DP, stating that it does not "*work as well as advertised*" for ML purposes since large datasets are usually needed.

Homomorphic Encryption. The general direction of posts is similar to the ones we have extracted from DP. Pointers to HE include suggestions to look into HE as a solution to the poster's issue. The related question rarely mentions HE. The pointers also include tutorials, papers, or blog articles and explain how HE might be suitable for the problem at hand. Some answers mention that HE might be applicable, but lacks maturity. Moreover, posters answer questions regarding HE's real life applications, e.g., banking and e-voting. Answers point out that it is possible in theory, but that an actual application of HE might take some time. Hence, some developers are knowledgeable about HE and aware of its potential. At the same time, most are also realistic about HE's limitations and that it is currently not a viable solution but might be in the future. Some have problems with the theory behind HE and answers try to explain the technique and point the users to HE. Both HE and DP are criticised, but while DP critique revolves mainly about the parameters and the added noise, criticism of HE revolves around its lack of maturity.

Secure Multi-party Computation. Answers are mostly replying to questions regarding the verification or exchange of secrets without revealing any information or hinting at the possibility of using SMPC for the respective problem. Only one technical solution, namely PySyft, is mentioned.

Summary and Answering RQ2. Experts and laypeople struggle with understanding DP [2,19,27]. Our investigation further reveals insecurities regarding applicability and accuracy of, e.g., FL. While usable libraries exist, they require expert knowledge to reap the benefits of privacy-preserving ML. Some perceive DP and FL as too complicated to use. Easy-to-use libraries and frameworks such as no-code solutions could solve this issue. DP is primarily used to increase the privacy-guarantee of FL. This shows that awareness for its originally intended use case—database privacy—is limited and most developers are interested in privacy-preserving ML, likely due to its current momentum.

Regarding HE and SMPC, limited usability is the main concern. HE is not mature enough to be used commercially and SMPC has a perceived unclear applicability. Interest in practical application of HE revolves mainly around searching in or comparison of ciphertexts. Developers mainly ask whether a specific technology can be applicable for their problem.

5 Discussion

We now discuss our findings, their implications for research and practitioners, and address limitations to our study.

5.1 Differential Privacy and Machine Learning

The reason that our analysis resulted in a comparatively high amount of DP questions is because DP can be used within TFF, which is the largest driver for DP questions. As we can expect that ML and privacy will become even more important in the future, we anticipate a rising interest in DP, especially when used in ML. However, some answers suggest that DP does not work as well as developers would hope. This is likely due to the amount of data needed to keep the distribution useful. For example, Google has successfully deployed FL with DP, which is only possible due to the vast amount of data Google can work with [59]. Most problems deal with the adjustment of parameters and perceived complexity—thereby confirming issues identified in a previous study [19]. Previous research also shows that increased awareness correlates with the willingness to use PPC techniques [28] and another study likewise recommends increasing awareness of privacy-enhancing methods to avoid confusion [15]. Therefore, to tackle these issues, (1) DP could be explained more thoroughly in the documentations and (2) DP should be taught to aspiring programmers. Moreover, research and developers could focus on developing easy-to-use libraries, such as, e.g., no-code solutions which have been proposed for FL [60].

Using DP in ML is not without problems. Blanco-Justicia et al. showed that using DP in ML does not lead to an increase in privacy protection [7]. Reasons are the unsafe privacy parameters, i.e., a too high value for ϵ, and the use of unreasonable relaxations on the model. Both are done in order to improve the model's accuracy; however, the privacy protection is consequently reduced.

5.2 The Maturity of Encryption PPC Methods

Apart from making fully HE functional and actually usable, research should continue along the path of investigating programmer-friendly HE solutions like [4]. While still underused, the high number of use cases could also increase SMPC's adoption in the industry [28]. Current examples include EPIC [33] which combines ML with SMPC but the authors state that it can also be extended using HE. Moreover, Lee et al. proposed a privacy-preserving ML solution using fully HE [30]. We see from examples such as Zama [57] and Intel [23] that these advanced encryption methods are actively discussed and used in the industry.

5.3 Recommendations

Missing privacy-related education has been identified by other works [6,39] and our results underscore their findings. Educators should not only teach about anonymization and pseudonymization, but also include DP in order to (1) increase awareness, (2) mitigate misconceptions early, and (3) teach the concepts. Currently available DP libraries have weaknesses [13,14] and are thus of limited usability for educators. Hence, improving the usability of these libraries is necessary in order to use them to teach the concept and the application of DP. Many DP use cases in our study focus on ML. In comparison, a previous study showed that in their sample, database requests are more important [19]. Still, educators could also focus on privacy-preserving ML and FL in particular. Similar to DP, there are many libraries that allow experimenting with FL in ML classes. Besides the increased familiarity, programmers would also profit from a realistic estimate of what FL can and cannot do. It is, for example, important to stress that using DP can lead to over-fitting [7] and that *Local Differential Privacy* (LDP) might be a viable alternative to FL [58]. While usable libraries for the encryption methods are rare, education could focus on the theory in order to avoid the misconceptions and false expectations that we reveal in our study.

Researchers and developers could focus on making DP and FL libraries more usable. As our results show, a lot of expert knowledge is currently required, thus, hindering adoption of PPC techniques. Lower perceived complexity of tools increases the willingness to use them [53]. Also, compatibility with currently used technologies is an important factor w.r.t. tool adoption [44,53].

5.4 Limitations

We acknowledge some limitations of our study. We assume that developers who have questions about PPC techniques also use their names or variations of them in their queries. We have focused on SO because it is the most popular Q&A site for developers. Other distributions and topics may be found on other sites, such as Reddit. Developers increasingly use large language models to fix bugs and ask questions about implementation issues and might not ask their questions on SO. As very few users mention their occupational status we cannot assess their level of expertise and whether they are developers or, e.g., security architects.

6 Conclusion

Privacy-preserving software development affects every developer who deals with personal data. Even though PPC techniques exist and the number of usable libraries is increasing, our analysis shows that many developers struggle during implementation and lack critical knowledge about those methods. The more libraries and frameworks are available, the more developers also discuss implementation-related topics. However, concepts which are not yet market-ready, such as HE, still enjoy some popularity. This shows that fully functioning HE would be adopted by many software developers. ML and cloud computing are currently two of the main areas of software development. Moreover, due to the worldwide rise of privacy regulations, privacy should already be incorporated during the design phase of software development. This means, that techniques that allow for privacy-preserving ML and cloud computing will be even more relevant in future. Currently, expert knowledge is necessary to incorporate FL or DP into ML projects and results therefore are not as expected. Hence, it is necessary to research and develop easy-to-use libraries. Educators can use our results to increase awareness and knowledge about PPC techniques in their curricula in order to prepare future programmers for privacy-preserving software development. Future research can evaluate the topics that surfaced during our analysis by, e.g., concretely investigating FL implementation issues.

References

1. Acar, Y., Fahl, S., Mazurek, M.L.: You are not your developer, either: a research agenda for usable security and privacy research beyond end users. In: IEEE Cybersecurity Development (SecDev) (2016)
2. Agrawal, N., Binns, R., Van Kleek, M., Laine, K., Shadbolt, N.: Exploring design and governance challenges in the development of privacy-preserving computation. In: Proceedings of the 2021 ACM Conference on Human Factors in Computing Systems (CHI) (2021)
3. Ahmad, A., Feng, C., Li, K., Asim, S.M., Sun, T.: Toward empirically investigating non-functional requirements of iOS developers on stack overflow. IEEE Access (2019)
4. Archer, D.W., et al.: RAMPARTS: a programmer-friendly system for building homomorphic encryption applications. In: Proceedings of the 7th ACM Workshop on Encrypted Computing and Applied Homomorphic Cryptography (2019)
5. Atwood, J., Spolsky, J.: Stack overflow - where developers learn, share, and build careers. https://stackoverflow.com/. Accessed November 2023
6. Bednar, K., Spiekermann, S., Langheinrich, M.: Engineering privacy by design: are engineers ready to live up to the challenge? Inf. Soc. (2019)
7. Blanco-Justicia, A., Sánchez, D., Domingo-Ferrer, J., Muralidhar, K.: A critical review on the use (and misuse) of differential privacy in machine learning. ACM Comput. Surv. (2022)
8. Borking, J.J.: Why adopting privacy enhancing technologies (PETs) takes so much time. In: Computers, Privacy and Data Protection: an Element of Choice (2011)
9. Braun, V., Clarke, V.: Thematic analysis. American Psychological Association (APA) (2012)
10. Castelluccia, C., et al.: Data protection engineering—from theory to practice (2022). https://www.enisa.europa.eu/publications/data-protection-engineering
11. Coopamootoo, K.P.L.: Usage patterns of privacy-enhancing technologies. In: Proceedings of the 2020 ACM Conference on Computer and Communications Security (SIGSAC) (2020)

12. Dechand, S., Naiakshina, A., Danilova, A., Smith, M.: In encryption we don't trust: the effect of end-to-end encryption to the masses on user perception. In: Proceedings of the 2019 IEEE European Symposium on Security and Privacy (EuroS&P) (2019)
13. Desfontaines, D.: Differential privacy primitives use insecure noise generation (2023). https://github.com/prestodb/presto/issues/23002. Accessed March 2025
14. Desfontaines, D.: Insecure noise primitives should be marked as such and/or removed entirely (2024). https://github.com/IBM/differential-privacy-library/issues/94. Accessed March 2025
15. Diepenbrock, A., Fleck, J., Sachweh, S.: An analysis of stack exchange questions: identifying challenges in software design and development with a focus on data privacy and data protection. In: Proceedings of the 18th International Conference on Availability, Reliability and Security (ARES) (2023)
16. Dwork, C.: Differential privacy. In: Proceedings of the 33rd International Colloquium on Automata, Languages, and Programming (ICALP) (2006)
17. Fischer-Hübner, S., Lindskog, H.: Teaching privacy-enhancing technologies. In: Proceedings of the IFIP WG 11.8 2nd World Conference on Information Security Education (2001)
18. Gan, M.F., Chua, H.N., Wong, S.F.: Privacy enhancing technologies implementation: an investigation of its impact on work processes and employee perception. Telemat. Inform. (2019)
19. Garrido, G.M., Liu, X., Matthes, F., Song, D.: Lessons learned: surveying the practicality of differential privacy in the industry. In: Proceedings on Privacy Enhancing Technologies (PoPETS) (2023)
20. Geierhaas, L., Ortloff, A.M., Smith, M., Naiakshina, A.: {Let's} hash: helping developers with password security. In: 18th Symposium on Usable Privacy and Security (SOUPS) (2022)
21. Gentry, C.: Fully homomorphic encryption using ideal lattices. In: Proceedings of the 41st Annual ACM Symposium on Theory of Computing (STOC) (2009)
22. Hadar, I., et al.: Privacy by designers: software developers' privacy mindset. Empir. Softw. Eng. (2018)
23. Intel: better together: privacy-preserving machine learning powered by intel SGX and intel DL boost. https://community.intel.com/t5/Blogs/Tech-Innovation/Artificial-Intelligence-AI/Better-Together-Privacy-Preserving-Machine-Learning-Powered-by/post/1335716
24. Iwaya, L.H., Babar, M.A., Rashid, A.: Privacy engineering in the wild: understanding the practitioners' mindset, organisational aspects, and current practices. IEEE Trans. Softw. Eng. (2023)
25. Juma'h, A., Alnsour, Y.: The effect of data breaches on company performance. Int. J. Account. Inf. Manage. (IJAIM) (2020)
26. Kühtreiber, P., Pak, V., Reinhardt, D.: A survey on solutions to support developers in privacy-preserving IoT development. Pervasive Mob. Comput. (PMC) (2022)
27. Kühtreiber, P., Pak, V., Reinhardt, D.: Replication: the effect of differential privacy communication on German users' comprehension and data sharing attitudes. In: Proceedings of the 18th Symposium on Usable Privacy and Security (SOUPS) (2022)
28. Kühtreiber, P., Pak, V., Reinhardt, D.: "A method like this would be overkill": developers' perceived issues with privacy-preserving computation methods. In: Proceedings of the 22nd IEEE International Conference on Trust, Security and Privacy in Computing and Communications (TrustCom) (2023)

29. Landis, J.R., Koch, G.G.: The measurement of observer agreement for categorical data. Biometrics (1977)
30. Lee, J.W., et al.: Privacy-Preserving machine learning with fully homomorphic encryption for deep neural network. IEEE Access (2022)
31. Li, T., Louie, E., Dabbish, L., Hong, J.I.: How developers talk about personal data and what it means for user privacy: a case study of a developer forum on reddit. In: Proceedings of the ACM on Human-Computer Interaction (2021)
32. Linares-Vásquez, M., Dit, B., Poshyvanyk, D.: An exploratory analysis of mobile development issues using stack overflow. In: Proceedings of the 10th Working Conference on Mining Software Repositories (MSR) (2013)
33. Makri, E., Rotaru, D., Smart, N.P., Vercauteren, F.: EPIC: efficient private image classification (or: learning from the masters). In: Proceedings of the Cryptographers' Track at the RSA Conference (2019)
34. Mattsson, U.: Privacy-preserving analytics and secure multiparty computation (2021). https://www.isaca.org/resources/isaca-journal/issues/2021/volume-2/privacy-preserving-analytics-and-secure-multiparty-computation
35. May, R., Biermann, C., Zerweck, X.M., Ludwig, K., Krüger, J., Leich, T.: Vulnerably (mis) configured? Exploring 10 years of developers' Q&As on stack overflow. In: Proceedings of the 18th International Working Conference on Variability Modelling of Software-Intensive Systems (2024)
36. McMahan, B., Moore, E., Ramage, D., Hampson, S., y Arcas, B.A.: Communication-efficient learning of deep networks from decentralized data. In: Artificial Intelligence and Statistics (2017)
37. Meals, D.W., Spooner, J., Dressing, S.A., Harcum, J.B.: Statistical analysis for monotonic trends. Tech Notes (2011)
38. Naiakshina, A., Danilova, A., Tiefenau, C., Herzog, M., Dechand, S., Smith, M.: Why do developers get password storage wrong? A qualitative usability study. In: Proceedings of the ACM Conference on Computer and Communications Security (SIGSAC) (2017)
39. Peixoto, M., et al.: The perspective of Brazilian software developers on data privacy. J. Syst. Softw. (JSS) (2023)
40. Research, M.: Microsoft SEAL (release 4.1.1) (2023). https://github.com/Microsoft/SEAL. Accessed November 2023
41. Rivers, C.M., Lewis, B.L.: Ethical research standards in a world of big data. F1000Research (2014)
42. Rivest, R.L., Adleman, L., Dertouzos, M.L., et al.: On data banks and privacy homomorphisms. Found. Secure Comput. (1978)
43. Rubinstein, I.S.: Regulating privacy by design. Berkeley Technol. Law J. (BTLJ) (2011)
44. Senarath, A., Grobler, M., Arachchilage, N.: Will they use it or not? Investigating software developers' intention to follow privacy engineering methodologies. ACM Trans. Priv. Secur. (TOPS) (2019)
45. Senarath, A.R., Arachchilage, N.A.G.: Understanding user privacy expectations: a software developer's perspective. Telemat. Inform. (2018)
46. Squire, M.: "Should we move to stack overflow?" measuring the utility of social media for developer support. In: Proceedings of the 37th IEEE International Conference on Software Engineering (ICSE) (2015)
47. Tahaei, M., Bernd, J., Rashid, A.: Privacy, permissions, and the health app ecosystem: a stack overflow exploration. In: Proceedings of the 2022 European Symposium on Usable Security (2022)

48. Tahaei, M., Vaniea, K., Saphra, N.: Understanding privacy-related questions on stack overflow. In: Proceedings of the 2020 ACM Conference on Human Factors in Computing Systems (CHI) (2020)
49. T.A.N. Brandão, L., Peralta, R.: Privacy-enhancing cryptography to complement differential privacy (2021). https://www.nist.gov/blogs/cybersecurity-insights/privacy-enhancing-cryptography-complement-differential-privacy
50. Team, U.P.P.T.T.: UN handbook on privacy-preserving computation techniques (2020). https://unstats.un.org/bigdata/task-teams/privacy/UN%20Handbook%20for%20Privacy-Preserving%20Techniques.pdf
51. Villanes, I.K., Ascate, S.M., Gomes, J., Dias-Neto, A.C.: What are software engineers asking about android testing on stack overflow? In: Proceedings of the 31st Brazilian Symposium on Software Engineering (SBES) (2017)
52. Votipka, D., Fulton, K.R., Parker, J., Hou, M., Mazurek, M.L., Hicks, M.: Understanding security mistakes developers make: qualitative analysis from build it, break it, fix it. In: Proceedings of the 29th USENIX Security Symposium (USENIX Security) (2020)
53. Witschey, J., Xiao, S., Murphy-Hill, E.: Technical and personal factors influencing developers' adoption of security tools. In: Proceedings of the ACM Workshop on Security Information Workers (2014)
54. Witschey, J., Zielinska, O., Welk, A., Murphy-Hill, E., Mayhorn, C., Zimmermann, T.: Quantifying developers' adoption of security tools. In: Proceedings of the 10th Joint Meeting on Foundations of Software Engineering (FSE) (2015)
55. Yang, X.L., Lo, D., Xia, X., Wan, Z.Y., Sun, J.L.: What security questions do developers ask? A large-scale study of stack overflow posts. J. Comput. Sci. Technol. (JCST) (2016)
56. Yao, A.C.: Protocols for secure computations. In: Proceedings of the 23rd Annual Symposium on Foundations of Computer Science (SFCS) (1982)
57. Zama: build applications with fully homomorphic encryption. https://www.zama.ai
58. Zheng, H., Hu, H., Han, Z.: Preserving user privacy for machine learning: local differential privacy or federated machine learning. IEEE Intell. Syst. (2020)
59. Zheng, X., Yanxiang, Z.: Advances in private training for production on-device language models (2024). https://blog.research.google/2024/02/advances-in-private-training-for.html
60. Zhuang, W., Gan, X., Wen, Y., Zhang, S.: EasyFL: a low-code federated learning platform for dummies. IEEE Internet of Things J. (2022)
61. Zou, J., Xu, L., Guo, W., Yan, M., Yang, D., Zhang, X.: Which non-functional requirements do developers focus on? An empirical study on stack overflow using topic analysis. In: Proceedings of the 12th Working Conference on Mining Software Repositories (MSR) (2015)
62. Zou, J., Xu, L., Yang, M., Zhang, X., Yang, D.: Towards comprehending the non-functional requirements through developers' eyes: an exploration of stack overflow using topic analysis. Inf. Softw. Technol. (2017)

Facing the Challenge of Leveraging Untrained Humans in Malware Analysis

Benjamin Zi Hao Zhao[1(✉)], Hassan Jameel Asghar[1], Muhammad Ikram[1], Mohamed Ali Kaafar[1], Sean Lamont[2], and Daniel Coscia[2]

[1] Macquarie University, Sydney, Australia
{ben_zi.zhao,hassan.asghar,muhammad.ikram,dali.kaafar}@mq.edu.au
[2] Defence Science and Technology Group, Adelaide, Australia
{sean.lamont2,daniel.coscia1}@defence.gov.au

Abstract. Software binary analysis, tools and machine learning aid security analysts in interpreting data, by automated means that filter, prioritize, and arrange pertinent information for skilled analysts. In this work, we revisit cooperative human-machine teams and evaluate the possibility of enabling untrained humans to assist machines and skilled analysts in their analysis of software binaries. Specifically, we propose a pipeline to transform a complex input domain into facial images on which untrained individuals make similarity decisions. Our faces include realistic human, animal, artistic, and anime faces that preserve inherent distances between data points of the input domain. Our approach is evaluated through a human study, where untrained respondents with minimal training successfully flag machine misclassifications. The untrained human does not replace the machine or skilled analyst, instead, utilized in a triage setting, to identify samples without historical precedence, deferring the decision to the skilled analyst for deeper inspection.

Keywords: Malware · Binaries · Data Visualization · Human · Faces · Rapid · Triage

1 Introduction

It is a longstanding problem in cyber security to swiftly and automatically distinguish between benign or malicious intentions of a software binary [5,11]. Proposed automated methods still require detailed analysis of suspicious software by human analysts who supply the necessary ground truth data used by these tools [39]. This setting creates a unique human-machine team in which both parties work in conjunction with each other to detect malicious software. However, skilled analysts are in short supply [13], making it hard to scale such a workforce in line with the ever increasing volume of malicious software [6]. Further, recently proposed attacks against such teams show that this human bottleneck can be targeted to increase their workload, thus further exacerbating the issue [31].

L. Nemec Zlatolas et al. (Eds.): SEC 2025, IFIP AICT 745, pp. 61–75, 2025.
https://doi.org/10.1007/978-3-031-92882-6_5

Quick triage of incoming software binaries is important so that limited resources can be focused on priority cases. Naturally, one would resort to automated triaging techniques, as human expertise is scarce. However, in this work, we are interested in knowing whether humans without domain expertise can contribute to the workflow of a triage task. An affirmative answer to this question would mean that triaging could be crowdsourced, thus alleviating the issue of resource scarcity to a large extent.

Traditional binary analysis requires significant domain expertise, extending to the interpretation of results from machine analysis. In this work, we propose representing high-dimension numeric data (extracted from software binaries) that would typically be difficult for untrained humans to interpret into accessible image representations. Specifically, we represent software binaries as faces (which include humans, animals, stylized art, and anime faces), and task humans to decide if a group of images appear similar. The humans effectively flag when novel, unseen software samples occur, as the displayed images would be dissimilar. Thereby presenting a unique opportunity where untrained humans could assist the machine in identifying out-of-distribution samples by flagging new unseen samples for closer human inspection.

This transformation seeks to preserve relative feature distances between software binaries in the dataset. A distance preserved into the face domain, manifesting as varying facial features whereas smaller inter-cluster variations are presented as subtle visual variations. It is important to note that while the machine seeks to preserve inherent relationships with the existing data, it does not classify samples before displaying the faces to humans.

When deciding similarity within a group, there are two decisions. If the unseen sample is deemed similar, the sample may be handled in the same manner as known existing samples. For example, if the reference samples are known malware, the same urgency and course of action may be applied to the new sample. The alternative, dissimilarity functions as a request for further analysis on the original binary by trained domain experts. This is particularly useful for new software, emergent malware families, and advanced persistent threats of which there is limited prior experience within the system. It is important to note that dissimilarity is neither a positive nor negative decision by the human.

We summarize our contributions in this paper as follows:

- The first proposal to transform numeric data into high-fidelity faces to make complex data more engaging for users and facilitate alternative approaches to create data-driven insights.
- We propose the use of humans in an an image similarity problem to improve an automated process by leveraging the human in identifying novel out-of-distribution samples.
- We provide a user study to evaluate untrained human contributions on malware images, a domain typically reserved for domain experts and machines.

2 Related Works and Background

2.1 Related Works

In this section, we shall review related works in techniques used for dataset visualization, and prior attempts to convey numeric data to human senses.

Dataset Visualization. The most closely related area of bringing numeric data into a visual format exists in dataset visualization. A core objective of this task is to present high-dimensional data in a format that is simple to inspect the relationships between data points within a wider dataset. This is typically achieved with an informed dimension reduction onto either a 1D, 2D or 3D space. Common techniques to achieve this include, but are not limited to, Principal Component Analysis (PCA) [37], Linear Discriminant Analysis (LDA) [30], t-distributed Stochastic Neighbor Embedding (t-SNE) [20], and Uniform Manifold Approximation and Projection (UMAP) [21]. In this paper, we are not performing dataset visualization to display the relationship of every data point against each other. We instead provide a visual representation of each individual data point in a relatively higher dimension.

Improving Accessibility of Data for Humans. The seminal work to represent higher-dimensional data as faces is the Cheroff Face [3]. Each of the data input dimensions directly controls a physical parameter of the simple line-drawn faces (e.g. eye diameter, lip curvature), Cheroff et al. tasked human participants to cluster all data points into distinct groups. Extensions to Cheroff faces were investigated by Flury and Riedwyl [9], with the incorporation of additional parameterization and asymmetric control of the face. The closest work to our own objective of triaging malware is Vanhoudnos et al. where Cheroff Faces and Stick Figures were used to represent malware API call graphs reduced to a lower dimension through PCA, their test samples contain malware belonging to only one of three classes of malware families [34]. This work focuses on static analysis of binaries, with explicit direction to avoid human respondents making a final classification decision to avoid potential bias in photo-realistic faces.

Image Synthesis. Cheroff faces [3] were printed on a Calcomp Plotter. In the 50 years since this work, computing can now produce realistic-high-fidelity facial representations seen in this work. A facilitating development being Generative Adversarial Networks (GAN) [10]. GANs are constructed with two competing networks, the generator, and the discriminator, where the former is tasked to generate realistic images images, and the latter to detect synthetic/fake images from a set of real images and generator outputs. With each iteration, the generator is updated with knowledge of it's outputs that were not sufficiently realistic, and the detector updated against the truth of separating the real and synthetic images, progressively improving both networks.

Malware Analysis. Malware Analysis can be broken down into two overarching categories, static analysis and dynamic analysis. Static analysis inspects the binary under question without directly executing any code, this typically involves decompiling the machine code of the binary into a language of greater abstraction [22,26], from which malicious routines could be identified by human analysts. Dynamic analysis on the other hand executes the binaries to observe and scrutinize the behavior and actions of the program [25].

2.2 Background

We first describe the Library to Instrument Executable Formats (LIEF) representation in which our binaries are initially represented. We then describe three binary imaging/visualization methods that convert binaries directly to images which will be our performance baseline.

Library to Instrument Executable Formats (LIEF) Features [32]**.** Executable formats share descriptive features useful for characterizing program operations, and thus if they are malicious. LIEF [32] provides an abstraction on these features for analysis independent of the underlying format. The set of LIEF features we leverage were first defined in the standardized malware benchmarks of EMBER [1], with later adoption by the SOREL [12] benchmark dataset. Specifically, this vector contains 2381 numeric features containing information about the binary's byte and byte entropy distributions, strings within the binary, and binary metadata including header, section, import and export information.

Lanczos Resampling [35]**.** The first binary to image baseline applies Lanczos filters. This technique sequentially arranges the bianry's raw byte values in a rectangular manner, and applies a Lanczos filter to reduce the byte array to a fixed size. Lanczos resampling obtains new points from a normalized `Sinc` function windowed by a secondary `Sinc` function. Unlike [35] we do not apply a final color map as none was specified in [35].

Markov Chain Matrix [40]**.** A Markov chain matrix [24] is a n by n matrix where n is the number of states within the system to capture the likelihood of values changing from one value to another. When created from the sequential bytes from the start to the end of the compiled binary, each byte represents a state ($n = 2^8 = 256$). This matrix is 2 dimensional axes for the origin byte value (i), and subsequent byte value (j). Each transition is counted, and normalized by the total number of transitions for a probability i.e. $P_{j|i} = P_{i,j}$. The resulting 256×256 array can be shown as a greyscale image, the probability within each cell as greyscale value of the corresponding pixel.

Similarity based Hashing of binary instructions (Simhash) [23]**.** When disassembling binaries the resulting opcodes form a bag of words on which, a Simhash function may be applied to capture the internal structure of the binary's instructions. As such binaries with similar instructions used to perform their function, will have similar resulting hashes (from Simhash). However, instead of directly comparing hashes, the hashes can be transformed into images. Constrained by the length of Simhash, the largest Simhash images have a size of 1024-bits reshaped into 32×32 pixels (SimHash–1024 [23]) from the concatenation of SHA–512, SHA–384, and MD5 hashes of the opcode bag.

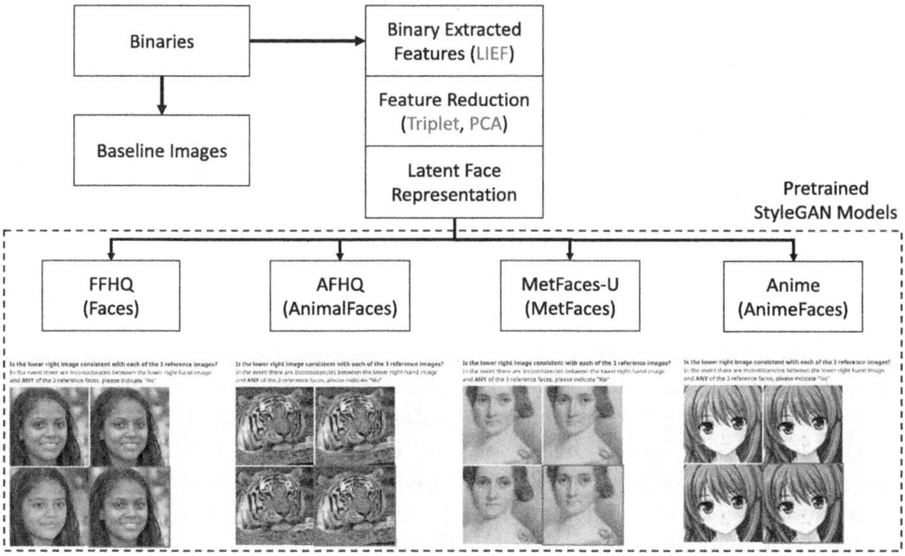

Fig. 1. Proposed pipeline of transforming software binaries to face representations. The baseline images can be viewed in Fig. 2. In each set of 4 faces, they correspond to the same 4 underlying binary samples.

3 Representing Numeric Data as Images

In this section, we propose our pipeline for representing numeric data as human, animal, artistic, and anime faces. We shall first describe the dataset used in our training and evaluation, followed by details of the proposed image pipeline, before providing a machine classification baseline to quantify the amount of discriminatory information remaining in the generated images. This is followed by the introduction of the proposed similarity comparison task, geared for humans, and a user study on the performance of leveraging humans in the similarity task. Our generated faces will be evaluated alongside existing malware image representations of Lanczos, Markov, and Simhash. (c.f. Sect. 2.2)

Dataset. For our evaluation, we use disjoint samples of the SOREL dataset [12]. We use 100K samples tagged as Malware, and a further 100K samples tagged as benign to form the basis of our dataset, resulting in a balanced dataset of 200K. For testing purposes, we further sample 5K Malware and 5K Benign from the remainder of the SOREL dataset. The SOREL dataset labels each software binary with a label including: malware, adware, flooder, ransomware, dropper, spyware, packed, crypto miner, file infector, installer, worm, and downloader.

3.1 Pipeline Methodology

In this section, we shall detail the proposed pipeline for face (human, animal, artistic, and anime faces) generation. The face pipeline is visually displayed in

Fig. 1, and shall be described from the Vector representation, conversion to latent face space, and the actual face image generation.

Vector Representation of Malware. To transform software binaries to faces, the data processing pipeline first involves the static analysis extraction of features from the binaries. To start our pipeline, a software binary can be represented as a sequence of raw bytes, or as an engineered vector of features extracted from the binary contents.

One such representations we leverage are the LIEF features, a set of binary characteristics including byte distributions, header metadata, external software imports [32]. We remark that other numeric representations of binaries exist, including (Attributes) Control Flow Graphs (CFG) [38], Graph Neural Network (GNN) Embeddings [2], or Dynamic Analysis features [14]. However, we opt for LIEF features as large labeled software datasets [1,12] containing software binaries with their respective LIEF features already extracted exist. The specific version of features are defined by [1]'s aggregation of features leveraged by multiple prior malware analysis works [27–29].

Converting Vectors to Latent Space. With LIEF features as our numeric starting point, generating face images can be broken up into two phases, (1) Transforming input features into a latent space compatible with a face generator. (2) Generating an image from the latent representation. This overall pipeline is displayed in Fig. 1, with visual examples of the similarity question grid for each of the evaluated face generators to be described later in Sect. 4.

In *phase 1*, the input features are to be transformed into a 512-wide latent face space. To this end, we evaluate two possible approaches. The first, an embedding network trained on a disjoint set of 200K software binaries. This embedding network is trained as a triplet loss Siamese network [8] that maximizes the distance between dissimilar classes, and minimize the distance between samples of the same class. We leverage all possible unique combinations of meta-classes provided by SOREL (c.f. 3), as the training classes. The second approach is Principal Component Analysis (PCA) [37].

Generating Face Images. The final phase generates the image. With the binary in the latent image space, a pre-trained generator outputs an image. For our evaluation, we employ generators based on StyleGAN [16–18], with an input latent space of 512. This generator follows a standardized structure, allowing drop-in evaluation of multiple pre-trained generators, each with different training datasets, and output image domains. These include, Human Faces (FFHQ) [17], Animal Faces (AFHQ) [4], Metropolitan Art Faces (MetArt) [15], and Anime Faces (Anime)[1]. Different pre-trained generators may output different image resolutions, so we resample all images to 256×256 pixels.

[1] https://huggingface.co/akiyamasho/stylegan3-anime-faces-generator, https://github.com/bchao1/Anime-Face-Dataset.

3.2 Baseline Image Methods

The software binary-to-image baselines described in Sect. 2.2 are incorporated alongside evaluations in the remainder of the paper. Visual examples of these baselines are provided in Fig. 2. We note that as the SOREL dataset only contains hashes, and pre-extracted LIEF features, the corresponding binaries (neccesary for baseline images) were obtained directly from VirusTotal [33]. In our disjoint evaluation dataset of 10K binaries, we were only able to recover 9,129 original binaries, of which 4,993 and 4,136 are benign and malicious respectively. Further for SIMHASH, a few binaries could not be decompiled, leaving us with 9,040 binaries, of which 4,972 and 4,068 are benign and malicious, respectively.

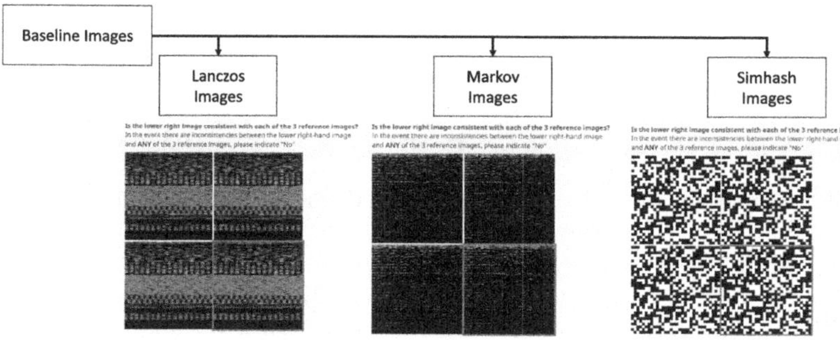

Fig. 2. Pipeline of baseline image representation created directly from software binaries, methods described in Sect. 2.2.

4 User Study - Similar Faces

4.1 Similarity Question

Now that we have established the creation of images to represent numeric data, we evaluate our images on humans. For this we introduce the similarity task. This task presents to a human participant four "similar" samples, of which one includes a hypothetical unseen sample. It is up to the human participant to decide if all four images are consistent with each other, or if there are observable differences. The specific question asked of the human participants is: "Is the lower right image consistent with each of the 3 reference images?". Further instruction is provided in a sentence: "In the event there are inconsistencies between the lower right-hand image and ANY of the 3 reference faces, please indicate"No". Asides from this prompt, no other training was provided to the human participants.

The decision outcome is to be able to flag if a new unseen sample has been presented to the system, to warrants further analysis by trained human analysts. The approach we use to select the most similar faces is Euclidean distance applied on the initial input LIEF features, the 3 most similar samples within the reference dataset (the remainder of the 10K test set) are used for these reference images. These 4 images form a single similarity question. We opt for similarity on the LIEF features, as each of the downstream face generations can be evaluated on the same set of similar samples albeit with different resulting faces due to differences in the generator.

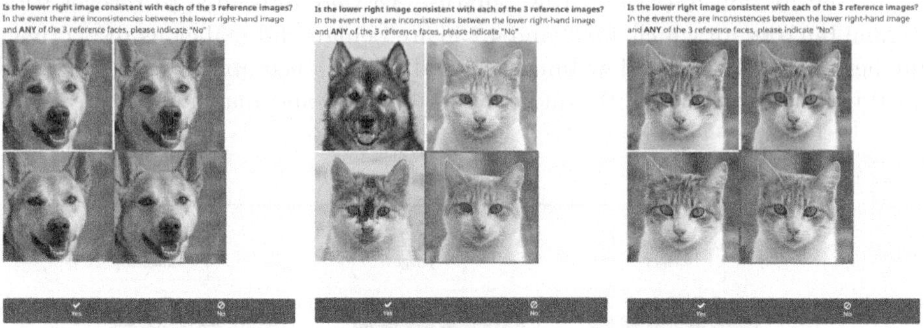

(a) Similar animal question (b) Dissimilar animal question (c) Subtle dissimilar animal question

Fig. 3. Example similarity questions in similar and dissimilar settings. Users are presented with the same simple question, with two check boxes, Yes and No. Not pictured is a next button below the selection that will record the respondent's answer, and proceed to the next question. The anticipation is a user would select No for (a), and Yes for (b), with mixtures of both for (c).

With four faces to a question, they are presented in a 2×2 grid with the unseen face highlighted by a red border. We use this arrangement to not overburden the user with a flood of stimuli, while also providing more opportunities to make comparisons, 3 references in contrast to the setting with only one or two reference images. An example of the question and input interface of animal faces is presented in Fig. 3.

4.2 User Study

We now perform a user study where human participants are tasked with determining if there is a sufficient representation of an unseen sample within the reference dataset. Overall, we have a total of 8 configurations, and 3 baseline image configurations within our pipeline as previously described in Sect. 3.1.

We are limited in the number of questions we can ask our participants, as it is infeasible to evaluate all 100K examples. Thus, select a representative set of samples. For this we settled on subsampling from when the machine classifier made Correct Malware (CM) and Correct Benign (CB) decisions, in addition to False Malware (FM) and False Benign (FB) decisions. The benefit gained would be if humans are able to flag FM and FB samples as needing further analysis,

Table 1. Resulting performance of human decisions in flagging 60 (15 in each of CM, FM, CB, FB) machine made decisions as requiring further analysis. For the CM and CB columns, an ideal result is 1, in this setting all questions were deemed by the humans as being similar. In contrast for FM and FB, results closer to 0 are ideal as incorrect classifications should not be flagged as similar. Positive samples are Malicious, while negative samples are benign. #R denotes the number of respondents.

60 Each	Sample Type	#R	CM	FM	CB	FB	60 Each	Sample Type	#R	CM	FM	CB	FB
Network	Faces	9	1.000	0.133	0.667	0.667	PCA	Faces	10	0.667	0.067	0.333	0.667
	AnimalFaces	8	1.000	0.400	0.733	0.800		AnimalFaces	11	0.667	0.133	0.333	0.733
	MetFaces	10	1.000	0.133	0.733	0.733		MetFaces	16	0.867	0.133	0.400	0.733
	AnimeFaces	11	1.000	0.267	0.800	0.800		AnimeFaces	13	0.667	0.067	0.333	0.733
2nd Trial	Faces	29	1.000	0.067	0.600	0.600	Baseline	Lanczos	10	0.667	0.067	0.333	0.400
Network	MetFaces	29	1.000	0.200	0.733	0.667		Markov	14	0.733	0.133	0.333	0.600
								Simhash	11	0.800	0.333	0.733	0.786

and not prompting for further analysis if the machine had answered correctly. 15 unseen samples from each type of machine decision (CM, CB, FM, FB) were subsampled for a total of 60 questions. We remark for 18 baseline images missing binaries, and 4 binaries that could not be decompiled for Simhash. In these examples, the authors referred to the equivalent face images and substituted to the closest appearing image within the remaining valid samples. One baseline question was missing an unseen sample and was excluded from the 60 questions for baselines only. The human participants are unaware of how these sample were selected, nor any prior machine decision, simply 4 faces.

We recruit participants from Amazon's Mechanical Turk [7], who were compensated USD$1 for the completion of 60 questions. The aggregated results (majority) from each set of users is used as the final similarity decision for a given sample. E.g. With 10 responses if 8 users agree on similarity, and 2 reject similarity, the final decision is agree. In the case of an even number of decisions, we favor agree. This aggregation of users leverages the 'Wisdom of the crowds' to minimize the influence of spurious errors produced by the participants, while we use approximately 10 users to make a decision on each sample, as the number of participants increase, the result will only grow more stable.

4.3 Results

We detail the overall results in Table 1, from which we find improvements to be gained. Considering the samples classified as FM and FB would have been incorrectly decided by the machine anyway, humans are able to divert a portion of these samples for further analysis.

Of particular note is the strong ability for the human participants to flag unseen ground truth benign samples. This task is observed to be more difficult when dealing with ground truth malicious samples. Further from the table, every network embedding generated faces permit the humans to identify with 100%

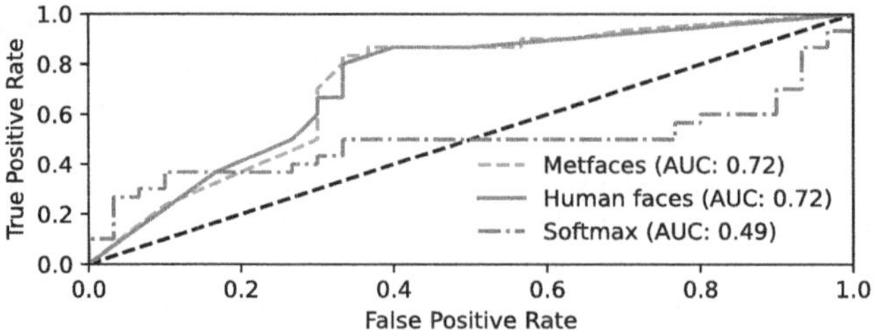

Fig. 4. Receiver Operator Curve (ROC) of humans correctly flagging incorrectly classified samples for further analysis. Where CM/CB samples should be flagged as similar, and FM/FB samples flagged as dissimilar for further analysis.

accuracy on CM. There is however a blurring of the lines that separate genuinely CB samples and malware that has been misclassified as benign.

When comparing the PCA and network faces, it is clear that the faces synthesized through PCA have reduced amounts of CM and CB, with comparable FM and FC, thereby solidifying the network approach for dimensionality reduction prior to face generation.

The 2nd Trial of Faces and MetFaces plotted as a Receiver Operator Curve (ROC) in Fig. 4, we can observe that there is a clear distinction that human inputs contribute positively in the identification of misclassified samples (CM, CB from FM, FB), with 0.72 AUC for both MetFaces and Human faces. The softmax precursor for classification is also shown to contrast the behavior. With this new set of results it is clear that the response of humans is stable from the previous MTurk respondents when contrast against a larger set of verified participants. We hypothesis this is a behavior of the overall flagging decision being not left to any individual respondent, instead formed the collective set of respondents, allowing for minor individual errors/uncertainties to be covered by other respondents.

User Consensus on Similarity

Previously a majority decision was displayed, however, each question will have varying degrees of consensus on similarity. In Fig. 5 the vertical axis denotes the proportion of respondents for a given question that agreed the images were similar, while the horizontal axis contains the classifier's softmax output, a proxy for the confidence of the machine in its classification decision.

In the networked faces, we observe an interesting occurrence whereby closer to 0 softmax, higher discord is present between respondents. Discord is lowered in the PCA faces, a potential indicator that the PCA faces will fall to either extreme of all being similar, or very dissimilar. The baselines do not exhibit any strong consensus between the respondents.

Response Timing. The time taken for respondents to complete their decision is also representative of the difficulty of a given similarity task. The timing results are displayed in Fig. 6. We note that outlier timings exceeding 10 times

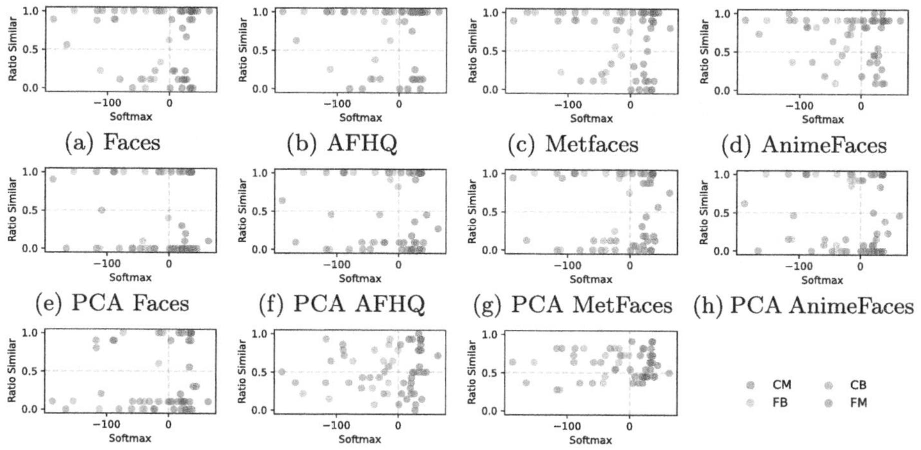

(a) Faces (b) AFHQ (c) Metfaces (d) AnimeFaces
(e) PCA Faces (f) PCA AFHQ (g) PCA MetFaces (h) PCA AnimeFaces
(i) Lanczos (j) Markov (k) Simhash (l) Scatter Legend

Fig. 5. Consensus of users in each question when deciding similarity scattered against softmax output of machine classifier decision. Softmax values greater than 0 indicate a machine prediction of the positive class (malware), and a softmax value less than 1 indicates a classifier negative prediction (benign).

the Median Absolute Deviation (MAD) [19] were excluded to remove potential distractions, or prolonged pauses in completing the survey.

From Fig. 6, we can observe that across all pipelines, a human decision falls within 10 s. Contrasting network and PCA faces, respondents completed faster decision on PCA faces, albeit as we have previously seen, with less success in appropriately flagging/not flagging samples for review. Clearly similar, and non-similar cases, prompted rapid responses. However, for networked faces, more questions with middling discord between users, reflects the increased time to carefully interpret the question.

5 Discussion

In this section, we discuss implications and potential future avenues from the conclusions of this paper.

Applications Beyond Software Analysis. This paper presents a use case of visualizing malware data as faces, however, the data pipeline is sufficiently general to take any numeric data. For example, website fingerprinting to ensure the average web user is viewing the intended webpage, the browser may render a visual image of certificates or domain.

Human Classifiers. We have refrained from requesting the human in the loop to make a distinct classification. If input is mapped to a face without restriction, to request a classification task of humans, the respondent must be trained to understand subtle facial variations describing each output class. For example,

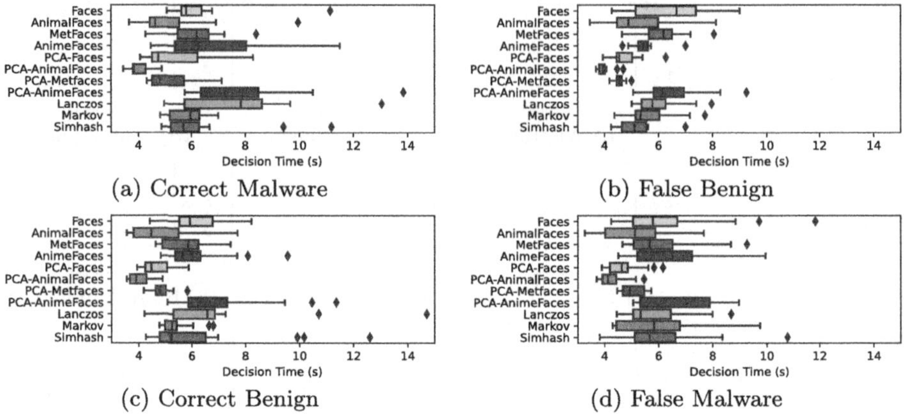

(a) Correct Malware (b) False Benign (c) Correct Benign (d) False Malware

Fig. 6. Timing of users in deciding similarity separated by machine classifier decision, and by generated image.

the presence of glasses or a emotion would mark a class, however, sensitive facial characteristics may manifest for a class, for example, race, age, and gender. When coupled with inherent connotations of class labels, negative stereotypes may emerge. For example, a particular skin color may correspond to benign/malicious software. Animals and Artistic faces may reduce such biases.

Obfuscation. Transforming data into a new domains, like faces can provide a level of data security by obscuring its true origins. This is useful if the underlying input domain is of a disturbing nature, and there exists a desire to minimize analyst exposure to this input domain, for example child abuse material, or if the input domain is to remain confidential. In this confidentiality scenario, the security of the original data is only as strong as the security of the transformation network, akin to the encryption half of a cryptographic operation.

Sourcing Human Input. CAPTCHA [36] has demonstrated the decomposition of difficult machine tasks to be repeated at scale by many humans. Like CAPTCHA, our proposed task could leverage a large pool of humans at a relatively low cost.

Ethics. This project has received IRB approval to perform human evaluations of the produced representation of numeric data as faces.

6 Conclusion

Works preceding this work have sought to represent software binaries as images optimized for machine classification, overlooking a significant advantage images have in improving accessibility for humans. In this work, we have presented the first proposal to transform numeric data into high-fidelity face images, a workflow to enable untrained humans to assist machines by identifying previously novel, unseen inputs. We have performed a user study to evaluate the ability of untrained humans to perform similarity decisions on our proposed and existing software images. Finally, we also initiate an important discussion cautioning against the use of untrained humans in "following" machine decisions. We hope that this work will spur further research to increase the cooperation between human and machine decisions for improved overall outcomes.

References

1. Anderson, H.S., Roth, P.: EMBER: an open dataset for training static PE malware machine learning models. arXiv preprint arXiv:1804.04637 (2018)
2. Busch, J., Kocheturov, A., Tresp, V., Seidl, T.: NF-GNN: network flow graph neural networks for malware detection and classification. In: 33rd International Conference on Scientific and Statistical Database Management, pp. 121–132 (2021)
3. Chernoff, H.: The use of faces to represent points in k-dimensional space graphically. J. Am. Stat. Assoc. **68**(342), 361–368 (1973)
4. Choi, Y., Uh, Y., Yoo, J., Ha, J.W.: StarGAN v2: diverse image synthesis for multiple domains. In: Proceedings of the IEEE/CVF Conference on Computer Vision and Pattern Recognition, pp. 8188–8197 (2020)
5. Cohen, F.: Computer viruses: theory and experiments. Comput. Secur. **6**(1), 22–35 (1987)
6. CrowdStrike: Crowdstrike 2023 global threat Report (2023). https://www.crowdstrike.com/global-threat-report/
7. Crowston, K.: Amazon mechanical turk: a research tool for organizations and information systems scholars. In: Shaping the Future of ICT Research. Methods and Approaches: IFIP WG 8.2, Working Conference, Tampa, FL, USA, 13–14 December 2012. Proceedings, pp. 210–221. Springer (2012)
8. Dong, X., Shen, J.: Triplet loss in Siamese network for object tracking. In: Proceedings of the European Conference on Computer Vision (ECCV) (2018)
9. Flury, B., Riedwyl, H.: Graphical representation of multivariate data by means of asymmetrical faces. J. Am. Stat. Assoc. (1981)
10. Goodfellow, I., et al.: Generative adversarial networks. Commun. ACM **63**(11), 139–144 (2020)
11. Gopinath, M., Sethuraman, S.C.: A comprehensive survey on deep learning based malware detection techniques. Comput. Sci. Rev. **47**, 100529 (2023)
12. Harang, R., Rudd, E.M.: SOREL-20M: a large scale benchmark dataset for malicious PE detection (2020)
13. ISC^2: (ISC) ^{2} 2022 cybersecurity workforce study (2022)
14. Jindal, C., Salls, C., Aghakhani, H., Long, K., Kruegel, C., Vigna, G.: Neurlux: dynamic malware analysis without feature engineering. In: Proceedings of the 35th Annual Computer Security Applications Conference, pp. 444–455 (2019)
15. Karras, T., Aittala, M., Hellsten, J., Laine, S., Lehtinen, J., Aila, T.: Training generative adversarial networks with limited data. Adv. Neural. Inf. Process. Syst. **33**, 12104–12114 (2020)
16. Karras, T., et al.: Alias-free generative adversarial networks. In: Proceeding Neural Information Processing System (2021)
17. Karras, T., Laine, S., Aila, T.: A style-based generator architecture for generative adversarial networks. In: Proceedings of the IEEE/CVF Conference on Computer Vision and Pattern Recognition, pp. 4401–4410 (2019)

18. Karras, T., Laine, S., Aittala, M., Hellsten, J., Lehtinen, J., Aila, T.: Analyzing and improving the image quality of StyleGAN. In: Proceedings of the IEEE/CVF conference on computer vision and pattern recognition (2020)
19. Leys, C., Ley, C., Klein, O., Bernard, P., Licata, L.: Detecting outliers: do not use standard deviation around the mean, use absolute deviation around the median. J. Exp. Soc. Psychol. **49**(4), 764–766 (2013)
20. Van der Maaten, L., Hinton, G.: Visualizing data using t-SNE. J. Mach. Learn. Res. **9**(11) (2008)
21. McInnes, L., Healy, J., Melville, J.: UMAP: uniform manifold approximation and projection for dimension reduction. arXiv preprint arXiv:1802.03426 (2018)
22. National Security Agency: ghidra. https://github.com/NationalSecurityAgency/ghidra
23. Ni, S., Qian, Q., Zhang, R.: Malware identification using visualization images and deep learning. Comput. Secur. **77**, 871–885 (2018)
24. Norris, J.R.: Markov Chains, vol. 2. Cambridge University Press (1998)
25. Or-Meir, O., Nissim, N., Elovici, Y., Rokach, L.: Dynamic malware analysis in the modern era—a state of the art survey. ACM Comput. Surv. (CSUR) (2019)
26. Rays, H.: Idapro. https://hex-rays.com/ida-pro/
27. Saxe, J., Berlin, K.: Deep neural network based malware detection using two dimensional binary program features. In: 2015 10th International Conference on Malicious and Unwanted Software (MALWARE), pp. 11–20. IEEE (2015)
28. Schultz, M.G., Eskin, E., Zadok, F., Stolfo, S.J.: Data mining methods for detection of new malicious executables. In: Proceedings 2001 IEEE Symposium on Security and Privacy, S and P 2001, pp. 38–49. IEEE (2000)
29. Shafiq, M.Z., Tabish, S.M., Mirza, F., Farooq, M.: A framework for efficient mining of structural information to detect zero-day malicious portable executables. 1Next Generation Intelligent Networks Research Center (nexGIN RC), Technical report (2009)
30. Sugiyama, M.: Dimensionality reduction of multimodal labeled data by local fisher discriminant analysis. J. Mach. Learn. Res. **8**(5) (2007)
31. Tag, B., et al.: DDoD: dual denial of decision attacks on human-AI teams. IEEE Pervasive Comput. **22**(1), 77–84 (2023)
32. Thomas, R.: LIEF - library to instrument executable formats (2017). https://lief.quarkslab.com/
33. Total, V.: Virus total. https://www.virustotal.com
34. VanHoudnos, N., et al.: This malware looks familiar: laymen identify malware runtime similarity with Chernoff faces and stick figures. In: 10th EAI International Conference on Bio-inspired Information and Communications Technologies (2017)
35. Vasan, D., Alazab, M., Wassan, S., Naeem, H., Safaei, B., Zheng, Q.: IMCFN: image-based malware classification using fine-tuned convolutional neural network architecture. Comput. Netw. **171**, 107138 (2020)
36. von Ahn, L., Blum, M., Hopper, N.J., Langford, J.: CAPTCHA: using hard AI problems for security. In: Biham, E. (ed.) EUROCRYPT 2003. LNCS, vol. 2656, pp. 294–311. Springer, Heidelberg (2003). https://doi.org/10.1007/3-540-39200-9_18
37. Wold, S., Esbensen, K., Geladi, P.: Principal component analysis. Chemom. Intell. Lab. Syst. **2**(1–3), 37–52 (1987)
38. Xu, P., Zhang, Y., Eckert, C., Zarras, A.: HawkEye: cross-platform malware detection with representation learning on graphs. In: Farkaš, I., Masulli, P., Otte, S., Wermter, S. (eds.) ICANN 2021. LNCS, vol. 12893, pp. 127–138. Springer, Cham (2021). https://doi.org/10.1007/978-3-030-86365-4_11

39. Yakdan, K., Dechand, S., Gerhards-Padilla, E., Smith, M.: Helping Johnny to analyze malware: a usability-optimized decompiler and malware analysis user study. In: 2016 IEEE Symposium on Security and Privacy (SP), pp. 158–177. IEEE (2016)
40. Yuan, B., Wang, J., Liu, D., Guo, W., Wu, P., Bao, X.: Byte-level malware classification based on Markov images and deep learning. Comput. Secur. (2020)

Post-processing in Local Differential Privacy: An Extensive Evaluation and Benchmark Platform

Alireza Khodaie, Berkay Kemal Balioglu, and M. Emre Gursoy(✉)

Department of Computer Engineering, Koç University, Istanbul, Turkey
{akhodaie22,bbalioglu23,emregursoy}@ku.edu.tr

Abstract. Local differential privacy (LDP) has recently gained prominence as a powerful paradigm for collecting and analyzing sensitive data from users' devices. However, the inherent perturbation added by LDP protocols reduces the utility of the collected data. To mitigate this issue, several post-processing (PP) methods have been developed. Yet, the comparative performance of PP methods under diverse settings remains underexplored. In this paper, we present an extensive benchmark comprising 6 popular LDP protocols, 7 PP methods, 4 utility metrics, and 6 datasets to evaluate the behaviors and optimality of PP methods under diverse conditions. Through extensive experiments, we show that while PP can substantially improve utility when the privacy budget is small (i.e., strict privacy), its benefit diminishes as the privacy budget grows. Moreover, our findings reveal that the optimal PP method depends on multiple factors, including the choice of LDP protocol, privacy budget, data characteristics (such as distribution and domain size), and the specific utility metric. To advance research in this area and assist practitioners in identifying the most suitable PP method for their setting, we introduce LDP^3, an open-source benchmark platform. LDP^3 contains all methods used in our experimental analysis, and it is designed in a modular, extensible, and multi-threaded way for future use and development.

Keywords: Local differential privacy · post-processing · data privacy

1 Introduction

Over the last few years, local differential privacy (LDP) has become a popular notion for privacy-preserving data collection and analysis. In LDP, users perturb their sensitive data locally and then send it to a data collector. The added perturbation disables the data collector from making inferences regarding any particular user, but the data collector can still estimate population-level statistics from aggregates of perturbed data. This feature of LDP makes it well-suited for data collection in decentralized settings. Consequently, LDP has seen widespread adoption in various research fields [4,7,10,12,16] as well as industry products, e.g., Google Chrome, Apple iOS, and Microsoft Windows [6,8,13].

Published by Springer Nature Switzerland AG 2025
L. Nemec Zlatolas et al. (Eds.): SEC 2025, IFIP AICT 745, pp. 76–90, 2025.
https://doi.org/10.1007/978-3-031-92882-6_6

With the emerging popularity of LDP, numerous LDP protocols have been developed in the literature [5,9,14]. However, since these protocols inherently introduce perturbation to ensure privacy, the population-level statistics estimated by the data collector become noisy, leading to utility loss. To reduce utility loss, several post-processing (PP) methods were proposed [11,15], e.g., Base-Pos, Norm, Norm-Cut, Norm-Sub, Norm-Mul, Power, and Power-NS. In essence, PP methods take as input the estimation results and process them in different ways to improve utility. On the other hand, although PP methods have been utilized in specific contexts or tested with specific protocols, to the best of our knowledge, there is no benchmark or detailed analysis of how different PP methods behave comparatively under diverse settings, e.g., under different combinations of LDP protocols, data characteristics, and utility metrics.

In this paper, we create an extensive setup containing 6 LDP protocols, 7 PP methods, 4 utility metrics, and 6 datasets to benchmark the behaviors and optimality of PP methods under diverse settings. We perform an experimental analysis using our benchmark setup and report (a subset) of our results in the paper. Our results and analyses yield several interesting findings. First, we find that PP methods indeed yield substantial utility benefits when the privacy budget ε is small (strict privacy), but their utility results converge as ε becomes larger, and their benefits decrease. Second, we find that the best-performing PP method (in terms of utility improvement) is not static, but rather, it depends on a variety of factors including the LDP protocol, ε budget, data characteristics (e.g., statistical distribution, domain size), and utility metric. Third, we find that the best-performing PP method is more consistent when ε is small, but it becomes more inconsistent as ε increases.

Next, considering there are multiple factors that influence the performance of PP methods and the choice of optimal PP method, we ask the following question: Can we design a practical system that helps a practitioner choose the best PP method for their setting, i.e., data, protocol, budget, and utility metric? To address this question, we design and develop LDP^3 (pronounced LDP-Cube): an open-source benchmark platform containing the implementations of all protocols, PP methods, utility metrics, and datasets used in our benchmark. LDP^3 is designed in a modular and extensible way so that new protocols, PP methods, utility metrics, etc. can be added in the future. Furthermore, it supports multi-threaded execution to reduce execution times so that researchers and practitioners can perform fast benchmarking of PP methods.

Contributions. In short, in this paper we make three main contributions:

- We create a benchmark setup with 6 LDP protocols, 7 PP methods, 4 utility metrics, and 6 datasets to analyze the behaviors and optimality of PP methods under diverse settings.
- We perform an experimental analysis and show that the best-performing PP method depends on a variety of factors, including the LDP protocol, ε budget, data characteristics (e.g., statistical distribution, domain size), and utility metric. We show that when these factors are different, the best-performing PP method can also be different.

- To advance research in this area and to assist researchers and practitioners in selecting the best PP method for their setting, we develop an open-source benchmark platform called LDP[3] which contains all protocols, PP methods, metrics, and datasets used in our analysis.

Related Work and Main Differences. While there exist a few past works in benchmarking LDP protocols or developing open-source LDP platforms, our work has some key differences. Earlier works such as [14] and [15] focus solely on protocols without post-processing or evaluate post-processing only on a single protocol. PURE-LDP proposed in [5] contains a subset of the LDP protocols and PP methods that exist in LDP[3]. The MULTI-FREQ-LDP package was proposed in [3]; however, its focus is on multi-dimensional and longitudinal frequency estimation [1,2] rather than post-processing. LDPLENS was proposed in [9]; however, it is focused on protocols' adversarial analysis and does not contain post-processing. Overall, our work differs in terms of its emphasis on post-processing as well as the novel experimental analysis and take-away messages concerning post-processing methods.

Paper Organization. The rest of the paper is organized as follows. In Sect. 2, we provide background information related to LDP, LDP protocols, and PP methods. In Sect. 3, we provide information regarding our experiment setup. In Sect. 4, we present and discuss our experiment results; additionally, we summarize the main take-away messages from our experimental analysis. In Sect. 5, we describe the design and implementation of LDP[3]. Finally, Sect. 6 concludes the paper.

2 LDP and Post-processing Methods

2.1 Local Differential Privacy (LDP)

Local differential privacy (LDP) is a popular notion for collecting data while protecting individuals' privacy. In a typical LDP setup, there are multiple users (clients) and a server (data collector). We denote the user population by $\mathcal{P}$, a user by $u \in \mathcal{P}$, and the user's true value by $v_u \in \mathcal{D}$, where $\mathcal{D}$ is the domain of allowed values. To satisfy LDP, each user encodes and perturbs their v_u locally on their device using a randomized algorithm ψ. The user then sends the perturbed value to the server. After gathering data from all users, the server applies estimation methods to compute statistics about the overall population $\mathcal{P}$. However, since each user's data is perturbed using ψ, the server cannot infer exact information about any particular user's v_u.

Definition 1 (ε-LDP). *A randomized mechanism ψ satisfies ε-LDP if and only if, for any two values $v_1, v_2 \in \mathcal{D}$:*

$$\forall y \in Range(\psi): \quad \frac{Pr[\psi(v_1) = y]}{Pr[\psi(v_2) = y]} \leq e^{\varepsilon} \tag{1}$$

where $Range(\psi)$ denotes the set of all possible outputs of ψ.

ε-LDP guarantees that, given the perturbed value y, the server cannot distinguish whether the user's true value was v_1 or v_2 with a probability ratio greater than e^{ε}. The strength of privacy protection is determined by the parameter ε, often referred to as the *privacy budget*, where smaller ε indicates stronger privacy.

The popularity of LDP has led to the development of various LDP protocols [5,9,14]. These protocols are often used as building blocks in more complex data analysis tasks and downstream applications. An LDP protocol can be characterized by two main components: (i) user-side encoding and perturbation to satisfy LDP, and (ii) server-side aggregation and estimation to recover population-level statistics. In this paper, we utilize six state-of-the-art LDP protocols: GRR, BLH, OLH, RAPPOR, OUE, and SS. Due to the page limit, we do not provide technical descriptions of each protocol; instead, we refer the readers to [9,14] which explain the user-side and server-side processes of the protocols in detail.

2.2 Post-Processing (PP) Methods

For $v \in \mathcal{D}$, let $f(v)$ denote the true occurrence frequency of v in the user population $\mathcal{P}$. After server-side estimation, the server recovers estimated frequencies $\hat{f}(v)$. However, $\hat{f}(v)$ is typically different from $f(v)$ because of LDP's perturbation, which causes utility loss (error) in downstream analyses and tasks. To improve utility, server-side post-processing (PP) methods have been proposed [11,15] which take as input $\hat{f}(v)$ and produce post-processed frequencies $\tilde{f}(v)$. Different PP methods result in varying trade-offs between utility increase and bias. In this paper, we use the following 7 state-of-the-art PP methods.

Base-Pos: Frequencies must be non-negative by definition; however, due to the perturbation in LDP, $\hat{f}(v)$ may be negative for some $v \in \mathcal{D}$. Base-Pos addresses this problem by converting all negative estimations to 0.

$$\forall v \in \mathcal{D} : \tilde{f}(v) = \begin{cases} \hat{f}(v) & \text{if } \hat{f}(v) \geq 0 \\ 0 & \text{otherwise} \end{cases} \tag{2}$$

Norm: The sum of frequencies across all $v \in \mathcal{D}$ should equal 1; however, this may not hold due to the perturbation in LDP. Norm addresses this problem by adding a constant σ to each frequency so that the sum will equal 1.

$$\forall v \in \mathcal{D} : \tilde{f}(v) = \hat{f}(v) + \sigma, \quad \text{such that} \quad \sum_{v \in \mathcal{D}} \tilde{f}(v) = 1 \tag{3}$$

Norm-Cut: Norm-Cut converts negative and small positive frequencies to 0, and it also ensures that the sum of frequencies equals 1. That is:

$$\forall v \in \mathcal{D} : \tilde{f}(v) = \begin{cases} 0 & \text{if } \hat{f}(v) \leq \theta \\ \hat{f}(v) & \text{if } \hat{f}(v) > \theta \end{cases} \tag{4}$$

where θ is a threshold value. The value of θ is chosen such that $\sum_{v \in \mathcal{D}} \tilde{f}(v) = 1$ is ensured.

Norm-Sub: Norm-Sub converts negative frequencies to 0. Then, it adds a constant δ to the frequencies to ensure that the sum of frequencies equals 1.

$$\forall v \in \mathcal{D} : \tilde{f}(v) = \begin{cases} 0 & \text{if } \hat{f}(v) < 0 \\ \hat{f}(v) + \delta & \text{if } \hat{f}(v) \geq 0 \end{cases} \tag{5}$$

Here, the value of δ is chosen such that $\sum_{v \in \mathcal{D}} \tilde{f}(v) = 1$ is ensured.

Norm-Mul: Norm-Mul converts negative frequencies to 0. Then, instead of an additive factor, it uses a multiplicative factor to the remaining frequencies so that their sum becomes 1.

$$\forall v \in \mathcal{D} : \tilde{f}(v) = \begin{cases} 0 & \text{if } \hat{f}(v) < 0 \\ \alpha \hat{f}(v) & \text{if } \hat{f}(v) \geq 0 \end{cases} \tag{6}$$

Here, α is the multiplicative factor. Its value is chosen such that $\sum_{v \in \mathcal{D}} \tilde{f}(v) = 1$ is ensured.

Power: The rationale of Power is that many real-world datasets follow a statistical distribution such as a Gaussian or power law distribution. Therefore, Power fits a distribution to the estimated frequencies and aims to minimize the expected square error. For example, with $\tilde{f}(v) \sim P$ where P is a power law distribution, the goal is to minimize:

$$\min_P \mathbb{E}\left[\sum_{v \in \mathcal{D}} \left(\hat{f}(v) - \tilde{f}(v)\right)^2\right] \tag{7}$$

Power-NS: Power-NS first applies Power and then uses Norm-Sub on Power's outputs to obtain the final result.

3 Benchmark Setup

We used Python to implement all LDP protocols, PP methods, and experiments. Each experiment was conducted 20 times for statistical significance.

3.1 Datasets

We used three real-world datasets (BMS-POS, Kosarak, Adult) and three synthetically generated datasets (Zipfian, Gaussian, Uniform) that are also commonly used in the DP and LDP literatures for experimentation.

Adult is a well-known dataset in the privacy literature, consisting of 45,222 records and 14 features. We downloaded it from the UCI ML Repository[1]. The features relate to individuals' census information such as age, education, workclass, marital status, race, and gender. In our experiments, we used *age* values

[1] https://archive.ics.uci.edu/dataset/2/adult.

as users' true values. Ages in the dataset ranged between 17 and 90; therefore, we have $|\mathcal{D}| = 74$.

Kosarak contains click-stream data of a Hungarian online news portal. We downloaded it from the SPMF Dataset Repository[2]. Each row in the dataset corresponds to one user's URL visit sequence. Due to many URLs having few occurrences (e.g., one or two), we pre-processed the dataset by identifying the top 128 most visited URLs and removed the rest, i.e., $|\mathcal{D}| = 128$. For users who had more than one URL in their resulting stream, the most frequently occurring URL in their stream was picked as their v_u.

BMS-POS includes market basket sales data from a major electronics retailer, consisting of 515,596 transactions and 1,657 unique items sold. We downloaded it from the public Github repository[3] and pre-processed it in a similar fashion to Kosarak by keeping only the top 256 most frequently purchased items.

Gaussian: We synthetically generated multiple Gaussian datasets in which users' true values are sampled from a Gaussian distribution with mean $\mu = 50$ and standard deviation $\sigma = 1, 5, 10$, and 20. In all Gaussian datasets, the domain size is fixed to $|\mathcal{D}| = 100$ and the population size is fixed to $|\mathcal{P}| = 100{,}000$.

Zipfian: We generated Zipfian datasets in which users' true values are sampled from a Zipfian distribution. The Zipfian distribution is characterized by a skewness parameter s. In our datasets, we fixed $s = 1.5$ and $|\mathcal{P}| = 1{,}000{,}000$, and varied the domain sizes $|\mathcal{D}| = 32, 64, 128, 256, 512, 1024$, and 2048.

Uniform: Finally, we generated Uniform datasets in which users' true value distribution follows a Uniform distribution. We used $|\mathcal{P}| = 100,000$ by default and the domain size $|\mathcal{D}|$ is varied.

3.2 Utility Metrics

We utilized four utility metrics to measure the errors between the true frequencies $f(v)$ and the post-processed frequencies $\tilde{f}(v)$: ℓ_1 distance, ℓ_2 distance, Kullback-Leibler Divergence (KL), and Earth Mover's Distance (EMD). Unless otherwise stated, ℓ_1 distance is the default utility metric used when reporting results.

ℓ_1 **distance**, also known as Manhattan distance, measures error using the absolute value norm. It is defined as:

$$\ell_1\text{distance} = \sum_{v \in \mathcal{D}} \left| \tilde{f}(v) - f(v) \right| \tag{8}$$

ℓ_2 **distance**, also known as Euclidean distance, measures error using the squared norm. It is defined as:

$$\ell_2\text{distance} = \sqrt{\sum_{v \in \mathcal{D}} \left(\tilde{f}(v) - f(v) \right)^2} \tag{9}$$

[2] https://www.philippe-fournier-viger.com/spmf/index.php?link=datasets.php.
[3] https://github.com/cpearce/HARM/blob/master/datasets/BMS-POS.csv.

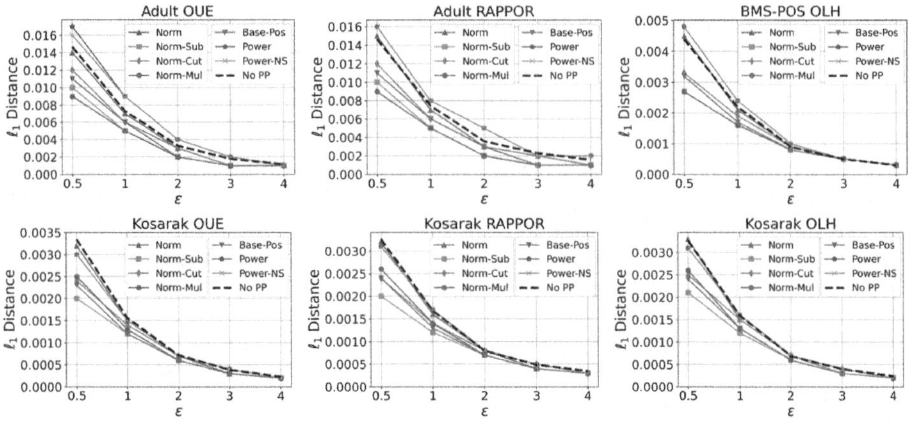

Fig. 1. Average utility loss (measured via ℓ_1 distance) of different PP methods under different datasets, protocols, and ε budgets.

Kullback-Leibler divergence is used to measure how much one probability distribution diverges from another. In this context, $f(v)$ and $\tilde{f}(v)$ are treated as probability mass functions, and KL-divergence is defined as:

$$\text{KL-divergence} = \sum_{v \in \mathcal{D}} f(v) \log \left(\frac{f(v)}{\tilde{f}(v)} \right) \tag{10}$$

Earth Mover's Distance (EMD) measures the minimum cost of transforming one distribution into another. It can be interpreted as the amount of work required to transform the original frequency distribution $f(v)$ into the post-processed distribution $\tilde{f}(v)$. Mathematically, it is defined as:

$$\text{EMD} = \min_{\pi} \sum_{v_1, v_2 \in \mathcal{D}} \pi(v_1, v_2) \cdot |v_1 - v_2| \tag{11}$$

where $\pi(v_1, v_2)$ represents the amount of mass moved from v_1 to v_2, and $|v_1 - v_2|$ is the distance between v_1 and v_2.

4 Results and Discussion

4.1 Impacts of LDP Protocols and Privacy Budgets

In Fig. 1, we present the ℓ_1 distance results of different PP methods under varying datasets, protocols, and ε budgets. Results in this figure are the average ℓ_1 distances over 20 runs. We observe from the plots in Fig. 1 that when ε is smaller (such as 0.5 or 1), there exist larger differences between the ℓ_1 distances of different PP methods. Furthermore, the benefits of using the best-performing PP method compared to not using PP (represented by the dashed line titled "No PP") or using a suboptimal PP method are substantial. For example, on

Table 1. Best-performing PP method in terms of ℓ_1 distance under varying datasets (BMS-POS, Kosarak, Adult), LDP protocols (GRR, BLH, OLH, RAPPOR, OUE, SS), and ε budgets.

ε		**GRR**	**BLH**	**OLH**	**RAPPOR**	**OUE**	**SS**
$\varepsilon = 0.5$	BMS-POS	Norm-Mul	Norm-Mul	Norm-Mul	Norm-Mul	Norm-Mul	Norm-Mul
	Kosarak	Norm-Sub	Norm-Sub	Norm-Sub	Norm-Sub	Norm-Sub	Power
	Adult	Norm-Mul	Norm-Mul	Norm-Mul	Norm-Mul	Norm-Mul	Norm-Mul
$\varepsilon = 1$	BMS-POS	Norm-Mul	Norm-Sub	Norm-Sub	Norm-Sub	Norm-Sub	Norm-Sub
	Kosarak	Norm-Sub	Norm-Sub	Norm-Sub	Norm-Sub	Norm-Sub	Norm-Sub
	Adult	Norm-Mul	Norm-Mul	Norm-Mul	Norm-Mul	Norm-Mul	Norm-Mul
$\varepsilon = 2$	BMS-POS	Norm-Sub	Norm-Sub	Norm-Sub	Norm-Sub	Norm-Mul	Norm-Mul
	Kosarak	Norm-Sub	Norm-Sub	Norm-Sub	Norm-Sub	Norm-Sub	Norm-Sub
	Adult	Norm-Mul	Norm-Mul	Norm-Mul	Norm-Mul	Norm-Mul	Power
$\varepsilon = 3$	BMS-POS	Norm-Mul	Norm-Mul	Norm-Mul	Norm-Mul	Norm-Sub	Norm-Mul
	Kosarak	Norm-Sub	Norm-Sub	Base-Pos	Norm-Sub	Norm-Sub	Norm-Sub
	Adult	Power	Norm-Mul	Norm-Sub	Norm-Mul	Norm-Sub	Power
$\varepsilon = 4$	BMS-POS	Norm-Mul	Norm-Sub	Base-Pos	Norm-Sub	Norm-Mul	Norm-Mul
	Kosarak	Base-Pos	Norm-Sub	Norm	Norm-Sub	Norm	Norm-Cut
	Adult	Power	Norm-Mul	Norm-Sub	Norm-Sub	Norm-Sub	Power

the Adult dataset, the best-performing PP method under $\varepsilon = 0.5$ is Norm-Mul, and its ℓ_1 distance is almost half of No PP, Power, and Power-NS. However, as ε increases, we observe that the ℓ_1 distances of all PP methods converge, and they become similar to No PP. Considering that increased ε implies reduced perturbation, these results suggest that the need for PP methods is also reduced in the case of larger ε values. Since many PP methods converge as ε increases, achieving the best utility also becomes less dependent on the PP method used. Combining these results, we arrive at the following take-away message.

PP methods can yield substantial utility benefits, especially when ε is small. As ε becomes larger, PP methods' utility results converge to one another, and their benefits (over not using PP) decrease.

In Table 1, we provide results regarding which PP method performs best under varying datasets, ε budgets, and LDP protocols. The name of the best-performing PP method is written in each corresponding cell. Note that the cells are colored. We use darker colors to indicate how frequently, across 20 experiment runs, the best-performing PP method ends up being the best performer. For example, the cells corresponding to GRR and $\varepsilon = 0.5$ are quite dark for all three datasets. This means that across 20 experiment runs, the PP methods written inside the cells (Norm-Mul and Norm-Sub) were the best performers in close to 20 of the runs. In contrast, the cells corresponding to OLH, RAPPOR, OUE, and SS with $\varepsilon = 4$ are light-colored. This means that across 20 experiment runs, the PP methods written inside those cells were the best performers in fewer runs – although they are still the best, other PP methods perform closely.

We observe from Table 1 that Norm-Sub and Norm-Mul usually perform better than others, especially when $\varepsilon = 0.5$, 1, and 2. Yet, they are not always the best. Power, Base-Pos, Norm, and others can be preferred under different settings. Thus, there is no single PP method that beats others in all settings. Furthermore, we observe that when ε is low (such as 0.5), the best PP method is relatively clear and consistent. Norm-Mul emerges as the best method for BMS-POS and Adult datasets, whereas Norm-Sub emerges as the best method for the Kosarak dataset. Considering the levels of darkness in the cells, we can conclude that both Norm-Mul and Norm-Sub are consistently the best performers. However, as ε gradually increases, two important trends emerge. First, the dominance of a single PP method starts to diminish. A single method does not outperform all others across different LDP protocols, i.e., different LDP protocols begin to favor different PP methods. This shift indicates that, as privacy levels increase, the preference of PP methods may become more protocol-dependent. Second, with larger values of ε, the frequency with which the best PP method produces the lowest ℓ_1 distance significantly decreases. It can be observed that there are many more dark-colored cells when $\varepsilon = 0.5$ compared to much lighter-colored cells when $\varepsilon = 4$. This indicates that with larger values of ε, the effectiveness of PP methods becomes more variable, making it challenging to find a consistent PP method that performs better in a given setting.

We also highlight that the results obtained in Table 1 agree with the results in Fig. 1 in terms of which PP method performs best. Also, the convergence trend of different PP methods in Fig. 1 can help explain the lighter-colored cells in Table 1 when $\varepsilon = 3$ or 4. In Fig. 1, we found that PP methods produce similar ℓ_1 distances when ε is large. Thus, the fact that the best-performing PP method changes frequently and the best-performing method is usually inconsistent in Table 1 can be explained by this finding from Fig. 1. Considering all results and discussion in this subsection, we can arrive at the following take-away message.

> Although Norm-Sub and Norm-Mul typically perform well, the best-performing PP method can be different under different protocols, ε values, and datasets. The best-performing PP method is more consistent when ε is small, but becomes inconsistent as ε increases.

4.2 Impacts of Data Characteristics

In this section, we analyze the impacts of two data-related characteristics: data distribution and domain size. To measure the impacts of the data distribution, we utilize the Gaussian and Uniform datasets. We generate Gaussian datasets with varying standard deviations ($\sigma = 1$, 5, 10, and 20) to experiment with varying degrees of non-uniformity in $f(v)$, and a Uniform dataset which in which all $f(v)$ are equal. Smaller σ means the data distribution is more concentrated around the mean, and therefore there is higher non-uniformity.

Table 2. Best-performing PP method under varying Gaussian and Uniform datasets.

	Protocols	Standard Deviation				
		$\sigma = 1$	$\sigma = 5$	$\sigma = 10$	$\sigma = 20$	Uniform
$\varepsilon = 1$	GRR	Norm-Cut	Norm-Cut	Norm-Mul	Norm-Mul	Norm-Mul
	BLH	Norm-Cut	Norm-Cut	Norm-Cut	Norm-Mul	Norm-Mul
	OLH	Norm-Cut	Norm-Cut	Norm-Cut	Norm-Mul	Norm-Mul
	RAPPOR	Norm-Cut	Norm-Cut	Norm-Cut	Norm-Mul	Norm-Mul
	OUE	Norm-Cut	Norm-Cut	Norm-Sub	Norm-Mul	Norm-Mul
	SS	Norm-Cut	Norm-Cut	Norm-Sub	Norm-Mul	Norm-Mul

Table 3. Best-performing PP method under Zipfian datasets with varying $|\mathcal{D}|$.

	Protocols	Domain Size $\|\mathcal{D}\|$						
		32	64	128	256	512	1024	2048
$\varepsilon = 1$	GRR	Base-Pos	Norm-Sub	Norm-Sub	Norm-Sub	Norm-Cut	Norm-Cut	Norm-Cut
	BLH	Norm	Norm-Sub	Norm-Sub	Norm-Sub	Norm-Sub	Norm-Sub	Norm-Cut
	OLH	Norm	Norm-Sub	Norm-Sub	Norm-Sub	Norm-Sub	Norm-Cut	Norm-Cut
	RAPPOR	Norm	Norm-Sub	Norm-Sub	Norm-Sub	Norm-Sub	Norm-Cut	Norm-Cut
	OUE	Norm	Norm-Sub	Norm-Sub	Norm-Sub	Norm-Sub	Norm-Cut	Norm-Cut
	SS	Norm-Cut	Norm-Mul	Norm-Sub	Power	Norm-Sub	Norm-Cut	Norm-Cut

The results of this experiment are shown in Table 2. We use the same representation and color coding as in Table 1. The ε value is 1. We observe from Table 2 that Norm-Cut is consistently the best-performing PP method for smaller σ values such as $\sigma = 1$ and 5. However, as σ increases to 10 and 20, PP methods such as Norm-Mul and Norm-Sub start becoming more preferable. For $\sigma = 20$ and the Uniform dataset, Norm-Mul becomes the best choice consistently. This progression reveals a clear trend: as non-uniformity changes, the best-performing PP method changes. Norm-Cut is the better choice when the data is non-uniform, whereas Norm-Mul becomes the better choice when the data is more uniform. This observation can be explained via the mathematical definitions of the PP methods as follows. When the data is uniform, $f(v)$ of all $v \in \mathcal{D}$ are similar and there do not exist values with substantially lower frequencies than others. In this case, the multiplicative correction applied by Norm-Mul is sufficient to ensure consistency and reduce error. On the other hand, when data is non-uniform, there exist some values v such that $f(v)$ is 0 or close to 0. After LDP, some of these values end up with non-zero but low $\hat{f}(v)$. Norm-Cut applies the rule $\tilde{f}(v) = 0$ if $\hat{f}(v) \leq \theta$ to them, i.e., these values' frequencies are post-processed to 0. Thus, it reduces error especially in datasets with high non-uniformity.

In our second experiment, we analyze the impact of domain size $|\mathcal{D}|$. For this experiment, we generate Zipfian datasets with varying $|\mathcal{D}| = 32$, 64, 128, 256, 512, 1024, and 2048. We conduct a similar analysis to Tables 1 and 2. The results are shown in Table 3. For the smallest domain size $|\mathcal{D}| = 32$, different

Table 4. Best-performing PP method under varying utility metrics. Kosarak dataset and $\varepsilon = 1$ are used.

	Protocols	Utility Metric			
		ℓ_1 distance	ℓ_2 distance	KL-divergence	EMD
$\varepsilon = 1$	GRR	Norm-Sub	Norm-Sub	Norm-Sub	Norm
	BLH	Norm-Sub	Norm-Sub	Norm-Sub	Norm
	OLH	Norm-Sub	Norm-Sub	Norm-Sub	Norm-Sub
	RAPPOR	Norm-Sub	Norm-Sub	Norm-Sub	Norm-Sub
	OUE	Norm-Sub	Norm-Sub	Norm-Sub	Norm-Sub
	SS	Norm-Sub	Norm-Sub	Power	Power-NS

protocols may favor different PP methods and the cells are not dark-colored, suggesting that a single PP method does not consistently outperform the others. As $|\mathcal{D}|$ increases to 64, 128, and 256, Norm-Sub becomes more dominant for most protocols. When $|\mathcal{D}|$ is further increased to 1024 and 2048, Norm-Cut emerges as the best-performing method. For the largest domain size $|\mathcal{D}| = 2048$, Norm-Cut becomes the best-performing protocol consistently. The superior performance of Norm-Sub and Norm-Cut for larger $|\mathcal{D}|$ agrees with results from Table 2, since both Norm-Sub and Norm-Cut post-process negative frequencies and low frequencies to 0. When $|\mathcal{D}|$ is large, as $|\mathcal{P}|$ is constant, there is a higher likelihood of obtaining low-frequency values $v \in \mathcal{D}$, whose frequencies may remain low or become negative after LDP perturbation. Norm-Sub and Norm-Cut help in reducing the errors in these cases. Overall, the results also demonstrate that the best PP method changes when $|\mathcal{D}|$ is changed, e.g., multiple PP methods perform well for small domain sizes, Norm-Sub emerges as the best approach for medium-sized domains (128 to 512), and Norm-Cut is the best for large domains (> 1024). Considering the results and discussion in this subsection, we arrive at the following take-away message.

> The best-performing PP method is dependent on data characteristics, e.g., data distribution (non-uniformity) and domain size.

4.3 Impacts of the Utility Metrics

In the experiments reported so far, ℓ_1 distance was used as the utility metric. In this section, we examine how the choice of utility metric impacts the performance of PP methods. We use all four of the utility metrics described in Sect. 3.2: ℓ_1 distance, ℓ_2 distance, KL-divergence, and EMD. We report experiments with varying protocols, but fixed $\varepsilon = 1$ and the Kosarak dataset. The results are given in Table 4. The same format and color coding as the previous tables are used.

For most protocols, ℓ_1 distance and ℓ_2 distance metrics consistently favor Norm-Sub. This observation underscores that the ℓ_1 and ℓ_2 distance metrics, which are similar in nature, agree in terms of the favorable PP method. In contrast, KL-divergence exhibits slightly more variability compared to ℓ_1 and ℓ_2. While Norm-Sub still performs well for most protocols, there are notable deviations. For example, for SS, Power is consistently the best-performing PP method. The reduced darkness of the cells corresponding to KL-divergence further highlights the varying nature of KL-divergence in comparison to ℓ_1 and ℓ_2 distance. On the other hand, EMD diverges even more significantly from ℓ_1 and ℓ_2, favoring a more distributed selection of methods. Norm-Sub still remains a leading contender but with substantially reduced consistencies, as seen in protocols like OLH, RAPPOR, and OUE. In the remaining protocols (GRR, BLH, SS), alternative PP methods such as Norm and Power-NS perform the best.

Overall, the results indicate that the best-performing PP method is indeed influenced by the choice of utility metric. Metrics that are inherently similar to one another tend to prefer the same PP methods, whereas different metrics (such as EMD) tend to prefer different PP methods.

> Norm-Sub typically performs well across multiple utility metrics, but the optimal PP method can change according to the choice of metric.

5 LDP³: An Open-Source Benchmark Platform

The results of our experimental analysis show that the optimal choice of PP method depends on multiple factors, including the LDP protocol, ε budget, data characteristics (e.g., statistical distribution, domain size), and utility metric. When these factors are different, the best-performing PP method is also different. This motivated the following question: Can we design a practical system that helps a researcher or practitioner choose the best PP method for their setting, i.e., for their choice of data, protocol, budget, and utility metric?

We designed and developed LDP^3 to address this need (pronounced LDP-Cube, stands for: **L**ocal **D**ifferential **P**rivacy with **P**ost **P**rocessing). LDP^3 is an open-source benchmark platform available on Github[4]. It contains implementations of 6 LDP protocols, 7 PP methods, 4 utility metrics, and 6 datasets in a multi-threaded setup. It aims to offer a comprehensive and extensible platform for researchers and practitioners to evaluate combinations of different LDP protocols and PP methods using their desired datasets, privacy budgets, and utility metrics. The results obtained from LDP^3 can assist researchers and practitioners in choosing the best-performing PP method in their custom settings.

The architectural design of LDP^3 is shown in Fig. 2. As it can be observed from Fig. 2, LDP^3 consists of the following modules:

[4] https://github.com/alrzakh/LDPcube.

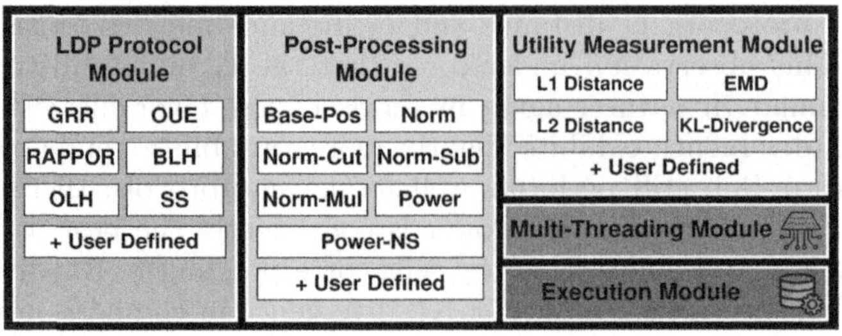

Fig. 2. LDP^3 system architecture.

- The LDP Protocol Module contains implementations of 6 state-of-the-art LDP protocols: GRR, BLH, OLH, RAPPOR, OUE, and SS. It is extensible to accommodate new protocols, e.g., protocols can be added by implementing the functionalities for user-side perturbation and server-side estimation.
- The Post-Processing Module contains implementations of 7 PP methods explained in Sect. 2.2. All methods take as input the estimated frequencies $\hat{f}(v)$ and produce post-processed $\tilde{f}(v)$. New PP methods can also be added in the future.
- The Utility Measurement Module contains implementations of utility metrics to measure the differences between $f(v)$ and $\tilde{f}(v)$. Currently, the 4 utility metrics explained in Sect. 3.2 are implemented in this module.
- The Multi-Threading Module leverages Python's concurrency features to parallelize the simulation of data perturbation and aggregation processes. It is useful when LDP^3 is run on multi-threaded or multi-core CPUs. In essence, it enables $\mathcal{P}$ to be divided into the number of available threads, simulates data collection for each subset of $\mathcal{P}$ in a different thread in parallel, and eventually combines the results from the different threads.
- Finally, the Execution Module facilitates the handling of datasets (e.g., reading or generating datasets from Sect. 3.1) and provides a command-line interface to run experiments.

6 Conclusion

In this paper, we performed an experimental analysis of PP methods and showed that PP methods can significantly improve utility in LDP, especially under strict privacy regimes (small ε). However, we also showed that this benefit is neither universal nor static: the optimal PP method depends on a combination of factors, including the LDP protocol, privacy budget, data characteristics (e.g., statistical distribution, domain size), and the specific utility metric. We then designed and developed an open-source benchmark platform for LDP protocols and PP methods called LDP^3, which integrates all components used in our experimental analysis. By making LDP^3 modular, extensible, and multi-threaded, we aimed to provide a platform that is helpful for both LDP researchers and practitioners.

There are several avenues for future work. First, we plan to integrate additional LDP protocols and PP methods into LDP^3 to further increase its breadth. Second, we plan to add a new module to evaluate protocols' adversarial aspects, e.g., privacy attacks and poisoning attacks. Third, we plan to design a graphical user interface (GUI) for LDP^3 and conduct human studies to test how convenient it is for non-experts to use LDP^3 for protocol and PP method selection.

Acknowledgments. This study was supported by the Scientific and Technological Research Council of Türkiye (TUBITAK) under Grant Number 123E179. The authors thank TUBITAK for their support.

References

1. Arcolezi, H.H., Couchot, J.F., Al Bouna, B., Xiao, X.: Random sampling plus fake data: multidimensional frequency estimates with local differential privacy. In: Proceedings of the 30th ACM International Conference on Information and Knowledge Management, pp. 47–57 (2021)
2. Arcolezi, H.H., Couchot, J.F., Al Bouna, B., Xiao, X.: Improving the utility of locally differentially private protocols for longitudinal and multidimensional frequency estimates. Digit. Commun. Netw. (2022)
3. Arcolezi, H.H., Couchot, J.F., Gambs, S., Palamidessi, C., Zolfaghari, M.: Multi-freq-LDPy: multiple frequency estimation under local differential privacy in python. In: Computer Security – ESORICS 2022, pp. 770–775. Springer (2022)
4. Cormode, G., Jha, S., Kulkarni, T., Li, N., Srivastava, D., Wang, T.: Privacy at scale: local differential privacy in practice. In: Proceedings of the 2018 International Conference on Management of Data, pp. 1655–1658 (2018)
5. Cormode, G., Maddock, S., Maple, C.: Frequency estimation under local differential privacy. Proc. VLDB Endow. **14**(11), 2046–2058 (2021)
6. Ding, B., Kulkarni, J., Yekhanin, S.: Collecting telemetry data privately. Adv. Neural Inf. Process. Syst. **30** (2017)
7. Du, Y., et al.: LDPtrace: locally differentially private trajectory synthesis. Proc. VLDB Endow. **16**(8), 1897–1909 (2023)
8. Erlingsson, Ú., Pihur, V., Korolova, A.: RAPPOR: randomized aggregatable privacy-preserving ordinal response. In: Proceedings of the 2014 ACM SIGSAC Conference on Computer and Communications Security, pp. 1054–1067 (2014)
9. Gursoy, M.E., Liu, L., Chow, K.H., Truex, S., Wei, W.: An adversarial approach to protocol analysis and selection in local differential privacy. IEEE Trans. Inf. Forensics Secur. **17**, 1785–1799 (2022)
10. Gursoy, M.E., Tamersoy, A., Truex, S., Wei, W., Liu, L.: Secure and utility-aware data collection with condensed local differential privacy. IEEE Trans. Dependable Secure Comput. **18**(5), 2365–2378 (2019)
11. Jia, J., Gong, N.Z.: Calibrate: Frequency estimation and heavy hitter identification with local differential privacy via incorporating prior knowledge. In: IEEE Conference on Computer Communications (INFOCOM), pp. 2008–2016. IEEE (2019)
12. Kim, J.W., Lim, J.H., Moon, S.M., Jang, B.: Collecting health lifelog data from smartwatch users in a privacy-preserving manner. IEEE Trans. Consum. Electron. **65**(3), 369–378 (2019)

13. Thakurta, A.G., et al.: Emoji frequency detection and deep link frequency. US Patent App. 15/640,266 (2017)
14. Wang, T., Blocki, J., Li, N., Jha, S.: Locally differentially private protocols for frequency estimation. In: 26th USENIX Security Symposium, pp. 729–745 (2017)
15. Wang, T., Lopuhaa-Zwakenberg, M., Li, Z., Skoric, B., Li, N.: Locally differentially private frequency estimation with consistency. In: Proceedings of the Network and Distributed System Security (NDSS) Symposium (2020)
16. Yang, M., Guo, T., Zhu, T., Tjuawinata, I., Zhao, J., Lam, K.Y.: Local differential privacy and its applications: a comprehensive survey. Comput. Stand. Interfaces 103827 (2023)

Rubber Ducky Station: Advancing HID Attacks with Visual Data Exfiltration

August See(✉), Thimo Grußendorf, Jona Laudan, and Mathias Fischer

University of Hamburg, Hamburg, Germany
{richard.august.see,mathias.fischer}@uni-hamburg.de,
{thimo.grussendord,jona.laudan}@studium.uni-hamburg.de

Abstract. Human Interface Device (HID) automation represents a frequently overlooked yet highly effective cyberattack vector. In this paper, we present the Rubber Ducky Station (RDS), an advanced HID-based attack tool that builds upon and surpasses the functionality of traditional Rubber Ducky devices. By integrating screen-capturing capabilities and a local network interface, the RDS enables non-intrusive data exfiltration through the duplication and recording of screen output, all without the victim's awareness. The RDS leverages visual feedback to adapt dynamically to varying conditions, such as device types, operating systems, and keyboard layouts. Furthermore, it uses visual signals as a stealthy exfiltration channel, eliminating the need for code execution on the target system. This approach allows the RDS to bypass detection mechanisms, including antivirus software and intrusion detection systems. A prototype of the RDS, developed at an approximate cost of 60 USD, integrates keyboard emulation, screen recording, and OCR capabilities, along with a local Wi-Fi network interface for seamless data exfiltration. We evaluate the RDS across multiple operating systems and compare its functionality to existing Rubber Ducky devices and Remote Access Trojans (RATs). The results demonstrate successful attacks on widely used platforms, including Ubuntu, Debian, Windows, and Android, as well as against various antivirus and Endpoint Detection and Response (EDR) solutions, such as Citrix Workspace, Windows Defender, Avira, Avast, Kaspersky, and Sophos.

Keywords: rubber ducky · HID emulation · HID attack · data exfiltration

1 Introduction

As research into network intrusions and malware progresses, the risks posed by less conventional attack vectors, such as malicious USB devices, are often underestimated. The most well known is likely the Rubber Ducky, a device disguised as a USB drive that simulates keyboard inputs. When connected to a computer, it executes pre-defined scripts that can manipulate both the operating system and software applications as if an attacker were physically present. This method

Published by Springer Nature Switzerland AG 2025
L. Nemec Zlatolas et al. (Eds.): SEC 2025, IFIP AICT 745, pp. 91–103, 2025.
https://doi.org/10.1007/978-3-031-92882-6_7

exploits the inherent trust that operating systems place in user input, but it also exposes significant limitations in the traditional Rubber Ducky's design.

To exfiltrate data, current implementations of the Rubber Ducky necessitate either the execution of onboard programs, such as SSH, or the installation of supplementary software on the target device. These actions can often be blocked by security measures such as firewall settings or restrictive permissions set by centralized administration using tools like Active Directory. Additionally, traditional Rubber Duckies cannot adapt their scripts to react dynamically to changes in the environment, such as login prompts, language settings, or user interventions, which limits their effectiveness in varied operational contexts[1].

The main contribution of this paper is the introduction of the Rubber Ducky Station (RDS), an advanced cyber-attack tool that not only retains the capabilities of its predecessors but also incorporates significant enhancements like screen capturing and a local network interface, which address the aforementioned weaknesses. The improvements presented in the RDS include:

- A passive data exfiltration method through screen capturing, which enables the RDS to remain undetected by, e.g., firewalls or Intrusion Detection Systems. Further, the RDS can adapt dynamically to different environments such as varying devices, operating systems, and language settings by using the on-screen information. For instance, the RDS can duplicate displays invisibly and record the screen's content or operate through keyboard inputs only when it detects the user's absence (e.g., when there has been no screen change for an extended period).
- A prototype implemented using a Raspberry Pi, which keeps the total hardware cost around 60 USD. The design and specifications of this prototype are made available as open source[2].
- Evaluation of the RDS against traditional Rubber Duckies and software-based remote access tools. Our findings demonstrate the RDS's superior capabilities in terms of data exfiltration, and its effectiveness in remotely controlling devices via Virtual Network Computing (VNC).
- An analysis of the defense mechanisms currently employed by operating systems, anti-virus software, and Intrusion Detection and Prevention Systems. Additionally, the paper discusses potential countermeasures such as USB port blocking and heuristic detection techniques, which highlight the ongoing challenge of balancing security with usability in system design.

The paper is structured as follows. Section 2 introduces our requirements for automation attacks on systems and presents related work, establishing the context and identifying the gaps the RDS aims to fill. Section 3 details the design and implementation of the RDS, covering hardware. Section 4 describes possible attack scenarios using the RDS. Section 5 provides an in-depth examination of

[1] https://shop.hak5.org/products/usb-rubber-ducky
https://github.com/whid-injector/WHID
https://hackingtoolscenter.com/product/usbninja/.

[2] https://github.com/8mas/rubber-ducky-station.

the new attack vectors enabled by the RDS, compares it with existing tools, and discusses potential countermeasures. Finally, Sect. 6 concludes the paper.

2 Requirements and Related Work

2.1 Requirements

We define the following requirements for the detection and capabilities that an attack on systems should fulfill.

Minimal Privileges Required (R1): The attack should operate without requiring administrative privileges or special capabilities, such as internet access on Android systems. This ensures functionality on managed devices or locked-down systems where software installation is restricted.

Stealthy and Passive Operation (R2): The attack should be designed to avoid triggering antivirus (AV) software, conducting its activities without active interference and maintaining a low profile on the target system. A normal user should not notice that the system is under attack. With a minimal detection surface, the attack should remain hidden from traditional security measures.

Stealthy Data Exfiltration (R3): Data should be exfiltrated without triggering firewalls or AV software in heavily locked-down systems, and without the victim's awareness or direct interaction.

Environmental Reactivity (R4): The attack should adapt to dynamic conditions such as varying device types, operating systems (e.g., Windows, macOS, Linux), and keyboard languages without requiring tailored modifications.

Dynamic Reactions or Remote Control Capabilities (R5): The attack should autonomously search for interesting data or be remotely controllable to do so. It can be used on systems where the data to exfiltrate is not yet known. If remotely controllable, the connection should be stealthy as well.

2.2 Related Work

The related work is grouped into three areas: software attacks (e.g., RATs), in-person HID attacks, and defenses against HID threats. These areas capture the main threats and countermeasures relevant to rubber ducky devices. RATs and HID attacks are discussed here, with defenses covered in Sect. 5.2. Table 1 summarizes our approach against prior work.

Remote Access Trojans. Remote Access Trojans are software applications that enable an attacker to control a system remotely. Examples include a trojan that includes Virtual Network Computing (VNC) software or Secure Shell (SSH) access. RATs offer significant advantages for attackers due to their ability to provide persistent access and control. Once installed, RATs can operate in the background, often undetected for extended periods. They can record keystrokes,

Table 1. Comparison of Rubber Ducky (RD), Remote Access Trojan (RAT), and Rubber Ducky Station (RDS).

Requirements	RD	RAT	RDS
Least Privileges Required	●	○	●
Stealthy and Passive Operation	◐	○	●
Stealthy Data Exfiltration	○	◐	●
Environmental Reactivity	○	●	●
Dynamic Reactions or Remote Control Capabilities	○	●	●

◐partially fulfilled ●fulfilled ○not fulfilled

capture screenshots, and activate cameras and microphones [13]. RATs typically require either an exploit or social engineering tactics for installation. However, their deployment is often not easily possible on managed systems that restrict software installations or are heavily secured. The installation process generally necessitates some level of interaction with the target system, such as opening a malicious email attachment or exploiting a vulnerability. These actions are increasingly difficult on systems with robust security measures, like those found in corporate environments with strict IT policies and antivirus protections [3].

The presence of RATs can often be identified through various indicators, such as unusual network activity, unauthorized software running in the background, and unexpected changes in system behavior. Security tools and practices, including endpoint detection and response (EDR) systems, can help identify and mitigate the presence of RATs. Despite these defenses, RATs continue to evolve, employing obfuscation techniques to evade detection.

In-Person Attacks Using Malicious Human Interface Devices. One of the most renowned tools for in-person attacks is the Rubber Ducky. It resembles a standard USB flash drive but functions as a highly effective HID attack device. The Rubber Ducky can execute pre-programmed scripts and commands as if they were manually entered by the user. It requires physical access to the target computer to be effective. Upon insertion, it can perform various malicious activities such as disabling firewalls, downloading and installing additional malware, or exfiltrating sensitive information. The primary advantage of the Rubber Ducky is its ability to bypass traditional security measures due to the inherent trust given to HID devices by the operating systems.

The Rubber Ducky's simplicity and effectiveness have made it a popular tool among penetration testers and malicious actors alike. Its scripts are written in a straightforward scripting language, making it easy to craft and execute attacks. However, this simplicity also imposes significant limitations. The Rubber Ducky cannot ascertain the current state of the system, such as whether it is locked or the specific operating system version running. This necessitates meticulous reconnaissance, planning and scripting, with a thorough understanding of the target environment. Additionally, data exfiltration via the Rubber Ducky typically requires the use of the victims network, which can trigger antivirus or firewall defenses. The Rubber Ducky is relatively inexpensive, retailing at approximately 80 USD[3], making it easily accessible.

Several variants of the Rubber Ducky exist, offering different methods of HID attacks. The WiFi HID Injector allows for wireless deployment of HID attacks by connecting to the Rubber Ducky via WiFi, enabling remote execution of malicious scripts without physical access[4]. The USB Ninja, disguised as a regular USB charging cable, operates similarly to the Rubber Ducky[5].

The study by Nicho and Sabry [9] provides a comprehensive analysis of the threats and vulnerabilities associated with malicious HIDs. The research emphasizes the significant risk posed by these devices due to the inherent trust operating systems place in them, allowing malicious HIDs to execute privileged actions as if they were genuine users. The paper categorizes malicious HIDs into wireless communication malicious HIDs, HID interface composite devices, and pure HIDs, and discusses various examples such as the USB Ninja, WiFi HID injector, and Rubber Ducky.

Building upon these studies, our paper seeks to extend HID attacks by incorporating screen-capturing capabilities. The potential for new threats through such capabilities is underscored by Chen et al. [6], who propose using deep learning to extract graphical user interface elements from screenshots. Coupled with advanced scene text recognition techniques, such as those proposed by Atienza [4], these methods facilitate passive cyber-attacks.

3 Rubber Ducky Station

This paper presents a hardware prototype of a Remote-access Rubber Ducky with screen-capturing capabilities, alongside an operating software that implements the attack vectors described in Sect. 4.

Our approach diverges from traditional methods by leveraging the non-intrusive nature of screen capturing to perform covert surveillance and data collection without direct interaction with the target system.

3.1 Software Design

In developing the RDS, we aim to meet the outlined requirements (R1–R5).

Requirement Fulfillment

Least Privileges Required (R1): We satisfy this requirement by implementing a basic HID and display driver. Specifically, we configure our device to function as

[3] https://shop.hak5.org/products/usb-rubber-ducky.
[4] https://github.com/whid-injector/WHID.
[5] https://hackingtoolscenter.com/product/usbninja/.

USB gadgets, such as a mouse, keyboard, and external display, upon connection to a computer[6]. This approach does not necessitate code signing and remains indistinguishable and undetectable by software. To enhance stealth, we can simulate characteristics of known USB gadgets, including vendor name, product ID, serial number, and manufacturer details.

Stealthy and Passive Operation (R2): By utilizing our simulated mouse and keyboard, we maintain stealth and avoid detection by antivirus software. Although attackers could choose to install a RAT using our RDS, this is beyond the current scope of our research.

Stealthy Data Exfiltration (R3): This requirement is fulfilled by using a virtual display. We can clone the display without the user's knowledge, record it, and save the data to our device. Additionally, we can create a local WiFi network with our RDS, allowing attackers to connect remotely and extract data, thereby bypassing firewalls. This capability can also be integrated with other ad-hoc networks. Depending on the hardware budget, a SIM card or eSIM could be used to enable mobile internet.

Environmental Reactivity (R4): We achieve this without violating R1 and R2 by using a backchannel via the display. This allows automated scripts or remote attackers to evaluate the environment (e.g., operating system) and react accordingly.

Dynamic Reactions or Remote Control Capabilities (R5): Our remote control capabilities fulfill this requirement. We leverage advancements in machine learning for automated blind attacks via Optical Character Recognition (OCR). In the future, more powerful devices could include local AI to identify interesting programs and data and navigate the user interface.

3.2 Hardware Design

The hardware components must support the software requirements, including USB port functionality to emulate mouse, keyboard, and monitor, as well as WiFi capabilities to establish a local network. Additionally, sufficient computational power is necessary to host a local web server for remote control, perform OCR tasks, and execute automated AI attacks.

To maintain cost-effectiveness and simplicity, we selected the Raspberry Pi as the base for our prototype. There are also smaller options available, but they tend to be more expensive. The hardware components of the prototype, illustrated in Fig. 1, are as follows:

[6] https://www.kernel.org/doc/Documentation/usb/gadget_configfs.txt.

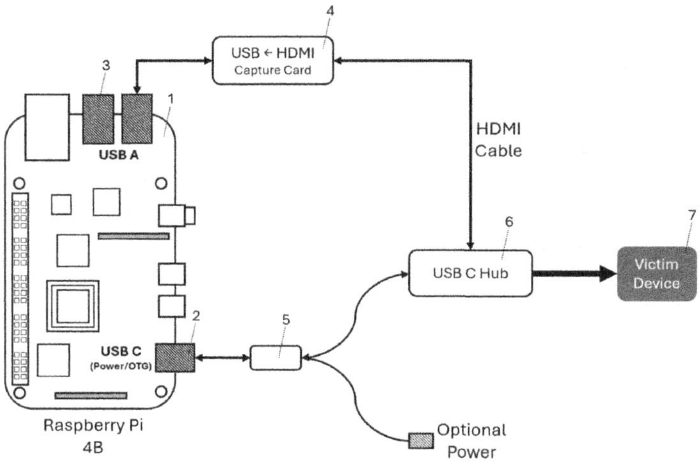

Fig. 1. Hardware layout of the prototype

1. **Raspberry Pi 4B or Zero W**
   USB-Host Capability: The Raspberry Pi Zero and 4B models include a USB hub chip, allowing the RDS to emulate input devices like keyboards and mice. *Network Interface*: Both models feature integrated Bluetooth and WiFi chips, enabling wireless communication for remote access and data exfiltration.
   Computational Power: The Raspberry Pi 4B is chosen for its superior processing power, necessary for on-device machine learning algorithms such as OCR on HD images. It operates within the power limits provided by USB 2.0 (2.5 W) or USB 3.0 (4.5 W) connections, ensuring efficient task execution. Additionally, the Raspberry Pi 4B includes USB A ports, which accommodate the capture card without requiring an additional USB adapter.
2. **USB-C (Power/OTG)** interface of the Raspberry Pi 4B.
3. **USB A**: 2x USB 3.0 (4.5 W), 2x USB 2.0 (2.5 W) ports of the Raspberry Pi.
4. **HDMI to USB Capture Card**
   This card converts HDMI video signals into MJPG video streams, enabling real-time on-device image processing for high-definition outputs from the target machine.
5. **Optional USB-C OTG/Power Splitter**
   An additional power supply can be used to operate local image processing faster.
6. **USB-C Hub**
   The hub consolidates HDMI and USB connections into a single interface, simplifying setup and enhancing device stealth.

The prototype employs the ubiquitous USB-C interface to function as a human input device for operating a keyboard or mouse and capturing the screen as video data. USB-C is chosen due to its availability on most modern PCs, laptops, and mobile devices. The collected video data is processed in real-time on the processing unit, which also facilitates command and control operations via a network interface. This combination of hardware components ensures that the RDS can perform a wide range of tasks while remaining cost-effective and easy to deploy.

In the absence of budget constraints, the prototype could be further miniaturized and could integrate a SIM card for mobile data, enabling remote control and offloading computationally intensive computer vision tasks. The use of a SIM card would allow for uninterrupted remote access, even in environments where WiFi networks are monitored or restricted, providing a significant advantage for stealth operations.

4 Attack Vectors

This section outlines two hypothetical scenarios that demonstrate the RDS versatility in covert operations and highlight associated security risks. A comparison to the standard rubber ducky and a software based remote access trojan is shown in Table 2.

4.1 Email Harvesting in an Open Workspace

In this scenario, the RDS is discreetly deployed in an open workspace, connected to a docking station or under-desk PC. When a victim connects their laptop, the RDS activates and executes an email harvesting attack. Key steps include:

- **Deployment:** The RDS blends in, avoiding suspicion.
- **Initiation:** Triggered when a victim connects their device.
- **Execution:** The RDS collects emails, attachments, and screenshots.
- **Exfiltration:** Data is sent via WiFi.

The RDS operates autonomously, navigating the system through GUI interactions without executing code, reducing forensic traces. It adapts to the system's language and settings, ensuring seamless operation.

4.2 Credential Harvesting in a Corporate Environment

Here, the RDS is deployed in a corporate break room disguised as a charging station. When employees connect their devices, the RDS passively clones the screen to capture credentials and sensitive information. Key steps include:

- **Deployment:** Strategically placed as a benign charging station.
- **Initiation:** Triggered when a user connects a device.
- **Execution:** Passive screen cloning records user activity.
- **Exfiltration:** Captured data is sent via WiFi.

This approach works across devices, including laptops and smartphones, without requiring software installation, making it stealthy and difficult to detect.

These scenarios underscore the RDS's covert capabilities and highlight the importance of proactive security measures to mitigate such threats.

Table 2. Comparison of Attack Vectors: Standard Rubber Ducky (RD), Remote Access Trojan (RAT), and Rubber Ducky Station (RDS)

Feature	RD	RAT	RDS
Capabilities	HID input	All	HID input, screen capturing, local WiFi
OS Support	All[a]	Depends on Development	All[a]
Physical Access Required	Yes	No	Yes
Screen Capturing	No	Yes	Yes
Remote Control	No	Yes	Yes, Local WLAN
Attack Vectors	Script-based input automation	Full system control	Script-based input automation, stealthy data exfiltration

[a] As long as they support keyboards

5 Evaluation

This evaluation assesses the enhancements introduced by the Rubber Ducky Station (RDS) in comparison to traditional Rubber Ducky (RD) devices and software-based Remote Access Trojans (RATs). We evaluate the RDS's effectiveness across various operating systems and analyze potential countermeasures in terms of the requirements outlined in Sect. 2. For reproducibility, we have made the hardware specifications available in Sect. 3.2 and the software accessible[7].

5.1 System Compatibility

Given that malicious HID devices are known threats, it is important to understand their interactions with different operating systems, which serve as the logical defense by controlling access. We aim to explore how various modern OS react to the presence of our RDS. Note, we did not obfuscate our characteristics, meaning we did not clone the information, such as the serial number, manufacturer, and product details, of already used keyboards.

Table 3 systematically compares the responsiveness of various operating systems, Windows 11, MacOS 14, Ubuntu 23.10, Debian 12.5, and Android 14.

Instant Connection. Instant connection is crucial for executing payloads without user intervention. Windows 11 provides immediate connectivity but displays a small notification that can be closed programmatically by the RDS. MacOS 14 requires user approval, which can delay or prevent the execution of an attack.

[7] https://github.com/8mas/rubber-ducky-station.

Table 3. Comparison of Operating Systems for Instant Connection, Screen Capture, HID Emulation, OCR, and Traces using the Rubber Ducky Station

Feature	Windows 11	MacOS 14	Ubuntu 23.10	Debian 12.5	Android 14[a]
Instant Connection	Yes[b]	No[c]	Yes	Yes	Yes
Mouse Emulation	Yes	Yes	Yes	Yes	Yes
Keyboard Emulation	Yes	Yes	Yes	Yes	Yes
Screen Capture	Yes	Yes	Yes	Yes	Yes

[a] Depends on the manufacturer and Android flavor. Tested with Pixel 8, Pixel 9, Samsung S22, Samsung S24. At the time of writing, external monitors were disabled by Google for all Pixel phones.
[b] small notification.
[c] needs approval.

Both Ubuntu 23.10 and Debian 12.5 support instant connection, facilitating immediate payload execution. Android 14's response varies by manufacturer, with most devices supporting instant connection, although external monitor support is disabled on some devices like Google Pixel phones at the time of writing.

HID Emulation. HID emulation is consistent across all tested operating systems, supporting both mouse and keyboard inputs. This uniformity allows the RDS to deploy its HID capabilities effectively, regardless of the target system. However, specific configurations, such as server setups (e.g., Debian Server), may not support mouse input by default, necessitating tailored payloads that adapt to the operating system's characteristics.

Screen Capture. Screen capture capability is essential for passive data exfiltration. The RDS supports screen capturing on all tested systems. For Android devices, this feature is manufacturer-dependent; for instance, Google Pixel phones do not support external displays at the time of writing. Despite this, screen capturing on other Android devices, such as Samsung models, is feasible.

Traceability. Traceability refers to the ability to detect and log the presence of the RDS. All operating systems maintain system logs that record new HID device connections and monitor activities. These logs are accessible on all systems but require root access on Android devices. Although these logs exist, users typically do not monitor them regularly, reducing the likelihood of detecting the RDS.

Managed Systems. On centrally managed systems, such as those utilizing Active Directory and critical systems using Citrix Workspace, which restricts actions like screenshots, it was initially believed that the RDS would be only partially effective. However, testing revealed that the RDS could still add and clone monitors, indicating that hardware-based attack vectors pose significant threats even in tightly controlled environments.

Further tests were conducted against several AV systems, including Windows Defender, Avira, Avast, Kaspersky, and Sophos. The test involved plugging in the RDS and remotely controlling it via the WiFi module. None of these systems responded to the RDS attack vector, highlighting a significant gap in current defensive capabilities against hardware-based threats.

5.2 Countermeasures

The previous section demonstrated the RDS's ability to exploit novel attack vectors and its broad compatibility across systems. This section discusses countermeasures against such exploits, drawing from existing research. Countermeasures can be broadly divided into prevention and detection strategies.

Prevention Techniques. Existing prevention strategies primarily target traditional rubber ducky devices. Key approaches include:

- **USB Driver Limitation:** Restricting generic USB driver execution, e.g., by enforcing user-defined policies or limiting functionality, has proven effective [1, 8].
- **Behavioral Detection:** Identifying abnormal behavior in autonomous HID devices, as explored by Arora et al. [2], Tyutyunnik et al. [12], and Tyler et al. [10], often relies on heuristic-based detection of anomalous patterns.

For the RDS, USB-blocking appears to be the most effective prevention measure. Passive attacks, which involve actions like registering virtual screens without sending malicious keystrokes, evade heuristic detection. Furthermore, Hetzel et al. [7] demonstrated that machine learning-based methods can emulate human typing patterns, complicating behavioral detection further.

USB Port Blocking. Completely disabling USB ports, as proposed by Neuner et al. [8], prevents generic HID or virtual screen connections but severely impacts usability. Cryptographic solutions, such as those proposed by Benadjila et al. [5], selectively allow only trusted USB devices, offering a more balanced approach. Tian et al. [11] further suggests fine-grained filtering by instrumenting the USB stack, enabling precise control over device interfaces.

Monitoring and Anomaly Detection. Monitoring HID data and employing anomaly detection can be an effective approach. For example, the RDS's ability to spawn multiple active devices in compromised docking stations can be detected with proper monitoring. However, the USB HID protocol allows for arbitrary field configurations, enabling the RDS to masquerade as legitimate devices, complicating detection efforts.

Post-attack Detection. Post-attack detection is inherently challenging, as HID emulation is universally supported across operating systems. Detection capabilities vary significantly: for instance, Windows 11 provides detailed event logs for post-incident analysis, while Android does not grant non-root users access to USB or display device histories. This inconsistency highlights the varying ease of post-incident analysis across platforms.

Limitations of Current Approaches. All existing strategies are most effective in controlled, static environments with minimal variability. Techniques such as USB filtering often introduce significant user friction. For instance, filtering certain USB devices and interfaces may enhance security but can disrupt workflow, limiting their practicality in dynamic, real-world settings.

6 Conclusion

This paper introduced the Rubber Ducky Station (RDS), an enhanced HID-based attack tool that combines mouse and keyboard emulation with screen-capturing and WiFi capabilities. Unlike the standard Rubber Ducky, the RDS enables dynamic, situation-aware attacks and stealthy data exfiltration through screen recording and a local WiFi interface. This combination shows the need for updated security protocols and increased awareness of HID-based threats. While the RDS introduces additional attack capabilities, many of its functionalities already exist in tools such as the standard Rubber Ducky. However, its ability to go beyond traditional keyboard and mouse emulation by incorporating screen cloning raises further security concerns. We hope this research increases awareness of HID-based attacks that extend beyond input manipulation to include more advanced techniques such as screen capture. Future work will involve evaluating the RDS against more comprehensive defensive systems, including intrusion detection and prevention systems, as well as endpoint protection solutions.

References

1. Angel, S., et al.: Defending against malicious peripherals with cinch. In: 25th USENIX Security Symposium (USENIX Security 2016), pp. 397–414 (2016)
2. Arora, L., Thakur, N., Yadav, S.K.: USB rubber ducky detection by using heuristic rules. In: 2021 International Conference on Computing, Communication, and Intelligent Systems (ICCCIS), pp. 156–160. IEEE (2021)
3. Aslan, Ö.A., Samet, R.: A comprehensive review on malware detection approaches. IEEE Access **8**, 6249–6271 (2020)
4. Atienza, R.: Vision transformer for fast and efficient scene text recognition. In: International Conference on Document Analysis and Recognition, pp. 319–334. Springer (2021)
5. Benadjila, R., Michelizza, A., Renard, M., Thierry, P., Trebuchet, P.: WooKey: designing a trusted and efficient USB device. In: Proceedings of the 35th Annual Computer Security Applications Conference, pp. 673–686 (2019)
6. Chen, J., et al.: Object detection for graphical user interface: old fashioned or deep learning or a combination? In: Proceedings of the 28th ACM Joint Meeting on European Software Engineering Conference and Symposium on the Foundations of Software Engineering, pp. 1202–1214 (2020)
7. Hetzel, L., Dudley, J., Feit, A.M., Kristensson, P.O.: Complex interaction as emergent behaviour: simulating mid-air virtual keyboard typing using reinforcement learning. IEEE Trans. Visual Comput. Graphics **27**(11), 4140–4149 (2021)

8. Neuner, S., Voyiatzis, A.G., Fotopoulos, S., Mulliner, C., Weippl, E.R.: USBlock: blocking USB-based keypress injection attacks. In: Data and Applications Security and Privacy XXXII: 32nd Annual IFIP WG 11.3 Conference, DBSec 2018, Bergamo, Italy, 16–18 July 2018, Proceedings 32, pp. 278–295. Springer (2018)
9. Nıcho, M., Sabry, I.: Threat and vulnerability modelling of malicious human interface devices. Eurasia Proc. Sci. Technol. Eng. Math. **21**, 241–247 (2022)
10. Thomas, T., Piscitelli, M., Nahar, B.A., Baggili, I.: Duck hunt: memory forensics of USB attack platforms. Forensic Sci. Int. Digit. Invest. **37**, 301190 (2021)
11. Tian, D.J., Scaife, N., Bates, A., Butler, K., Traynor, P.: Making {USB} great again with {USBFILTER}. In: 25th USENIX Security Symposium (USENIX Security 2016), pp. 415–430 (2016)
12. Tyutyunnik, A., Lazarev, A.: Intelligent system for preventing rubber ducky attacks using deep learning neural networks. In: 2021 International Russian Automation Conference (RusAutoCon), pp. 497–502. IEEE (2021)
13. Xue, M., Gu, C., Liu, W., Yu, S., O'Neill, M.: Ten years of hardware trojans: a survey from the attacker's perspective. IET Comput. Digit. Tech. **14**(6), 231–246 (2020)

PrivTru: A Privacy-by-Design Data Trustee Minimizing Information Leakage

Lukas Gehring(✉) and Florian Tschorsch

Technische Universität Dresden, 01062 Dresden, Germany
{lukas.gehring,florian.tschorsch}@tu-dresden.de

Abstract. Data trustees serve as intermediaries that facilitate secure data sharing between independent parties. This paper offers a technical perspective on data trustees, guided by privacy-by-design principles. We introduce PrivTru, an instantiation of a data trustee that provably achieves optimal privacy properties. Therefore, PrivTru calculates the minimal amount of information the data trustee needs to request from data sources to respond to a given query. Our analysis shows that PrivTru minimizes information leakage to the data trustee, regardless of the trustee's prior knowledge, while preserving the utility of the data.

Keywords: Data Trustee · Privacy by design · Privacy Engineering

1 Introduction

The concept of a data trustee (or sometimes data trust) facilitates a data economy that aligns with privacy goals and data protection regulations, particularly in the EU [2,3,13]. It addresses challenges in sharing data between independent data sources and data receivers. This is particularly relevant in fields such as medicine, public administration, mobility, and other domains where data can drive innovation and create value. Politically, data trustees are presented as an alternative to the dominance of data platforms, which risk creating a "data oligopoly" that centralizes power and limits competition [13].

Most discussions have focused on the organizational aspects [3], situating data trustees as a third party between data sources (entities who *have* data) and data receivers (entities who *want* data). A core idea of the concept is that sources and receivers are independent systems, operated by any entity, enabling data sharing (and potentially linking) across institutional boundaries. To fulfill this role, a data trustee needs to be constituted as an independent organization, which has no interest in the data itself. As such it can reasonably balance the interests of the involved parties. The primary task of a data trustee is, thus, to manage data "on behalf of and in the interest of" [13] the data sources.

The literature [2,13] categorizes trustees into two types: *data stewards* and *data exchange*. In the former, the trustee stores the data, whereas in the latter, the trustee facilitates matching between sources and receivers and relays the data without storing it.

Published by Springer Nature Switzerland AG 2025
L. Nemec Zlatolas et al. (Eds.): SEC 2025, IFIP AICT 745, pp. 104–118, 2025.
https://doi.org/10.1007/978-3-031-92882-6_8

In this paper, we answer the question of how a privacy-first data trustee can be designed from a technical perspective. Hereby we focus specifically on data stewards and data exchanges and restrict ourselves to static, relational data as a starting point. This work addresses a gap in the discussion on data trustees, which has largely been explored from organizational, political, and legal perspectives. By applying Hoepman's privacy design strategies [9], we identify the challenges of implementing privacy-respecting data trustees and demonstrate that the *data exchange* model is preferable from a privacy-centric standpoint.

We then introduce *PrivTru*, a data exchange designed to be private by design. To this end, we extend relational algebra, enabling the formulation of individual subqueries for generalized data from the data sources. By leveraging this approach, PrivTru outsources pre-processing tasks to the data sources, ensuring that only the necessary information is retrieved to answer a given query. We further prove that our instantiation is optimal in minimizing the information the data trustee learns about the provided data. The proposed solution achieves this without any loss of utility and remains optimal regardless of the prior knowledge the central exchange may have about the input data. Accordingly, our contributions can be summarized as follows:

- We formulate a technical perspective on data stewards and data exchanges, the two primary types of data trustees (Sect. 2).
- We use Hoepman's privacy design strategies [9] to analyze the privacy properties of the proposed models (Sect. 3).
- We introduce *PrivTru*, an instantiation of a data exchange aligned with privacy engineering principles (Sect. 4).
- We analyze the information gain of the central data exchange in *PrivTru* and prove that it is minimal compared to all other relational data exchange implementations (Sect. 5).

2 Technical Perspective on Data Trustees

In this section, we provide a technical perspective on the notion of a *data trustee* by introducing two models capturing its main variations: *data steward* and *data exchange*. To encompass most concepts covered by this notion, the models focus on the core functionality of a data trustee, which is providing access to data from *data sources* to *data receivers*. Apparently, given the broad understanding of a data trustee, there may be some instantiations of data trustees, stewards, and exchanges that are not compatible with our model. We additionally consider the question of bootstrapping the connection between sources, receivers, and the trustees, notably the implementation of access control, to be out of scope. Nevertheless, the models are designed to be extensible, allowing for adaptation to specific organizational and legal requirements of data trustees or to provide better guidance for practical implementation.

In the data trustee model, the third party sitting between the sources and the receivers is a *steward* or an *exchange*. These are differentiated by their mandate

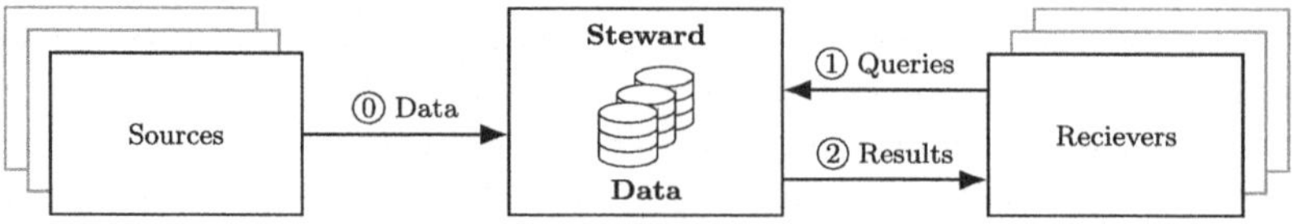

Fig. 1. Illustration of a data steward.

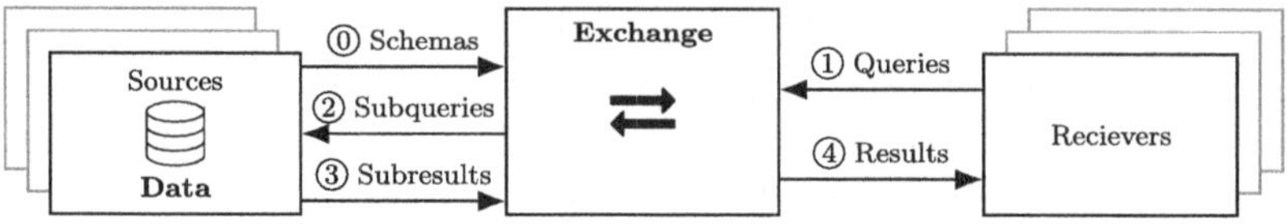

Fig. 2. Illustration of a data exchange.

to store the processed data, which leads to distinct data flows when in operation. A *steward* stores data on behalf of the sources, while an *exchange* merely processes the information from the sources, without storing any data. Figure 1 illustrates the architecture and functionality of a data steward. In the setup phase, all sources send *all* of their data to the steward (Step ⓪), which then stores it centrally. Subsequently, the steward provides one or more API endpoints for the receivers to query the data (Step ①). It processes these queries by sending results back to the corresponding receiver (Step ②).

The architecture of a data exchange is depicted in Fig. 2. During the bootstrapping process (Step ⓪), the central entity only receives the schema of the data provided by the sources. Exchanges provide the same interface as stewards, enabling receivers to query information and obtain results (Steps ① and ④). However, unlike stewards, exchanges do not store any data. Instead, upon receiving a query (Step ①), they generate subqueries for each data source and assembles the subresults to answer the full query (Steps ② and ③).

3 Privacy Analysis of Data Trustees

A system that prioritizes privacy should be designed with respect to *privacy-by-design* strategies. Note, that these go beyond the traditional security model of defending the systems against an attacker. A data trustee is – as the name implies – not an attacker, and still we want it to have e.g., as little data as possible. In this section, we apply these design strategies to our two data trustees models and argue that *data exchanges* are preferable to *data stewards* under these principles.

Privacy Design Strategies. To bridge the gap between privacy requirements for IT systems driven by ethical and legal requirements and software development, Hoepman proposed eight privacy design strategies [9]. According to this perspective, a system's design plays a significant role in shaping its level of privacy. Therefore, privacy considerations should be taken into account from the very beginning, when the foundational concepts and ideas for a new system are first being developed, which includes our models of data trustees. His contributions are categorized into data-oriented strategies and process-oriented strategies. Since we focus on the technical side of data trustees, our analysis is limited to the former. Of course, process-oriented strategies must also be considered when deploying a data trustee. The data-oriented privacy strategies as formulated by Hoepman [9] are as follows:

- MINIMIZE: The amount of personal data that is processed should be limited to the minimal amount possible.
- HIDE: Any personal data, and their relationships, should be concealed from plain view.
- SEPARATE: Personal data should be processed in a distributed manner, using separate compartments whenever possible.
- AGGREGATE: Personal data should be processed at the highest level of aggregation and with the least detail necessary for it to remain useful.

Comparing Data Stewards and Data Exchanges. In the following analysis, we compare the data trustee models (as outlined in Sect. 2) based on the data-oriented privacy strategies. Hereby we focus on the differences between the two models and always assume the same premises when possible.

MINIMIZE: Data trustees generally allocate information from multiple data sources to be jointly provided to one or more data receivers. This is a problem for data minimization because when two or more personal data points concerning one individual are joined, the generated information is in most cases more privacy-sensitive than the two data points alone since it increases the risk of *re-identification attacks* [14]. Still, one can argue that the data is sufficiently minimized if two requirements are fulfilled. Firstly, the data sources need to make sure, that the data they provide is already minimized. Secondly, the purpose of the whole system is formulated broadly. So that it encompasses all use cases where any data might be requested. If the sources give their consent to the possible wide range of data usage, such usage is not a privacy violation. If a data trustee satisfies these conditions, we can consider the system to be in line with MINIMIZE. In the data exchange model, data sources can minimize queries locally, thereby enhancing privacy when compared to data stewards.

HIDE: For data trustees, it is essential to ensure that data remains confidential. Encrypting connections secures the content during transfer. However, when data requests involve only a subset of sources, it may also be necessary to obscure traffic patterns—especially when a single data source corresponds to an individual or a small group, a challenge that solely affects data exchanges. In such cases, obfuscation techniques can mitigate risks. This leaves data exchanges with a slight but manageable disadvantage compared to data stewards.

SEPARATE: Organizational data trustees are formulated as centralized systems, which opposes the SEPARATE design strategy. As discussed in Sect. 2, a centralized organizational concept does not necessarily demand a centralized technical model. The data exchange model is fundamentally embracing the SEPARATE strategy, while the data steward model is breaking it. This is especially true if a data exchange is instantiated by a distributed protocol between the data source and receivers, and not through a centralized service. Regarding SEPARATE, data exchanges are to be favored over data stewards.

AGGREGATE: Data aggregation can occur at the data sources or by the data steward/exchange. For certain techniques, such as k-anonymity [14], access to all data points is critical for a reasonable privacy-utility tradeoff. Thus, aggregation strategies must be carefully tailored to each use case. Data exchanges are generally preferred due to their flexibility in determining aggregation levels per query, whereas the data steward model requires defining these levels during the bootstrapping phase.

Summary of Comparison. Summarizing the analysis, we observe that data exchanges are mostly preferable from a privacy perspective. This is largely due to the SEPARATE strategy, which data exchanges fully implement and data stewards compromise by default. For HIDE, both models are comparable, although data exchanges are more prone to information leakage via side channels. MINIMIZE & AGGREGATE can be achieved by both models; however, the data exchange model conceptually offers more flexibility, as the data sources can minimize or aggregate the data on a per-query basis.

4 PrivTru: Minimizing Information Leakage

In this section, we introduce *PrivTru*, an instantiation of a data trustee designed with *privacy-by-design* principles. Our analysis revealed that designing PrivTru as a data exchange is preferable for aligning with privacy principles. Yet, implementing MINIMIZE and AGGREGATE poses challenges. In our work, we focus on MINIMIZE and argue that AGGREGATE can be addressed similarly in Sect. 7. We specifically examine how queries to PrivTru are structured and how subqueries are derived.

Data and Query Format. For PrivTru, we adopt the commonly used relational database model, where data is stored in tables T, also referred to as *relations*. Each table consists of multiple columns, identified by a set of *attributes* $\mathbb{A}(T) = \{A_1, \dots A_n\}$, with $n > 0$. Each attribute A_i is associated with a *domain* $\mathbb{D}(A_i)$, which defines the set of permitted values in this column. Accordingly, the datapoints t in T are the rows of the table. Formally, they are tuples of length n with $t_i \in \mathbb{D}(A_i)$ for $i = 1, \dots n$. In the system model of data exchanges, there are multiple data sources $S_1, \dots S_s$, each providing a portion of the data. For readability, we assume that each source S_i contributes exactly one table T_i to the system. In addition, the attributes across all tables are assumed to be pairwise distinct, meaning that every attribute in the system is present in exactly one table. Note, that data trustees are not tied to a specific data model.

Using relational databases as our data model naturally leads to relational algebra as the foundation for our query model. Specifically, we adopt the relational algebra as introduced by Codd [7].

Definition 1 (Relational Algebra [1]**).** *The* relational algebra *consists of three primitive operators, working on tables (or relations) T.*

(a) Selection*: $\sigma_F(T)$ selects tuples in T that fulfill a given propositional formula F. The formula F consists of the logical operators $\wedge, \vee, \neg$, connecting literals of the form* `true`*,* `false`*, $A\theta B$, and $A\theta c$ with $A, B \in \mathbb{A}(T), c \in \mathbb{D}(A)$, and $\theta \in \{=, <\}$.*

(b) Projection*: $\pi_{(A_1,\dots A_n)}(T)$ outputs a new relation containing the columns identified by $A_1, \dots A_n$ in T.*

(c) Join*: ($T \bowtie S$) outputs a relation O with $\mathbb{A}(O) = \mathbb{A}(T) \cup \mathbb{A}(S)$. Where every o over $\mathbb{A}(O)$ is in O if and only if its restrictions are in the original table, that is, $o[\mathbb{A}(T)] \in T$ and $o[\mathbb{A}(S)] \in S$. In case that $\mathbb{A}(T) \cap \mathbb{A}(S) = \emptyset$, the join operator is equal to calculating the cross-product.*

We now present an extension of the relational algebra, which we will use in the next subsection to achieve MINIMIZE in PrivTru. This extension enables data sources to evaluate basic propositions on their local entries and to communicate the corresponding truth-values without revealing the underlying data. To enhance readability, we write $(\neg)$, to represent optional negations. As a result, the following $(\neg)$ are also evaluated as negation in the given context.

Definition 2 (Relational Algebra with Propositional Projections). *The* relational algebra with propositional projections (RAPP) *consists of the three primitive operators of the relational algebra, where the* projection *operator is replaced by the following: $\pi_{(A_1,\dots A_n)}(T)$ outputs a new relation containing the columns identified by $A_1, \dots A_n$ in T. Additionally, any A_i can have the form $p : \bigvee_i (\neg)\gamma_i$, where p is any string and all γ_i are literals of the form* `true`*,* `false`*, $A\theta B$ or $A\theta c$, with $A, B \in \mathbb{A}(T), c \in \mathbb{D}(A)$ and $\theta \in \{=, <\}$. In this case, the resulting relation $R = \pi_{(A_1,\dots A_n)}(T)$ consists of a new column identified by p, where each tuple in R holds* `true` *or* `false` *depending on the evaluation of $\bigvee_i (\neg)\gamma_i$ on that tuple in T.*

For example, Table 1 shows a table of persons with their names, ages, and income. Using the propositional projections of RAPP, we can query this data to produce a table that indicates only whether each person is older than 30 (see Table 2). This projection is also supported in modern SQL dialects.

Calculating Subqueries for Relational Data Exchanges. Every data exchange compatible with our model must have a strategy to derive subqueries from the main query. We formally define this problem as follows.

Table 1. T

Name	Age	Income
Alice	30	44k
Bob	33	40k
Carol	50	52k
Eve	42	66k

Table 2. $\pi_{\text{Name, over\_30: age>30}}T$

Name	over_30
Alice	`false`
Bob	`true`
Carol	`true`
Eve	`true`

Problem 1 (CalculateSubqueries (CS-Problem))
Input: *Query q in the language of relational algebra over relations $T_1, \dots T_s$.*
Output: *For $i = 1, \dots s$, subqueries $\widehat{q_i}$ in the language of RAPP over T_i and a collecting query $\widehat{q}$ over the relations $R_1, \dots R_s$. So that for every set of tables $T_1, \dots T_s$, the evaluation of q on $T_1 \dots T_s$ is equal to the evaluation of $\widehat{q}$ on $R_1, \dots R_s$, where R_i is the result of the evaluation of $\widehat{q_i}$ on T_i.*

Every algorithm $\mathcal{A}$ that solves Problem 1 can be canonically transferred into a data exchange, given we have algorithms for evaluating queries in relational algebra and RAPP. For this, the exchange calculates $\widehat{q_1}, \dots \widehat{q_s}$ from the input query q (using $\mathcal{A}$) and sends these subqueries to the respective data sources $S_1, \dots S_s$. Each source evaluates its query on its local data and returns the results $R_1, \dots R_s$ to the exchange. The exchange then evaluates $\widehat{q}$ over $R_1, \dots R_s$ and sends the result back to the data receiver.

A trivial algorithm to solve Problem 1 is to set $\widehat{q_i} := T_i$ and set $\widehat{q}$ to q. In this case, the exchange requests all data from all sources, enabling it to calculate q locally. However, this solution directly contradicts the privacy analysis in Sect. 3. It violates MINIMIZE and undermines the spirit of SEPARATE, since the exchange gains complete knowledge of the data on any query.

To develop a more privacy-friendly solution, we first need to introduce some theoretical preliminaries. Definition 3 defines a form for expressing queries in relational algebras, based on the commonly used normal form [1]. Lemma 1 then presents rewrite rules for these queries.

Definition 3 (Extended Normal Form). *A query q in the language relational algebra is in* extended normal form *if:*

(a) q is in normal form, which means q can be written as $q = \pi_\beta \sigma_F(T_1 \bowtie \dots \bowtie T_k)$.
(b) F is in conjunctive normal form, meaning it can be written as $F := \bigwedge_i x_i := \bigwedge_i \bigvee_j (\neg)\gamma_{i,j}$, where x_i are clauses that are disjunctions of the literals $\gamma_{i,j}$.
(c) If F is not a trivial tautology ($F =$ `true`) or trivially not satisfiable ($F =$ `false`), then F is satisfiable and not a tautology and every clause x in F is satisfiable and not a tautology and every literal γ in F is satisfiable and not a tautology.

Database theory established that every query q can be rewritten in normal form, and every propositional formula F can be rewritten in conjunctive normal form [1]. Furthermore, Definition 3(c) can be achieved using rewrite rules and an algorithm that checks for satisfiability. Consequently, every query q can be expressed in extended normal form. Definition 3 makes the queries manageable in our system. Definition 3(c) is particularly useful, as it enables mapping literals to the tables that determine their values. More precisely, for any set of literals Γ used in a RAPP query, let $\mathbb{T}(\Gamma)$ be the set of tables T containing $A \in \mathbb{A}(T)$, which is used in a literal $\gamma \in \Gamma$. We sometimes omit parentheses when using $\mathbb{T}$. Since we assume that attributes are unique across all tables and because of Definitions 2 and 3(c), $1 \leqslant \mathbb{T}(\gamma) \leqslant 2$ holds for all γ in our scenario.

The following lemma provides useful rewrite rules for propositions and queries, which we will use to build an algorithm that solves Problem 1.

Lemma 1. *For every set of relations $R_1, \ldots R_s$, proposition formula F, literals $\gamma, \gamma_1, \ldots \gamma_m$, list of attributes β and $i \in \{1, \ldots s\}$:*

(a) If $F := F' \wedge (x)$, where $x = \bigvee_{i=1}^{m} (\neg_i)\gamma_i$ and $\mathbb{T}(\gamma_1, \ldots \gamma_m) = \{R_i\}$, then $\sigma_F(R_1 \bowtie \cdots \bowtie R_n) \equiv \sigma_{F'}(R_1 \bowtie \cdots \sigma_x(R_i) \cdots \bowtie R_n)$.
(b) If $F := F' \wedge (\neg_1)\gamma_1 \vee \cdots \vee (\neg_m)\gamma_m$ and for a subset $\Gamma \subset \{\gamma_1, \ldots \gamma_m\}, \mathbb{T}(\Gamma) = \{R_i\}$, then $\sigma_F(R_1 \bowtie \cdots \bowtie R_n) \equiv \sigma_{F' \wedge (\bigvee_{\gamma_i \in \{\gamma_1, \ldots \gamma_m\} \setminus \Gamma} (\neg_i)(\gamma_i) \vee p = true)}(R_1 \bowtie \cdots \pi_{p: \bigvee_{\gamma_j \in \Gamma} (\neg_j)(\gamma_j)} R_i \cdots \bowtie R_n)$.
(c) Let $\mathbb{A}(R_i, F, \beta)$ denote the set of attributes A in β and F, with $A \in \mathbb{A}(R_i)$, then $\pi_\beta \sigma_F(R_1 \bowtie \cdots \bowtie R_n) \equiv \pi_\beta \sigma_F(R_1 \bowtie \cdots \pi_{\mathbb{A}(R_i, F, \beta)}(R_i) \cdots \bowtie R_n)$.

We now introduce Algorithm 1 as a solution to Problem 1. In the algorithm, we treat attribute lists and propositional formulas as sets. More precisely, for a projection π_β in RAPP, β is a set of attributes and constructs of the form $p : \gamma$. Propositional formulas F (in conjunctive normal form) are viewed as a set of sets containing literals γ, where each inner set corresponds to a clause x. The conjunction F is formed by combining these clauses, while each clause represents a disjunction of its literals. Since Algorithm 1 repeatedly applies the rules of Lemma 1 til a fixpoint is reached, the algorithm is linear in the size of the input query. Still, getting queries into extended normal form adds complexity.

Theorem 1. *Algorithm 1 solves the CS-Problem, for all queries in extended normal form.*

Proof. We can easily see, that Algorithm 1 fulfills the syntactical requirements of Problem 1. It remains to show that q evaluated on $T_1, \ldots T_s$ is equal to $\widehat{q}$ evaluated on $R_1, \ldots R_s$, where R_i is the evaluation of $\widehat{q_i}$ on T_i. The proof is structured into substatements about the algorithm, utilizing Lemma 1. In the following, we will examine the query Q at different intermediate states of the algorithm. We assume that Q is constructed from the intermediate values of $\beta, \widehat{F}, \beta_i, F_i$ as defined in Statement 1. At the end of the algorithm, $Q = \widehat{q}$.

Statement 1. Q is from the form $\pi_\beta \sigma_{\widehat{F}}(\bowtie_{i=1}^{s} \pi_{\beta_i} \sigma_{F_i}(T_i))$, making Lemma 1 generally applicable to it.

Algorithm 1: Query Distribution

Data: Query $q = \pi_\beta \sigma_F(T_1 \bowtie \ldots \bowtie T_s)$ in extended normal form with $F := \bigwedge_{k=0}^{n} x_k := \bigwedge_{k=0}^{n} \bigvee_{j=0}^{n_k} (\neg)\gamma_{k,j}$.

if $F = \mathit{false}$ **then**
  return $q^\varnothing, \ldots q^\varnothing$; // $s+1$ times the empty query $q^\varnothing$
$\widehat{q} \leftarrow \varnothing$;
$\widehat{F} \leftarrow F$;
foreach $i \in \{1, \ldots s\}$ **do**
  $\widehat{q_i} \leftarrow \varnothing$; $\beta_i \leftarrow \varnothing$; $F_i \leftarrow \varnothing$; $\Gamma_i \leftarrow \varnothing$;
foreach $x \in F$ **do** // x is a set representing a clause
  if $|\mathbb{T}(x)| = 1$ **then** // Use Lemma 1(a)
    foreach $T_i \in \{T_1, \ldots T_s\}$ **do**
      if $\mathbb{T}(x) = \{T_i\}$ **then**
        $F_i \leftarrow F_i \cup \{x\}$;
        $\widehat{F} \leftarrow \widehat{F} \setminus \{x\}$;
  else // Use Lemma 1(b)
    foreach $(\neg)\gamma \in x$ **do** // Consider only literals in x
      if $\mathbb{T}(\gamma) = \{T_i\}$ **then**
        $\Gamma_i \leftarrow \Gamma_i \cup \{(\neg)\gamma\}$;
    foreach $i \in \{1, \ldots s\}$ **do**
      if $\Gamma_i \neq \varnothing$ **then**
        $\beta_i \leftarrow \beta_i \cup \{p_{x,i} : \bigvee_{(\neg)\gamma \in \Gamma_i} ((\neg)\gamma)\}$;
        $\widehat{x} \leftarrow x \setminus \Gamma_i \cup \{p_{x,i} = \mathtt{true}\}$;
        $\widehat{F} \leftarrow \widehat{F} \cup \{\widehat{x}\}$;
        $\widehat{F} \leftarrow \widehat{F} \setminus \{x\}$;
foreach $x \in \widehat{F}$ **do**
  foreach $(\neg)A\theta B \in x$ **do** // Literals written as $A\theta B$ $(\theta \in \{=, >\})$
    $\{T_i, T_j\} \leftarrow \mathbb{T}(A\theta B)$;
    $A_i \leftarrow \mathbb{A}(T_i) \cap \{A, B\}$;
    $A_j \leftarrow \mathbb{A}(T_j) \cap \{A, B\}$;
    $\beta_i \leftarrow \beta_i \cup A_i$;
    $\beta_j \leftarrow \beta_j \cup A_j$;
foreach $A \in \beta$ **do**
  $i \leftarrow \{i | A \in \mathbb{A}(T_i)\}$;
  $\beta_i \leftarrow \beta_i \cup A$;
foreach $i \in \{1, \ldots s\}$ **do**
  if $F_i = \emptyset$ **then**
    $F_i \leftarrow \{\{\mathtt{true}\}\}$;
  $\widehat{q_i} \leftarrow \pi_{\beta_i} \sigma_{F_i}(T_i)$;
  if $\beta_i = \emptyset$ **then**
    $\widehat{q_i} \leftarrow q^\varnothing$;
$\widehat{q} \leftarrow \pi_\beta \sigma_{\widehat{F}}(R_1 \bowtie \cdots \bowtie R_s)$;
return $\widehat{q}, \widehat{q_1}, \ldots \widehat{q_s}$

This follows directly from Lines 36 and 39, the construction of Q, and the fact that R_i is the evaluation of $\pi_{\beta_i}\sigma_{F_i}\widehat{q_i}$ on T_i.

Statement 2. The foreach-loop in Line 7 preserves equivalence for Q.

Let Q_0 be the intermediate query before the start of the foreach-loop and Q_k the intermediate query after the k-th round. We need to show that for $k = 1, \dots n$, it holds that $Q_{k-1} \equiv Q_k$. Let $k \in \{1, \dots n\}$ and x_k be the clause of the k-th round. If there is a $T_i \in \{T_1, \dots T_s\}$ with $\mathbb{T}(x_k) = \{T_i\}$, Lines 8–12 rewrites Q_{k-1} to Q_k according to Lemma 1 (a). If x_k can not be fully evaluated in one table the code in Lines 13–22 repeatedly rewrites Q_{k-1} using Lemma 1 (b). In Line 17 every Γ_i only holds γ with $\mathbb{T}(\gamma) = \{T_i\}$. As such the Γ_i are subsets, as defined in Lemma 1 (b). The Lines 18–22 only execute the Lemma for each of the subsets Γ_i, making Q_k equivalent to Q_{k-1}.

Statement 3. The code from Line 23 to Line 32 is preserves equivalence for Q.

This property holds because at Line 23 $\widehat{F}$ contains only literals γ with $|\mathbb{T}(\gamma)| = 2$, as literals with $|\mathbb{T}(\gamma)| = 1$ are removed in Lines 12 and 22. Consequently, in Line 30, every β_i holds the attributes that $\widehat{F}$ uses from table T_i ($i = 1, \dots s$). The foreach-loop starting at Line 30 ensures that $\beta_i = \mathbb{A}(T_i, F, \beta) \cup P_i$ where $\mathbb{A}(T_i, F, \beta)$ is as defined in Lemma 1 (c) and P_i are values held β_i before Line 23. Since for projections $\pi_A\pi_B$ can be replaced by $\pi_{A\cup B}$ for every pair of sets A, B, Statement 3 follows by using Lemma 1 (c) for all $i \in \{1, \dots s\}$.

The theorem follows from Statements 1 to 3.

5 Analysis of Information Leakage

In this section, we quantify the information leakage incurred by a central exchange when solving an instance of Problem 1. We show that Algorithm 1 minimizes leakage, regardless of the exchange's prior knowledge.

To measure leakage, we assess the probability of the data exchange correctly reconstructing the full tables $T_1, \dots T_s$ based on $R_1 = \widehat{q_1}[T_1], \dots R_s = \widehat{q_s}[T_s]$. We consider T_i as a set of tuples over the cross-product of its attribute domains, $\mathbb{D}(T_i) := \times_{A\in\mathbb{A}(T_i)}\mathbb{D}(A)$, disregarding row order. The exchange's assumptions about T_i are modeled by the probability measure p^i, sampling from all possible tables $\tilde{T} \in \mathbb{D}(T_i)^2$. We consider only discrete p^i, where $p^i(\tilde{T}) > 0$ holds for a finite number of $\tilde{T}$, reflecting real-world scenarios where attribute domains are naturally finite. A relational exchange updates its assumptions for T_i upon receiving a result R_i. The updated assumptions are modeled by $p^i_{R_i}$. To determine the optimal solution for Problem 1, we evaluate the deviation of $p^i_{R_i}$ for all $i \in \{1, \dots s\}$ from correctly guessing T_i, where R_i is the (implicit) output of a solution.

To quantify the difference between two probabilities p and q, we use the Kullback-Leibler Divergence [11].

Definition 4. (Discrete Kullback-Leibler Divergence [5]). *For two discrete probability measures p and q with sample set X, where $q(x) = 0$ implies $p(x) = 0$, the* Kullback-Leibler Divergence *of p and q (with $0 \log(0) := 0$) is defined as:*

$$D(p||q) = \sum_{x \in X} p(x) \log \frac{p(x)}{q(x)}.$$

For our case, we calculate the divergence between $p^i_{R_i}$ and $p^i_{T_i}$, where $p^i_{T_i}$ fully reveals T_i. Specifically, $p^i_{T_i}(T_i) = 1$ and $p^i_{T_i}(\tilde{T}) = 0$ for all $\tilde{T} \in \mathbb{D}(T_i)^2 \setminus \{T_i\}$. From

$$D(p^i_{T_i}||p^i_{R_i}) = \sum_{\tilde{T} \in \mathbb{D}(T_i)^2} p^i_{T_i}(\tilde{T}) \log \left(\frac{p^i_{T_i}(\tilde{T})}{p^i_{R_i}(\tilde{T})} \right) = \log \left(p^i_{R_i}(T_i)^{-1} \right) \tag{1}$$

the divergence depends only on the value of $p^i_{R_i}$ at T_i.

Calculating $p^i_{R_i}$. Intuitively, $p^i_{R_i}$ should correspond to the initial probability p^i under the condition that R_i is the result of the evaluation of $\widehat{q}_i$. However, using plain conditional probability $p^i(X|R_i)$ is not feasible. This is because R_i is not guaranteed to be an element of $\mathbb{D}(T_i)^2$, as $\widehat{q}_i$ might utilize projections. Nonetheless, the information gained from R_i can be used to minimize the set of possible candidates $\tilde{T} \in \mathbb{D}(T_i)$. Since R_i is queried from T_i, all entries in R_i must have exactly one compatible entry in $\tilde{T}$. For compatibility, two conditions must be satisfied: (1) For all attributes of R_i that do not result from propositional projections, compatible entries must have the same values projected on these attributes in $\tilde{T}$. (2) For all columns originating from propositional projections, the truth-value in that entry must match the evaluation of that entry in $\tilde{T}$. Formally, we define the possible candidates for T_i given R_i as:

$$\begin{aligned} C^i(R_i) = \{\tilde{T} \in \mathbb{D}(T_i)^2 | \exists \text{ injective } m : R_i \hookrightarrow \tilde{T}, \\ \forall x \in R_i : \pi_{\mathbb{A}(R_i) \cap \mathbb{A}(T_i)} x = \pi_{\mathbb{A}(R_i) \cap \mathbb{A}(T_i)} m(x) \wedge \\ \forall p : \bigvee_i ((\neg)\gamma_i) \in \mathbb{A}(R_i) : \pi_p(x) = \bigvee_i (\neg)\gamma_i[m(x)]\}. \end{aligned} \tag{2}$$

This allows us to define $p^i_{R_i}$ as the probability of p^i under the condition $C^i(R_i)$:

$$p^i_{R_i}(X) := p^i(X \mid C^i(R_i)) = \frac{p^i(X \cap C^i(R_i))}{p^i(C^i(R_i))} \tag{3}$$

Note that if R_i is part of a solution to Problem 1, where T_i is part of the input, then $T_i \in p^i(C^i(R_i))$. As such, $p^i(C^i(R_i)) \neq 0$ if $p^i(T_i) > 0$.

Solving the CS-Problem with Minimal Information Leakage. We can now prove that Algorithm 1 is the optimal solution for Problem 1.

Theorem 2. *Let* $q = \pi_\beta \sigma_F(\bowtie T_i)$ *be a query in RAPP in extended normal form over* $T_1, \ldots T_s$. *Let* $\widehat{q}, \widehat{q_1}, \ldots \widehat{q_s}$ *with* $R_1, \ldots R_s$ *be the solution of Problem 1 given* q *produced by Algorithm 1. Let* $\tilde{q}, \tilde{q_1}, \ldots \tilde{q_s}$ *with* $\tilde{R}_1, \ldots \tilde{R}_s$ *be any other solution of Problem 1 given* q. *For any set of discrete probability measures* $p^1, \ldots p^s$ *over* $\mathbb{D}(T_1)^2, \ldots \mathbb{D}(T_s)^2$ *respectively with* $p^i(T_i) > 0$ *for any* $i \in \{1, \ldots s\}$:

$$D(p^i_{T_i} || p^i_{R_i}) \geq D(p^i_{T_i} || p^i_{\tilde{R}_i})$$

Proof. Let $i \in \{1, \ldots s\}$. With $T_i \in C^i(\tilde{R}_i)$, Eqs. (1) and (3), and the additive property of probability measures, the following holds:

$$D(p^i_{T_i} || p^i_{R_i}) \geqslant D(p^i_{T_i} || p^i_{\tilde{R}_i}) \Leftrightarrow p^i(C^i(R_i)) \geqslant p^i(C^i(\tilde{R}_i)) \Leftrightarrow \sum_{\tilde{T} \in C^i(R_i)} p^i(\tilde{T}) \geq \sum_{\tilde{T} \in C^i(\tilde{R}_i)} p^i(\tilde{T}).$$

Because of this, it suffices to show that $C^i(R_i) \supseteq C^i(\tilde{R}_i)$. We will show this by proving four substatements.

Statement 1. $\mathbb{A}(R_i) \cap \mathbb{A}(T_i) \subseteq \mathbb{A}(\tilde{R}_i) \cap \mathbb{A}(T_i)$

Let $A \in \mathbb{A}(R_i) \cap \mathbb{A}(T_i)$. By definition of $R_i = \pi_{\beta_i} \sigma_{F_i}(T_i)$, it follows that $A \in \beta_i$. From the construction of β_i in Lines 30–32 of Algorithm 1, it holds that $A \in \beta$. Since $q(\bowtie T_i) = \tilde{q}(\bowtie R_i) = \tilde{q}(\bowtie \tilde{q}_i(T_i))$, it follows that $A \in \mathbb{A}(\tilde{R}_i) \cap \mathbb{A}(T_i)$.

Statement 2. For every $x \in F$ with $\{T_i, T_j\} \subseteq \mathbb{T}(x), (j \neq i)$ and every $e \in \tilde{R}_i$ there must exist a projection π_p such that $\pi_p e =$ `true` iff $\bigvee_{(\neg)\gamma \in \Gamma_i} (\neg)\gamma(e) =$ `true`, where $\Gamma_i = \{(\neg)\gamma \in x \,|\, \mathbb{T}(x) = \{T_i\}\}$. Furthermore, $\pi_{p \cup \mathbb{A}(\tilde{R}_i)} \tilde{R}_i$ is also a solution to Problem 1.

This statement directly follows from the fact that $\tilde{R}_i$ is part of a solution to Problem 1 for q. Since x depends on values from at least T_i and T_j, $\tilde{R}_i$ must indicate, for each of its entries e, whether that entry sets x to `true`. By definition, this is the case if $\bigvee_{(\neg)\gamma \in \Gamma_i} (\neg)\gamma(e)$ is `true`.

Statement 3. For all $\tilde{T} \in C^i(\tilde{R}_i)$, there exists β and F such that $\pi_\beta \sigma_F(\tilde{T}) = \tilde{R}_i$.

Let $\beta = (\mathbb{A}(\tilde{R}_i) \cap \mathbb{A}(\tilde{T})\ ) \cup \{p : (\neg)\gamma | p : (\neg)\gamma \in \mathbb{A}(\tilde{R}_i)\}$ and F be defined as $F(e) =$ `true` iff $e \in Img(\tilde{m})$. Here, $Img(\tilde{m})$ represents the image of the function $\tilde{m} : \tilde{R}_i \hookrightarrow \tilde{T}$, as defined in eq. (2).

Statement 4. Let $M_i : R_i \hookrightarrow T_i$ and $\tilde{M}_i : \tilde{R}_i \hookrightarrow T_i$ be the functions for $T_i \in C^i(R_i) \cap C^i(\tilde{R}_i)$ in eq. (2). Then, $Img(M_i) \subseteq Img(\tilde{M}_i)$.

We prove this statement by contradiction. Let $e \in Img(M_i) \setminus Img(\tilde{M}_i)$. Let β', F', $\tilde{\beta}_i$, and $\tilde{F}$ be such that $\pi_{\beta'} \sigma_{F'}(T_i) = R_i$ and $\pi_{\tilde{\beta}_i} \sigma_{\tilde{F}}(T_i) = \tilde{R}_i$ (as shown in Statement 3). By construction, $F'(e) =$ `true` and $\tilde{F}(e) =$ `false`. Since R_i and $\tilde{R}_i$ are part of solutions of Problem 1, it holds that $q(\bowtie T_i) = \widehat{q}(\bowtie R_i) = \tilde{q}(\bowtie \tilde{R}_i)$. Therefore, e cannot be a part of the evaluation of $q(\bowtie T_i)$. More precisely, for every $t \in q(\bowtie T_i)$ with $\pi_{\mathbb{A}(e)} t = e$: $F(t) =$ `false`. Since this needs to hold independently of the other $T_j (j \neq i)$, there exists a clause $x \in F$ with $\mathbb{T}(x) = \{T_i\}$ and $x(e) = \texttt{false}$. Let x be such a clause. We now look at the construction of R_i in Algorithm 1. By Line 11, $x \in F_i$. Hence, $e \notin R_i$. This is a contradiction with $F'(e) = \texttt{true}$.

Given the four statements, we can show that $C^i(R_i) \subseteq C^i(\tilde{R}_i)$. Let $\tilde{T} \in C^i(\tilde{R}_i)$ with $\tilde{m} : \tilde{R}_i \hookrightarrow \tilde{T}$ and $M_i, \tilde{M}_i$ as described in Statement 4. We need to show that there exists an $m : R_i \hookrightarrow \tilde{T}$ satisfying the properties in Eq. (2). We argue that $m : x \mapsto \tilde{m}(\tilde{M}_i^{-1}(M_i(x)))$ is such a function. The function is well-defined due to Statement 4. Its domain is $\tilde{T}$, and it is injective as a concatenation of injective functions. The expression $\pi_{\mathbb{A}(R_i)\cap\mathbb{A}(T_i)} x = \pi_{\mathbb{A}(R_i)\cap\mathbb{A}(T_i)} m(x)$ is only a problem when mapping $M_i(x)$ to $\tilde{M}_i^{-1}(M_i(x))$. However, since $\tilde{M}_i^{-1}$ satisfies the required property, it holds that $\pi_{\mathbb{A}(\tilde{R}_i)\cap\mathbb{A}(T_i)} \tilde{M}_i^{-1}(M_i(x)) = \pi_{\mathbb{A}(\tilde{R}_i)\cap\mathbb{A}(T_i)} M_i(x)$, and the property follows from Statement 1. From the construction of R_i in Algorithm 1, we know that R_i only has propositional projections if there exists a clause $x \in F$ with $\{T_i, T_j\} \subseteq \mathbb{T}(x), (j \neq i)$, and all have the form $p_{x,i} : \bigvee_{(\neg)\gamma\in\Gamma_i} (\neg)\gamma$. To fulfill the second property of Eq. (2), we assume WLOG that $\tilde{R}_i$ has attributes $\tilde{p}_{x,i}$ for all $p_{x,i}$ which are true iff the disjunction of $p_{x,i}$ above is `true` (as described in Statement 2). With this, m satisfies the second property of Eq. (2), because $\tilde{m}$ satisfies it.

6 Related Work

A similar architecture to the one described in this paper is used by DJoin [12], a system which provides differential private counting queries over multiple data sources. DJoin utilizes query rewriting similar to ours, which are also used in late materialization techniques to enhance performance in database management systems [6]. Furthermore, Kolain and Malavi [10] discuss a data trustee in the medical field which needs to be able to share non-relational data. Extracting only the minimum required information from such data remains a significant challenge.

The concept of data trustees aligns with models used in distributed database systems, where data is managed across multiple sources. Unlike distributed databases, which often replicate data across nodes, data trustees typically manage unique data from different sources. An overview of distributed database principles can be found in [15].

Beyond the privacy strategies implemented in our work, systems can be evaluated using frameworks such as the LINDUNN [4] or the privacy protection goals proposed in [8]. We believe PrivTru fulfills their requirements as well.

7 Conclusion

In this paper, we introduced PrivTru, a privacy-by-design data trustee, which facilitates data exchange from data sources to data receivers for static, relational data. We contributed to the ongoing discussion on whether data trustees should act as data stewards (storing data) or as data exchanges (relaying information). We argue that data exchanges are preferable, as they comply with the SEPARATE design strategy while also adhering to the principles of HIDE, MINIMIZE, and AGGREGATE. PrivTru exemplifies an instantiation of data exchanges, achieving MINIMIZE by ensuring that each data source provides only the minimum data necessary to answer a query. We proved that this property holds regardless of the exchange's prior knowledge. While we did not explore AGGREGATE in detail, it can be achieved by allowing queries with aggregation functions to be evaluated at the data sources, as done with other operations in PrivTru. In summary, our work establishes a foundation for designing data trustees that balance data utility with robust privacy protection, contributing to a more trustworthy data economy.

Acknowledgements. This research has been funded by the Federal Ministry of Education and Research of Germany (BMBF, Project 16KISA038).

References

1. Abiteboul, S., Hull, R., Vianu, V.: Foundations of databases (1995)
2. Blankertz, A.: Designing data trusts. Why we need to test consumer data trusts now (2020). https://www.interface-eu.org/storage/archive/files/designing_data_trusts_e.pdf. Accessed 11 Dec 2024
3. Blankertz, A., Specht, L.: What regulation for data trusts should look like (2021). https://www.interface-eu.org/storage/archive/files/regulation_for_data_trusts_0.pdf. Accessed 11 Dec 2024
4. Cavoukian, A.: Privacy by design [leading edge]. IEEE Technol. Soc. Mag. **31**, 18–19 (2012). https://doi.org/10.1109/MTS.2012.2225459
5. Chambert-Loir, A.: Information Theory: Three Theorems by Claude Shannon. UNITEXT, vol. 144. Cham (2022). https://doi.org/10.1007/978-3-031-21561-2
6. Chernishev, G., Galaktionov, V., Grigorev, V., Klyuchikov, E., Smirnov, K.: A comprehensive study of late materialization strategies for a disk-based column-store. In: DOLAP, pp. 21–30 (2022)
7. Codd, E.F.: A relational model of data for large shared data banks. Commun. ACM **13**, 377–387 (1970). https://doi.org/10.1145/362384.362685
8. Hansen, M., Jensen, M., Rost, M.: Protection goals for privacy engineering. In: IEEE Security and Privacy Workshops (2015). https://doi.org/10.1109/SPW.2015.13
9. Hoepman, J.-H.: Privacy design strategies. In: Cuppens-Boulahia, N., Cuppens, F., Jajodia, S., Abou El Kalam, A., Sans, T. (eds.) SEC 2014. IAICT, vol. 428, pp. 446–459. Springer, Heidelberg (2014). https://doi.org/10.1007/978-3-642-55415-5_38
10. Kolain, M., Molavi, R.: Zukunft Gesundheitsdaten (2019). https://www.bundesdruckerei-gmbh.de/files/dokumente/pdf/studie_zukunft-gesundheitsdaten.pdf. Accessed 11 Dec 2024
11. Kullback, S., Leibler, R.A.: On information and sufficiency. Ann. Math. Stat. **22**, 79–86 (1951). https://doi.org/10.1214/aoms/1177729694

12. Narayan, A., Haeberlen, A.: DJoin: differentially private join queries over distributed databases. In: 10th USENIX Symposium on Operating Systems Design and Implementation (OSDI 12), pp. 149–162 (2012)
13. Reiberg, A., Appelt, D., Kraemer, P.: Data trusts, data intermediation services and Gaia-X (2023). https://gaia-x-hub.de/wp-content/uploads/2023/11/GX-White-Paper-Data-Trusts.pdf. Accessed 29 May 2024
14. Samarati, P., Sweeney, L.: Protecting privacy when disclosing information: k-anonymity and its enforcement through generalization and suppression. In: Proceedings of the IEEE Symposium on Research in Security and Privacy (1998)
15. Xu, Q., Yang, C., Zhou, A.: Native distributed databases: problems, challenges and opportunities. Proc. VLDB Endow. 4217–4220 (2024)

Industrial and Critical Infrastructure Security

Uncovering Robot Joint-Level Controller Actions from Encrypted Network Traffic

Cheng Tang(✉), Diogo Barradas, Urs Hengartner, and Yue Hu

University of Waterloo, Waterloo, Canada
{c225tang,dbarrada,urs.hengartner,yue.hu}@uwaterloo.ca

Abstract. This study examines the privacy risks faced during the teleoperation of robots which are controlled via commands exchanged through encrypted network communications. From the perspective of an adversary able to eavesdrop network traffic, we explore the potential to infer sensitive robotic actions by analyzing the metadata of encrypted traffic, such as packet timing, size, and direction. We investigate this threat in realistic setups, using a smartphone's Inertial Measurement Unit (IMU) to control a robotic arm via three joint-level modalities—position, velocity, and torque—to perform four distinct actions. First, by leveraging state-of-the-art traffic analysis attacks to examine robot teleoperation traffic, we uncover that an adversary can accurately identify the actions performed by the robot. Second, by prototyping a defense against such attacks, we analyze the performance and privacy trade-offs across the robot control modalities. Our findings highlight the importance of integrating privacy considerations into robotics APIs, and encourage further exploration of factors influencing the security of teleoperated systems.

Keywords: Encrypted traffic analysis · Privacy · Robot teleoperation

1 Introduction

Current research is pushing towards the adoption of teleoperated robots, particularly robot arms, in everyday settings, including homes [1] and production lines [4]. In this setting, the robot and the controller (i.e., the computer on which the control software is run) are typically connected to a network, often the internet [2,12], and the network traffic exchanged between the controller and the robot can typically be encrypted for preventing a network adversary to read or tamper with the commands sent by the controller.

Despite these safeguards, observers can still try to infer the content of encrypted messages by analyzing communication metadata, such as the size, direction, and timing of network packets. For instance, inference techniques have previously succeeded in identifying the websites users visit through encrypted tunnels [5,16] that aim to hide one's browsing patterns. However, this threat remains underexplored in robot teleoperation scenarios. If these inference techniques were as effective on encrypted robot/controller traffic as on web traffic,

Published by Springer Nature Switzerland AG 2025
L. Nemec Zlatolas et al. (Eds.): SEC 2025, IFIP AICT 745, pp. 121–135, 2025.
https://doi.org/10.1007/978-3-031-92882-6_9

adversaries could gain unauthorized access to private information which, in sensitive settings like home care, could reveal information about an individual's care regimen and health status (such as medication dispensing or physical therapy).

The *first objective* of our research is to showcase the practical feasibility of inferring robot actions from encrypted network traffic patterns. We leverage an intrinsic property of robotic teleoperation traffic: the unique network traffic pattern generated by each command and its associated feedback. For example, the completion time of a motion can be reflected by observing the frequency between network packets with specific lengths. Even with encryption, certain characteristics of this traffic pattern, such as the timing between packets, may allow an observer to differentiate between commands.

To experiment with these inference attacks, we employ a smartphone as the teleoperation interface [13,20] (similarly to [11]). We use the phone's Inertial Measurement Unit (IMU)'s gyroscope and accelerometer to control a collaborative robot arm. The smartphone is connected to a computer that is connected to the same network as the robot and commands the motions to the robot via three types of joint-level controllers: position, velocity, and torque. For instance, the end-effector (EE) of the robot arm follows the movements of the smartphone - if the smartphone is moved up and down, the robot arm's EE also moves up and down. For robot arms, all control strategies essentially boil down to joint-level controllers, which set specific values (e.g., positions, velocities, or torques) at joint level depending on the desired outcome. For instance, torque control might be more desirable when physical interactions with human users may occur, while position control might be prioritized for precision in movement.

The *second objective* of our research is to identify how different control strategies impact the privacy of teleoperated robotic systems. We posit that different joint-level controllers influence the type and granularity of data inferable from encrypted network traffic. For example, a controller adjusting joint positions predictably may make action inference easier from network metadata, compared to a torque-based control scheme that produces more variable traffic patterns. To the best of our knowledge, we are the first to study the prediction of robot actions from encrypted joint-level controller traffic.

In our experiments, we execute four distinct movements 100 times each using each of the three controllers and collect the encrypted network traffic transferred between the computer and the robot. We analyze different features of this network traffic, using them to train and evaluate different classifiers.

Contributions. We deliver the following main contributions:

- We investigate encrypted network traffic patterns from various angles, including the effects of command frequency (i.e., the frequency at which the robot is requested to perform a movement as part of an action) on packet sizes and arrival times, as well as the time it takes to complete commands.
- We assess the effectiveness of several traffic pattern recognition methods and identify reliable techniques for deducing robot actions from encrypted traffic.
- We explore the consequences of our research for the design of new privacy-preserving robot teleoperation APIs.

2 Related Work

2.1 Analysis of Encrypted Network Traffic

In communications established across the network, encryption protocols (e.g., TLS) ensure that data remains confidential and secure against unauthorized tampering. Despite the use of encryption, it is still possible to infer privacy-sensitive information pertaining to these data exchanges through the analysis of the *communication metadata*; characteristics such as the size, timing, and frequency of network packets comprising encrypted communications reveal patterns that allow external observers to infer communications' contents [7].

Traffic *fingerprinting* is a sub-category of network traffic analysis. In a fingerprinting attack, an adversary's goal is to re-identify the occurrence of a certain event in the network, based on the similarity to past events labeled by the adversary, i.e., a set of traffic "fingerprints" [5]. These attacks have been widely researched in the context of website fingerprinting [10,21], where an adversary wishes to uncover which website a client is accessing through an encrypted tunnel (e.g., Virtual Private Networks (VPNs) [21] or Tor [10]) that hides the website's IP address from a local network observer.

2.2 Fingerprinting Encrypted Robotic Teleoperation Traffic

Teleoperated robots are controlled remotely via network commands, facing privacy challenges that bear a notable resemblance to those encountered in website fingerprinting. Specifically, traffic fingerprinting techniques in robotic teleoperation can expose fine-grained aspects of robot operations, ranging from movement patterns to user interactions, thereby posing a considerable privacy risk to users. Shah et al. [14] demonstrated that robot movements can be identified from encrypted traffic using deep neural network-based analysis. Adversaries can extract detailed operational sequences of robots, potentially revealing sensitive information, or unauthorized replication of tasks. In earlier work [17], we classified robot actions using higher-level APIs like Cartesian commands, achieving high accuracy through signal processing and traffic statistics analysis. However, these studies did not explore classifying daily actions and tasks using joint-level controllers, the most fundamental type of robotic arm controllers, thus leaving a critical gap in existing research.

As it stands, not all tasks can use high-level descriptions, especially in dynamic environments like homes or care facilities where human-robot interaction may occur. Unlike industrial robots, robots in these settings must adjust in real-time, needing to target delicate handling, human contact, or complex environments. For example, in rehabilitation, a robot assisting with arm lifting needs to continuously adapt its torque and position based on the patient's movements, requiring low-level control for smooth and safe interaction. In these cases, high-level controller commands need to be translated into precise joint-level position/velocity/torque commands that call for real-time sensor feedback. While Shah et al. [14] inferred low-level motions from encrypted traffic, they did not explore the inference of high-level actions through the composition/analysis of low-level motions, raising the

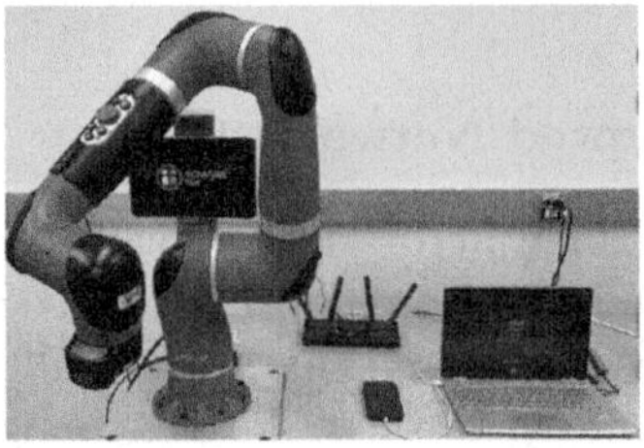

Fig. 1. The smartphone sends signals to the robot control software on a computer via cable, and the computer communicates with the robot over the same network.

question of whether and to which degree such relationships can be established. In our work, we show that it is possible to predict high-level actions from encrypted network traffic using joint-level controllers.

3 Experimental Setup

3.1 Hardware and Software Configurations

Our experimental setup leverages a smartphone equipped with an accelerometer, gyroscope, and magnetometer, which we use to teleoperate a commercial collaborative robot arm (Sawyer from Rethink Robotics) as depicted in Fig. 1.

Controllers Used in Teleoperation. We implemented teleoperation using the three types of joint-level controllers available on the Sawyer: position, velocity, and torque control, commonly used in commercial robot arms to move robot arms, where position and velocity control are desired for precision tasks and torque control for tasks requiring interactions with humans and/or delicate objects. The IMU data are collected from the smartphone to estimate its position and velocity, then, depending on the desired controller, translated into the robot arms' joint position, velocity, and torques for the arm to move with the smartphone. Ultimately, we used a single phone to collect network traffic generated via teleoperation (see Sect. 3.3). Despite variations in sensor performance, our goal is to capture valid trajectories. Minor sensor differences do not affect overall motion, ensuring coherent trajectories for analysis.

Teleoperation Software and Secure Communication. The control of Sawyer is facilitated through API[1] that enables the generation of command patterns for effective robot operation. To establish an encrypted communication channel between the robot and the computer, we used the built-in OpenVPN features of a commercial-off-the-shelf router. Commands are processed on this computer, running Ubuntu 20.04 LTS, which communicates with the robot via ROS (Robotic Operating System) Noetic, a standard framework in robotics. The robotic arm and computer are connected to the same router via Ethernet, ensuring reliable data transmission and real-time command execution/feedback.

[1] https://rethinkrobotics.github.io/intera_sdk_docs/5.1.0/index.html.

3.2 Threat Model

Our threat model assumes a network adversary who is able to intercept the encrypted network traffic flowing between the computer and the robotic arm (e.g., by wiretapping a physical Ethernet link). The adversary aims at identifying the (potentially privacy-sensitive) actions being performed by the robot but is unable to break the cryptographic assumptions that would allow it to reveal the actual content of the encrypted communication channel.

To uncover the actions performed by the robot, the adversary will resort to encrypted traffic analysis techniques based on the inspection of the communication metadata exchanged between the controller and the robot, e.g., the timing, command frequency, and size of network packets exchanged in the communication, as well as the overall volume of exchanged data. Similar to the website fingerprinting literature, we assume that the adversary can replicate the operational setup of their target – in this case, including network conditions, the use of the same robot models, and the use of the same encryption techniques to establish a secure communication channel between the controller and the robot.

In particular, the adversary will attempt to re-identify the occurrence of a set of actions by the target robot as follows: First, the adversary generates a comprehensive database of network traces ("fingerprints") by executing a set of actions that closely resemble the ones that may be executed by the target robot in the future. Then, the adversary waits for the target robot to perform an action whose information is exchanged via the encrypted tunnel, collects the robot's traffic, and attempts to match it with one of the fingerprints in its database. This matching is performed via machine learning [5] and deep learning [10,16] techniques, which help automate and enhance the fingerprinting's effectiveness.

Traffic fingerprinting typically focuses on two different scenarios (referred to as *closed-* and/or *open-world* [16]), depending on the information made available to the adversary. In this work, we assume a *closed-world* scenario, where an adversary is given the knowledge about a limited set of actions a robot is able to perform (also known as the *monitored* set). While the set of monitored actions is limited, it may be sufficient to allow an adversary to infer a robot's activity in specific contexts. For instance, one may assume that a caregiving robot would perform a few pre-determined actions for helping a patient with reduced mobility, but that a different set of actions would be more relevant for a visually impaired patient. Should the adversary know which condition afflicts a patient, they could reasonably create a database of actions expected to be performed by the robot.

3.3 Dataset Collection

Choice of Robotic Actions. We collected network traces [18] while the robot performed *four* distinct actions: (a) picking up and placing an object; (b) pouring water; (c) pressing a key, and; (d) turning on a switch. This set of actions was selected based on the assumption that the robot may be operating in a private setting, where the four selected actions are highly representative of recurring daily routine actions. While these actions may seem basic, they may reveal user habits, leading to the exposure of private information and user profiling.

Among the four actions, *pour water* is mostly similar to *pick and place*, while *press key* is mostly similar to *turn on switch*. We deliberately chose two pairs of actions that could be considered dissimilar to one another, while internally similar within each pair. This approach allows for exploring how subtle differences in the network traffic generated by joint-level commands can help distinguish between similar actions, as well as demonstrating clear distinctions between different types of movements. This selection helps us evaluate the effectiveness of fingerprinting across varied, yet closely related, robot behaviors (Sect. 5.2).

Robotic Actions' Trajectories. To ensure our traces provide a robust basis for assessing fingerprinting performance, we collected each action sample following a *different trajectory*. In essence, action trajectories are generated via the execution of several sub-tasks (e.g., move to a given location, press/lift an object, etc.) that are chained together and executed at different instants in time. Each sub-task may be configured to operate at different robot movement speeds, to assume disparate movement waypoints and object locations, and other task-specific parameters (e.g., pouring angles). In addition, each trajectory may involve additional variability due to minor variations in sensor readings (see Sect. 3.1).

For each action class, we collected and interpolated 100 sample motion trajectories using the phone, each lasting 10 to 30 s, totaling 400 data samples. One traffic sample encompasses the entire network data exchanged between the robot and the controller PC when completing an instance of the desired action.

Per-Controller Data Acquisition. We used the interpolated motion samples to operate the robot using our three different controllers: position, velocity, and torque. During these operations, we captured the network traffic exchanged between the robot and the computer. This process resulted in 400 network traffic trace samples for each type of controller, amounting to a total of 1200 network traffic trace samples. We acquired the network traces by running the Linux `tcpdump` utility on the robot's controller computer, which allows us to record the encrypted data exchanges between the robot and the controller.

4 Characterization of Robot Actions Traffic

In our testbed, the command and feedback messages necessary for teleoperation are encrypted by VPN software, preventing adversaries from reading their content. However, different actions might produce distinct network patterns. Commands requiring more parameters may generate larger packets; different actions may require different command sequences, resulting in varying packet sizes; and different actions might require command and feedback exchanges at different frequencies, affecting packet inter-arrival times. These possibly disparate traffic patterns could allow an adversary to match them to specific actions.

To better visualize the existence of such patterns in teleoperation traffic, Fig. 2 presents a set of example network traces collected during the execution of different actions. (The traces comprising each action/controller combination

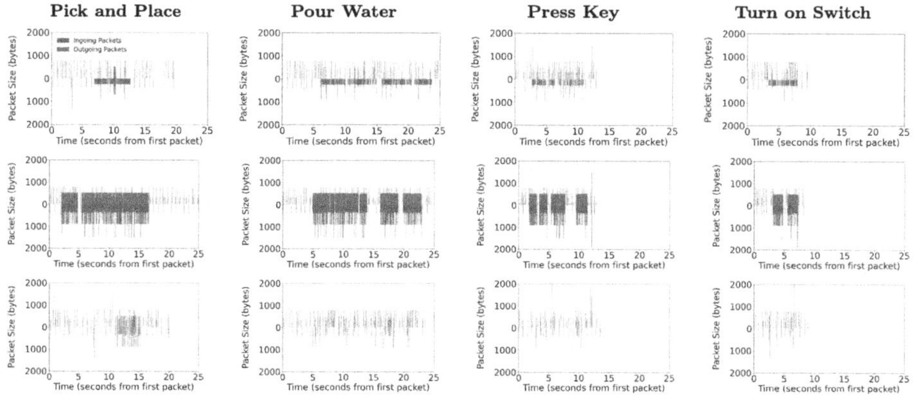

Fig. 2. Examples of four actions' packet lengths over time. (First row – position controller; second row – velocity controller; third row – torque controller).

were found to be rather stable.) Each row of the figure depicts the packet sizes and timing relationship for the position, velocity, and torque controllers. In this figure, "incoming" refers to the packets sent by the controller and received by the robot, while "outgoing" refers to packets sent in the reverse direction.

Different Controller/Action Combinations Produce Disparate Traffic Patterns. A closer analysis of Fig. 2 allows us to pinpoint two major observations: a) row-wise, each controller originates a different traffic pattern across each of the actions, and; b) column-wise, for the same action, each controller originates a different network traffic pattern. Overall, this means that each action performed by each different controller will exhibit a different traffic pattern in the network, potentially allowing traffic fingerprinting techniques to identify the traces produced by a specific controller/action combination.

Consider, for instance, the first row of Fig. 2, which showcase the traffic patterns produced by the position controller over each of the four actions. For each action, we can see that not only each action is performed in a different amount of time, but also that the frequency of packets exchanged between the robot and its controller is quite disparate. For instance, for the *pick and place* action, there is a high concentration of incoming packets from around 7 s to 12 s in the trace, while incoming packets for the *pour water* action form four individual clusters after 5 s into the trace, where these packets are more concentrated. The traffic patterns generated by other controllers given the same action follow a similar trend, i.e., the length of the packet exchange, as well as the frequency of packets exchanged at different points in the trace is indicative of the action being performed. Now, consider also the first column of Fig. 2, showcasing the traffic patterns for the *pick and place* action across three different controllers. We can observe that each controller will also produce a different pattern.

Packet Sizes Reflect the Number of Joints Being Commanded. Figure 3 depicts a comparative analysis of command transmissions when controlling a

(a) Command one joint. (b) Command all joints.

Fig. 3. Packet lengths over time when commanding a different number of joints.

single joint versus all seven joints of the robot. Note that sending one command to a given joint essentially requires the controller to specify a value for one key in a dictionary. Thus, the more joints are controlled simultaneously, the more information needs to be conveyed by the controller to the robot. Indeed, we can observe from the figure that packet lengths experience a noticeable increase when all seven joints are being controlled. This trend is also consistent across position, velocity, and torque control modes. Interestingly, this means that network traffic analysis techniques can also focus on these particularities to infer whether simpler/more complex actions are being performed, depending on the number of joints used by the robot at any given time. For instance, in a simple horizontal motion of the arm, only one joint needs to be moved. In this case, the controller would send smaller packets for commanding the movement of a single joint.

5 Evaluation of Fingerprinting Attacks

5.1 Traffic Analysis Attacks and Metrics

Classical ML-Based Attacks. These attacks work by analyzing a set of manually-engineered features extracted from encrypted network traffic. These features include summary statistics such as the average packet size and percentiles of inter-packet timing and are used to identify patterns that can distinguish different types of traffic despite encryption. We use three ML-based classifiers (initially proposed for website fingerprinting) that operate on summary statistics, including k-Fingerprinting [5], CUMUL [9], and k-Nearest Neighbors (kNN) [19]. We also devised our own classifier based on gradient-boosted decision trees (XGBoost), resorting to summary statistics focusing the frequency distribution of packet sizes and timing, as well as each action's communication volume.

Deep Learning Attacks. Unlike classical ML attacks which require manual feature engineering, deep learning-based attacks automatically extract features from network traces by using kernels as filters during the backpropagation process. These methods are generally more resource-intensive, requiring significant computational power and large training datasets. While acquiring such datasets is relatively straightforward in domains like website fingerprinting, it proves challenging in the context of robotic operations, where collecting large amounts of real-world data requires extensive work [8]. Nevertheless, we explore these classifiers within our study, considering their success in network traffic classification.

We use two deep learning attacks based on Convolutional Neural Networks (CNNs), named deep fingerprinting (DF) [16] and Tik-Tok [10]. While both classifiers share the same neural network architecture, they use different input representations of the network data they are trained/tested on. Specifically, DF leverages an input vector formed by the *direction and size* of traffic (e.g., [+50, −50, +80] denotes a trace formed by an outgoing packet of size 50, an incoming packet of size 50, and an outgoing packet of size 80). Instead, Tik-Tok considers a *directional timing* input representation (e.g., [0, −0.02, +0.34] denotes a trace formed by the first outgoing packet that is sent to the network, followed by an incoming packet that arrives 0.02 s after the first packet was sent, and so on).

In addition to the "vanilla" inputs for both classifiers, we generated two alternative input representations. Specifically, we started by generating an alternative input representation for Tik-Tok, where we simply use raw packet timings (e.g., [0, 0.02, 0.54] denotes a trace where the second packet exchanged in the connection was sent after 0.02 s of the start of the connection). Then, for assessing the potential benefits of including all three of the metadata dimensions we consider for a network packet (direction, timing, and size), we crafted new input vectors containing these dimensions. We feed this hybrid feature vector into the generic DF/Tik-Tok architecture for building a new classifier we refer to as DF-Tok.

Lastly, we use another recent attack known as Robust Fingerprinting (RF) [15]. This attack aggregates the direction and timing information of packets (according to fixed-length time intervals) into a matrix and uses a CNN-based classifier.

Classification Metrics and Setup. We evaluate the success of each attack through its *accuracy* and use *confusion matrices* to examine predictions across different classes. We used 10-fold cross-validation when experimenting with classical ML classifiers and, due to computational demands, used an 80% training/10% validation/10% testing splits when evaluating our deep learning classifiers. All results refer to the accuracy obtained on each classifier's testing set.

5.2 Attack Results

Table 1 depicts the accuracy of each attack when identifying the action performed by the robot under a given controller. These results showcase significant privacy risks (accuracy surpassing 80%), suggesting that an adversary could potentially identify the actions executed by the robot by using already existing fingerprinting attacks. Below, we describe our main findings.

Table 1. Accuracy of each attack in distinguishing between the four different actions across each of the controllers.

Attack	Position (%)	Velocity (%)	Torque (%)
k-Fingerprinting	77.2	63.5	72.5
KNN	33.2	31.0	27.5
CUMUL	63.6	61.0	63.8
XGBoost	83.2	81.2	80.5
DF (direction, sizes)	67.5	62.5	48.8
Tik-Tok (direction, timing)	28.8	27.5	28.8
Tik-Tok (timing)	28.8	27.5	28.8
DF-Tok (direction, timing, sizes)	67.5	63.2	55.0
RF (direction, timing)	38.0	37.8	37.4

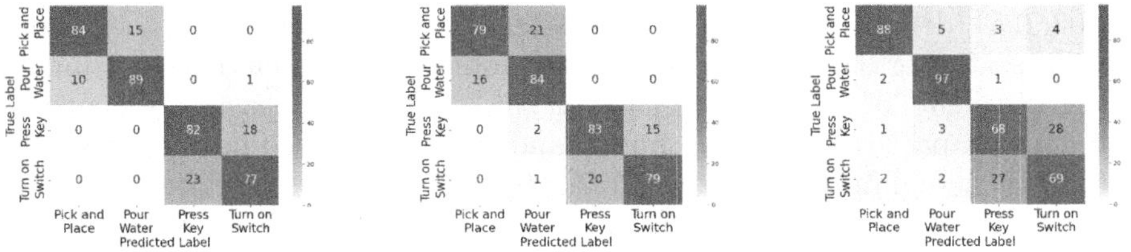

(a) Position Controller. (b) Velocity Controller. (c) Torque Controller.

Fig. 4. XGBoost's confusion matrices for the three controllers.

XGBoost Performs Best in Uncovering Robot Actions from Encrypted Network Traffic. Figure 4 displays the confusion matrices for the three controllers using the XGBoost classifier, which yielded the highest accuracy. The actions of picking and placing an object and pouring water tend to overlap in terms of their characteristic patterns, which can lead to these actions being more easily confused with one another during classification. Similarly, the actions of pressing a key and the tapping motion involved turning on a switch and exhibit a higher likelihood of being mixed up. This observation aligns with the intuitive understanding that actions sharing similar physical movements or operational characteristics are more challenging to distinguish based on traffic patterns.

The Performance of Deep Learning Attacks was Subpar When Compared to Those Based on Classical ML. Despite the theoretical advantages of CNNs, the performance of the deep learning attacks we considered may have been limited by several factors. First, these attacks were proposed for the website fingerprinting setting, where data collection is a rather easy process to automate and conduct at scale, whereas this is not the particular case for teleoperation. Second, while Tik-Tok and RF take packet timing into consideration, they forego packet sizing information, thus being unable to build important context about the trace by distinguishing between different packet types composing a trace (and

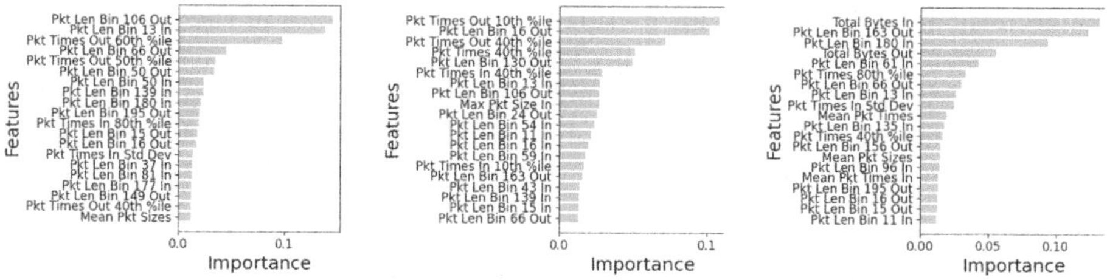

(a) Position Controller. (b) Velocity Controller. (c) Torque Controller.

Fig. 5. Top 20 feature importance for three controllers using XGBoost.

which may only be distinguishable according to their size). This may present a challenge to these classifiers, since, alongside the command messages we rely on to characterize each action, the controller and the robot exchange maintenance and feedback messages that are not useful for action identification. Indeed, DF-Tok's results suggest that timing information appears to provide only limited gains on top of DF with packet direction and size information. However, performance gains were evident when applied to the torque controller (∼6% increase).

In contrast, attacks that jointly consider statistics about both packet sizes and timing have demonstrated a compelling potential to unveil sensitive data. Classical ML attacks, including k-Fingerprinting or our XGBoost-based classifier, were effective in uncovering the actions executed by the teleoperated robot.

Different Controllers Produce Different Sets of Traffic Characteristics Useful for Action Identification. Fig. 5 showcases the top 20 most important features for classifying actions across the three different controllers, as determined by our XGBoost classifier. It can be observed that the position, velocity, and torque controllers are all influenced by the number of packets exchanged in a trace, featuring a mix of useful packet size ranges that are both shared and distinct across controllers. This is also true for some indicators of timing information between packets. Additionally, the total in/out bytes transmitted in the connection are relevant for the torque controller, but not for the other controllers. This is consistent with the third row of Fig. 2, where it can be seen that different actions tend to produce traffic sequences of varying length (e.g., the tap action is relatively short, under 10 s, whereas the pour water action is longer, over 20 s), suggesting that longer action sequences also generate a larger amount of packets, providing useful information to the classifier.

Some Actions Share Common Feature Distributions. When delving into the per-class distribution of the most important feature for each controller, we identified an overlap in the feature distributions for some classes, revealing some of the inherent difficulties in distinguishing between the network traces of different actions. For instance, consider the *10th percentile of outgoing packets' times* feature, identified as the most important feature for distinguishing actions performed with the velocity controller (Fig. 5b). We observed a clear similarity between the distribution of this feature among the samples of the *pick and place* and *pour water* actions (both ranging from 4 to 6 milliseconds), and also between *press key* and *turn on switch* (2 to 4 milliseconds), whereas there is an observable difference between these two groups of actions. This is further evidenced by the results shown in the confusion matrix of Fig. 4b.

6 Towards Effective Fingerprinting Defenses

6.1 Requirements for Teleoperation Traffic Analysis Defenses

In designing software APIs for teleoperated robotic systems, several strategies can be considered to enhance privacy. As an inspiration, the literature on website fingerprinting is already prolific with the development of defenses to scramble traffic patterns so as to make fingerprinting attacks unsuccessful [6].

Accommodating Real-Time Constraints. Ideally, defense mechanisms should avoid compromising a robot's operational effectiveness. For instance, while strategies involving the padding of command packets to the same size and forcing packet delays might deter an adversary from identifying the robotic actions being performed, the bandwidth and latency overheads imposed by such strategies should not compromise the correct and timely operation of the robot. In contrast to web traffic, robot teleoperation is often ruled by real-time requirements which are not amenable to fingerprinting defenses that introduce latency. In general, if any data at the joint control level is delayed even by milliseconds, this would cause either the robot to stop (if such a feature is implemented on the onboard computer) or the controller could become unstable.

Zero-Delay Defenses. Defenses that avoid introducing delays have been recently explored in the website fingerprinting literature. For instance, FRONT [3] foregoes bandwidth savings, altering traffic patterns by introducing dummy packets. Another strategy could entail sending a set of commands to all joints, at a fixed rate, even in the absence of updates. This could mask the number of joints involved in motion execution (an information leak we underlined in Sect. 4).

6.2 Prototyping a Command Size Padding Defense

We prototyped a simple simulator for a zero-delay defense against robot traffic fingerprinting, applying it on the traces we have previously collected (Sect. 3.3).

Since our earlier feature analysis (see Fig. 5) suggested that packet sizes are amongst the most important features for classification, we built a defense that artificially pads joint-level command packets to their nearest multiple of n bytes. We applied the defense in several configurations, including n = 200B, 400B, 800B, or 1800B. Given that the largest command packets we observed are in a size range of 1600–1700B, the 1800B padding configuration essentially turns all command packets into the same size. Thus, this modification removes any useful information that could be extracted from the size of individual command packets

Table 2. XGBoost attack accuracy and bandwidth overhead (% of extra transmitted bytes) on padded command packets.

Padding (B)	Position		Velocity		Torque	
	Acc. (%)	OH (%)	Acc. (%)	OH (%)	Acc. (%)	OH (%)
200	80.7	121.1	72.9	132.9	79.7	120.7
400	79.7	136.1	72.5	164.5	79.3	137.1
800	78.5	182.2	73.4	252.2	78.7	182.6
1800	78.0	300.6	72.9	495.3	78.8	302.2

alone. Padding increases bandwidth consumption (see Table 2), but does not affect packet transmission time nor adds extra packets to the link.

We assess the ability of the XGBoost classifier to distinguish actions protected by the defense by training and testing the classifier on the same (but now defended) subsets of the data used to train/test the original attacks in Sect. 5.2. The results of this experiment, shown in Table 2, reveal that padding command traffic alone appears to be largely ineffective for preventing the fingerprinting of position and torque controllers, even when padding all command packets to the same size, imposing a maximum ~8% accuracy degradation when classifying actions using the velocity controller. According to our feature importance analysis, this may be explained by the fact that, while the size of individual command messages is padded to the same length, the communication volume and amount of command packets exchanged in each direction of the communication still reveal sufficient information for the classifier to identify different actions. Overall, these findings call for a comprehensive exploration of defense mechanisms that can withstand fingerprinting while ensuring the robot's operational effectiveness.

7 Considerations on Generalizability

Robot Characteristics. Different robots may use different joint-level control APIs and control modes, as well as different networking protocols to exchange data. This may result in different command formats and structure of associated messages/network packets. While we find that the Sawyer robotic arm is vulnerable to traffic fingerprinting (and likely, other ROS-based robots as well), we aim to conduct future work that extends our study to a wider set of robots.

Sets of Actions. Additional sets of actions included in our dataset may result in differences on the ability of adversaries to correctly fingerprint robotic actions. However, while admittedly far from comprehensive, our work suggests that even relatively similar actions (e.g., *turn on switch* and *press key*) can be successfully distinguished through traffic analysis.

Network Conditions. Different network conditions may affect the traffic patterns observed on the communication between a robot and its controller. For instance, degraded conditions may cause packets to be dropped and retransmissions to occur, altering packet delivery rates or causing the exchange of additional messages. We aim to extend our study to more complex networking setups.

8 Conclusions

Our study uncovered significant privacy risks in robot teleoperation, particularly by analyzing encrypted network traffic data of joint-level controller actions exchanged between a collaborative robot arm and the computer that runs the controller. One possible step to address this issue is to integrate traffic scrambling methods in API design for robots, while balancing the integration of these privacy-preserving techniques with the efficiency of robot operations.

Acknowledgments. This work was supported in part by a seed grant jointly awarded by the University of Waterloo's Cybersecurity and Privacy Institute and RoboHub. We thank RoboHub for providing us with access to the Sawyer robotic arm.

Disclosure of Interests. The authors have no competing interests to declare that are relevant to the content of this article.

References

1. Cabrera, M.E., Bhattacharjee, T., Dey, K., Cakmak, M.: An exploration of accessible remote tele-operation for assistive mobile manipulators in the home. In: Proceedings of IEEE RO-MAN (2021)
2. DeMarinis, N., Tellex, S., Kemerlis, V.P., Konidaris, G., Fonseca, R.: Scanning the internet for ROS: a view of security in robotics research. In: Proceedings of ICRA (2019)
3. Gong, J., Wang, T.: Zero-delay lightweight defenses against website fingerprinting. In: Proceedings of USENIX Security (2020)
4. González, C., Solanes, J.E., Munoz, A., Gracia, L., Girbés-Juan, V., Tornero, J.: Advanced teleoperation and control system for industrial robots based on augmented virtuality and haptic feedback. J. Manuf. Syst. **59** (2021)
5. Hayes, J., Danezis, G.: k-fingerprinting: a robust scalable website fingerprinting technique. In: Proceedings of USENIX Security (2016)
6. Mathews, N., Holland, J.K., Oh, S.E., Rahman, M.S., Hopper, N., Wright, M.: SoK: a critical evaluation of efficient website fingerprinting defenses. In: Proceedings of IEEE S&P (2023)
7. Nguyen, T.T., Armitage, G.: A survey of techniques for internet traffic classification using machine learning. IEEE Commun. Surv. Tutor. **10**(4) (2008)
8. Open X-Embodiment Collaboration, et al.: Open X-embodiment: robotic learning datasets and RT-X models. https://arxiv.org/abs/2310.08864 (2023)
9. Panchenko, A., Lanze, F.: Website fingerprinting at internet scale. In: Proceedings of NDSS (2016)
10. Rahman, M.S., Sirinam, P., Mathews, N., Gangadhara, K.G., Wright, M.: Tik-Tok: the utility of packet timing in website fingerprinting attacks. Proc. Priv. Enhanc. Technol. **2020**(3) (2020)

11. Rodriguez, D., Perez, C., Jagersand, M., Figueroa, P.: A comparison of smartphone interfaces for teleoperation of robot arms. In: Proceedings of CLEI (2017)
12. Romeo, L., Petitti, A., Marani, R., Milella, A.: Internet of robotic things in smart domains: applications and challenges. Sensors **20**(12) (2020)
13. Sankar, G., Djamasbi, S., Li, Z., Xiao, J., Buchler, N.: Systematic literature review on the user evaluation of teleoperation interfaces for professional service robots. In: Proceedings of HCI International (2023)
14. Shah, R., Ahmed, C.M., Nagaraja, S.: Can you still see me?: identifying robot operations over end-to-end encrypted channels. In: Proceedings of ACM WiSec (2022)
15. Shen, M., Ji, K., Gao, Z., Li, Q., Zhu, L., Xu, K.: Subverting website fingerprinting defenses with robust traffic representation. In: Proceedings of USENIX Security (2023)
16. Sirinam, P., Imani, M., Juarez, M., Wright, M.: Deep fingerprinting: undermining website fingerprinting defenses with deep learning. In: Proceedings of ACM CCS (2018)
17. Tang, C., Barradas, D., Hengartner, U., Hu, Y.: On the feasibility of fingerprinting collaborative robot traffic. arXiv preprint arXiv:2312.06802 (2023)
18. Tang, C., Barradas, D., Hengartner, U., Hu, Y.: Network traces for Sawyer's joint-level controller actions (2025). https://doi.org/10.5281/zenodo.15007304
19. Wang, T., Cai, X., Nithyanand, R., Johnson, R.: Effective attacks and provable defenses for website fingerprinting. In: Proceedings of USENIX Security (2014)
20. Wu, L., Alqasemi, R., Dubey, R.: Development of smartphone-based human-robot interfaces for individuals with disabilities. IEEE Robot. Autom. Lett. **5**(4) (2020)
21. Xue, D., et al.: OpenVPN is open to VPN fingerprinting. In: Proceedings of USENIX Security (2022)

Artefact Provenance Graphs for Anomaly Inference in Industrial Control Systems

Marco M. Cook(✉) and Dimitrios Pezaros

University of Glasgow, Glasgow, Scotland
{marco.cook,dimitrios.pezaros}@glasgow.ac.uk

Abstract. The digitalisation of Critical National Infrastructure (CNI) to improve automation has resulted in the underlying Industrial Control Systems (ICS) becoming increasingly interconnected. This sudden connectivity combined with a lack of inherent security controls in ICS components such as Programmable Logic Controllers (PLCs) has enabled sophisticated cyber adversaries to disrupt physical processes. Detecting and analysing attacks is therefore essential for ICS operators to ensure the continuous availability of critical systems. However, existing research has made limited advances into data provenance for anomalies occurring in ICS networks. This is fundamental for enabling rapid triaging of cyber incidents. In this paper, we introduce a novel vendor-independent approach for representing the behaviour of PLC states using graphs for anomaly detection. Through the modelling of dependencies between memory and network data artefacts, we facilitate the data provenance of different types of PLC attack scenarios using graph-based metrics as a generalisable feature set for accurate state and node classification. We evaluate our approach using two physical ICS testbeds with real PLCs to demonstrate generalisability across industrial vendors and environments. The results reveal high, achieving up to 98.9% and 98.7% accuracy for anomalous state and node detection, respectively.

Keywords: Cyber-Security · Anomaly Classification · Anomaly Detection · Industrial Control Systems · Machine Learning · Programmable Logic Controllers

1 Introduction

Modern society relies on the continuous operation of complex inter-dependent systems that underpin Critical National Infrastructure (CNI) sectors, such as water treatment and energy generation. The underlying *Operational Technologies (OT)* and *Industrial Control Systems (ICS)* that manage physical processes in CNI have witnessed systemic digitisation driven by the rise of Industry 4.0 and remote connectivity. Despite being such critical systems, the integration of security into ICS at design time has often been overlooked. Furthermore, increasing OT network connectivity to internet-facing networks has enabled adversaries

Published by Springer Nature Switzerland AG 2025
L. Nemec Zlatolas et al. (Eds.): SEC 2025, IFIP AICT 745, pp. 136–150, 2025.
https://doi.org/10.1007/978-3-031-92882-6_10

to conduct cyber campaigns that aim to manipulate the operations of Programmable Logic Controllers (PLCs) connected to physical apparatus. Conventional ICS attacks have involved sophisticated malware targeting specific models of PLCs [4,15]. Recent threats have indicated a change in attack vectors where adversaries use existing capabilities of ICS networks and components [8] to cause significant disruption such as attacks targeting energy infrastructure [10]. Hence, developing approaches for accurate normal behaviour and anomaly profiling is critical in enabling the detection of current and future threats.

Machine Learning (ML) models have recently been used to facilitate effective ICS anomaly detection, achieving high detection accuracy with low inference times [1,2,7]. Current state-of-the-art solutions for ICS primarily focus on detection, and lack methods for providing granular explanations with evidence of anomalous behaviours. Demonstrating the *provenance* of underlying data artefacts is one approach that can provide benefits for attack analysis and enable rapid incident triaging, ensuring the continuity of critical systems. Moreover, there are challenges with generalising data extracted from specific systems to perform normal behaviour profiling. For instance, many existing studies use sensor and actuator measurements derived from specific physical process setups [2,13], which may not be representative of other environments.

In this paper, we introduce a novel vendor-independent approach for normal behaviour profiling of PLC states to achieve effective anomaly inference and data provenance for incident analysis. We examine how PLC states that manifest from changes in memory registers can be represented as heterogeneous graphs comprising different types of data. Moreover, we define PLC state graphs to nodes as data artefacts, including memory registers and network packets extracted from industrial communication flows. We introduce the notion of *PLC Artefact Provenance Tracing* (PAPT) to model dependencies between packets of industrial network protocols to represent edges between nodes. We propose that artefact tracing can provide benefits for data provenance since connections between anomalous data artefacts can be established to assist incident analysis. Furthermore, we explore the use of a generalisable feature vector for anomaly detection by abstracting away from environment-specific measurements such as raw sensor data, and use graph centrality and clustering metrics derived from the PLC state graph structures. We evaluate the performance of anomalous state and node detection using different unsupervised ML algorithms over two physical ICS testbeds that use real PLCs controlling industrial equipment to demonstrate generalisability across different PLC networks. Our key contributions can be summarised as follows:

1. We propose a novel approach for normal behaviour profiling of PLC states through heterogeneous graph-based structures.
2. We introduce an algorithm for tracing dependencies within PLC data artefacts, including network packets to enable data provenance of anomalies.
3. We evaluate the performance of first-order graph metrics as a generalisable approach for PLC anomaly detection feature sets using real PLCs.

This paper is structured as follows. We start in Sect. 2 by presenting the state-of-the-art work and discussing the existing shortcomings. In Sect. 3 we introduce our approach for graph-based PLC artefact provenance, providing the required background and algorithmic descriptions. We then provide results and evaluations of our approach in Sect. 4, as well as the threat model. Finally, in Sect. 5 we conclude this paper and provide directions for future work.

2 Related Work

Previous research has proposed using graph-based modelling for profiling normal operational behaviour for ICS and demonstrated how ICS states can be represented as time-series automata for anomaly detection [14]. More recent work has demonstrated how spatio-temporal properties of industrial environments can be modelled with graph neural networks for effective monitoring [17]. However, the authors focus their approach on sensor and actuator data to identify anomalous equipment in the industrial process, which can be challenging to generalise to different environments. Further research has explored effective approaches for the diagnosis of different anomalous behaviours that can occur in ICS [6,7]. Conversely, our approach aims to enhance the detection process by identifying the anomalous artefacts within PLC data traces to assist with attack attribution. Hence, we demonstrate how PLC attacks are taking place rather than what specific sensors or actuators an attack is targeting. Outside of anomaly detection, graphs have previously been used to model dependencies in PLC firmware code to achieve non-intrusive vulnerability patching [16], and to represent control logic data flows for security testing [5]. Such studies demonstrate the proficiency of using graphs to establish data dependencies within ICS, however not for real-time detection. Several existing studies provide adequate solutions for ICS anomaly detection, however they are often evaluated using single types of attack such as False Data Injection (FDI) or Denial of Service (DoS) scenarios [14,18]. However, other types of attack are prominent [8] and could also provide early indicators of compromise, such as network reconnaissance attacks.

3 PLC Artefact Provenance Graphs

3.1 Multi-State Instance Formulation

PLCs are fundamental embedded components within ICS that control and monitor physical processes by interfacing with sensors and actuators. To perform these functions, PLCs use different register areas to generate dynamic variables that typically change during the operation of the physical process under control. We defined R as the super-set of registers that a PLC uses from the three common register areas used for basic PLC operations: Inputs I, Outputs Q, and Holding bits H; $R\{I, Q, H\}$. Each register area has a predefined finite number of registers assigned to it, which is determined primarily by the PLC model. We define each register area as: $I\{i_1, i_2, \ldots, i_v\}$, $Q\{q_1, q_2, \ldots, q_w\}$, $H\{h_1, h_2, \ldots, h_x\}$. All register sets I, Q, H have a subset of active (ac) and inactive (in) registers at any point in time, which we combine into single R^{ac} and R^{in} subsets, respectively:

$$R^{ac} = \{I^{ac} \frown Q^{ac} \frown H^{ac}\} \tag{1}$$

$$R^{in} = \{I^{in} \frown Q^{in} \frown H^{in}\} \tag{2}$$

The operation of an ICS and PLCs can be described using Deterministic Finite State Machines (DFSM) which models the evolution of system states. A PLC has a finite set of defined states S, which are dependent upon how the PLC has been programmed and the number of sensors and actuators connected to that PLC. We define a single PLC state s_n at time point t as a unique combination of R^{ac} and R^{in}: $s_n^t\{R^{ac} \frown R^{in}\}$. A transition of multiple PLC states is represented as $S\{s_1, s_2, \ldots, s_k\}, k \in \mathbb{N}$, where k is the number of states a particular PLC has. As industrial processes are often relatively deterministic compared to usage patters of an IT infrastructure, a PLC state is likely to be repeated over a period of time. Therefore, each manifestation of a PLC state s_n can be referred to as a *state instance* ($si \in s_n$), which represents a single occurrence of a particular *master state* $s \in S$:

$$s_1\{si_{1.1}, si_{1.2}, \ldots, si_{1.m}\}, s_2\{si_{2.1}, si_{2.2}, \ldots, si_{1.n}\} \ldots \tag{3}$$

Collecting data artefacts from multiple instances of the same state can provide more comprehensive profiling of normal behaviour for that particular state than if we only included one instance. In other words, we obtain a larger set of data samples and therefore are less likely to miss subtle conditions that exist within a state.

3.2 PLC Artefact Provenance Tracing (PAPT)

Provenance refers to the origin of data and can describe how it was generated within the wider system and network context. Enabling data provenance of anomalies can improve the subsequent triaging process by assisting root-cause analysis mechanisms and provide rapid system recovery. Hence, we establish PLC artefact provenance by examining the relationships between individual pieces of

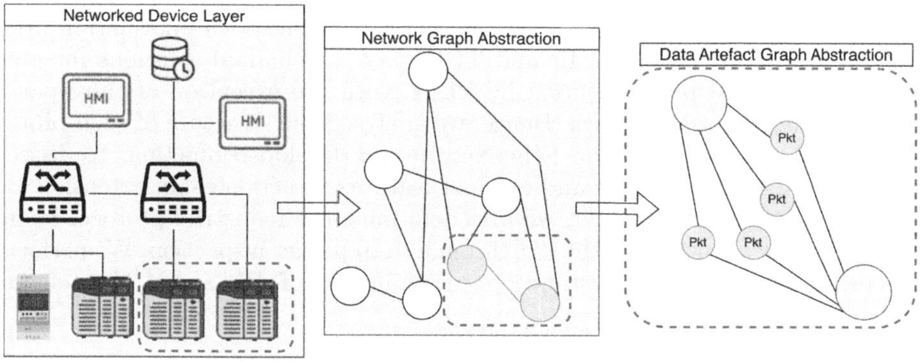

Fig. 1. Graph-based Extraction of PLC Artefacts

data either created by or sent to a target PLC as illustrated in Fig. 1 and model these relationships using graphs.

Artefact Acquisition. For each state instance, we acquire a set of related artefacts which we can define as $si_k(A\{a_1, a_2, \ldots, a_j\})$, where $si_k\{A\}$ is the full set of artefacts for one particular state instance k. To acquire data from the PLCs, we use open-source communication libraries that contain a set of defined scripts to perform data requests on PLCs using specific industrial protocols. For example, for Siemens we use the Snap7 library[1] which provides functionality to interface with Siemens PLCs running over the S7 Communication protocol, whereas for Allen-Bradley PLCs we use the PyLogix[2] library that enables data access over EtherNet/IP and the Common Industrial Protocol (CIP). To passively acquire the network traffic, we implement a packet sniffer through the Scapy Python framework to capture any packets related to the IP address of the PLC. Minimal filtering is conducted at this stage to avoid omitting packets that may be important to establishing the provenance of PLC data artefacts.

Artefact Generation. The resulting artefacts are extracted from a combination of PLC memory register vectors and network packet capture (pcap) files that are generated while that particular state instance is active. Memory register artefacts (A^{reg}) are extracted from the R^{ac} subset for each state, and include information on the register area and memory address as defined previously in Sect. 3.1. As PLC states are defined as a unique combination of $\{R^{ac}, R^{in}\}$, the set of si^{reg} for each state instance from the same master state, for example ***S1.1*** and ***S1.2*** etc., are identical. For network traces, we extract individual packets from the pcap file collected for a given state instance by matching either the source or destination IP addresses of packets to that of the target PLC. From this process, we obtain a set of packets that represents the network artefacts (A^{net}) for each state instance: $si\{pkt_1, pkt_2, \ldots, pkt_p\}$.

Subsequently, we perform packet dissection to extract key features related to each packet, including packet size (in bytes), the source and destination IP addresses, the protocol, and packet function codes that are specific to the industrial protocol. While Scapy provides functions to extract such information from generic IT protocols such as IP and TCP, there are limited solutions for proprietary industrial protocols used by PLCs, with the exception of third-party protocol parsers for Wireshark. Hence, we analysed the structure of such protocols, specifically S7Comm and EtherNet/IP and developed functions to dissect packets from these protocols and conduct feature extraction as an extension for Scapy. Therefore, for each pkt, we first determine the industrial protocol being used and subsequently pass the pkt through deep packet inspection. We perform this process for every state instance, resulting in a set of A^{reg} and A^{net} artefacts:

$$si_k(A\{A^{reg} \frown A^{net}\}) \tag{4}$$

[1] http://snap7.sourceforge.net.

[2] https://github.com/dmroeder/pylogix.

Artefact Dependency Tracing. For each artefact, we then examine its dependencies and how it related to PLC operations. We define two possible conditions for artefact dependencies, expressed in terms of distance d an artefact node a has from the associated *state node* s (root node) of a provenance graph: $d(s, a)$. A single artefact may only satisfy the properties for one of these conditions:

1. **State Dependency** ($Dep1$): $d(s, a) = 1$, where artefact a is connected to the state node s, and is the first in a sequence of one or more related artefacts, typically a data request packet or a memory register.
2. **Artefact Dependency** ($Dep2$): $d(s, a) > 1$, where the artefact generated in response to a proceeding artefact, either by the PLC or another device with a communication link to the PLC.

Algorithm 1. PLC Artefact Provenance Tracing (PAPT)

Input: Set of artefacts for single state instance $si_k\{A\}$: $A^{reg} = \{reg_1, reg_2, \ldots\}$, $A^{net} = \{pkt_1, pkt_2, \ldots\}$
Output: Set of artefact dependencies $Dep\{A^{reg}\}, Dep\{A^{net}\}$

for reg in A^{reg} **do**
  $reg \Rightarrow State$ ▷ Dependency = $Dep1$
end for
for pkt in A^{net} **do**
  if $pkt = pkt^{req}$ **then**
    $pkt \Rightarrow State$ ▷ Dependency = $Dep1$
  else if $pkt = pkt^{res}$ **then**
    for $pkt\_request$ in A^{net} **do**
      if $pkt\_request(seq\_no) = pkt(seq\_no)$ **then**
        $pkt \Rightarrow pkt\_request$ ▷ Dependency = $Dep2$
      end if
    end for
  end if
end for

For each memory register artefact $a^{reg} \in A^{reg}$, we assign the target PLC as the dependency since it is generated due to the change in PLC state. Hence, the artefact dependency is always $Dep1$. Conversely, $a^{net} \in A^{net}$ artefacts are assigned a dependency type based on the packet type and its origin within the network. For instance, a set of a^{net} artefacts may be generated from a communication link between the PLC and an HMI, where the HMI is requesting tag data from the PLC in order to display real-time measures for a particular sensor. The resulting response network packet (pkt^{res}) that contains the tag values sent to the HMI is generated as a result of the first request packet (pkt^{req}), and therefore is dependent ($\Rightarrow$) on it. Hence, we can say that $pkt_x^{res} \Rightarrow pkt_x^{req}$, indicating an artefact dependency. The process for performing artefact tracing is presented in Algorithm 1.

To achieve this, we perform deep packet inspection using the industrial protocol dissectors introduced earlier in Sect. 3.2 to obtain reference values that indicate which response packet(s) result from an initial request packet(s). For instance, packets from the S7Comm protocol contain two fields in the packet header that indicate the packet function and the sequence it belongs to. Firstly, the *Remote Operating Service Control* (ROSCTR) field value indicates whether the packet is a *job* request (0×01), or an *acknowledgement* – *data* response (0×03) containing the reply to a specific job request. Secondly, we can then extract the *Protocol Data Unit (PDU) Reference*, which is generated by the transmission creator and copied into the response. Hence, the PDU reference can be used to link packet responses to their requests. This packet tracing process can be achieved with other industrial protocols, for example EtherNet/IP by matching CIP sequence numbers, and is therefore generalisable to different PLC vendors. We will explore this further in Sect. 4.

3.3 Artefact Provenance Graph Representation

We generate a provenance graph for each PLC state using artefacts and dependencies derived from the PAPT process. Therefore, we define a PLC provenance graph as a heterogeneous undirected graph G_t comprising a 3-tuple of $\{S,A,E\}$ extracted at time t where: S is the state as defined in Sect. 3.1, with each *state node* representing a root vertex in the graph. Vertices (A) are the set of artefact nodes defined in Sect. 3.2, where node $a \in A$ can be either a memory register or network packet. We define E as the set of edges that represent dependencies between artefact nodes; $E\{e_1, e_2, \ldots, e_l\}$, which are determined through the PAPT process. An artefact node a_n is embedded with a set of features B and dependency edges E: $A\{B, D\}$ where $E\{e_1, e_2, \ldots, e_l\}$ is a set of relations between $a^1 \in A$ and $s \in S$ or $a^2 \in A$.

3.4 Anomaly Detection

The anomaly detection process comprises two phases: i) *State detection*, and ii) *Node detection*. In this paper, we specifically explore how graph-based metrics can be derived from PLC state formulations as a generalisable approach to detect anomalies. Hence, for each state and individual artefact node within a provenance graph, we calculate a series of centrality graph measurements that describes how each node is related to other nodes. These measurements are then embedded within graph nodes as detection features.

Anomalous State Detection. We firstly employ an ML novelty detection algorithm for state detection that uses general features derived from network traces in synergy with the graph-based metrics extracted from the provenance graphs of each individual state instance. We train the detector model with only normal operating behaviour since the aim is to detect whether a new sample is an outlier. Novelty detection has particular advantages in the context of ICS as generating datasets comprising of both normal and abnormal data, such as attack data points, is much more challenging due to the safety and availability requirements of the underlying physical processes that could be impacted when generating such data.

Anomalous Node Detection. While state detection aims to detect anomalous states using aggregated measurements, node detection is used to identify individual anomalous data artefacts. For each state instance, we generate a set of network and memory register artefacts which have a combination of artefact-specific and graph-based features, similar to state instances. The key aim of node detection is to provide greater granularity for data provenance by indicating the anomalous artefacts related to a state.

4 Evaluation

4.1 Threat Model

Our threat model focuses on attack scenarios targeting PLCs. The attacks assume an adversary position of either an outsider who has gained remote access to the control network through exploited credentials as seen in previous real-world ICS cyber attacks [15], or an insider who already has legitimate access to the engineering workstations. We therefore make the following assumptions, all of which are plausible based on observations of existing ICS cyber threats:

- The attacker has no prior knowledge of the physical process, however they have performed reconnaissance to identify specific PLC models.
- The attacker can access the engineering workstation that has a physical connection to the PLC network.

Table 1. PLC Attack Scenarios with related ICS MITRE attack techniques [3] used for each test scenario

Attack Type	ICS MITRE Technique(s)
A_1 Reconnaissance scan attack	I/O Image, Network Connection Enumeration, Network Sniffing, Remote System Discovery
A_2 Random PLC register manipulation	Brute Force I/O
A_3 Targeted PLC register manipulation	I/O Image, Brute Force I/O
A_4 Man in the middle	Network Sniffing, Denial of Service, Block Command Message, Block Response Message

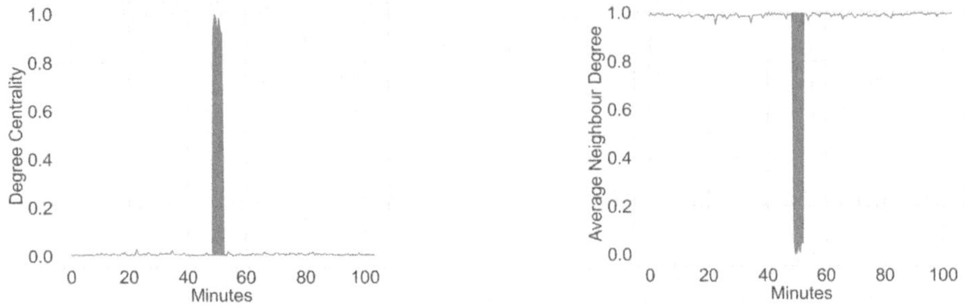

(a) Degree Centrality (b) Average neighbour degree

Fig. 2. Time-series detection of PLC attacks based on graph metrics. Highlighted areas indicate attack period after approx. 45 minutes of normal operating behaviour.

Based on these assumptions, we define four PLC attack scenarios, summarised in Table 1. To develop the attacks, we used the MITRE ICS attack framework [3] to construct generalisable PLC attack vectors using techniques extrapolated from existing real world ICS cyber attacks. For instance, many of the attack techniques we used have been identified in the recent Pipedream [8] and FrotyGoop [10] attacks.

4.2 Experiment Setup and Datasets

While there are several publicly available ICS dataset repositories, these primarily provide process measurement data extracted from sensors and actuators, and do not contain PLC memory register data. Hence, we generated our own datasets using two representative physical ICS testbeds comprising real PLCs and industrial equipment. These ICS testbeds represent different CNI use-cases; specifically a water treatment facility through the Glasgow University Liquid Purification (GULP) testbed, and a Motor Cooling System emulation (MCSys). Apart from the physical process being controlled, the key differences between these testbeds are the PLC models used and the size of the industrial network. GULP contains a Siemens S7-300 and a Rockwell Allen-Bradley ControlLogix (AB-CLX), hence enabling us to evaluate the generalisability of our approach. Conversely, the MCSys testbed comprises multiple Siemens S7-1200 PLCs.

4.3 State Detection Performance

We first evaluate how PLC attacks manifest perturbations within the underlying graph-based metrics derived from PLC states. An initial experiment was performed on the GULP testbed in which the S7-300 PLC was targeted with a register manipulation attack. The results demonstrated how centrality graph measurements can deviate from a known-good baseline over time during anomalous behaviour. The time-series plots in Fig. 2 illustrate approximately 45 minutes of normal behaviour before the attack scenario is performed over several minutes

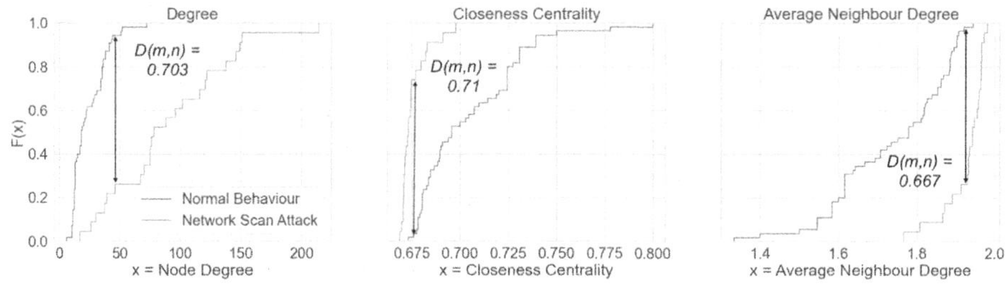

(a) PLC Scan Attack (A_1)

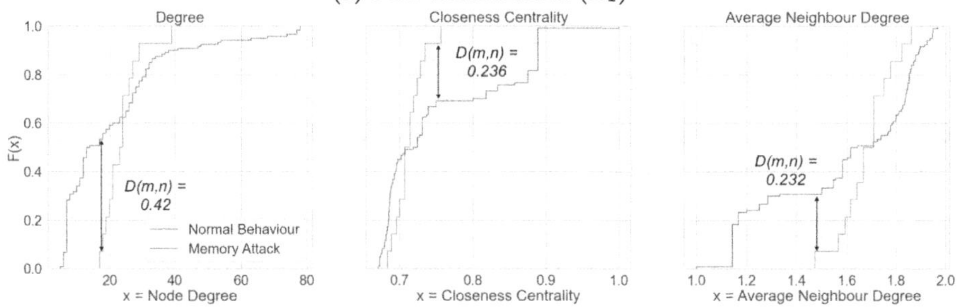

(b) Register Manipulation Attack (aggregated from A_2 and A_3.

Fig. 3. Cumulative Distribution Functions (CDFs) of graph-based metrics for different attack types compared with normal behaviour demonstrating that individual graph features can differentiate attacks.

that causes substantial deviations in degree centrality and average neighbour degree measurements, respectively. These deviations are caused because the state graph comprises additional node clusters generated from an increase in network packets that would not exist under normal operation. Moreover, the increase in degree centrality is caused by a higher number of nodes within the graph, whereas the decrease in average neighbour degree is a result of an imbalance of increased edges to the state node. Specifically, as the number of packets connected to a state graph increases, the average number of connections decreases since the degree of the state node does not substantially increase. This is an effect of the PAPT process introduced earlier in Sect. 3.2 where packets that are part of the same communication flow are linked through packet session identifiers.

To evaluate the probability that graph metrics deviations will result from attacks, we examine the Cumulative Distribution Functions (CDFs)for normal and attack data. A two-sample Kolmogorov-Smirnov (K-S) statistical test is used to quantify the distances ($D(m, n)$) between the resulting CDFs for normal behaviour (F_1) and attacks (F_2) for each graph metric feature (x), where m and n are the number of observations in F_1 and F_2, respectively.

We identified that perturbations from different attack types can be differentiated from normal behaviour, demonstrated by the K-S distances ($D_{m,n}$) presented for each graph in Fig. 3. However, the suitability for using graph-based metrics for PLC anomaly detection depends on the attack type taking place. For

Table 2. F1 scores of attack scenarios detected for each PLC using two different novelty detection algorithms for a 10 s sample rate (A_1 - A_4 are the four attack scenarios defined earlier in Table 1).

	Isolation Forest			Local Outlier Factor		
Attack	S7-300	S7-1200	ABCLX	S7-300	S7-1200	ABCLX
A_1	0.95	0.99	0.95	0.95	0.95	0.94
A_2	0.92	0.98	0.98	0.90	0.95	0.94
A_3	0.95	0.98	0.99	0.91	0.94	0.95
A_4	0.98	0.96	0.95	0.99	0.98	0.92
Avg.	0.95	0.98	0.97	0.94	0.96	0.94

Table 3. Comparison with existing ICS anomaly detection approaches (* indicates an average score over multiple tests).

Approach	Tabor [14]	SCAPHY* [12]	SensitiveHUE [9]	*Our Work**
F1 Score	0.823	0.872	0.968	0.957

instance, we see in Fig. 3a that the distance ($D_{m,n}$) between normal and abnormal behaviour during a network scan attack for all three graph measurements is greater than for a memory register manipulation attack shown in Fig. 3b. As an example, the Closeness Centrality measurement demonstrates $D_{m,n} = 0.71$ for scan attacks compared with 0.236 for memory manipulation attacks, indicating that the latter attacks are more easily detected.

We evaluate the performance of unsupervised attack detection when using such measurements in synergy. Two popular outlier detection algorithms are used as unsupervised ML novelty detectors, Isolation Forest (IF) and Local Outlier Factor (LOF), where only normal behaviour is used during model training. Both IF and LOF are particularly suited to training data comprising fully of normal operating behaviour, which is advantageous within the context of ICS since obtaining abnormal data, for instance attack samples, is practically challenging in real systems. The results presented in Table 2 demonstrate that both IF and LOF models perform well, achieving over 0.90 F1 score in most cases. Furthermore, the F1 detection scores are also reasonably consistent and stable across different PLC models and attack types, indicating that graph-based metrics can provide a generalisable feature set that abstract from the configuration of specific systems. The IF model outperforms LOF in almost all like-for-like cases, likely because IF is more suitable for detecting global outliers cause by the deviation in anomalous state behaviours when compared to normal behaviour.

In Table 3 we compare our approach with existing state-of-the-art ICS anomaly detection literature. The results demonstrate that the PAPT algorithm achieves performance that is competitive and in most cases outperforms similar solutions. Most existing approaches are evaluated using the SWaT dataset

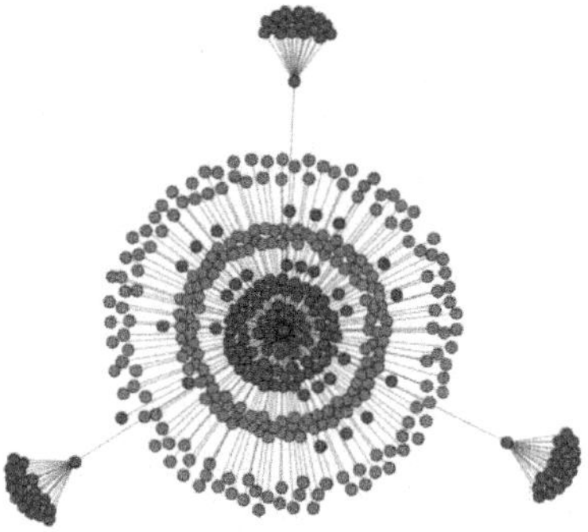

(a) Network scan attack (A_1)

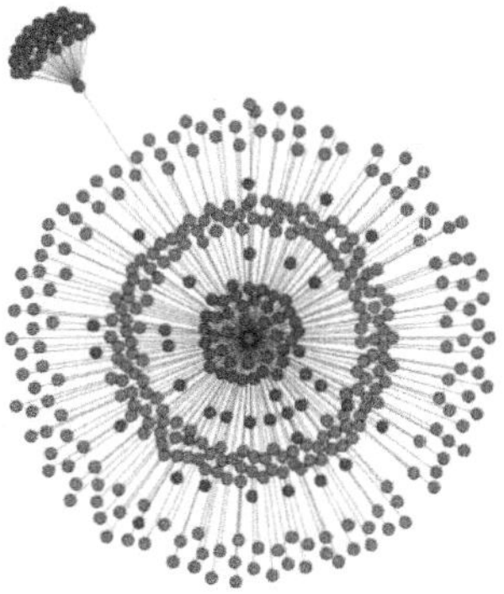

(b) Memory manipulation attack (A_3)

Fig. 4. Artefact Provenance graphs demonstrating baseline and attacks on S7-1200 PLC where anomalous artefact nodes are highlighted red as a result of node detection

Table 4. Accuracy and F1 scores for anomalous node detection using datasets collected with a 10 s sample rate - here we do not include attack scenario A_4 since no anomalous nodes are induced and the graph becomes sparse.

		Isolation Forest			Local Outlier Factor		
PLC Model		A_1	A_2	A_3	A_1	A_2	A_3
S7-300	*Acc*	0.964	0.981	0.963	0.91	0.931	0.841
	F1	0.979	0.984	0.973	0.944	0.957	0.899
S7-1200	*Acc*	0.936	0.945	0.933	0.984	0.987	0.985
	F1	0.904	0.820	0.814	0.952	0.981	0.933
AB-CLX	*Acc*	0.711	0.691	0.716	0.637	0.712	0.772
	F1	0.795	0.749	0.787	0.744	0.862	0.822

[11] which includes both network and sensor measurement data extracted from the physical process. In comparison, we focus on network traffic features which we believe can detect a wider range of ICS threats, such as network scanning attacks.

4.4 Node Detection Performance

The second phase of detection identifies the data artefacts that are associated with the anomalous state behaviour of the PLC. Figure 4 illustrates two example artefact provenance graphs generated from anomalous states of the S7-1200 PLC that visually demonstrate anomalous artefact nodes. Artefacts are clustered together based on their similarity determined by the dependencies extracted through the PAPT process. Anomalous network packet nodes typically cluster tightly around the root state node in the centre of the graph and connect to dendrite-like clusters containing packets from the same network flow.

To evaluate node detection accuracy we used the same ML models as state detection, however with different hyper-parameter optimisations. We can see from the results presented in Table 4 that there is greater variation of performance, particularly between PLC models. The Siemens S7-300 and S7-1200 models generally perform well achieving high F1 and accuracy scores across all attack types, including low false positive and negative rates of $<1\%$ and $<0.26\%$, respectively. However, performance drops significantly for AB-CLX PLC, particularly with the LOF model. We attribute this reduction in performance to the sensitivity of the ML models and the size of the AB-CLX network compared to the other PLCs that generate larger volumes of traffic. It is important to note that the lower performance is generally due to misclassification of normal traffic, resulting in high quantities of false positives rather than false negatives, which would mean that attacks were potentially being missed.

5 Conclusions

There are challenges with the analysis of ICS cyber attacks with limited existing approaches addressing the provenance of anomalous data artefacts. In this paper, we introduced a novel vendor-independent approach for normal behaviour profiling to enable anomaly inference and data provenance of PLC attacks. We proposed a method for establishing dependencies between data artefacts that are generated through PLC states, represented by graph structures. Extensive evaluations over different ICS testbeds using multiple PLC models achieve high F1 scores over 0.98 for anomaly detection based on deviations in state behaviours. Moreover, we demonstrated that our approach can accurately identify individual data artefacts that contribute to anomalous state behaviour, enabling the triaging of cyber incidents. We identified how graph-based metrics can be used as effective and generalisable features for ML-based anomaly detection models.

For future work, a natural step is for us to consider extending the proposed approach to use Graph Neural Networks (GNNs) to improve node detection performance. We anticipate that GNNs will efficiently handle larger graph structures and identify more subtle changes in graph structure compared with classical ML algorithms. Furthermore, we will investigate the logical and network interdependencies between different industrial components such as PLCs, to establish more comprehensive network graphs to detect more sophisticated attack scenarios.

Acknowledgements. This work was supported by the Royal Academy of Engineering under grant number RCSRF2223-1645, Dstl under order number DSTL 0000014002 and EDF under order number 4840659490, UK Engineering and Physical Research Sciences Research Council (EPSRC) under reference EP/Z533221/1, and UK Research and Innovation (UKRI) under reference 10091225.

References

1. Ahmed, C.M., Ochoa, M., Zhou, J., Mathur, A.: Scanning the cycle: timing-based authentication on PLCs, pp. 886–900. Association for Computing Machinery, New York, NY, USA (2021)
2. Ahmed, C.M., Prakash, J., Qadeer, R., Agrawal, A., Zhou, J.: Process skew: fingerprinting the process for anomaly detection in industrial control systems. In: Proceedings of the 13th ACM Conference on Security and Privacy in Wireless and Mobile Network, pp. 219–230. WiSec '20, Association for Computing Machinery, New York, NY, USA (2020)
3. Alexander, O., Belisle, M., Steele, J.: Mitre Att&ck® for Industrial Control Systems: Design and Philosophy. The MITRE Corporation, Bedford, MA, USA (2020)
4. Arora, P., Kaur, B., Teixeira, M.A.: Security in industrial control systems using machine learning algorithms: an overview. In: Fong, S., Dey, N., Joshi, A. (eds.) ICT Analysis and Applications, pp. 359–368. Springer Nature Singapore, Singapore (2022)
5. Castellanos, J.H., Ochoa, M., Zhou, J.: Finding dependencies between cyber-physical domains for security testing of industrial control systems. In: Proceedings of the 34th Annual Computer Security Applications Conference, pp. 582–594. ACSAC '18, Association for Computing Machinery, New York, NY, USA (2018)
6. Cook, M., Patterson, C., Marnerides, A.K., Pezaros, D.: Anomaly diagnosis in cyber-physical systems. In: IEEE ICC. IEEE, Seoul, South Korea (2022)
7. Cook, M.M., Marnerides, A.K., Pezaros, D.: PLCPrint: fingerprinting memory attacks in programmable logic controllers. IEEE Trans. Inf. Forensics Secur. **18**, 3376–3387 (2023)
8. Dragos: Pipedream: Chernovite's emerging malware targeting industrial control systems. Tech. rep., Dragos, Inc. (2022)
9. Feng, Y., Zhang, W., Fu, Y., Jiang, W., Zhu, J., Ren, W.: Sensitivehue: multivariate time series anomaly detection by enhancing the sensitivity to normal patterns. In: Proceedings of the 30th ACM SIGKDD Conference on Knowledge Discovery and Data Mining, pp. 782–793 (2024)
10. Forscout Research: "ICS malware 'FrostyGoop/BUSTLEBERM': Insights others missed" (2024). https://www.forescout.com/blog/ics-malware-frostygoopbustleberm-insights-others-missed/
11. Goh, J., Adepu, S., Junejo, K.N., Mathur, A.: A dataset to support research in the design of secure water treatment systems. In: Havarneanu, G., Setola, R., Nassopoulos, H., Wolthusen, S. (eds.) Critical Information Infrastructures Security, pp. 88–99. Springer International Publishing, Cham (2017)
12. Ike, M., Phan, K., Sadoski, K., Valme, R., Lee, W.: Scaphy: detecting modern ics attacks by correlating behaviors in scada and physical. In: 2023 IEEE Symposium on Security and Privacy (SP), pp. 20–37. IEEE (2023)
13. Kim, B., Alawami, M.A., Kim, E., Oh, S., Park, J., Kim, H.: A comparative study of time series anomaly detection models for industrial control systems. Sensors **23**(3), 1310 (2023)
14. Lin, Q., Adepu, S., Verwer, S., Mathur, A.: Tabor: a graphical model-based approach for anomaly detection in industrial control systems. In: Proceedings of the 2018 on Asia Conference on Computer and Communications Security, pp. 525–536 (2018)
15. Miller, T., Staves, A., Maesschalck, S., Sturdee, M., Green, B.: Looking back to look forward: lessons learnt from cyber-attacks on industrial control systems. Int. J. Crit. Infrastruct. Prot. **35**, 100464 (2021)

16. Rajput, P.H.N., Doumanidis, C., Maniatakos, M.: {ICSPatch}: automated vulnerability localization and {Non-Intrusive} hotpatching in industrial control systems using data dependence graphs. In: 32nd USENIX Security Symposium, pp. 6861–6876 (2023)
17. Wang, Y., Peng, H., Wang, G., Tang, X., Wang, X., Liu, C.: Monitoring industrial control systems via spatio-temporal graph neural networks. Eng. Appl. Artif. Intell. **122**, 106144 (2023)
18. Yang, K., Li, Q., Lin, X., Chen, X., Sun, L.: iFinger: intrusion detection in industrial control systems via register-based fingerprinting. IEEE J. Sel. Areas Commun. **38**(5), 955–967 (2020)

Certified Secure Updates for IoT Devices

Alberto Tacchella(✉), Emanuele Beozzo, Bruno Crispo, and Marco Roveri

Università degli studi di Trento, Trento, Italy
{alberto.tacchella,emanuele.beozzo,bruno.crispo,marco.roveri}@unitn.it

Abstract. Current firmware update workflows are geared towards ensuring integrity and confidentiality in the face of untrusted servers mediating the communication process. However, they cannot ensure that the update's content preserves deployment-specific security properties, potentially allowing vulnerabilities or malicious code if third-party components compromise or alter the firmware. There is also no guarantee that the new firmware retains the old one's security properties, a crucial requirement in safety-critical environments. We propose an enhancement of the SUIT standard which ensures that software updates preserve a formally-specified set of behavioral properties in the affected components. We demonstrate the feasibility of the proposed workflow in some realistic use cases.

Keywords: Secure Update · IoT Security · Firmware Distribution · Formal Methods

1 Introduction

Internet-of-Things (IoT) devices are becoming increasingly prevalent in modern infrastructure, with applications spanning from industrial automation to safety critical systems like autonomous transportation and smart grids. The native software stack running on these devices (often referred to as *firmware*) must be updated regularly to introduce new functionalities or to address existing bugs and vulnerabilities. The security of the firmware update process is critical as it can become a potential attack vector, especially if weak verification mechanisms are employed. As many recent surveys have revealed (e.g. [25]), it is very common to find IoT devices in the wild that lack a secure firmware update system. The recently approved EU Cyber Resilience Act [23] highlights the significance of this issue, including remote update capabilities as a strict requirement for device manufacturers wishing to sell in the EU market after 2027.

In this context, the IETF Software Updates for Internet of Things (SUIT) Working Group proposed a new standard [20] to enhance the security of software updates for IoT devices. In the SUIT framework, an Fiemware Author (FA)

Published by Springer Nature Switzerland AG 2025
L. Nemec Zlatolas et al. (Eds.): SEC 2025, IFIP AICT 745, pp. 151–165, 2025.
https://doi.org/10.1007/978-3-031-92882-6_11

generates an update package consisting, for example, of a firmware image with the device's operating system and application containing the core functionality of the IoT device. The FA then uploads the package to a Firmware Server (FS), which distributes it to affected devices using over-the-air (OTA) or wired technologies. The SUIT process is carefully designed to ensure the integrity and confidentiality of the updates, guaranteeing end-to-end security from the FA to the device, even when an untrusted FS is involved. However, there are no guarantees about the impact that the update may have on the existing security and safety properties of the installed firmware. This limitation means that authentic and bug-free image updates can unintentionally introduce violations to the security policies regulating the software installed on a specific device. Recent incidents that involved major players such as ASUS, HP and Siemens[1], show striking examples of this risk.

In this paper we address this problem by means of the following contributions. First, we propose an extension of the SUIT standard architecture that integrates within the SUIT manifest [19] a list of formal proofs, which we call the *Behavioral Certification Manifest* (BCM). Each proof in the BCM attests that the update does not violate a corresponding security or behavioral property. Examples of relevant properties are the correctness of the configuration parameters and conditions on the control flow of the updated binaries to ensure that an attacker has not injected calls to malicious functions.

Second, we extend the SUIT update workflow to take into account the new addition to the update manifest. The new flow requires first extracting the BCM from the SUIT manifest and checking whether the proofs contained in it are valid and comply with the security policy adopted by the device. If verification of any proof fails, the update is rejected; otherwise, the update is installed. To take into account the possibly limited computation resources of the IoT device, the revision considers two approaches for the verification of the proofs: directly on the device, or delegated to a trusted verification server.

Third, we consider in detail two broad classes of behavioral properties: *correctness of configuration parameters*, and *binary instrumentation enforcement*. For each property, we provide an encoding into a Satisfiability Modulo Theory (SMT) problem [5], to enable for the verification and generation of a proof certificate whose validity can be subsequently checked with third party proof checkers. This approach does not necessarily require the source code and, therefore, can also be applied to third-party libraries available only in binary.

Finally, to demonstrate the applicability of the proposed framework, we developed a prototype implementation that uses the cvc5 SMT solver and its proof extraction capabilities [2]. The prototype has been validated on several standard real-world benchmarks taken from the literature to demonstrate the feasibility of the approach and assess its scalability. The results show that the approach can be successfully applied to real use cases of different sizes.

The paper is organized as follows. Section 2 contains a brief review of the existing research literature on the topic, highlighting the differences with our

[1] See CVE-2021-3166, CVE-2024-2209, and CVE-2024-39872, respectively.

approach. Section 3 describes the main points of the SUIT standard and its limitations. Section 4 explains the high-level architecture of the present proposal, including a detailed workflow for the update generation and installation phases. Section 5 discusses in detail the two classes of behavioral properties described above. Section 6 describes our implementation and reports on its performance evaluation. Finally, Sect. 7 provides some concluding remarks.

2 Related Work

This section offers a brief survey of the existing literature on secure update proposals, focusing in particular on *over-the-air* and *general-purpose* approaches (i.e., excluding the proposals which are designed to work only in specific settings, like sensor networks or the automotive domain). The reader may consult [12, 16] for more comprehensive reviews on the topic.

The Update Framework (TUF) [24] provides an open source specification for OTA updates that focuses in particular on key security issues. However, this approach does not seem adequate for resource-constrained IoT devices. Chandra et al. [8] present an OTA update system that provides a low-power mesh protocol, route discovery, and route establishment. The solution is based on the Lightweight Mesh network protocol (LWMesh) over a peer-to-peer mesh architecture (P2PMesh). However, in addition to the proprietary aspect, the proposal ignores the security aspects. Doddapaneni et al. [10] propose an OTA update scheme for IoT devices based on a secure object format called Firmware Object Signing and Encryption (FOSE). The main goal is to solve the problems of integrity and security. However, the paper addresses only the case where there is an intermediary application between the end-device and the device manager. Asokan et al. [1] design an architecture (ASSURED) for a secure update framework of realistic embedded devices. The proposal is an enhancement of the TUF architecture and adopts the same terminology as proposed by the SUIT Working Group. However, the authors do not take into account the scalability issues when dealing with hundreds of IoT devices (for instance, to guarantee the attestation of update installation) and the case of very constrained devices. The UpKit proposal [17] is a lightweight and portable software update framework for restricted IoT devices that aims to cover all phases of the update process, from generation to installation. This scheme guarantees the freshness and integrity of the firmware image, but does not cover the functional properties of the deployed update. Giarretta et al. [13, 14] propose a *security by contract* framework (S×C4IoT) which allows to formally bind a behavioral description of a device to its firmware. In their scheme, the proof verification step is performed by the network each time a new device joins it, whereas we also envisage the possibility of executing this step directly on device. Finally, the *IoT Application Verification* (IoTAV) framework of Dejon et al. [9] is a security analysis toolchain for (binary) software updates based on the ANGR binary analysis tool (to extract the Control Flow Graph from a binary image) and the PRISM probabilistic model checker (to analyse whether the generated CFG is compliant with some specified security policy, expressed in terms of sequences of API calls). Our approach is more general, in that we take into account any behavioral property which is amenable to formal verification; furthermore, the IoTAV framework also does not consider the possibility of performing proof verification locally.

3 Background

Currently, there is no consensus on a standard for firmware updates in the IoT world [7]. Many solutions have been proposed, with various use cases and scenarios in mind. In industry practice, different manufacturers follow different approaches depending on their tools, infrastructures, and strategies [12].

3.1 The SUIT Standard

The IETF Software Updates for Internet of Things (SUIT) working group has developed an Internet standard, described in RFC 9019 [20], for a new firmware update architecture that uses state-of-the-art security and can be deployed even on devices with very limited resources. The architecture is based on a metadata structure, known as the *manifest*, which is sent to the devices affected by the update. The information contained in the manifest is used for authentication and authorization purposes, to retrieve and validate the new firmware image, and to fulfill any other requirement that the process might have. The architecture is designed to be flexible enough to be applied in many situations, but at the same time can be made robust with regard to functionality and security. An information model for the SUIT manifest has been described in RFC 9124 [18], and a proposal for a concrete encoding scheme is currently in an advanced draft stage [19]. Moreover, the standard allows for possible extensions to the manifest in order to implement optional capabilities, including firmware encryption, trust domains, update management, inclusion of a Manufacturer Usage Description (MUD) specification, and secure methods for a device to report on the firmware update status.

The architecture of the SUIT update process involves four main components:

- an IoT device, or more specifically, a component inside the device that needs to receive the firmware update, called the **Firmware Consumer** (FC);
- a **Firmware Server** (FS) that can store manifests and firmware images and make them available upon request;
- a **Status Tracker Server** (STS) that keeps track of software and hardware information about each device on the network and the availability of updates;
- a **Status Tracker Client** (STC) running on the IoT device and communicating with the Status Tracker Server.

The update process can be triggered by the STS (push mode) as soon as a new firmware image is available or by the STC (pull mode) by periodically querying the server. Once the update is initiated, the FC receives the manifest and must validate the signature to confirm its authenticity. Then the FC must parse the manifest to verify the validity of the update, identify if it applies to the device, and perform the required integrity checks. The manifest can also specify how to perform the update, where to store the firmware, and so on. Finally, the firmware image is fetched depending on the device's capabilities; it can be downloaded using a URI in the manifest, embedded in the manifest itself, or delivered through physical means. The obtained image is then verified and installed according to the instructions contained in the manifest.

3.2 Limitations of SUIT

The SUIT workflow has been designed to enforce the integrity and confidentiality of the software update even if an untrusted server mediates the process. This ensures end-to-end security between the Firmware Author and the device. However, it provides no guarantees on the effective content of the update.

For instance, there is no mechanism to prevent the distribution of a firmware image containing security vulnerabilities or malicious behaviors unbeknownst to the Firmware Author. This opens the door to any scenario in which an attack is carried out by injecting malicious software components inside the firmware, either directly at the source level, as in recent xzutils backdooring attempt (CVE-2024-3094), or by tampering with a third-party binary-only component linked by the firmware. In the same vein, there is no mechanism to ensure that the new firmware preserves the same security properties as the old one. This is particularly relevant in safety-critical settings, where an update can introduce a new functionality that impacts a security or behavioral policy imposed on the software running on the device (see Sect. 5 for an example of such a scenario).

To address these limitations, we propose an extension of the SUIT standard that provides a mechanism to guarantee the preservation of the behavioral properties of a software component that is subject to an update and runs on a specific device, with a solid foundation based on the usage of formal verification methods. Our proposal can be seen as an instantiation of the seminal *Proof-Carrying Code* scheme [22], adapted to the specific setting of firmware updates targeting resource-constrained devices subject to strict behavioral policies.

4 Proposed Architecture

This Section describes the architecture of our proposal in detail. The Behavioral Certification Manifest is defined in Subsect. 4.1, while detailed workflows for the update generation and installation phases are presented in Subsect. 4.2. Finally, in Subsect. 4.3 the algorithm for proof verification is discussed.

4.1 Extensions to the SUIT Information Model

To describe our extensions to the SUIT manifest, we adopt the same terminology as in RFC 9124, which defines the information model for the original SUIT

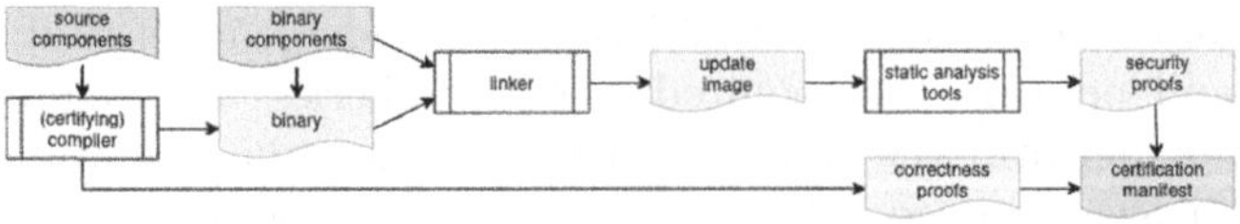

Fig. 1. Workflow for the generation of the Behavioral Certification Manifest.

manifest; therefore, we speak of *manifest information elements*, leaving their concrete encoding to be determined by the particular data model adopted.

We propose a new required information element, the **Behavioral Certification Manifest** (BCM), containing a structured list of formal properties satisfied by the contents of the update package, together with the corresponding proof certificates that allow the device to directly verify the validity of such properties before performing the update. We shall distinguish between a *proof certificate*, which is a textual representation of a formal proof written in some specific formal language [3], and a *proof descriptor*, which is a data structure that encapsulates a proof certificate together with all the information needed to verify it.

The BCM consists of a list of proof descriptors. Each proof descriptor is a record consisting of the following elements:

- A **property identifier**, which is used to uniquely identify the formal property to which the proof descriptor refers. Each property identifier must appear only once in the BCM.
- A list of **component identifiers**, used to select which components affected by the update are targeted by the considered proof. Each element of this list must match the identifier of a corresponding software component affected by the update, as defined in the basic SUIT standard.
- A **language identifier**, which is used to specify the formal language in which the proof is expressed. By requiring each proof descriptor to define the language used in the corresponding proof, our proposal can remain fully agnostic about the tools used to generate proof certificates.
- The **proof certificate** itself, expressed in the formal language designated by the language identifier.
- A **locality constraint**, a Boolean flag that, when set, enforces the proof verification step to be performed on the device. This possibility can be useful for sufficiently powerful devices that have no or very restricted access to the Internet, or when a verification server cannot be set up in a trusted way.
- A list of suggested **verification servers**. Each element is the URI of an external server that can be queried to verify the associated proof certificate. Again, specifying the servers on a proof-by-proof basis is useful because some languages and/or proof techniques may be supported only by some of the available backends. This list is meant to be advisory only; the owner of the device can always opt for a trusted server of his choice when it is available.

Proof certificates can be generated at two different stages: directly from the update source code (when available), by means of a *certifying compiler* [21] (see

[6] for an application of the concept to embedded systems), or alternatively at the binary image level using *static analysis tools* [11]. In Sect. 5 we discuss some examples of behavioral properties and how to verify them.

4.2 Update Workflows

This subsection describes in more detail the proposed workflow for update generation and update delivery.

Update Generation. The workflow for generating the BCM is shown in Fig. 1. The Firmware Author (FA) starts by compiling the source code of the update, if it is available, possibly using a certifying compiler. The results of this step are a binary image and zero or more proof certificates generated by the compilation process. The compiled binary is then linked together with every other component whose sources are either not available or not under the control of the FA. The resulting binary image is then subject to the appropriate static analysis tools such as model checkers [15], which generate further proof certificates to be bundled with the update. Finally, all proof artifacts are collected in the BCM, and the corresponding proof descriptors are populated accordingly (as described in Subsect. 4.1).

Once the BCM is ready, the FA adds it to the regular SUIT manifest, along with all other metadata necessary for the update process. The manifest is then signed and packaged with any other payload (including the binary image, in case it should be distributed together with the manifest) to create the SUIT envelope. Finally, the FA sends the envelope to the Firmware Server, in order to enable distribution of the update, and notifies the Status Tracker Server of the availability of the update.

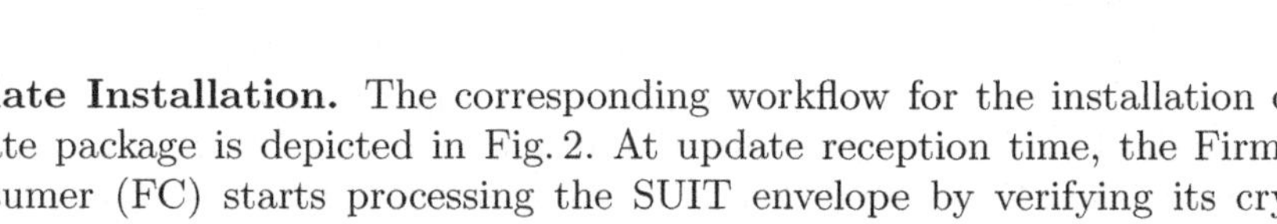

Fig. 2. Workflow for update installation.

Update Installation. The corresponding workflow for the installation of an update package is depicted in Fig. 2. At update reception time, the Firmware Consumer (FC) starts processing the SUIT envelope by verifying its cryptographic signature. If this basic integrity check passes, the FC can proceed further and extract the manifest itself and the integrated firmware image (if present). Then the FC extracts the formal proofs packaged in the manifest and verifies them one by one by feeding each proof to an appropriate proof checker. This step can either be performed directly on the device (if the available resources allow it) or offloaded to an external server, as described in the next subsection. If any of the proofs fails to verify, the update is rejected. If all the proofs are successfully verified, the FC can proceed with the regular SUIT installation workflow, either using the binary image embedded in the update envelope or fetching it from the URI specified in the manifest.

When an update is rejected as invalid, an appropriate notification must be sent to the Status Tracker Server and to any relevant authority in charge of the update process. In particular, the device owner is expected to register a way to receive notifications about the results of the update. These notifications must contain both the identifier of the component/property whose proof certificate check failed, and the reason for the failure (e.g. vulnerable component, bad proof certificate, server timeout, etc.).

4.3 Checking Proof Certificates

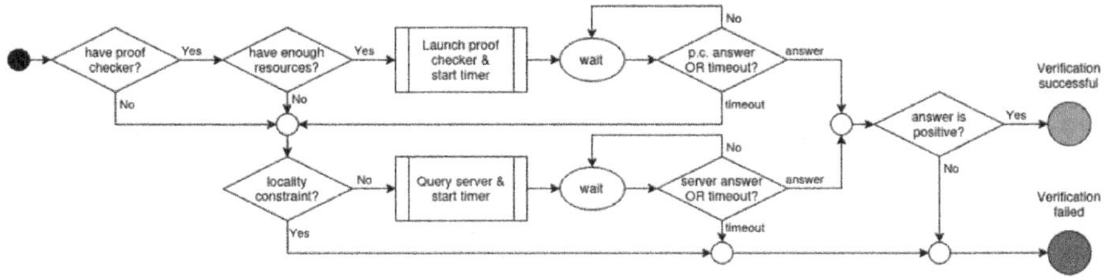

Fig. 3. Workflow for the verification of a single proof.

Figure 3 shows the suggested activity diagram for the verification of each proof contained in the BCM. The task can be decomposed into the following steps. First, the Firmware Consumer must decide whether it can perform the check locally or not. To do it, the following two conditions must be met: 1. a proof checker for the formal language selected by the language identifier field in the corresponding proof descriptor must be locally available, and 2. the device must have sufficient resources to perform the check. The second condition involves both the current state of the device and the characteristics of the proof certificate. For instance, the check could be as simple as verifying that the available memory is greater than the size of the proof certificate multiplied by a fixed constant (to be chosen using some appropriate heuristics, perhaps involving the formal language used and/or the kind of property which must be verified).

If the check can proceed locally, the appropriate proof checker is launched and a timer is set. If the proof checker terminates within the chosen time bound, its answer is processed and the corresponding action is taken; otherwise the proof checker process is killed. If the local verification is not successful, there is still the possibility of checking the proof using a remote server, assuming that this has been allowed by the update author (i.e., the locality constraint flag is not set). In this case, the FC queries either a known server or one of the remote server(s) specified by the proof descriptor itself and waits for the result. Again, the process should abort if the answer does not arrive within a given time limit, which now should also take into account network latency effects.

5 Generating Behavioral Certification Artifacts

Behavioral properties aim to formally specify which properties are expected to hold about the contents of the update. These properties can concern the safety, security, or other behavioral aspects of the object component. In this Section, we consider two broad classes of examples of behavioral properties that are amenable to a formal verification process. In each case, we show how to formally specify such properties, how to check them on a given program (either in source code or object code form), and how to produce a *behavioral certification artifact* that witnesses the truth of that property.

5.1 Static Checking of Configuration Parameters

In many applications, especially in IoT and embedded settings, a firmware may depend on a set of statically determined *configuration parameters* describing, for instance, memory maps, partitioning of resources, and so on. The correctness of these parameters can be checked at compile time by defining a formal specification for the allowed values of these parameters as a Satisfiability Modulo Theory (SMT) formula [5], whose validity is then verified by an SMT solver as part of the compilation pipeline. The resulting proof certificate can be used as a guarantee of the correctness of the configuration deployed by the update.

As a paradigmatic example of this kind of property, consider a firmware defining a *memory map* that partitions the device memory into a certain number of regions $R_1, \ldots, R_n$, which are required to be disjoint (non-interference condition). Every configuration that does not meet this criterion must be rejected at compilation time. In order to formalize this requirement, suppose that the configuration parameters defining each memory region are contained in an array $\mathsf{regions}$ whose elements are records containing two unsigned integer fields start and end (with $\mathsf{start} < \mathsf{end}$) that specify the start and end addresses of each region. Then the predicate $\mu_i(x) := \mathsf{regions}[i].\mathsf{start} \leq x < \mathsf{regions}[i].\mathsf{end}$ is true exactly when the integer variable x belongs to the i-th memory region. The correctness specification for the configuration parameters may thus be expressed by the formula

$$\varphi := \forall x. \forall i. \forall i'. (i < i' \rightarrow \neg(\mu_i(x) \wedge \mu_{i'}(x))), \quad (1)$$

formalizing the requirement that no pair of distinct regions overlap. Note that the index i ranges over a finite domain, so every universal quantification over it can be replaced with a finite conjunction. Thus, the only essential variable in formula (1) is the integer variable x.

It is straightforward to translate these formulae into the theory of Quantifier-Free Linear Integer Arithmetic (QF_LIA), which is typically very well supported by every state-of-the-art SMT solver. Since our goal is to *verify* a specification, that is, to prove that the formula (1) is *valid* for every possible value of x, the SMT solver must be queried for a proof that the *negation* of that formula is not satisfiable. Therefore, the logical formula to be encoded is

$$\neg\varphi \equiv \neg\forall x.\forall i.\forall i'.\,(i < i' \rightarrow \neg(\mu_i(x) \wedge \mu_{i'}(x))) \tag{2}$$

that is, pushing the negation inside the quantifiers and using De Morgan rules,

$$\exists x.\exists i.\exists i'.\,(i < i' \wedge \mu_i(x) \wedge \mu_{i'}(x)). \tag{3}$$

The behavioral certification artifact in this case is just a proof certificate for the unsatisfiability of the formula (3). Figure 4 shows the SMT-LIB encoding of this check for a simple configuration with three distinct memory regions, where the constants `r1_start`, etc. are to be replaced with the concrete values extracted from the firmware configuration.

```
(set-logic QF_LIA)
(declare-fun x () Int)
(assert (let ((mu_1 (and (<= r1_start x) (< x r1_end)))
              (mu_2 (and (<= r2_start x) (< x r2_end)))
              (mu_3 (and (<= r3_start x) (< x r3_end))))
             (or (and mu_1 mu_2) (and mu_1 mu_3) (and mu_2 mu_3))))
(check-sat)
```

Fig. 4. SMT-LIB encoding of non-interference for a configuration with three regions.

5.2 Verifying Binary Code Instrumentation

Many approaches to software hardening use *compile-time instrumentation* techniques to automatically generate binary images that enforce security properties such as memory safety or control flow integrity. It is thus of interest to be able to independently verify the presence of such instrumentation on a given binary, whether the corresponding source is available (to check the output of the instrumented compiler) or not. In order to verify this property using an SMT solver, we can convert it into a satisfiability problem in the theory QF_S of strings and regular languages (recently added to the SMT-LIB standard [4]), as follows. Let s_{pre} denote the string containing the assembly source of the routine which is subject to instrumentation (in a specified ISA), and let s_{post} denote the string containing the assembly source of the same routine after instrumentation. As an additional input, we require a formal specification of the instrumentation process in the form of a pair of regular expressions (R_1, R_2), where R_1 is the *trigger expression* and R_2 is the *replacement template*. The instrumentation process shall replace each occurrence in s_{pre} of a substring that matches the trigger expression R_1 with a substring that matches the replacement template R_2. Then the correctness of the instrumented code can be checked simply by comparing the result of this operation, applied to the non-instrumented code s_{pre}, with the string s_{post} describing the result of the instrumentation.

```
(set-logic QF_S)
(define-const s_pre String ...)  ; omitted for brevity
(define-const s_post String ...) ; omitted for brevity
(declare-const r String)
(declare-const x String)
(declare-const y String)
(define-const R_reg RegLan ...)  ; omitted for brevity
(define-const R1 RegLan (re.++ (str.to_re "call ") (str.to_re r)))
(define-const R2 RegLan (re.++ (str.to_re "mov ") (str.to_re r)
                               (str.to_re ", r6|call safe_call")))
(assert (and (str.in_re r R_reg)
        (str.in_re s_pre (re.++ (str.to_re x) R1 (str.to_re y)))
        (not (str.in_re s_post (re.++ (str.to_re x) R2 (str.to_re y))))))
(check-sat)
```

Fig. 5. SMT-LIB encoding of the instrumentation policy described in the text.

As an example, let us consider a *control flow integrity* scheme in which indirect calls (i.e., calls whose target is contained in a register) are instrumented to allow control transfer to legitimate routines only, in order to prevent any possible diversion of the control flow by an attacker that has gained write access to the machine registers. Let R_{reg} denote a regular expression that matches all the (canonical) register names for the selected ISA. A possible formal description (R_1, R_2) of such an instrumentation is as follows:

$$R_1 = \texttt{call}\ R_{\text{reg}} \qquad R_2 = \texttt{mov}\ R_{\text{reg}}\texttt{, r6; call safe\_call}$$

The replacement template substitutes the indirect call with a sequence of two instructions that pass the register that holds the call target to a function, named `safe_call`, which checks if the call target is legitimate. Figure 5 shows a possible SMT encoding to detect violations of this policy.

A simpler variant of the above problem may just require that an assembly source s does not contain any substring (i.e., an assembly instruction or sequence of instructions) that matches a particular regular expression R (e.g., a call to an insecure library function). In this case, it is not necessary to supply the string s_{pre}, since it is sufficient to verify that the regular expression R does not match any substring of the post-instrumentation code s_{post}.

6 Implementation and Evaluation

To verify the viability of our proposal, we implemented a prototype of our framework by extending an existing implementation of the SUIT standard with new routines to handle proof generation and proof verification. For the update generation phase, after evaluating the available options, we chose the official ARM tool, called SUIT-Tool[2]. This Python implementation handles the generation and signing of manifests starting from a JSON input file structured similarly to the resulting manifest. For proof generation, we leveraged the capabilities of the cvc5 SMT solver [3].

Once the device receives the update package, the installation process described in Subsect. 4.2 begins, performing tasks such as fetching the update

[2] https://gitlab.arm.com/research/ietf-suit/suit-tool.

image, parsing, and validating the manifest. As the target platform we selected a Raspberry Pi 4B, equipped with a quad-core ARM Cortex-A72 processor running at 1.5 GHz and 2 GB of RAM, as it is a widely used representative of high-end IoT devices. The manifest parser implementation is derived from the ARM reference SUIT-Parser[3], which includes functionalities to compute the digest of the manifest from the received message and verify its signature using the Public Key of the server, supporting various Elliptic Curve algorithms such as EdDSA and ES256/384/512. To perform proof-checking we used the ETHOS tool[4] by the same team that developed CVC5.

To evaluate the proposed implementation[5] on our target device, we generated a series of 10 test manifests that comprise a variable number of proof certificates, ranging in size between 10KB and 338KB (before compression). The proofs have been obtained by verifying properties of both classes described in Sect. 5. For the memory partitioning case, we wrote by hand some simple test configurations with 5 to 10 memory regions. For the code instrumentation case, we chose to focus on a very simple property, namely the absence of indirect calls in the disassembled code of an (independently-compiled) binary. To perform the code extraction step, we used the well-known ANGR binary analysis framework, whereas the binaries are taken from the standard MIBENCH test suite, freely available online[6].

The generated proofs were compressed using gzip to reduce their length; the gzip output was then encoded using Base64, a simple and lightweight encoding method that introduces a minimal increase in output size. The test manifests do not include any binary payload and only use remotely fetched binary images, as the goal of the tests is to assess the impact of the new fields not already part of the SUIT standard.

Table 1. Manifests size, maximum memory usage and execution time (in seconds).

# of proofs	Total size of manifest	Parsing time	Max parsing memory	Proof checking time	Max checking memory
1	43KB	0.06	1.50MB	10.91	171.97MB
2	84KB	0.07	1.50MB	18.28	171.97MB
3	122KB	0.08	1.63MB	30.89	213.50MB
3	86KB	0.07	1.50MB	18.58	171.97MB
4	124KB	0.08	1.63MB	31.19	213.50MB
4	88KB	0.07	1.50MB	18.87	171.97MB
5	185KB	0.10	1.63MB	32.31	213.50MB
5	126KB	0.08	1.63MB	31.48	213.50MB
6	194KB	0.10	1.63MB	32.74	213.50MB
6	135KB	0.10	1.63MB	31.91	213.50MB

The tests were carried out in two stages: first, parsing and verifying the update package and manifest, and second, validating the included proofs. Both

[3] https://gitlab.arm.com/research/ietf-suit/suit-parser.
[4] https://github.com/cvc5/ethos.
[5] https://github.com/CybersecurityUnitn/IoTSecureUpdate.
[6] https://vhosts.eecs.umich.edu/mibench/.

steps were executed locally, without relying on external servers. The results of the evaluation are summarized in Table 1. By combining them with some additional observations collected during the tests, we can gather the following key insights.

- The manifest parsing and signature verification phases do not constitute a bottleneck, as the processing requires a limited amount of computational resources and memory, while the proof verification phase is more demanding.
- Proof certificates for the non-interference property (Subsect. 5.1) are generally small (15–50 KB uncompressed) and not problematic to verify.
- Proof certificates for the code instrumentation property (Subsect. 5.2) are typically larger (empirically on the order of 3-6KB per analyzed instruction) and their verification does not scale well with the size: indeed, we observed the proof checker quickly exhausting the 2GB available on the Raspberry Pi when checking proof certificates with a size approaching 1MB.

Overall, the findings indicate that incorporating numerous smaller proofs in the Behavioral Certification manifest tends to be more effective than relying on a few larger ones. However, successful verification is not solely determined by the proof size: the type and characteristics of verified properties also play a critical role in resource consumption, and setting the threshold for local verification must take into account all these factors, as discussed in Subsect. 4.3.

7 Conclusions

In this paper we introduced a new scheme for the remote update of trusted, security- and safety-critical components in IoT devices. Our proposal is based on an extension of the SUIT standard that adds a *Behavioral Certification Manifest* to formally guarantee the preservation of the relevant safety and security properties of the updated software.

As future work we plan to extend the scope of our approach to new kinds of behavioral properties in addition to the ones considered in Sect. 5, such as safety or security properties that can be proven by model checking techniques. However, in order to do this, a model checker equipped with a proof-producing framework like the one described in [15] must be available. Furthermore, we would like to develop our current tools into a complete implementation of the SUIT standard which is able to run in realistic environments.

Acknowledgments. This research was funded by the European Union through the Next Generation EU PRIN 2022 Prot. n. 202297YF75, the MUR PNRR project PE SERICS - SecCO (PE00000014), CUP D33C22001300002, and the Horizon Europe Research and Innovation Program under Grant n. 101070537, project Cross-Platform Open Security Stack for Connected Devices (CROSSCON).

Disclosure of Interests. The authors declare that they have no competing interests.

References

1. Asokan, N., Nyman, T., Rattanavipanon, N., Sadeghi, A.R., Tsudik, G.: ASSURED: architecture for secure software update of realistic embedded devices. IEEE Trans. Comput. Aided Des. Integr. Circuits Syst. **37**(11), 2290–2300 (2018). https://doi.org/10.1109/TCAD.2018.2858422
2. Barbosa, H., et al.: CVC5: a versatile and industrial-strength SMT solver. Presented at the (2022). https://doi.org/10.1007/978-3-030-99524-9_24
3. Barbosa, H., et al.: Generating and exploiting automated reasoning proof certificates. Commun. ACM **66**(10), 86–95 (2023). https://doi.org/10.1145/3587692
4. Barrett, C., Fontaine, P., Tinelli, C.: The Satisfiability Modulo Theories Library (SMT-LIB) (2016). www.SMT-LIB.org
5. Barrett, C.W., Sebastiani, R., Seshia, S.A., Tinelli, C.: Satisfiability modulo theories. In: Handbook of Satisfiability, Frontiers in Artificial Intelligence and Applications, vol. 336, pp. 1267–1329. IOS Press (2021)
6. Blech, J.O., Périn, M.: Generating invariant-based certificates for embedded systems. ACM Trans. Embed. Comput. Syst. **11**(2), 34:1–34:22 (2012). https://doi.org/10.1145/2220336.2220346
7. Bradley, C., Barrera, D.: Towards characterizing IoT software update practices. In: Jourdan, G.V., et.al (eds.) Foundations and Practice of Security, pp. 406–422. LNCS, Springer Nature Switzerland, Cham (2023). https://doi.org/10.1007/978-3-031-30122-3_25
8. Chandra, H., Anggadjaja, E., Wijaya, P.S., Gunawan, E.: Internet of things: over-the-air (OTA) firmware update in Lightweight mesh network protocol for smart urban development. In: 2016 22nd Asia-Pacific Conference on Communications (APCC), pp. 115–118 (August 2016). https://doi.org/10.1109/APCC.2016.7581459
9. Dejon, N., Caputo, D., Verderame, L., Armando, A., Merlo, A.: Automated security analysis of IoT software updates. In: Laurent, M., Giannetsos, T. (eds.) Information Security Theory and Practice - 13th IFIP WG 11.2 International Conference, Paris, France. LNCS, vol. 12024, pp. 223–239. Springer, Cham (2019). https://doi.org/10.1007/978-3-030-41702-4_14
10. Doddapaneni, K., Lakkundi, R., Rao, S., Kulkarni, S.G., Bhat, B.: Secure FoTA object for IoT. In: 2017 IEEE 42nd Conference on Local Computer Networks Workshops (LCN Workshops), pp. 154–159 (October 2017). https://doi.org/10.1109/LCN.Workshops.2017.78
11. D'Silva, V., Kroening, D., Weissenbacher, G.: A survey of automated techniques for formal software verification. IEEE Trans. Comput. Aided Des. Integr. Circuits Syst. **27**(7), 1165–1178 (2008). https://doi.org/10.1109/TCAD.2008.923410
12. El Jaouhari, S., Bouvet, E.: Secure firmware over-the-air updates for IoT: survey, challenges, and discussions. Internet Things **18**, 100508 (2022). https://doi.org/10.1016/j.iot.2022.100508
13. Giaretta, A., Dragoni, N., Massacci, F.: IoT security configurability with security-by-contract. Sensors **19**(19), 4121 (2019). https://doi.org/10.3390/S19194121
14. Giaretta, A., Dragoni, N., Massacci, F.: S×C4IoT: a security-by-contract framework for dynamic evolving IoT devices. ACM Trans. Sens. Netw. **18**(1), 12:1–12:51 (2022). https://doi.org/10.1145/3480462
15. Griggio, A., Roveri, M., Tonetta, S.: Certifying proofs for SAT-based model checking. Form. Methods Syst. Des. **57**(2), 178–210 (2021). https://doi.org/10.1007/S10703-021-00369-1

16. Kolehmainen, A.: Secure firmware updates for IoT: a survey. In: IEEE International Conference on iThings and IEEE GreenCom and IEEE CPSCom and IEEE SmartData, Halifax, NS, Canada, pp. 112–117. IEEE (2018). https://doi.org/10.1109/CYBERMATICS_2018.2018.00051
17. Langiu, A., Boano, C.A., Schuß, M., Römer, K.: UpKit: an open-source, portable, and lightweight update framework for constrained IoT devices. In: 2019 IEEE 39th International Conference on Distributed Computing Systems (ICDCS), pp. 2101–2112 (July 2019)
18. Moran, B., Tschofenig, H., Birkholz, H.: A Manifest Information Model for Firmware Updates in Internet of Things (IoT) Devices. RFC 9124 (January 2022)
19. Moran, B., Tschofenig, H., Birkholz, H., Zandberg, K., Rønningstad, O.: A Concise Binary Object Representation (CBOR)-based Serialization Format for the Software Updates for Internet of Things (SUIT) Manifest. Internet-Draft draft-ietf-suit-manifest-25, Internet Engineering Task Force (February 2024). https://datatracker.ietf.org/doc/draft-ietf-suit-manifest/25/, work in progress
20. Moran, B., Tschofenig, H., Brown, D., Meriac, M.: A Firmware Update Architecture for Internet of Things. RFC 9019 (April 2021)
21. Necula, G.C., Lee, P.: The design and implementation of a certifying compiler. SIGPLAN Not. **33**(5), 333–344 (1998). https://doi.org/10.1145/277652.277752
22. Necula, G.C.: Proof-carrying code. In: Proceedings of the 24th ACM SIGPLAN-SIGACT Symposium on Principles of Programming Languages, pp. 106–119. POPL '97, Association for Computing Machinery, New York, NY, USA (January 1997). https://doi.org/10.1145/263699.263712
23. Parliament, E.: Cyber resilience act (March 2024). https://www.europarl.europa.eu/doceo/document/TA-9-2024-0130_EN.html. Accessed 14 Nov 2024
24. Samuel, J., Mathewson, N., Cappos, J., Dingledine, R.: Survivable key compromise in software update systems. In: Proceedings of the 17th ACM Conference on Computer and Communications Security, pp. 61–72. CCS '10, Association for Computing Machinery, New York, NY, USA (October 2010). https://doi.org/10.1145/1866307.1866315
25. Zandberg, K., Schleiser, K., Padilla, F.A., Tschofenig, H., Baccelli, E.: Secure firmware updates for constrained IoT devices using open standards: a reality check. IEEE Access **7**, 71907–71920 (2019). https://doi.org/10.1109/ACCESS.2019.2919760

LSAST: Enhancing Cybersecurity Through LLM-Supported Static Application Security Testing

Mete Keltek[1], Rong Hu[2(✉)], Mohammadreza Fani Sani[3], and Ziyue Li[1]

[1] University of Cologne, Cologne, Germany
meke00001@stud.uni-saarland.de, zlibn@wiso.uni-koeln.de
[2] Hunan University, Changsha, China
upupwords@hnu.edu.cn
[3] Microsoft, Development Center Copenhagen, Copenhagen, Denmark
mfanisani@microsoft.com

Abstract. The cybersecurity landscape has grown increasingly complex, with traditional Static Application Security Testing (SAST) tools often unable to capture emerging vulnerabilities due to their reliance on rule-based matching. Large Language Models (LLMs) offer promising code analysis capabilities, yet static training data and privacy concerns limit their effectiveness. To address these gaps, we propose LSAST, a novel integration of LLMs with SAST scanners, enhancing vulnerability detection. LSAST utilizes a locally hosted LLM with a dynamic knowledge retrieval system, ensuring up-to-date vulnerability insights while safeguarding data privacy. Our approach sets a new standard for static vulnerability analysis, bridging the capabilities of traditional scanners and advanced AI-driven methods. Evaluation results show that integrating SAST results into LLM analysis significantly enhances detection accuracy, capturing vulnerabilities that conventional methods miss.

Keywords: Vulnerability Scanning · Large Language Model · Static Application Security Testing

1 Introduction

With global cybercrime losses projected to escalate from $8.15 trillion in 2023 to $13.82 trillion by 2028 [6] and hackers initiating an attack every three seconds on average [2], cybersecurity has never been more critical. As the IT landscape expands, cyber threats have evolved into sophisticated, persistent risks, demanding robust cybersecurity measures.

Security scanning is a widely adopted measure for identifying vulnerabilities [3,11]. While Static Application Security Testing (SAST) [8] is a conventional method in code security, its rule-based pattern matching approach often falls short of detecting complex vulnerabilities. In contrast, Large Language Models (LLMs) [1,15] show promise in analyzing code and identifying vulnerabilities

Published by Springer Nature Switzerland AG 2025
L. Nemec Zlatolas et al. (Eds.): SEC 2025, IFIP AICT 745, pp. 166–179, 2025.
https://doi.org/10.1007/978-3-031-92882-6_12

due to their advanced contextual understanding and adaptability to emerging threats [16,17].

However, LLMs are constrained by static training data, which limits their ability to recognize new security threats, posing substantial security risks. Additionally, using third-party LLM providers for vulnerability scanning introduces privacy concerns, as sensitive code could be exposed to unauthorized access or repurposed for model training, raising the potential for training data extraction attacks.

This paper addresses these challenges by:

- enhancing LLMs for vulnerability detection through integration with static scanning results, creating a combined system that surpasses traditional methods;
- introducing knowledge retrieval techniques to supply LLMs with up-to-date threat data, advancing knowledge retrieval standards in security scanning;
- highlighting how irrelevant reports can detract from LLM performance in retrieval systems and addressing privacy concerns by utilizing open-source LLMs for secure vulnerability scanning;
- demonstrating that LSAST can detect vulnerabilities overlooked by traditional tools, affirming its value in security assessments.

The remainder of this paper is organized as follows: Sect. 2 provides background on security scanners and vulnerability information. Section 3 reviews related work on security testing tools, LLMs in vulnerability detection, and knowledge retrieval. Section 4 details the LSAST approach and its SAST-based optimizations. Section 5 presents experimental results and findings, and Sect. 6 concludes the paper.

2 Background

2.1 Types of Security Scanners

Security scanners are primarily divided into Dynamic Application Security Testing (DAST) and Static Application Security Testing (SAST) tools [5]. DAST scanners treat applications as black boxes, assessing vulnerabilities by interacting with the system during runtime. By sending crafted requests and analyzing responses, they simulate attacks like SQL Injection and Cross-Site Scripting to identify weaknesses. In contrast, SAST scanners analyze source code directly, without executing the application, to detect patterns associated with known vulnerabilities. These methods are complementary, as each detects vulnerabilities the other might miss, underscoring the importance of integrating both into comprehensive security frameworks.

2.2 Retrieval-Augmented Generation

With cybersecurity evolving rapidly, staying informed about new threats is crucial. Traditional static analysis tools struggle to keep pace with emerging vulnerabilities, and LLMs, despite their potential in identifying complex issues, are restricted by static training data. RAG addresses this limitation by dynamically incorporating external knowledge into LLM outputs. RAG enhances real-time awareness by storing external knowledge in vector-based databases and conducting similarity searches to retrieve the most relevant data during processing. This enables LLMs to access continuously updated vulnerability reports and insights, bridging the gap between static models and the need for current security intelligence.

3 Related Work

3.1 Challenges in Traditional Detection and LLM Opportunities

Traditional vulnerability detection relies heavily on SAST and DAST tools, but these methods face significant limitations, especially in detecting complex, context-specific vulnerabilities. SAST tools often use rule-based pattern recognition, resulting in high false positives and poor detection of novel vulnerabilities [9,13]. Machine learning integration has been explored, but traditional tools still lack the adaptability required for sophisticated analysis. Recent work [7] suggests LLMs could enhance static analysis but often applies only to narrow use cases.

LLMs have emerged as a promising alternative, especially for complex vulnerabilities that traditional tools miss. Research demonstrates LLMs' ability to analyze code and identify issues within context [10,12]. Despite this potential, key challenges persist-especially regarding privacy risks associated with third-party LLM providers and the limited adaptability of static training data. Privacy concerns have led some researchers [18] to advocate for locally hosted LLMs, though these models' effectiveness in static vulnerability scanning is not fully benchmarked. Additionally, the static nature of training data restricts LLMs' responsiveness to new threats, underscoring the need for real-time updates to maximize detection capability.

3.2 Enhancing LLMs with Knowledge Retrieval for Improved Detection

To address the limitations of static training data in LLMs, researchers are exploring knowledge retrieval systems. Retrieval-augmented systems can provide up-to-date threat data, enhancing the LLM's adaptability to new vulnerabilities. For example, retrieval-augmented scanning has been demonstrated to improve detection but often remains focused on specific applications, like smart contracts [14]. Other RAG-based approaches, such as in [4], incorporate real-time updates but lack functionality-specific searches and integration with SAST results.

Systematic integration of LLMs and SAST tools has remained limited, with existing approaches often focusing on single-use cases rather than broader application. CodeQL has been used for specific vulnerability querying [9], yet this approach lacks full integration with SAST outputs or comprehensive knowledge retrieval. By leveraging SAST data with LLMs in a retrieval-augmented framework, LSAST aims to provide real-time insights and improve detection coverage, establishing a more adaptive and robust vulnerability detection approach.

4 Methodology

4.1 Combining Conservative SAST Scanners with LLMs

To implement LSAST, we use the open-source Bearer SAST scanner[1] for its rapid response time and flexible output formats, which ease integration with the LLM. A simplified Bearer scan output is shown in Listing 1, detailing key information like the vulnerability type and affected lines. We format this data as shown in Listing 2 to create a concise output for the LLM prompt. The target code, shown in Listing 3, is also formatted with line numbers to facilitate cross-referencing with Bearer results, enhancing the LLM's ability to pinpoint vulnerabilities accurately.

```
{
    "cwe_ids": [
        "78"
    ],
    "id": "javascript_lang_os_command_injection",
    "title": "Unsanitized user input in OS command",
    "description": "Executing operating system commands with unsanitized
        ...",
    "line_number": 39,
    "full_filename": "/Users/User/repos/dvna/core/appHandler.js",
    "source": {
        "start": 39,
        "end": 44,
    }
}
```

Listing 1. single Bearer scan finding (simplified)

```
[
        'CWE-943 (line 59-65)',
        'CWE-943 (line 85-89)',
        'CWE-943 (line 107-111)',
        'CWE-943 (line 145-149)',
        'CWE-611 (line 235)',
        'CWE-78 (line 39-44)'
]
```

Listing 2. formatted output of Bearer scan results

```
line 1: var db = require('../models')
line 2:
line 3: module.exports.userSearch = function (req, res) {
line 4:     var query = "SELECT name,id FROM Users WHERE login='" + req.body.
    login + "'";
line 5:     db.sequelize.query(query, {
line 6:         model: db.User
line 7:     }).then(user => {
line 8:         if (user.length) {
line 9:             var output = {
...
```

Listing 3. target code with line information added

[1] https://github.com/Bearer/bearer.

In Listing 4, we integrate Bearer's scan findings and the target code into a structured LLM prompt, with instructions for detecting additional vulnerabilities. This setup ensures the LLM can analyze the target code contextually, flagging any missed vulnerabilities.

```
Code:
{target_code}

After scanning the code with a SAST Scanner we receive following
    vulnerabilities:
{bearer_result}

You are a very efficient vulnerability scanner.
Follow these tasks carefully:
- Evaluate whether the given code includes any more vulnerabilities other
    then the ones found by the SAST Scanner.
- Only output vulnerabilities that were not found by the SAST Scanner.
- There can be multiple vulnerabilities
- Only output vulnerabilites that are 100 percent certain to be present in
    the given code.
- If you don't find any additional vulnerabilties just answer: "no additional
    vulnerabilties found"
- If you find a vulnerability structure your answer like this:
"CWE-ID: <CWE-ID>
Reason: <reason why code is vulnerable>
line: <line number of vulnerable code>
code-snippet: <code-snippet that causes the vulnerability>"
```

Listing 4. LLM prompt with bearer results

4.2 Gathering and Preparing Vulnerability Reports

To provide the LLM with recent vulnerability information, we developed a Knowledge Retrieval System. This system aggregates vulnerability reports from the past year to ensure the LLM can address current threats. Using the Hacktivity API[2], we collected 873 JSON-formatted vulnerability reports. Each report contains relevant identifiers, severity ratings, and detailed vulnerability information, exemplified in Listing 5.

```
{
    "id": 2493548,
    "title": "Incorrect Type Conversion in interpreting IPv4-mapped IPv6
        addresses and below 'curl' results in indeterminate SSRF
        vulnerabilities.",
    "severity_rating": "critical",
    "cve_ids": [
        "CVE-2023-24329",
        "CVE-2024-22243"
    ],
    "cwe-id": "CWE-843",
    "cwe-title": "Type Confusion",
    "vulnerability_information": "## Summary:\nOctal Type Handling of Errors
        in IPv4 Mapped IPv6 Addresses in curl allows unauthenticated remote
        attackers to ....",
},
```

Listing 5. HackerOne vulnerability report (simplified)

[2] https://hackerone.com/hacktivity.

We optimize report delivery by employing LLM4Vuln [14] to perform similarity searches based on code functionality. Summarized vulnerability snippets are stored as vectors, enabling a rapid match against the target code's function (see Listing 6). For cases where functionality does not correlate directly with vulnerabilities, we developed an abstraction-based approach. In this method, code is minimized to structural patterns, allowing the LLM to match reports based on fundamental syntax (see Listing 7).

```
{target_code}

Given the code snippet, please remove all contextual information and variable
    names, leaving only the syntactic structure intact.
1. The task involves extracting the core syntactic structure of the code
   while removing all contextual information and variable names, leaving
   only the essential code pattern intact.
2. This process requires meticulous attention to detail and a thorough
   understanding of the code's structure.
3. Focus on identifying and preserving the fundamental syntax elements, such
   as loops, conditionals, function definitions, and method invocations,
   while disregarding any specific variable names, comments, or non-
   essential whitespace.
4. The resulting isolated code pattern will serve as a basis for further
   analysis and comparison, aiding in the identification of similar code
   patterns across multiple codebases or vulnerability reports.
5. Use the format: Code-Pattern:[xxxx], placing the extracted Code Pattern
   inside the brackets.
6. If there is no code only answer "code-Pattern:[no code]"
```

Listing 6. LLM prompt to get abstraction of target code

```
{target_code}

Follow these tasks:
1. Outline the operational purpose of the provided code using imperative
   language, such as 'Calculate bank account balance.' Your explanation
   should be brief, no more than one paragraph and within 40-50 words.
2. Ensure your description focuses solely on the functionality or business
   logic without referencing specific variables, functions, or expressions.
```

Listing 7. LLM prompt to get summarization of target code

4.3 Knowledge Retrieval Methods

To address the limitations of static LLM training data, we use a dynamic Knowledge Retrieval System. This section summarizes seven retrieval methods, combining functionality-based, abstraction-based, and SAST-specific approaches (Table 1). Each retrieval method progressively enhances LLM detection by integrating additional vulnerability information.

In the baseline RAW approach, the LLM queries only the *TC* without retrieval:

$$\text{llm-input} = \text{TC}, \tag{1}$$

shown in Fig. 1a. It relies solely on static training data, often missing newer or context-specific vulnerabilities.

Table 1. Definitions of Terms

Abbreviation	Description
TC	Target Code
SR	SAST-Scanner Result
VR	Vulnerability Reports
FVR	Functionality-similar Vulnerability Reports
CVR	Code-Abstraction-similar Vulnerability Reports
k	Value of top k in the similarity search

(a) RAW Own-Knowledge Approach.

(b) RAW Own-Knowledge LSAST-Approach.

Fig. 1. Own-Knowledge Approach.

RAW Own-Knowledge LSAST-Approach

$$\text{llm-input} = \text{TC} + \text{SR} \tag{2}$$

Building upon the baseline, we incorporate the SAST scanner result, *SR*, along with the *TC* into the LLM input as our raw LSAST approach, as shown in Fig. 1b. This allows the LLM gain initial insights into known vulnerabilities identified by traditional static analysis to enhance the overall detection accuracy.

Functionality-Based Retrieval Approach

$$\text{llm-input} = \text{TC} + \text{FVR} \tag{3}$$

As depicted in Fig. 2a , the LLM first summarizes the functionality of the *TC*. A similarity search is then conducted within a vector database containing functionalities of known vulnerable code snippets. The most relevant *FVR* are retrieved and provided to the LLM along with the target code.

Functionality LSAST-Approach

$$\text{llm-input} = \text{TC} + \text{FVR} + \text{SR} \tag{4}$$

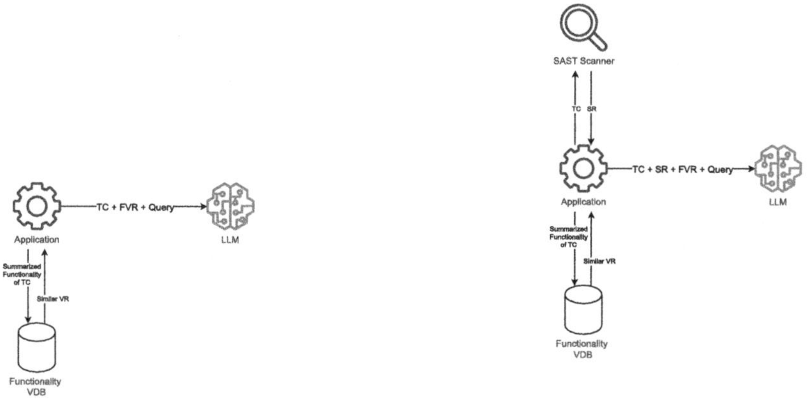

(a) RAW Functionality Approach.

(b) Functionality LSAST-Approach.

Fig. 2. Functionality Approach.

For the functionality, our approach utilizes Eq. (2) to extend the retrieval process by also incorporating SAST results (*SR*) alongside functionality reports (*FVR*) as shown in Fig. 2b. Combining the detailed vulnerability reports with SAST's known patterns provides a dual-layered context, improving the LLM's performance by cross-referencing functionality-driven insights with existing static analysis results.

Abstraction-Based Retrieval Approach

$$\text{llm-input} = \text{TC} + \text{CVR} \tag{5}$$

In the abstraction approach as shown in Fig. 3a, the LLM abstracts the *TC* into its fundamental structual components. A similarity search is conducted within a vector database of code abstractions, retrieving the closest matching *CVR*.

Abstraction LSAST-Approach

$$\text{llm-input} = \text{TC} + \text{CVR} + \text{SR} \tag{6}$$

As shown in Fig. 3b , our abstraction LSAST-approach combines the strengths of abstraction-based retrieval with *SR*, providing the LLM with a comprehensive input that includes both structural patterns and known vulnerabilities. This dual approach allows the LLM to validate structural vulnerabilities against established patterns found by SAST, enhancing detection accuracy, especially in complex or poorly documented code segments.

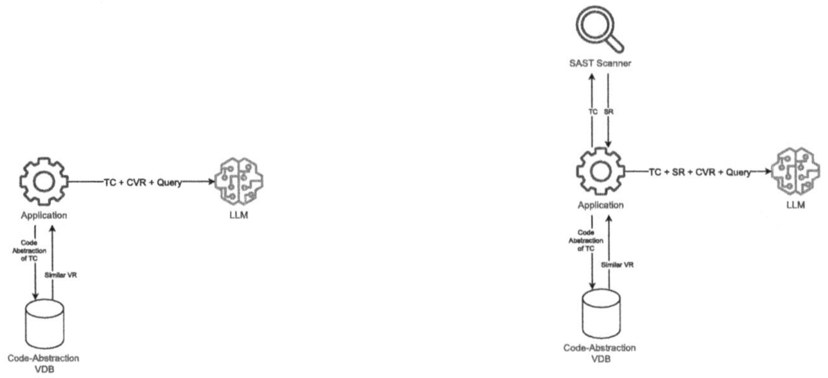

(a) RAW Abstraction Approach. (b) Abstraction LSAST-Approach.

Fig. 3. Abstraction Approach.

Combined Approach

$$\text{llm-input} = \text{TC} + \text{CVR} + \text{FVR} \tag{7}$$

This method combines both *FVR* and *CVR* with the target code, yielding a holistic view as shown in Fig. 4a. From each similarity search (Functionality and Pattern), the top k *VR's* are selected and provided to the LLM.

$$\text{llm-input} = \text{TC} + \text{CVR} + \text{FVR} + \text{SR} \tag{8}$$

The most comprehensive approach, Combined-LSAST, incorporates *TC* with functionality (*FVR*), abstraction (*CVR*), and SAST scanner results (*SR*), illustrated in Fig. 4b. This integration leverages the strengths of all previous methods, equipping the LLM with a well-rounded input that combines functionality, structure, and known vulnerabilities. Together, these inputs significantly enhance the LLM's capability for robust and accurate vulnerability detection.

5 Evaluation

Previous studies have established that LLMs are effective for vulnerability scanning, so we focused on structuring our evaluation efficiently. We used Llama-3-70B for all evaluations, as it provides high performance on mid-sized models and can be hosted without external cloud infrastructure or third-party LLM providers. First, we conducted a small-scale evaluation to determine the most effective RAG approach, then compared the best-performing RAG approach against raw models. For our environmental setup, we leveraged Hugging Face Inference Endpoints, which provide dedicated hosting and maintenance for deployed Large Language Models (LLMs). We specifically used the deployment of the meta-llama/Meta-Llama-3.1-70B-Instruct model.

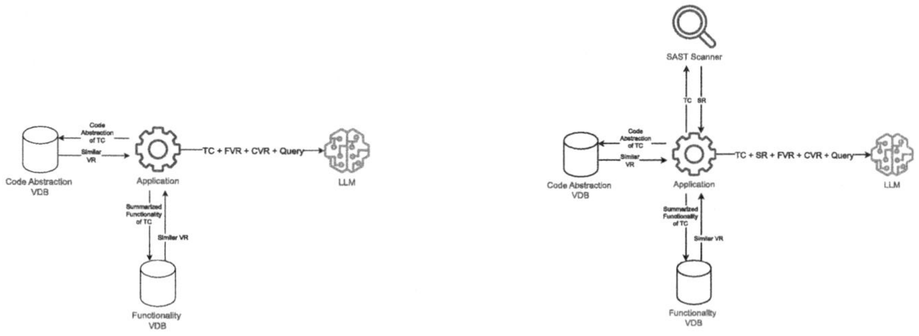

(a) RAW Combined Approach.

(b) Combined LSAST-Approach.

Fig. 4. Combined Approach.

Due to time constraints and the substantial manual effort required for evaluation, we focused our assessment on this single model.

Further the Bearer SAST scan results were assumed to be true positives due to the tool's established reputation for accuracy and its low false positive rate, as evidenced by independent evaluations.

5.1 Comparison of Abstraction, Functionality, and Combined Approaches

We began by testing the Abstraction (Eq. (5)), Functionality (Eq. (3)), and Combined (Eq. (7)) approaches without incorporating Bearer inputs into the prompts. We used four open-source security testing projects for evaluation:

1. **DVWA**[3]: A PHP/MySQL app with built-in vulnerabilities for testing.
2. **DVNA**[4]: A Node.js app with OWASP Top 10 vulnerabilities.
3. **OWASP Juice Shop**[5]: A JavaScript app (Node.js, Express, Angular) with vulnerabilities.
4. **WebGoat**[6]: A Java app designed to highlight Java-specific security risks.

These projects, covering Java, JavaScript, TypeScript, and PHP, included over 15 types of vulnerabilities across 10 files. Table 2 presents the evaluation metrics: True Positive Rate (TP-Rate), False Positive Rate (FP-Rate), Accuracy, Precision, and F1-Score, showing that the Combined Approach outperformed both Abstraction and Functionality. The FP-Rate was uniformly high since each file contained at least one vulnerability.

[3] https://github.com/digininja/DVWA.
[4] https://github.com/appsecco/dvna.
[5] https://owasp.org/www-project-juice-shop/.
[6] https://owasp.org/www-project-webgoat/.

Table 2. Comparison of Abstraction, Functionality, and Combined Approaches

Measure	Abstraction	Functionality	Combined
TP-Rate	23.81%	14.29%	**28.57%**
FP-Rate	100%	100%	100%
Accuracy	19.23%	10%	**24%**
Precision	50%	25%	**60%**
F1-Score	32.26%	18.18%	**38.71%**

Table 3. Comparison of Similarity Search for Abstraction and Functionality Approaches

Measure	Abstraction	Functionality
TP-Rate	**33.33%**	16.67%
FP-Rate	100%	100%
Accuracy	**12.50%**	6.90%
Precision	**16.67%**	10.53%
F1-Score	**22.22%**	12.90%

These results confirm that code abstraction correlates more strongly with vulnerabilities than functionality alone, as differing functions may share vulnerabilities and vice versa. The Combined Approach's superior performance suggests that added reports, even those not directly similar in abstraction, enrich the LLM's vulnerability detection (Table 3).

5.2 RAW vs. LSAST vs. LSAST-Combined

RAW Approach: Here we are asking the LLM directly to find vulnerabilities without using Bearer results or knowledge retrieval. (Eq. (1)).

LSAST-RAW: This approach uses Bearer results but does not incorporate knowledge retrieval. It assesses how many additional vulnerabilities the LLM can identify beyond those detected by Bearer (Eq. (2)).

Combined LSAST: This method integrates knowledge retrieval with Bearer results, aiming to maximize vulnerability detection by leveraging external vulnerability information (Eq. (8)).

The Combined Approach performed best among RAG approaches, so we next compared it against approaches without knowledge retrieval. We evaluated DVWA, DVNA, Juice Shop, and WebGoat. In the Combined and RAW LSAST methods, Bearer results were provided to the LLM to see how many new vulnerabilities it could identify beyond those found by Bearer. We manually classified scanner outputs as true positives, false positives, or false negatives.

As shown in Table 4, including Bearer findings significantly improves vulnerability detection. The RAW LSAST approach outperformed the Combined

Table 4. Comparison of Measures

Measure	RAW	RAW-LSAST	Combined-LSAST
TP-Rate	17.91%	**68.89%**	35.71%
FP-Rate	100%	100%	100%
Accuracy	24%	**62%**	32.61%
Precision	63.16%	**86.11%**	78.95%
F1-Score	38.71%	**76.54%**	49.18%

LSAST, while the RAW approach had the lowest performance. Our findings show that providing SAST results enables the LLM to focus on undiscovered vulnerabilities, improving accuracy. The drop in performance when utilizing RAG can be attributed to the irrelevant vulnerability reports provided to the LLM after the similarity search. These reports often failed to match the actual vulnerabilities in the code snippet, leading the LLM to search for non-existent vulnerabilities. This issue stems from the limited size and quality of the dataset, as well as the lack of comprehensive open-source vulnerability databases that include example code. Existing databases are often limited to specific languages, small, not actively maintained, or lack code snippets. Our research underscores the need for more robust and diverse open-source databases to improve the accuracy of RAG systems in vulnerability detection, as current limitations significantly impact system effectiveness when used for LLM vulnerability scanning.

5.3 Real-World Test

To validate LSAST in a real-world setting, we tested the Python package pyDust[7] and collaborated with the repository's authors on the findings. We ran the LSAST-Raw scans to identify real vulnerabilities that were not detected by using SAST or LLM methods alone. Following the LSAST scan, we systematically reviewed each finding, collaborating with the repository owner to manually classify them as true or false positives. This joint effort ensured accuracy during the triage process, minimizing errors and confirming that only genuine vulnerabilities were flagged as true positives. By combining automated scanning with expert human validation, we enhanced the reliability of our vulnerability assessment. LSAST identified 2 High-Risk, 1 Medium-Risk, and 3 Low-Risk vulnerabilities missed by conventional scanners, with potential risks of code injection and remote execution. It also reported 2 false positives, emphasizing the need to verify scanner results. This demonstrates the unique effectiveness of LSAST in combining SAST and LLM techniques, uncovering vulnerabilities that neither approach could detect independently. The findings underscore LSAST's distinctive capability to reveal security issues that would remain hidden when using SAST or LLMs alone, showcasing the critical importance of integrating these complementary methods for comprehensive vulnerability detection. Given pyDust's

[7] https://github.com/MondoAurora/pydust/tree/main/dust.

complexity, LSAST's success in identifying missed vulnerabilities demonstrates its effectiveness in practical scenarios.

6 Conclusion

This study presents LSAST, a novel integration of LLMs with static application security testing (SAST) to enhance vulnerability detection. By combining SAST outputs with a knowledge retrieval system, LSAST effectively identifies complex vulnerabilities that traditional scanners may overlook. The results demonstrate a significant improvement in detection accuracy through LLM-SAST integration, though success depends on the relevance of the retrieved data. LSAST's privacy-conscious approach and real-world validation on the Python package pyDust confirm its practical value in identifying high-risk vulnerabilities missed by conventional methods.

By leveraging an open-source model, LSAST shows that privacy concerns associated with third-party LLM providers can be effectively mitigated while still achieving beneficial results in vulnerability detection. This approach addresses data confidentiality issues and allows organizations to maintain control over their security analysis processes, ensuring that they can benefit from LLM integration without compromising on privacy.

Our evaluation assessed vulnerability detection capabilities across five widely used programming languages (Java, JavaScript, TypeScript, Python, and PHP). This diverse selection enables generalization within the web development context and extends to a broader spectrum of software development, encompassing both statically and dynamically typed languages. Future work will focus on refining knowledge retrieval strategies and exploring LLMs' integration with dynamic testing, with the aim of developing adaptive learning to keep models updated on emerging threats.

Acknowledgement. We would like to express our gratitude to Andras Kosztyu for his help in identifying and flagging vulnerabilities during the evaluation process. Furthermore, we thank Zsolt Horvath for generously providing the pyDust repository (https://github.com/MondoAurora/pydust/tree/main/dust) to facilitate the evaluation of LSAST efficiency in a practical setting, and for his valuable collaboration during the manual classification of the LSAST findings.

References

1. Achiam, J., et al.: Gpt-4 technical report. arXiv preprint arXiv:2303.08774 (2023)
2. Brooks, C.: More alarming cybersecurity stats for 2021. Forbes (2021). Accessed 19 June 2024
3. Dibbo, S.V., Chung, D.L., Mehnaz, S.: Model inversion attack with least information and an in-depth analysis of its disparate vulnerability. In: 2023 IEEE Conference on Secure and Trustworthy Machine Learning (SaTML), pp. 119–135. IEEE (2023)

4. Du, X., et al.: VUL-RAG: enhancing llm-based vulnerability detection via knowledge-level rag. arXiv preprint arXiv:2401.17011 (2024). Accessed 24 June 2024
5. Felderer, M., Büchler, M., Johns, M., Brucker, A.D., Breu, R., Pretschner, A.: Security testing: a survey. In: Advances in Computers, vol. 101, pp. 1–51. Elsevier (2016)
6. Fleck, A.: Expected cost of cybercrime until 2027. Statista (2023). Accessed 19 June 2024
7. Li, H., Hao, Y., Zhai, Y., Qian, Z.: The hitchhiker's guide to program analysis: a journey with large language models. In: Proceedings of the 2023 International Conference on Software Engineering (2023). Accessed 24 June 2024
8. Li, J.: Vulnerabilities mapping based on owasp-sans: a survey for static application security testing (sast). arXiv preprint arXiv:2004.03216 (2020)
9. Li, Z., Dutta, S., Naik, M.: LLM-assisted static analysis for detecting security vulnerabilities. arXiv preprint (2023). Accessed 24 June 2024
10. Mohajer, M.M., et al.: Skipanalyzer: a tool for static code analysis with large language models. In: Proceedings of the 2023 IEEE/ACM 45th International Conference on Software Engineering (2023). Accessed 24 June 2024
11. Nielsen, B.B., Torp, M.T., Møller, A.: Modular call graph construction for security scanning of node. js applications. In: Proceedings of the 30th ACM SIGSOFT International Symposium on Software Testing and Analysis, pp. 29–41 (2021)
12. Shestov, A., Levichev, R., Mussabayev, R., Maslov, E., Cheshkov, A., Zadorozhny, P.: Finetuning large language models for vulnerability detection. arXiv preprint (2024). Accessed 24 June 2024
13. Shivarpatna Venkatesh, A.P., Sabu, S., Mir, A.M., Reis, S., Bodden, E.: The emergence of large language models in static analysis: a first look through micro-benchmarks. In: Proceedings of the 2023 ACM SIGSOFT International Symposium on Software Testing and Analysis (2023). Accessed 24 June 2024
14. Sun, Y., et al.: Llm4vuln: a unified evaluation framework for decoupling and enhancing llms' vulnerability reasoning. arXiv preprint (2024). Accessed 24 June 2024
15. Team, G., et al.: Gemini: a family of highly capable multimodal models. arXiv preprint arXiv:2312.11805 (2023)
16. Torkura, K.A., Sukmana, M., Cheng, F., Meinel, C.: CAVAS: neutralizing application and container security vulnerabilities in the cloud native era. In: Beyah, R., Chang, B., Li, Y., Zhu, S. (eds.) SecureComm 2018. LNICSSITE, vol. 254, pp. 471–490. Springer, Cham (2018). https://doi.org/10.1007/978-3-030-01701-9_26
17. Zhou, X., et al.: Comparison of static application security testing tools and large language models for repo-level vulnerability detection. arXiv preprint arXiv:2407.16235 (2024)
18. Zhou, X., Zhang, T., Lo, D.: Large language model for vulnerability detection: emerging results and future directions. ACM Comput. Surv. (2023). Accessed 24 June 2024

FRAMICS: Functional Risk Assessment Methodology for Industrial Control Systems

Ahmed Elmarkez[1,2,3(✉)], Soraya Mesli-Kesraoui[1], Flavio Oquendo[2], and Pascal Berruet[3]

[1] Segula Engineering France, Lanester, France
ahmed.elmarkez@segula.fr
[2] IRISA - Université Bretagne Sud, Vannes, France
[3] Lab-STICC - Université Bretagne Sud, Lorient, France

Abstract. Industrial control systems (ICS), essential for managing critical infrastructure like energy, water, and transportation, are increasingly vulnerable to cyber threats due to the integration of Operational Technology (OT) with Information Technology (IT). This paper introduces FRAMICS, a novel risk assessment methodology for ICS, expanding beyond traditional approaches focusing only on logical components. It integrates technical functions with operational environment, using a new functional model and a customized threat modeling technique based on the STRIDE framework. FRAMICS also enhances risk evaluation by adapting the DREAD model to incorporate empirical data, offering a more objective and rigorous assessment. As a data-driven approach, it improves current ICS risk assessment practices. A use case study of a water treatment system showed that threats to availability and integrity were the highest risks, whereas confidentiality and repudiation risks were less significant due to their limited direct impact on system operations.

Keywords: Security-by-design · Functional security · Risk analysis · STRIDE · DREAD

1 Introduction

The risk to Industrial Control Systems (ICS) has steadily increased in recent years. The number of vulnerabilities in ICS has surged from 19 in 2010 [8] to 1,342 in 2022, with nearly 1,000 classified as high or critical severity [22]. In 2017, 64% of vulnerability patches applied to ICS failed to fully mitigate risks, as the components were inherently insecure by design [12].

Furthermore, failing to prioritize security early in the development lifecycle, starting from the functional analysis phase, makes it nearly impossible to **effectively** incorporate security requirements into a complex system, particularly since, in this type of system, "security requirements are often scattered and tangled throughout system functional requirements" [25]. Moreover, the functional

Published by Springer Nature Switzerland AG 2025
L. Nemec Zlatolas et al. (Eds.): SEC 2025, IFIP AICT 745, pp. 180–194, 2025.
https://doi.org/10.1007/978-3-031-92882-6_13

architecture is characterized by its longevity, particularly in ICS. Meanwhile, the physical architecture of such systems continues to evolve in tandem with technological advancements [23]. This implies that systems are not confined to existing, real-world components; rather, a system engineer can focus on what a system needs to do, rather than what it needs to be or look like [11]. This breakdown implies that, as long as the function remains unchanged, the architecture does not need to be redesigned each time a physical change occurs in the system [11]. Consequently, we can conclude that as long as the system retains the **same objectives (functions)**, it maintains the **same functional risks**. Thus, securing a functional architecture ensures **resilience to physical architecture changes**, whether due to technological advancements or maintenance requirements and constraints.

In this article, we introduce FRAMICS, a systematic risk assessment methodology to be integrated into functional analysis. This approach is based on the adaptation of two established methodologies—STRIDE and DREAD—to the context of ICS. FRAMICS identifies threats targeting a functional architecture and systematically assesses them based on their impact and likelihood. This assessment prioritizes key risks, informs security strategies, and helps address security gaps early to ensure compliance with standards [7].

The rest of this paper is organized as follows. Section 2 reviews related works. Section 3 presents the adapted methodology of STRIDE threat modeling methodology. In Sect. 4, the systematic threat assessment methodology is presented. Then, The proposed methodology is applied to a water treatment system use case in Sect. 5. The conclusion is presented in Sect. 6.

2 Related Work

Numerous standards and academic works have addressed risk assessment, particularly for IT systems, offering systematic approaches. However, many of these approaches face challenges in practical application, especially in the context of highly dynamic systems such as Cyber-Physical Systems (CPS) [16,27]. Consequently, our focus will be on methodologies related to the identification, analysis, and evaluation of risks within ICS.

The ISA 62443-3-2 standard [1] defines a security approach for segmenting ICS environments and integrating risk-based security requirements but lacks a systematic cybersecurity risk assessment procedure.

Several safety analysis methods have been adapted to security contexts to safeguard ICS from cyber threats. For instance, STPA-sec [34] extends STPA (Systems Theoretic Process Analysis) methodology by incorporating a cybersecurity analysis based on high-level control models. However, this method primarily addresses how hazards or failures can be triggered by cyber threats, without considering cyber threats that impact the system independently, such as those compromising non-repudiation and confidentiality properties. Similarly, Failure Mode and Effect Analysis (FMEA) [29], traditionally used to assess mechanical or system failures, has been applied in security contexts. FMEA identifies potential failure modes and their effects but focuses on system components (hardware and software) without directly addressing security threats.

The STRIDE methodology is commonly used to identify cyber threats in ICS. STRIDE, as defined in [31], stands for Spoofing ("pretending to be something or someone other than yourself"), Tampering (modifying something, typically on disk, on a network, or in memory"), Repudiation ("claiming you did not do something, or were not responsible for what happened"), Information disclosure ("allowing people to see the information they are not authorized to see"), Denial of service ("absorbing a resource that is needed to provide service"), and Elevation of privilege ("allowing someone to do something they're not authorized to do"). In [21], the authors applied STRIDE to distributed ICS, constructing comprehensive architectural models and utilizing data flow diagrams (DFDs) to map out the interactions between system components. While this approach facilitated threat identification, their focus remained on system components rather than functions. Moreover, their risk evaluation was not based on a systematic method but instead relied on expert judgment, utilizing the DREAD framework to assess STRIDE threats. Subsequent studies, such as [19], have attempted to apply STRIDE more systematically to CPSs, offering structured procedures for threat elicitation using an attack taxonomy. However, while the contributions of such studies advance threat identification in SCADA systems, they tend to prioritize case studies—such as an electric grid example—without offering a comprehensive, systematic methodology for evaluating the identified threats. Similarly, [18] and [17] employ STRIDE in their analysis of autonomous ships' cybersecurity, using generic logical architectures. These studies also lack a systematic threat assessment methodology, instead relying on qualitative expert analysis of impact and likelihood. In [30], Shaaban et al. propose strategic actions aimed at developing secure applications for unmanned aerial vehicles (UAVs) as CPSs, using a methodology that links STRIDE threats to the fundamental requirements of ISA 62443. However, their approach does not extend to evaluating the severity of the identified threats. The authors of [20] provide a lightweight STRIDE application for CPSs, wherein threats are identified based on expert-determined consequences before the threat elicitation stage. While promising, this method presents challenges for teams lacking expertise in both electrical and cybersecurity fields. Additionally, [26] presents a STRIDE case study in the context of industrial process control, prioritizing threats based on a risk assessment model that multiplies likelihood by impact. However, this study does not clarify how the likelihood values were determined.

Numerous comparative studies have concluded that the STRIDE methodology yields the most rigorous results compared to other threat modeling methodologies [15,32]. Therefore, we adapted it to detect functional cyber threats.

The novelty of this paper lies in two key contributions. First, to the best of our knowledge, no existing work systematically evaluates functional cyber threats. Prior studies predominantly address either system components or safety hazards. This paper bridges that gap by **introducing risk assessment into functional**

analysis granting a higher level of security-by-design. By focusing on securing the functional architecture, the methodology ensures resilience to physical changes, whether driven by technological advancements or maintenance requirements. Second, this work introduces a **systematic, data-driven methodology for assessing the severity of such threats**—a gap unaddressed by previous research, which has largely relied on expert judgment through the application of the DREAD framework to assess STRIDE threats.

3 Threat Modeling

Our objective here is to analyze the risks associated with various functions. First, we present our proposed reference functional architecture. It will be used in the identification and assessment of threats. The reference functional architecture of an ICS encompasses all functions that can be found in an ICS, and that ensure the necessary activities for acquiring, processing, monitoring, controlling, and interacting with the system while guaranteeing its reliability, safety, and performance. Functions' types have been synthesized from "French National Agency for the Security of Information Systems" (ANSSI) Profiles[1] of industrial systems and MITRE ATT&CK ICS[2].

Two categories of system elements are identified. The context elements which consist of **humans** (local and external to the system) and **external functions** that communicate with the system, and the **system functions** itself which are:

- *Maintenance Function*: corresponds to tasks that ensure the configuration, parameter setting, programming, testing, and diagnostics of all or part of the system.
- *Supervision Function*: corresponds to tasks that allow the industrial system operator to access system data and control the industrial process by sending commands or telemetry settings.
- *Acquisition Function*: consists of tasks that are in charge of exchanging information with field functions such as control functions, and with supervision functions to be visualized by operators.
- *Data Archiving Function*: refers to tasks that collect and store data—including telemetry, events, alerts, and alarms—about the operational process.
- *Control Function*: includes the tasks directly connected to the physical system through inputs and outputs, allowing direct control of the physical process.
- *Safety Function*: refers to tasks that ensure safety by bringing the process to a safe state when predetermined conditions are not met.
- *Service Function*: consists of tasks that act on the industrial process according to the instructions from the control functions and also measure physical properties, sending these measurements to the control functions.

---

[1] https://cyber.gouv.fr/publications/profils-de-protection-pour-les-systemes-industriels.

[2] https://attack.mitre.org/assets/.

- *Application Function*: includes task that ensure data analysis, optimization/scheduling of the industrial process, and the management of various application-related actions like patching, data processing, etc.

Functions may interact with other functions within the system or with a context function, which can be human (local or remote) or a function belonging to another system. Interactions between functions are represented by data flows. These data flows are categorized as either local, linking functions within the same system (such as between a local human and a service function, or between two service functions), or external, connecting an external function to a local one (such as a remote human or an external function interacting with a local function). This distinction is important because external data flows and local data flows have different threats severity.

The risk analysis follows an adapted STRIDE methodology, as outlined in Table 1. External functions and humans are treated as external entities, making them susceptible to spoofing or repudiation. Local functions are subject to all STRIDE threats, similar to processes in the original STRIDE method. Dataflows may be tampered with, disclosed, or made unavailable.

Table 1. Threat modeling matrix

ICS Element	S	T	R	I	D	E
Local Functions	X	X	X	X	X	X
External Functions	X		X			
Human	X		X			
Data flow		X		X	X	

4 Risk Assessment Estimation

Risk is the expected loss based on the likelihood of a threat exploiting a vulnerability [3]. Its evaluation combines impact and likelihood.

Quantitative risk assessment offers an objective, data-driven approach by assigning numerical values to factors like probability and impact, allowing precise risk comparison and informed decision-making. However, relying solely on attack probability can lead to ratings that may confuse or cause disagreements among stakeholders [16]. To address these challenges, the DREAD model [5] quantifies security threats using five criteria: **Damage** (assessing potential damage from a threat), **Reproducibility** (how often an attack might succeed), **Exploitability** (effort and expertise required for an attack), **Affected users/systems** (number of affected users or systems), and **Discoverability** (likelihood that a vulnerability will be exploited). Discoverability is difficult to estimate, so it's often assumed that any vulnerability will be exploited, focusing instead on other criteria [5].

Qualitative risk assessment methods, in contrast, are simpler and more accessible to non-technical or executive audiences, offering clear risk categorizations (e.g., extreme, high, medium, or low). In our proposed approach, we combine both qualitative and quantitative methodologies. This hybrid model links quantitative data to qualitative categories across the DREAD criteria, offering a more comprehensive yet understandable risk assessment. This integration ensures that complex data-driven insights are communicated in terms of easily understood risk levels, supporting better decision-making throughout the organization. The mapping between quantitative data and qualitative risk categories is informed by the authors' expertise and insights from ISA 62443-3-2.

The next subsection details the approach for determining each criterion. The impact is characterized by the *damage* and *affected systems*.

Damage. In ICS, the damage can cause safety, environmental and financial implications. Effects resulting from adversarial efforts to attack the ICS environment can manifest in the following damages (they were synthesized from the MITRE ATT&CK ICS impact tactic[3] and [3]):

- *Damage to property/ people/ Environment:* Adversaries may inflict damage and destruction on infrastructure, jeopardize the safety of individuals, and potentially trigger broader environmental catastrophes.
- *Impact on control:* attackers may target operators or function abilities to control the ICS.
- *Impact on view:* Adversaries may influence individuals involved in managing the ICS, affecting their ability to monitor and oversee the system's status.
- *Loss of productivity and revenue:* Attackers may undermine productivity and revenue by disrupting system availability, integrity or/and confidentiality.
- *Loss of Availability:*Adversaries may disrupt Service Functions to impair system control, visibility, or maintenance.
- *Loss of safety:* Adversaries may compromise safety systems essential for hazard mitigation and system protection.
- *Theft of Operational Information:* Adversaries may steal operational data for personal gain or to improve future attacks.

To estimate the damage of a threat, its score is calculated using formula 1:

$$\begin{aligned} Score(t,f) &= \sum_{i\in I} c_i.d_{i,t,f} \\ with \sum_{i\in I} c_i &= 4, c_i \in \mathbb{R} \\ and\ \ d_{i,t,f} &= \begin{cases} \text{1 if the damage i occurs when t menaces f} \\ \text{0 else} \end{cases} \end{aligned} \tag{1}$$

With **t** is a given STRIDE threat, **f** is a given function type, **I** is the set of different damages that may occur in an ICS, $(c_i)_{i\in I}$ is a coefficient that represents the system's sensitivity to a specific type of damage. More the coefficient is high more the damage type is not tolerable to happen. It is important to note that the

[3] https://attack.mitre.org/tactics/TA0105/.

values $d_{i,t,f}$ have been predefined and remain fixed, meaning we have identified, for each function type, the potential damages that could occur in the presence of a specific STRIDE threat (more details in [13]). Then the quantitative score is associated with the damage categories using Table 2.

Affected Systems. For this criterion, we estimate the spread of a threat that menaces an element, as illustrated in Table 3. If the threat consequences affect the entire system, the criterion is classified as high. When the impact is confined to elements communicating with the given elements, the criteria is rated as medium. Lastly, if only the concerned element is impacted, the criteria is considered low.

Impact Estimation. The impact of a threat that menaces a given function is calculated using the Table 4 by combining the damage and the affected systems criteria.

Table 2. Damage categories Estimation

Score	Estimation
between 3 and 4	Extreme
between 2 and 3	High
between 1 and 2	Medium
between 0 and 1	Low

Table 3. Affected systems categories estimation

Value	Estimation
Affects the entire system	High
Impacts directly connected elements	Medium
Affects only the corresponding function	Low

Table 4. Impact categories Estimation

Impact		Damage			
		Low	Medium	High	Extreme
Affected systems	High	Medium	High	Extreme	Extreme
	Medium	Low	Medium	High	Extreme
	Low	Low	Low	Medium	High

4.1 Likelihood

The likelihood is represented by *reproducibility* and *exploitability*.

Reproducibility. To estimate the reproducibility of a threat that targets a specific function type, our analysis relies on the number of previously documented exploits published in public databases. These exploits must be of the same nature as the given threat and must have targeted the same function type.

The procedure outlined in Figure 1 was utilized to quantify the number of exploits associated with a particular threat targeting a given function or interaction type. First, we map function types to their corresponding ICS assets (logical components) based on the MITRE ATT&CK ICS asset list. Relevant keywords for each asset are identified and used to search for historical exploits associated with those assets. The keyword lists are derived from MITRE ATT&CK ICS and related studies [14]. Next, we use the Cybersecurity and Infrastructure Security Agency (CISA)[4] advisories to search for prior exploits for each asset based on the associated keywords. Following the methodology in [14], we identify the affected assets and extract the reported Common Vulnerabilities and Exposures (CVEs). For each CVE, we determine the corresponding Common Weakness Enumerations (CWEs) exploited. We exclude non-architectural weaknesses, focusing on architectural weaknesses (CAWEs) defined in [28]. For each CAWE, we retrieve the common consequences, representing the affected security properties. Using Table 5, which links security properties to threats, we identify the associated STRIDE threats.

This process is repeated for all CISA advisories. We then calculate the number of threats linked to each keyword and sum the results to estimate the overall occurrence of threats for each asset. By aggregating these occurrences (They can be found in [13]), we estimate the threat reproducibility for a given function.

Quantitative data is mapped to qualitative categories using Table 6. Risks associated with human factors, such as errors, intentional actions, or negligence, exhibit high risk reproducibility, indicating a greater likelihood of recurrence.

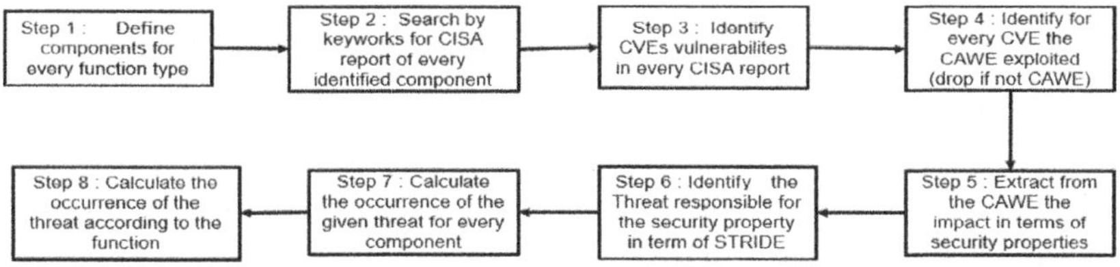

Fig. 1. Threat Reproducibility identification approach.

Table 5. Security properties and STRIDE threat mapping

Security property	STRIDE threat
Availability	Denial of service
Confidentiality	Information disclosure
Accountability	Repudiation
Authentication	Spoofing
Access Control	Elevation of privilege
Non-Repudiation	Repudiation
Integrity	Tampering

Table 6. Reproducibility categories estimation

Quantitative estimation	Qualitative estimation
more than 100	High
between 50 and 100	Medium
under 50	Low

Exploitability. This criterion evaluates two factors: the effort required and the level of expertise needed to execute an attack. Attack scripts are widely available

[4] https://www.cisa.gov/news-events/cybersecurity-advisories.

to the public, and there are databases that automate and replicate them (e.g., [2,6]), making the expertise factor negligible in our analysis.

Effort is assessed based on the potential number of attackers, as described in [5]. A threat exploitable by any remote, anonymous user is considered more exploitable than one requiring an on-site, highly authorized user. Thus, we define three values to evaluate this parameter based on the function's exposure. The greater the exposure to external networks, the higher the risk of exploitation. A function is considered directly exposed if connected to remote users or external functions. Indirect exposure occurs when the function is briefly connected to external networks, such as during local human interactions. A function is deemed not exposed if it is never connected to external networks.

Likelihood Estimation. The Likelihood of a threat that menaces a given function is calculated using the Table 7 by combining the exploitability and the reproductiliby criteria.

Table 7. Likelihood categories Estimation

Likelihood		Exploitability		
		Not Exposed	Indirect Exposure	Direct Exposure
Reproducibility	High	Likely	Very Likely	Very Likely
	Medium	Medium	Likely	Very Likely
	Low	Rare	Medium	Likely

4.2 Threat Criticality Estimation

The criticality of a threat that menaces a given function is estimated using Table 8 by combining the impact and the likelihood estimations. (All the necessary data is accessible within this repository [13]).

Table 8. Threat Criticality Estimation

Risk Criticality		Impact			
		Low	Moderate	High	Extreme
Likelihood	Very Likely	High	High	Extreme	Extreme
	Likely	Medium	High	Extreme	Extreme
	Medium	Low	Medium	High	High
	Rare	Low	Low	Medium	High

5 Water Treatment System Use Case

This section applies our methodology to a small-scale water treatment testbed based on [24] (Fig. 2), replicating key functions of urban plants. The system comprises six independently controlled stages, along with functions for supervision, data acquisition and archiving, and a maintenance feature.

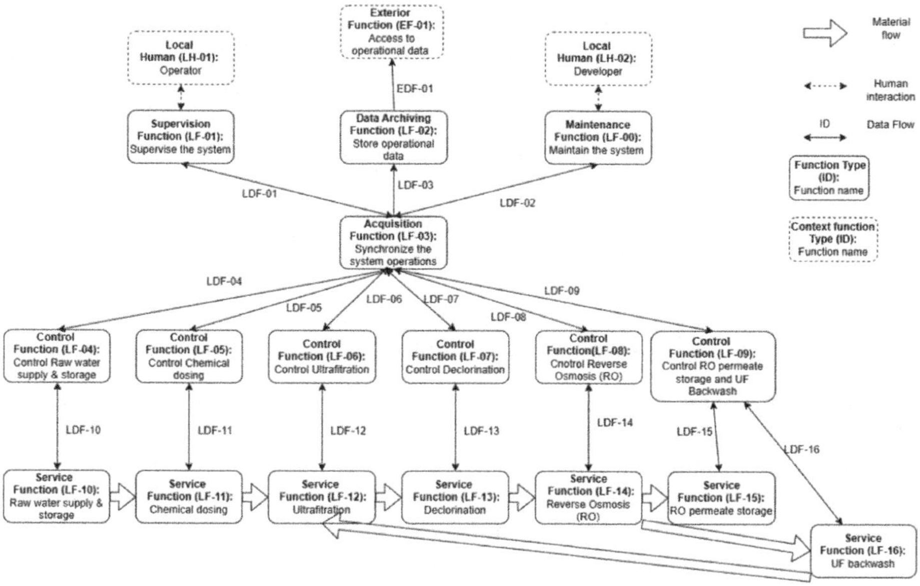

Fig. 2. Water Treatment System functional architecture based on [24].

5.1 Threat Identification

At the first stage of our threat modeling methodology, we first identify the list of different functions and context element with categorizing them into their abstract type (Local Function (LF), Local Human (LH), Local Data Flow (LDF), External Function (EF), External Human (EH) or External Data Flow (EDF)).

Based on Table 1, we identify threats for every system element.

Spoofing: An attacker could impersonate an operator (LH-01) to issue harmful commands, or a developer (LH-02) to alter critical configurations -such as the lower and upper set points for water storage, the dosage of chemicals- leading to dangerous outcomes. They might also spoof the external function (EF-01) to access sensitive industrial data or compromise the local network to impersonate local functions (LF-00 to LF-16), disrupting monitoring and control.

Tampering: This attack affects all local functions and their interactions. By compromising the maintenance function (LF-00), an attacker can inject or alter harmful configurations, destabilizing the system. Compromising acquisition (LF-03) or control functions (LF-04 to LF-09) allows manipulation of logic or set points, disrupting local and system-wide operations. Attacks on service functions (LF-10 to LF-16) can falsify data or commands, causing denial of view or control. Likewise, compromising the supervision function (LF-01) enables tampering with operator commands or visualized data, leading to errors and potential damage. Manipulating dataflows can also result in denial of view or control.

Repudiation: Without non-repudiation measures, local actors (LH-01 or LH-02) can deny responsibility for harmful actions. An attacker compromising the data archiving function (LF-02) could corrupt or delete data, hindering incident tracing and process optimization while concealing malicious activity. Additionally, a compromised local function could send falsified data or commands and deny involvement, complicating prevention and tracing efforts.

Information Disclosure: An attacker compromising the network (LDF-01 to LDF-16, EDF-01) or local functions (LF-00 to LF-16) could access operational and control information to analyze processes and plan further attacks. This data might be leaked to competitors, risking revenue loss. Additionally, sensitive security data like credentials and logs could be exploited in future attacks.

Denial of Service: This threat can severely impact system availability, safety, and protection, potentially endangering property and lives. All local functions (LF-00 to LF-16) and communications (LDF-01 to LDF-16) are vulnerable. An attacker might cause denial of service (DoS) by overloading the network, delaying or blocking real-time data like commands or sensor inputs, leading to a loss of view and control, hindering data transmission and command execution.

Elevation of Privilege: All local functions are vulnerable to attacks that may escalate privileges, enabling unauthorized actions. An attacker could manipulate actuators or issue unauthorized commands, bypassing control protocols and altering system behavior. They might also access sensitive information like system configurations or security credentials, compromising integrity and confidentiality. These breaches can lead to operational disruptions, data exfiltration, degraded performance, and significant security risks.

5.2 Threat Analysis and Evaluation

For each threat, we evaluate its impact in terms of potential damage and the systems it affects, as well as its likelihood, which depends on the threat's reproducibility and exploitability. Table 9 provides an overview of the number of threats across different assessment categories. The data highlights that Tampering and Denial of Service pose the greatest risks to ICS environments, emerging as the most critical threats. Due to pages limitations reasons, Table 10 illustrates a sample of this assessment. For damage coefficients, we assigned a value of 1 to 'Damage to property/people/environment' as this factor is critical, while other types of damage were given a coefficient of 0.5.

Table 9. Number of threats per assessment categories

Threats	Assessment categories			
	Extreme	High	Medium	Low
S	2	17	1	0
T	33	3	0	0
R	12	1	2	15
I	0	1	34	1
D	33	3	0	0
E	15	2	0	0

Table 10. Samples from threats assessment of water treatment system

Element ID	Concrete type	Threat	Impact		Likelihood		Threat assessment
			Damage	Affected systems	Reproducibility	Exploita-bility	
LF-01	Supervision Function	S	High	High	Low	Not Exposed	High
		T	Extreme	High	High		Extreme
		R	Medium	Medium	Medium		Medium
		I	Low	Low	High		Low
		D	Medium	High	High		Extreme
		E	High	High	High		Extreme

5.3 Discussion

This section discusses the accuracy of STRIDE threat assessments by comparing our results with findings from other studies and documented ICS cyber incidents.

Table 9 highlights the criticality of STRIDE threats across various function types, emphasizing the heightened risks of **denial of service (DoS)** and **tampering**. These threats are particularly severe in industrial cybersecurity due to their potential to disrupt essential system operations [10,33]. For instance, a DoS attack on functions responsible for monitoring or controlling system states can cause catastrophic failures, especially in systems reliant on real-time control of physical processes, such as water treatment plants or power grids [9]. In our use case, disruptions in critical functions, such as a dosing mechanism in a municipal water supply system, could pose significant public health risks. A DoS attack on the dosing function, which regulates chemical levels like chlorine or fluoride, could result in widespread exposure to contaminated water. Similarly, tampering attacks compromising the integrity of control signals or sensor data could cause underdosing, leaving pathogens in the water, or overdosing, introducing toxic chemical levels. These scenarios present severe threats to public health and safety. Safeguarding the integrity of control loops in critical infrastructure is essential, as breaches can trigger cascading failures extending beyond technical issues, with potential public health and safety consequences [24,33].

Elevation of privilege attacks, a critical threat in the STRIDE model, present similar risks to tampering. Unauthorized access to elevated control functions can allow attackers to issue malicious commands, compromising system integrity. In industrial systems, privilege escalation can enable attackers to alter critical operational parameters, leading to severe consequences.

Spoofing threats, though less commonly observed in past incidents, can be highly destructive. A spoofed operator or control function can issue fraudulent commands, mimicking tampering by sending false instructions that undermine system performance. In ICS, spoofed commands or identities could manipulate physical processes, resulting in safety and operational hazards [4].

In contrast, threats like **repudiation** and **information disclosure** typically present lower severity in industrial settings. While repudiation can obscure an attacker's actions, its direct impact is less critical compared to threats affecting system availability, integrity, or safety. Similarly, information disclosure threats are less severe in industrial contexts, as the focus is on system availability and integrity, not data privacy [10,33]. Yet, in intellectual property-heavy industries, exposing sensitive data could lead to significant financial and legal repercussions.

6 Conclusion and Future Work

This paper introduces FRAMICS, a risk assessment methodology for ICS that considers both technical functions and the operational environment, beyond traditional logical component-focused approaches. It uses an adapted STRIDE-based threat modeling technique and DREAD methodology, incorporating empirical data for a more objective risk assessment. A case study on a water treatment system demonstrates its applicability by assessing various threats.

The next phase of the research aims to mitigate risks by prioritizing them according to their severity, following the ISA-62443-3-3 standard, which organizes security requirements across multiple levels, with higher levels addressing more critical risks. Additionally, FRAMICS will be enhanced with further methodologies to capture relevant details and identify weaknesses and vulnerabilities introduced during the logical and physical development stages of the ICS development lifecycle.

References

1. ANSI/ISA-62443-3-2-2020, Security for industrial automation and control systems, Part 3-2: Security risk assessment for system design
2. GitHub - swisskyrepo/PayloadsAllTheThings: A list of useful payloads and bypass for Web Application Security and Pentest/CTF. https://github.com/swisskyrepo/PayloadsAllTheThings
3. ISA/IEC 62443 (ISA-99). https://www.isa-france.org/isa-99
4. A hacker tried to poison a Calif. water supply. It was as easy as entering a password (June 2021). https://www.nbcnews.com/tech/security/hacker-tried-poison-calif-water-supply-was-easy-entering-password-rcna1206

5. Threats - Microsoft Threat Modeling Tool - Azure (August 2022). https://learn.microsoft.com/en-us/azure/security/develop/threat-modeling-tool-threats
6. Redcanaryco/atomic-red-team (September 2024). https://github.com/redcanaryco/atomic-red-team, original-date: 2017-10-11T17:23:32Z
7. Aksu, M.U., et al.: A quantitative CVSS-based cyber security risk assessment methodology for IT systems. In: 2017 International Carnahan Conference on Security Technology (ICCST) (October 2017). iSSN: 2153-0742
8. Andreeva, O., et al.: Industrial control systems vulnerabilities statistics. Kaspersky Lab, Report (2016)
9. Asghar, M.R., Hu, Q., Zeadally, S.: Cybersecurity in industrial control systems: issues, technologies, and challenges. Comput. Netw. **165**, 106946 (2019)
10. Cheminod, M., Durante, L., Valenzano, A.: Review of security issues in industrial networks. IEEE Trans. Ind. Inform. **9**(1), 277–293 (2013). conference Name: IEEE Transactions on Industrial Informatics
11. Cline, J., Novell, S.: A Functional Reference Architecture and Assessment Thereof for the National Ignition Facility Industrial Controls Systems. Technical report. LLNL–TR-848125, 1971301, 1072223 (April 2023)
12. DRAGOS: Industrial control vulnerabilities:2017 in review (2018). https://www.dragos.com/wp-content/uploads/2017-Review-Industrial-Control-Vulnerabilities.pdf
13. Elmarkez, A., Mesli-Kesraoui, S., Oquendo, F., Pascal, B.: FRAMICS. https://shorturl.at/zOtxS
14. Gonzalez, D., Alhenaki, F., Mirakhorli, M.: Architectural security weaknesses in industrial control systems (ics) an empirical study based on disclosed software vulnerabilities. In: 2019 IEEE International Conference on Software Architecture (ICSA), pp. 31–40. IEEE, Hamburg, Germany (March 2019)
15. Hussain, S., Kamal, A., Ahmad, S., Rasool, G., Iqbal, S.: Threat modelling methodologies: a survey. Sci. Int. (Lahore) **26**, 1607–1609 (2014)
16. Kavallieratos, G., Katsikas, S.: Managing cyber security risks of the cyber-enabled ship (2020)
17. Kavallieratos, G., Katsikas, S.: Managing cyber security risks of the cyber-enabled ship. J. Mar. Sci. Eng. **8**(10), 768 (2020). number: 10 Publisher: Multidisciplinary Digital Publishing Institute
18. Kavallieratos, G., Katsikas, S., Gkioulos, V.: Cyber-attacks against the autonomous ship. In: Katsikas, S.K., et al. (eds.) SECPRE/CyberICPS -2018. LNCS, vol. 11387, pp. 20–36. Springer, Cham (2019). https://doi.org/10.1007/978-3-030-12786-2_2
19. Khalil, S.M., Bahsi, H., Dola, H.O., Korõtko, T., McLaughlin, K., Kotkas, V.: Threat modeling of cyber-physical systems - a case study of a microgrid system. Comput. Secur. **124**, 102950 (2023)
20. Khan, R., McLaughlin, K., Laverty, D., Sezer, S.: STRIDE-based threat modeling for cyber-physical systems. In: 2017 IEEE PES Innovative Smart Grid Technologies Conference Europe (ISGT-Europe), pp. 1–6 (September 2017)
21. Kim, K.H., Kim, K., Kim, H.K.: STRIDE-based threat modeling and DREAD evaluation for the distributed control system in the oil refinery. ETRI J. **44**(6), 991–1003 (2022)
22. Kovacs, E.: Siemens Drives Rise in ICS Vulnerabilities Discovered in 2022: Report (February 2023). https://www.securityweek.com/siemens-drives-rise-in-ics-vulnerabilities-discovered-in-2022-report/
23. Lamm, J.G., Weilkiens, T.: Functional Architectures in SysML. Tag des Systems Engineering (2010)

24. Mathur, A.P., Tippenhauer, N.O.: SWaT: a water treatment testbed for research and training on ICS security. In: 2016 International Workshop on Cyber-physical Systems for Smart Water Networks (CySWater), pp. 31–36 (April 2016)
25. Nguyen, P.H., Ali, S., Yue, T.: Model-based security engineering for cyber-physical systems: a systematic mapping study. Inf. Softw. Technol. **83**, 116–135 (2017)
26. Ramis Ferrer, B., Afolaranmi, S.O., Lastra, J.L.M.: Principles and risk assessment of managing distributed ontologies hosted by embedded devices for controlling industrial systems. In: IECON 2017 - 43rd Annual Conference of the IEEE Industrial Electronics Society, pp. 3498–3505 (Oct 2017)
27. Rosado, D.G., et al.: Managing cybersecurity risks of cyber-physical systems: the marisma-cps pattern. Comput. Ind. **142**, 103715 (2022)
28. Santos, J.C.S., Tarrit, K., Mirakhorli, M.: A catalog of security architecture weaknesses. In: 2017 IEEE International Conference on Software Architecture Workshops (ICSAW), pp. 220–223 (April 2017)
29. Schmittner, C., Gruber, T., Puschner, P., Schoitsch, E.: Security application of failure mode and effect analysis (FMEA). In: Bondavalli, A., Di Giandomenico, F. (eds.) SAFECOMP 2014. LNCS, vol. 8666, pp. 310–325. Springer, Cham (2014). https://doi.org/10.1007/978-3-319-10506-2_21
30. Shaaban, A.M., Jung, O., Fas Millan, M.A.: Toward applying the IEC 62443 in the UAS for secure civil applications. In: SAFECOMP 2014. LNCS, vol. 8666, pp. 45–52. Springer, Wiesbaden (2022). https://doi.org/10.1007/978-3-658-36295-9_7
31. Shostack, A.: Threat Modeling: Designing for Security. Wiley, Indianapolis, IN (2014). oCLC: ocn855043351
32. Sidi, F., et al.: A comparative analysis study on information security threat models: a propose for threat factor profiling. J. Eng. Appl. Sci. **12**(3), 548–554 (2017). number: 3 Publisher: Medwell Journals
33. Stouffer, K., et al.: Guide to Operational Technology (OT) Security. Technical report. NIST Special Publication (SP) 800-82 Rev. 3, National Institute of Standards and Technology (September 2023)
34. Young, W., Leveson, N.: Systems thinking for safety and security. In: Proceedings of the 29th Annual Computer Security Applications Conference, pp. 1–8. ACSAC '13, Association for Computing Machinery, New York, NY, USA (December 2013)

Data Transformation for IDS: Leveraging Symbolic and Temporal Aspects

Enzo Zamaï[1](✉), David Espes[1], Audrey C. Therrien[2], and Catherine Dezan[1]

[1] Université de Bretagne Occidentale, Brest, France
{enzo.zamai,david.espes,catherine.dezan}@univ-brest.fr
[2] Université de Sherbrooke, Sherbrooke, Canada
audrey.corbeil.therrien@usherbrooke.ca

Abstract. This paper introduces a novel data representation approach for Intrusion Detection Systems (IDS), which integrates temporal and symbolic dimensions by constructing 2D matrices that incorporate the history of packet flows while preserving their temporal order and enhancing contextual richness. These enriched representations are then processed by a custom lightweight Convolutional Neural Network (CNN) designed to capture complex patterns with high efficiency. We have developed a new pooling mechanism that emphasizes recent communication patterns, ensuring the relevance of temporal data, and the creation of a compact yet effective CNN architecture optimized for IDS tasks. The proposed model achieves state-of-the-art performance on the CICIDS2017 dataset, demonstrating superior detection accuracy and robustness across diverse attack classes. By reducing computational complexity and enhancing the contextual representation of network data, our approach offers a significant step forward in the design of effective and scalable IDS solutions.

Keywords: Data Transformation · Symbolic and Temporal Context · IDS · CNN · Network Security · Ponderate Pooling · CICIDS2017

1 Introduction

Interconnected devices are increasingly present in our day to day, and these devices have increasingly complex functions, in both civilian and military fields. These systems often need to communicate with their environment in order to function in a coordinated way. However, making these devices communicative and cooperative considerably increases the attack surface, with every connection point becoming a potential vulnerability to be exploited by attackers. To reduce these risks, it is essential to design these systems with robust defense mechanisms and proactive anticipation of attack vectors. This makes the integration of an Intrusion Detection System (IDS) [12] essential. These systems enable real-time monitoring of network activities and rapid detection of anomalies or intrusions, including complex and persistent attacks that exploit advanced vulnerabilities. By combining anomaly detection techniques with malicious behavior

Published by Springer Nature Switzerland AG 2025
L. Nemec Zlatolas et al. (Eds.): SEC 2025, IFIP AICT 745, pp. 195–209, 2025.
https://doi.org/10.1007/978-3-031-92882-6_14

identification capabilities, an IDS considerably enhances system resilience. This helps mitigate threats and improve security in an increasingly interconnected and exposed environment.

To ensure system security, it is crucial to understand the means of communication and the information that IDS uses to discriminate attacks. They generally exploit information from network traffic to identify abnormal or malicious activity. First, many IDSs focus solely on single network packets, analyzing their individual characteristics (e.g. IP addresses, ports or protocols). These approaches, often exploiting models such as Support Vector Machine (SVM), Naive Bayes classifier, Random Forest (RF), Logistic Regression (LR), extract features directly from packets and identify anomalies at this granular level [22]. Some more advanced methods also take into account temporal information by modeling network traffic as a time series. These approaches are based on architectures such as Recurrent Neural Networks (RNN), Long Short-Term Memory (LSTM), Gated Recurrent Unit (GRU) or transformers, which can capture temporal dependencies and detect complex attack patterns taking place over several stages [16,27]. The majority of previous models use 1D data, which represents a single vector, allowing efficient analysis of packages in isolation. On the other hand, some methods transform this 1D data into 2D representations, for example by organizing packet characteristics in matrix or image form, but without establishing any real logical link between the dimensions created [10].

Our contribution represents a major advance in network flow analysis, incorporating an innovative approach combining symbolic, temporal and organizational dimensions. By combining in-depth packet analysis with a study of the complex relationships between data flows, our method enhances the capabilities of IDS to detect sophisticated attacks. We also introduce innovative modeling that incorporates a communications history, enabling a 2D representation of interactions combining temporal and symbolic aspects. This enriched representation is exploited by a convolutional neural network (CNN) designed to capture complex patterns while reducing data dimensionality. Our results show that this model achieves some of the best performance for the detection and classification of different classes of attack, outperforming existing approaches on several key points. Moreover, the clever combination of CNN and our 2D representation of the data enables us to have small models compared with the latest AI architecture such as transformers.

We will begin the article with a contextualization of our work in relation to the literature. Then, we will justify and present our new history-based approach and its adaptation within the CNN model. Finally, we will look at the results obtained and compare them with the literature, with a view to drawing a general conclusion on this study.

2 Related Works

The vast majority of articles in the literature report on a large number of models that only take into account each sample independently of the others. These include a large number of classic machine learning models for IDS, such as Naive Bayes [6,26], Support Vector Machine (SVM) [6] or K-nearest neighbors (KNN) [7]. Other researchers have turned their attention to Deep Learning-based AI. A method proposed by [24] performs feature selection using the Artificial Bee Colony (ABC) algorithm. After that, they use a Deep Belief Network (DBF) based on a Deep Neural Network (DNN) for the detection. The researchers in [2] uses a DNN directly on sample characteristics. These models work well overall, but often show limited performance for the detection of underrepresented classes in the dataset. Their drawbacks and advantages, as well as those of other models, can be found in greater detail in the paper [14].

This is followed by time-series models, of which article [1] proposes a perfect transition to a two-stage model. First, normal traffic is separated from malicious traffic using four algorithms: SVM, Decision Tree (DT), Random Forest (RF) and Gradient Boosting Tree (GBT). Malicious samples are then sent to an LSTM CNN for sorting which uses short term memory architecture to analyze the time serie. Other researchers have also turned to RNN-based techniques for similar reasons [27]. However, their inference latency and tendency to forget long-term information sometimes limit their effectiveness. Lately, with the rise of NLP-type models such as ChatGPT, transformer-type models are becoming popular for IDS. In [16], transformer architecture is used to identify the long-term behavior and characteristics of networks. With positional encoding, they bring in a notion of time and order between different packets. They achieve better results than previous models, at the expense of very high computing power requirements.

A notable development concerns 2D models, which transform 1D data into matrix representations or images to take advantage of advances in image classification algorithms. In [25], a vector representing a network sample is structured as a matrix. Kim et al. [10] exploit transform-inspired techniques to convert packets into 2D images with multiple color channels. Despite the performance of 2D CNNs, these models rely on an artificial transformation of 1D data into 2D, without really enriching the information exploited. To compensate for this, [19] groups samples into time windows to create 2D representations. In this way, we add several samples that follow each other over a given period. This makes more sense than simply transforming 1D samples into 2D, but there is still room for improvement, particularly as different streams will be mixed. Finally, the approaches presented in articles [8,23] involve transforming 1D network samples into a session-based 2D representation. In this context, samples are grouped together according to their source and destination IP addresses, as well as their source and destination ports, to form these sessions. These sessions are then grouped together in 2D matrices, which contain the samples belonging to the same flow. This is highly relevant, as it incorporates all the important notions of network communication: the values of the various characteristics, the temporality and the context of the flow in question. However, this technique has a major limitation for real-time implementation: it is necessary to wait for all the samples in a session to be sent and received before being able to analyze and determine whether or not they are malicious. Another problem lies in the use of fixed-size matrices, which imposes a limit on the number of packets per stream, sometimes excluding part of the data.

In conclusion, this state of the art highlights several key points. First, classical models simply adapted for IDS show limited performance, particularly in detecting minority classes. Second, integrating temporality into models improves overall performance, but often at the cost of a significant increase in model size and complexity. Finally, the most advanced approaches, which take into account all the parameters of a communication (values, temporality and flow context), produce promising results. However, they suffer from significant limitations, notably their incompatibility with real-time use and their computational complexity, which hampers their implementation in constrained environments.

3 Proposed IDS Model

In the following section, we describe in detail the method used to build our model.

3.1 Connection Symbolism

Adapting an artificial intelligence model for IDS requires a deep understanding of network communications. First, we need to look at the temporal notion of samples, in particular their scheduling (the order in which they arrive). Secondly, we propose to group data by network flow, because, as with Brute Force attacks, it is the cumulative interactions and persistent abnormal behavior that characterize this attack. An isolated activity or a single connection is not enough to qualify as an attack in this context. We define a network flow as a set of data packets circulating through a computer network between specific points of communication (often called hosts or devices). Two machines communicating together will share the same source and destination IP address values, as well as source and destination port values, in both directions. Each flow will then uniquely possess these characteristics. More formally, we define:

- $\forall (i,j) \in [\![1,n]\!] \times [\![1,d]\!]$, we define the sample S_i by:

$$\mathbf{S}_i = (S_{i,1}, S_{i,2}, \ldots, S_{i,j}, \ldots, S_{i,d})^T = \begin{pmatrix} S_{i,1} \\ \vdots \\ S_{i,d} \end{pmatrix} \in \mathbb{R}^{d,1} \tag{1}$$

where n is the number of samples and d is the number of features in a sample. The values $S_{i,1}$, $S_{i,2}$, $S_{i,3}$, $S_{i,4}$ represent the source and destination IP addresses and the source and destination ports of sample i respectively. Thus, each sample belongs to a flow F_k according to the following conditions:

- $\forall k \in [\![1, l]\!],\ F_k =$

$$\left\{ S_i \mid \forall k' \in [\![1, l]\!], S_j \in F_{k'}, \begin{pmatrix} \min(S_{i,1}, S_{i,2}) = \min(S_{j,1}, S_{j,2}) \wedge \\ \max(S_{i,1}, S_{i,2}) = \max(S_{j,1}, S_{j,2}) \wedge \\ \min(S_{i,3}, S_{i,4}) = \min(S_{j,3}, S_{j,4}) \wedge \\ \max(S_{i,3}, S_{i,4}) = \max(S_{j,3}, S_{j,4}) \end{pmatrix} \Leftrightarrow (k = k') \right\} \tag{2}$$

where l is the number of flows and the values $\min(S_{i,1}, S_{i,2})$, $\max(S_{i,1}, S_{i,2})$, $\min(S_{i,3}, S_{i,4})$ and $\max(S_{i,3}, S_{i,4})$ represent the characteristics specific to flow k.

Finally, we define $m_k = |F_k|$ as the number of samples belonging to the same flow F_k. With these definitions in place, we can now present the way we structure the data in our model.

3.2 Transformation of Data Into 2D

Having defined the concepts of streams and samples, we can now examine how they work. Our approach consists in enriching samples with their context specific flow, while preserving the sample sequence from the network. To do this, we choose to concatenate the $S_i \in F_k$ within a $Save_k$ matrix, while respecting their order of arrival.

- $\forall (u, v) \in [\![1, m_k]\!]^2,\ (S_u, S_v) \in F_k^2\ ,\ u > v :$

$$Save_k = \begin{pmatrix} S_{m_k,1} & \cdots & S_{u,1} & \cdots & S_{v,1} & \cdots & S_{1,1} \\ S_{m_k,2} & \cdots & S_{u,2} & \cdots & S_{v,2} & \cdots & S_{1,2} \\ \vdots & \ddots & \vdots & \ddots & \vdots & \ddots & \vdots \\ S_{m_k,d} & \cdots & S_{u,d} & \cdots & S_{v,d} & \cdots & S_{1,d} \end{pmatrix} \in M_{d,m_k}(\mathbb{R}) \tag{3}$$

At the start of the process, there are no samples or flows; as samples are exchanged in the network, data fills the $Save$ matrices. Most artificial intelligence models require inputs of constant size. However, our representation implies a variation in the number of columns in the $Save$ matrices over time. To overcome this, we're going to create sliding window matrices $SW_k \in M_{d,d_{sw}}(\mathbb{R})$ which will keep only the d_{sw} first column of the $Save_k$ matrix as illustrated in Fig. 1.

This leaves us with the special case of initialization. When a flow contains fewer than d_{sw} packets (for example, at the start of the exchange), we complete the matrix by copying the existing packets as many times as necessary to fill the d_{sw} columns. This means that :

- In the case of a flow containing a single package, the matrix SW_k will be made up of d_{sw}identical columns.
- If the stream contains three packets, these will be alternated in order $P_3, P_2, P_1,\ P_3, P_2, P_1 \ldots$, until the target matrix size is reached.
- More generally, for n packages with $n < d_{sw}$, we construct a cyclic sequence $(P_n, P_{n-1}, \ldots, P_1)$, repeated as many times as necessary.

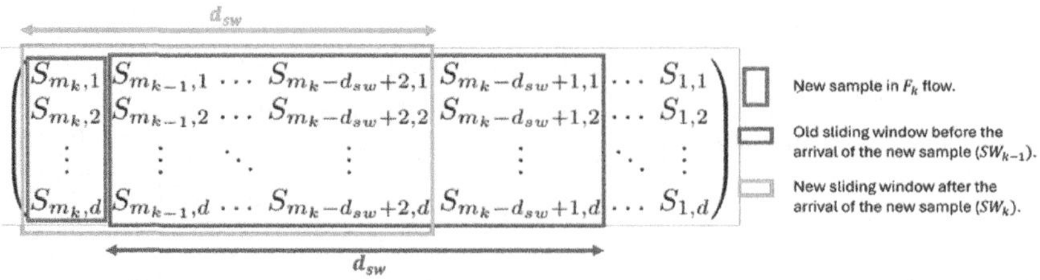

Fig. 1. Presentation of our sliding windows

This method guarantees a consistent, standardized representation of flows, while dynamically adapting matrices to available data. The overall matrix SW_k filling process is summarized in Fig. 2.

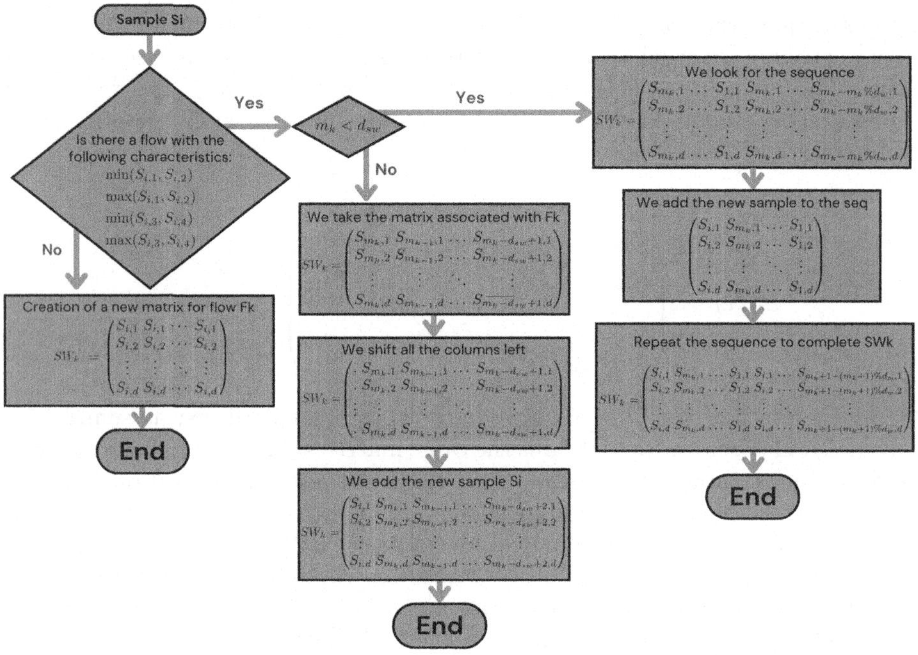

Fig. 2. Process to create our history

The dimension of all matrices SW_k will be the same, i.e., $\forall k \in [\![1, l]\!], SW_k \in M_{d,d_{sw}}(\mathbb{R})$. In this way, each sample S_i is transformed by the preceding process into a matrix containing the previous values of the samples of that same connection if it has occurred:

- $S_i \in \mathbb{R}^{d,1} \xrightarrow{\text{Our process}} M_i \in M_{d,d_{sw}}(\mathbb{R})$ (4)

The preceding work is deliberately generic so that it can be used by most AI models of interest in this context.

3.3 Our Convolutional Neural Network (CNN)

CNNs [28] are among the most effective models for processing 2D structured data, and form the core of our architecture. They consist of convolution layers that extract relevant patterns using learned filters, followed by pooling layers to reduce dimensionality while retaining key information. The resulting feature maps are flattened and passed through fully connected layers to produce output probabilities. In our case, CNNs are particularly suited to process the temporal-symbolic matrices we construct. Each matrix has around 80 rows (features) and a tunable number of columns d_{sw} (recent packets). CNNs can handle such structured data efficiently, with a limited number of parameters, making them ideal for our compact design. We further adapt the CNN to our data by introducing a custom pooling mechanism—ponderate pooling—that emphasizes recent packets via position-based weighting. This highlights the most relevant communication patterns for detection. These architectural choices make CNNs especially well-suited for our representation, balancing performance and efficiency better than generic MLPs or resource-heavy models like transformers.

Although our data has a 2D layout similar to images, it does have differences. First, in an image, a pixel and its neighbors are often coherent. The convolution extracts specific features and reduces the resolution. In our data, each matrix row corresponds to a sample feature such as Source Port, Packet length,... There is therefore no relationship between two successive lines. Consequently, we use 1D kernels to reduce our matrices on the columns only, as illustrated in Fig. 3.

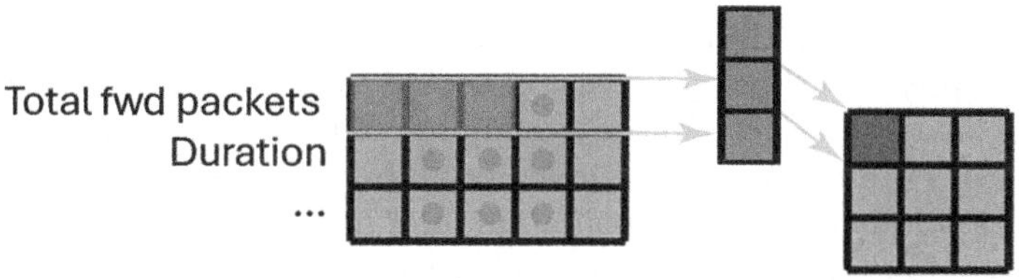

Fig. 3. Convolution operation to reduce our matrix

Depending on the number of convolution operations and the size of the kernels used, the result is a matrix with the same number of rows but a reduced number of columns.

Conventional pooling operations are of the max pooling or average pooling type, which doesn't take into account the pixel positioning in the images [11]. The data supplied as input to the CNN will contain the most recent samples from left to right. The logical approach is to give more weight to more recent samples than older ones. Indeed, the aim is that in the d_{sw} samples, the samples which contribute significantly to the prediction are not drowned out by the others during convolution. To this end, we adopted weighted average operation into our own polling operation called ponderate pooling.

Let X be the feature map resulting from the convolution operation of size $H \times W$, which we aim to reduce to a matrix Y of size $H \times W_{out}$ (with $W_{out} < W$). To achieve this, the columns of X are divided into groups of size k (W must be divisible by k), and a weighting is applied within each group using the vector $\alpha = (\alpha_1, \alpha_2, \ldots, \alpha_k) \in [0,1]^k$, where $\sum_{m=1}^{k} \alpha_m = 1$ and $\alpha_1 \leq \alpha_2 \leq \cdots \leq \alpha_k$. The formula for the output $Y(i,j)$ is given in Eq. 5.

$$Y(i,j) = \sum_{n=1}^{k} \alpha_n \cdot X\big(i, (j-1)k + n\big), \quad \text{where } j \in [1, W_{\text{out}}] \tag{5}$$

This pooling operation is very similar to that of average pooling, to which we have added different weights depending on the position of our values in the matrix. We illustrate it in Fig. 4.

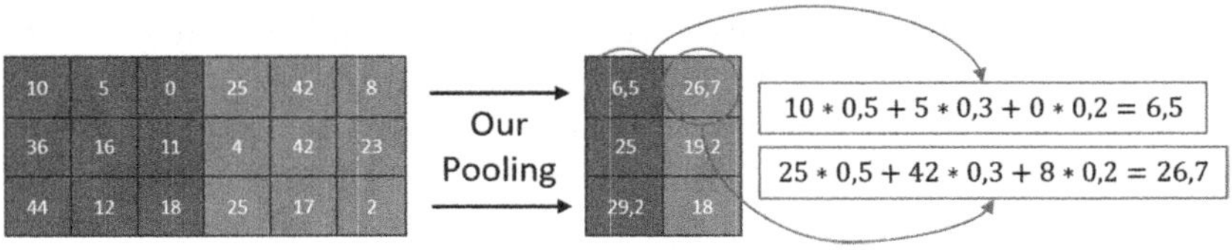

Fig. 4. Example of ponderate pooling with $k = 3$ and $\alpha = (0.5, 0.3, 0.2)$

Our approach therefore adapts the classical CNN model to the specificities of our data. By using 1D kernels to perform convolutions exclusively on the columns, we preserve the consistency of online features while reducing the size of the input matrices. This reduces the number of parameters, and thus compute complexity, of the neural network while retaining the relevant information.

In addition, our ponderate pooling method introduces a temporal hierarchy among the samples, placing greater emphasis on recent information. This mechanism improves the relevance of input data. By combining these adaptations, we obtain a model optimized for efficiently exploiting matrix-structured data, while meeting the constraints imposed by their network nature and dimensionality.

4 Experiments and Results

To evaluate the performance of our model, we designed a rigorous experimental protocol based on the CICIDS2017 dataset [4], a reference in the field of intrusion detection. The following section describes in detail the data preparation steps, the configuration of our model, and the training parameters used for our experiments.

4.1 Experimental Setup

For our experiments, we used the CICIDS2017 dataset, widely recognized for its completeness in IDS. This dataset contains network flows captured in real environments, including a variety of attacks such as DoS, DDoS, Botnet, PortScan, as well as normal benign activity. Each sample is defined by 84 attributes, including information such as Source Port, Destination IP, and Packet Length. We remove the first column representing the unique flow number, as well as the source and destination IP address columns, as they have been arbitrarily selected for each attack type in the CICIDS2017 dataset. This would bias the model, which would only learn which IP addresses source attacks. We also remove the labels and keep them in a new matrix. Finally, as there are 3 protocols used in CICIDS2017, we use one-hot encoding, which adds 2 columns. The result is 82 attributes for each sample. The samples were reworked to remove incorrect samples (missing values) and also to normalize the data (for each feature) to a range between 0 and 1.

Table 1. The layers of our CNN model

Step	Output Shape	Parameters
Conv1D (relu)	$82 \times 18 \times 16$	64
Our Pooling $\alpha = (0.6, 0.3, 0.1)$(relu)	$82 \times 6 \times 16$	0
Conv1D (relu)	$82 \times 5 \times 16$	528
Our Pooling $\alpha = (0.35, 0.25, 0.2, 0.1, 0.1)$ (relu)	$82 \times 2 \times 16$	0
Conv1D (relu)	$82 \times 1 \times 16$	528
Flatten	1312	0
Fully Connected (Dense)	32	42016
Fully Connected (Dense)	128	4224
Fully Connected (Dense)	128	16512
Fully Connected (Dense)	64	8256
Output Layer (Dense)	15	975

In our work, we structured these flows and attributes into 2D matrices, where each row represents a specific feature, and each column corresponds to a temporal sample of the flow. The CICIDS2017 has a very high number of ports, so to create the flow matrices, we only grouped together packets with the same source/destination ip and the same destination port. These dynamic matrices have a fixed length d_{sw} of 20 columns (determined after several trials). We applied SMOTE [5] to augment the class Infiltration. Finally, each matrix of size (82,20) maps to the input of our CNN model. The data were split into 2 groups, 70% for training and 30% for testing, applied to each class. Table 1 describes the layers of our CNN model.

The model was trained on a computer with the following characteristics: 2 x Intel Gold 6148 Skylake @ 2.4 GHz, 128 GB RAM, NVidia V100SXM2 (16 GB). After several experiments, we used the Adam optimizer with a learning rate of 5e–5 and a batch size of 256 for 75 epochs.

4.2 Evaluation Metrics

To evaluate the performance of our CNN on the CICIDS2017 dataset, we use four key metrics: Accuracy, Precision, Recall and F1 Score. **Accuracy** is the proportion of samples correctly classified, **Precision** represents the proportion of correctly identified positive cases among all those predicted as positive, **Recall** indicates the proportion of actual positive cases that are correctly detected, and **f1-score** represents the harmonic mean between precision and recall, balancing the two metrics within a single value. These metrics provide a comprehensive overview of model performance. In the context of network security intrusion detection, they help to minimize false positives and increase detection rates of true attacks, thus ensuring greater model reliability and efficiency.

4.3 Results and Comparison with State-of-the-Art

The literature on CICIDS2017 sometimes lacks specific information on the results obtained, in particular distinguishing between attacks, and the size of the AI model used [7,10,16,26,27]. First, we most often find global results on the entire dataset that do not distinguish between classes and that we provide in the Table 2. We considered it useful to insert the number of parameters of each model when this was provided in order to compare the different complexities of the models.

Z. K. Maseer and al. [17] proposes a benchmark of different machine learning models on the CICIDS2017 allowing us to give a basis of comparison for our model. We also propose to visualize the results of approaches based solely on 1D CNNs [9,20,21]. We find comparisons on the construction of 2D matrices and their applications (CNN, LSTM) [23,25]. Finally, we have displayed the results of interesting approaches by their construction and use of their models such as transformers in the article by Han et al. [8]. Many articles in the literature [8,13,17,22,23] do not give details of the number of parameters in their models, so in this case we will not compare ourselves with them on this point. Our model shows better performance than all models except in the case of precision, for which Kilichev and al. [9] are better. Additionally, our model size, where reported, is at the lower end, comparable with Qazi and al. [20], but our model shows better performance on all metrics.

In a second step, we display the details of our tests on the CICIDS2017 classes. For this part, in order to compare with the other papers, we group the 3 WebAttack classes into one; we do the same for Ddos as well as Patator. We give the results in Table 3.

Table 2. Comparison of overall results on CICIDS2017 dataset

Paper	Model	Parameters	Accuracy	Precision	Recall	F1-score
Z. K. Maseer and al. [17]	ANN	–	99,28%	99,37%	99,28%	99,17%
	DT	–	99,49%	99,43%	99,49%	99,42%
	KNN	–	99,52%	99,49%	99,52%	99,49%
	RF	–	99,30%	99,09%	99,30%	99,12%
	SVM	–	75,21%	99,16%	75,21%	76,60%
	K-means	–	25,59%	97,47%	25,59%	39,96%
V. R. Varanasi and al. [25]	CNN	125697	99,00%	99,00%	99,00%	–
	DNN	1435905	–	98,00%	98,00%	98,00%
Han and al. [8]	Transformer	–	97,87%	98,16%	97,59%	97,83%
T. Sowmya and al. [22]	RNN-BLSTM	–	98,48%	–	–	–
	Naive Bayes classifier	–	98,59%	–	–	–
Sun and al. [23]	CNN	–	98,44%	–	96,46%	93,11%
	LSTM	–	96,83%	–	94,21%	90,97%
	CNN+LSTM	–	98,67%	–	97,21%	93,32%
Rizvi and al. [21]	CNN 1D	118017	99,70%	–	–	–
Kilichev and al. [9]	Optimised cnn 1D	¿200000	99,71%	**100,00%**	99,00%	99,00%
Qazi and al. [20]	CNN 1D	73200	98,96%	98,70%	99,20%	98,94%
C. Liu and al. [13]	VAE CNN	–	98,38%	–	–	–
	VAE GRU	–	98,47%	–	–	–
Behiry and al. [3]	DNN	–	99,80%	98,70%	97,70%	98,70%
Our Model	CNN 1D, new data	**72575**	**99,81%**	99,85%	**99,85%**	**99,85%**

Table 3. Multiclass f1-score comparison on CICIDS2017 dataset

Article	Modèle	Benign	Bot	Ddos	DoS	Patator	Heartbleed	Infiltration	PortScan	WebAttack
Nawaz and al. [18]	LSTM + SMOTE	[94,5–95,4]%	[57,5–58,4]%	[98,5–99,4]%	[97,5–98,4]%	[91,5–92,5]%	[91,5–92,5]%	[94,5–95,4]%	[91,5–92,4]%	[92,5–93,4]%
Han and al. [8]	Transformer	97,51%	96,59%	92,96%	98,74%	98,63%	–	–	**99,83%**	95,37%
Long and al. [15]	Transformer	96,45%	**99,54%**	48,92%	93,95%	12,11%	–	13,23%	–	92,05%
	CNN	99,64%	–	–	97,86%	88,59%	80,88%	**97,75%**	98,51%	–
Sun and al. [23]	LSTM	99,63%	–	–	89,89%	89,19%	77,69%	97,17%	94,04%	–
	CNN+LSTM	99,61%	–	–	97,87%	89,16%	81,20%	97,54%	98,71%	–
Our Model	CNN 1D, new data	**99,91%**	84,06%	**99,91%**	**99,91%**	**99,80%**	50,00%	84,21%	98,85%	**95,90%**

For our AI model, we kept all the classes. The selected models from literature removed some classes from the dataset prior to training [8,15,23]. We can see that our model works very well for the major classes in the dataset, especially for normal traffic, but we have a little more difficulty with the minority classes, such as Bot, Heartbleed and Infiltration, with 587, 3 and 11 test values respectively. The precision of the different models is given in Table 4.

Table 4. Multiclass precision comparison on CICIDS2017 dataset

Article	Modèle	Benign	Bot	Ddos	DoS	Patator	Heartbleed	Infiltration	PortScan	WebAttack
Nawaz et al. [18]	LSTM + SMOTE	[99,5–100]%	[40,5–41,4]%	[97,5–98,4]%	[95,5–96,4]%	[84,5–85,4]%	[84,5–85,4]%	[90,5–91,4]%	[85,5–86,4]%	[91,5–92,4]%
Han et al. [8]	Transformer	95,21%	98,84%	99,41%	**99,98%**	**99,93%**	–	–	**99,98%**	**98,80%**
Long et al. [15]	Transformer	94,65%	**99,72%**	64,40%	99,29%	17,24%	-	44,26%	–	17,24%
Sun et al. [23]	CNN	99,56%	–	–	98,04%	86,43%	80,08%	97,91%	97,48%	–
	LSTM	99,55%	–	–	94,85%	84,59%	81,12%	96,80%	97,99%	–
	CNN+LSTM	99,52%	–	–	98,25%	89,67%	81,12%	98,07%	98,42%	–
Our Model	CNN 1D, new data	**99,84%**	88,25%	**99,95%**	99,92%	99,86%	**100,00%**	**100,00%**	99,87%	96,92%

With these values, we can see that our model is overall similar or better than others at predicting classes. Where it stands out is in its accuracy on normal traffic, with a difference of 0.3%. As this class has 681396 test values, the difference represents over 2000 more correct values. The low F1-scores are due solely to recall. We therefore propose to display our model's confusion matrix on Fig. 6, using the true values, to examine where it is incorrect. We summarize the model predictions in the confusion matrix showed on Fig. 5.

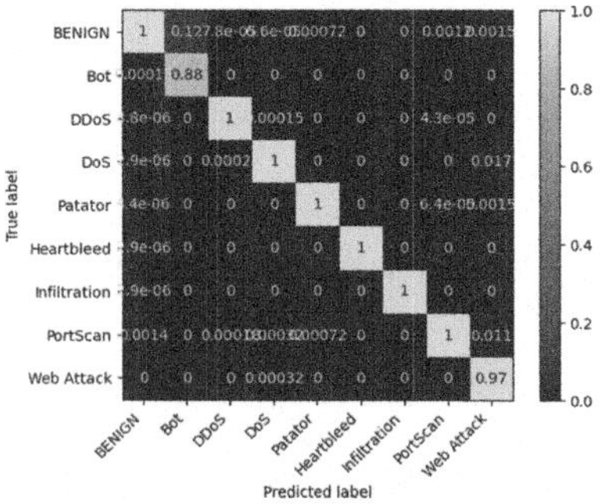

Fig. 5. Confusion matrix with predict labels

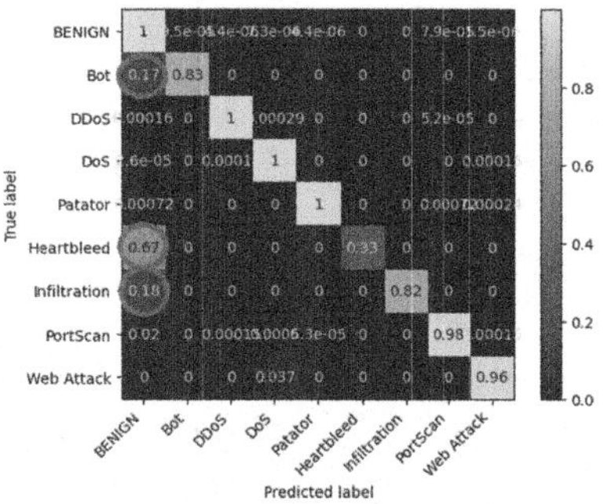

Fig. 6. Confusion matrix with true labels

This shows that normal traffic data is occasionnally detected as an attack, translating to lower recall values (highlighted by the red circles). This means this system will produce false alerts for normal traffic. It is preferable to have false positives than the other way round, where we wouldn't detect an actual attack that. However, a high rate of false positives could interfere with regular uage of the network, and must be kept as low as possible.

5 Conclusion and Future Work

In this paper, we propose a new approach to improve IDS performance by constructing matrices based on the network data which include temporal information to provide more context. To minimize the impact on model size, we propose a clever use of 1D CNN, particularly with the introduction of our own pooling function aimed at reducing the data size while maintaining a trace of the communication history. The results place us among the best in literature on the CICIDS2017 dataset using a CNN model (f1-score:99,85%, accuracy: 99,81%, precision: 99,85% and recall: 99,85%) with a very low number of parameters (around 72000).

In the short term, a complementary study using this method could be considered to test across the entire available datasets in the literature. Following this, it would be relevant to test this method in real-world conditions to see if the performance is affected. This would be followed by a medium-term study focusing on the storage of our backup matrices. Since the number of communication flows continues to grow, a maximum memory capacity should be defined, with the possibility of implementing a flow deletion routine if not used for several months. Finally, in the long term, the model should be retrained on future attack types.

References

1. Ashfaq Khan, M., Karim, R., Kim, Y.: A scalable and hybrid intrusion detection system based on the convolutional-lstm network. Symmetry **11**, 583 (2019). https://doi.org/10.3390/sym11040583
2. Awajan, A.: A novel deep learning-based intrusion detection system for iot networks. Computers **12**, 34 (2023). https://doi.org/10.3390/computers12020034
3. Behiry, M., Aly, M.: Cyberattack detection in wireless sensor networks using a hybrid feature reduction technique with ai and machine learning methods. J. Big Data **11** (2024). https://doi.org/10.1186/s40537-023-00870-w
4. Canadian Institute for Cybersecurity: CICIDS2017 intrusion detection dataset (2017). https://www.unb.ca/cic/datasets/ids-2017.html
5. Chawla, N.V., Bowyer, K.W., Hall, L.O., Kegelmeyer, W.P.: SMOTE: synthetic minority over-sampling technique. J. Artif. Intell. Res. **16**, 321–357 (2002). https://doi.org/10.1613/jair.953
6. Dixit, M., Moholkar, A., Limaye, S., Limaye, D.: Naive bayes and svm based nids. In: 2018 3rd International Conference on Inventive Computation Technologies (ICICT), pp. 527–532 (2018). https://doi.org/10.1109/ICICT43934.2018.9034411
7. Fauzi, M.A., Hanuranto, A.T., Setianingsih, C.: Intrusion detection system using genetic algorithm and k-nn algorithm on dos attack. In: 2020 2nd International Conference on Cybernetics and Intelligent System (ICORIS), pp. 1–6 (2020). https://doi.org/10.1109/ICORIS50180.2020.9320822
8. Han, X., Cui, S., Liu, S., Zhang, C., Jiang, B., Lu, Z.: Network intrusion detection based on n-gram frequency and time-aware transformer. Comput. Secur. **128**, 103171 (2023). https://doi.org/10.1016/j.cose.2023.103171
9. Kilichev, D., Kim, W.: Hyperparameter optimization for 1d-cnn-based network intrusion detection using ga and pso. Mathematics **11**, 3724 (2023). https://doi.org/10.3390/math11173724
10. Kim, T., Pak, W.: Deep learning-based network intrusion detection using multiple image transformers. Appl. Sci. **13**, 2754 (2023). https://doi.org/10.3390/app13052754

11. Lee, C.Y., Gallagher, P., Tu, Z.: Generalizing pooling functions in convolutional neural networks: mixed, gated, and tree (2015). https://doi.org/10.48550/arXiv.1509.08985
12. Liao, H.J., Richard Lin, C.H., Lin, Y.C., Tung, K.Y.: Intrusion detection system: a comprehensive review. J. Netw. Comput. Appl. **36**(1), 16–24 (2013). https://doi.org/10.1016/j.jnca.2012.09.004
13. Liu, C., Antypenko, R., Sushko, I., Zakharchenko, O.: Intrusion detection system after data augmentation schemes based on the vae and cvae. IEEE Trans. Reliab. **71**(2), 1000–1010 (2022). https://doi.org/10.1109/TR.2022.3164877
14. Liu, H., Lang, B.: Machine learning and deep learning methods for intrusion detection systems: a survey. Appl. Sci. **9**, 4396 (2019). https://doi.org/10.3390/app9204396
15. Long, Z., Yan, H., Shen, G., Zhang, X., He, H., Cheng, L.: A transformer-based network intrusion detection approach for cloud security. J. Cloud Comput. **13** (2024). https://doi.org/10.1186/s13677-023-00574-9
16. Manocchio, L.D., Layeghy, S., Lo, W.W., Kulatilleke, G.K., Sarhan, M., Portmann, M.: Flowtransformer: a transformer framework for flow-based network intrusion detection systems. Expert Syst. Appl. **241**, 122564 (2024). https://doi.org/10.1016/j.eswa.2023.122564
17. Maseer, Z.K., Yusof, R., Bahaman, N., Mostafa, S.A., Foozy, C.: Benchmarking of machine learning for anomaly based intrusion detection systems in the cicids2017 dataset. IEEE Access **9**, 22351–22370 (2021). https://doi.org/10.1109/ACCESS.2021.3056614
18. Nawaz, M.W., Munawar, R., Mehmood, A., Rahman, M.M.U., Abbasi, Q.H.: Multi-class Network Intrusion Detection with Class Imbalance via LSTM & SMOTE (2023). https://doi.org/10.48550/arXiv.2310.01850
19. Okey, O.D., Melgarejo, D.C., Saadi, M., Rosa, R.L., Kleinschmidt, J.H., Rodrìguez, D.Z.: Transfer learning approach to ids on cloud iot devices using optimized cnn. IEEE Access **11**, 1023–1038 (2023). https://doi.org/10.1109/ACCESS.2022.3233775
20. Qazi, E., Almorjan, A., Zia, T.: A one-dimensional convolutional neural network (1d-cnn) based deep learning system for network intrusion detection. Appl. Sci. **12**, 7986 (2022). https://doi.org/10.3390/app12167986
21. Rizvi, S., Scanlon, M., McGibney, J., Sheppard, J.: Deep learning based network intrusion detection system for resource-constrained environments. In: Goel, S., Gladyshev, P., Nikolay, A., Markowsky, G., Johnson, D. (eds.) Digital Forensics and Cyber Crime, pp. 355–367. Springer, Cham (2023). https://doi.org/10.1007/978-3-031-36574-4_21
22. Sowmya, T., Mary Anita, E.: A comprehensive review of ai based intrusion detection system. Meas. Sens. **28**, 100827 (2023). https://doi.org/10.1016/j.measen.2023.100827
23. Sun, P., et al.: DL-IDS: extracting features using CNN-LSTM hybrid network for intrusion detection system. Secur. Commun. Netw. **2020**, 1–11 (2020). https://doi.org/10.1155/2020/8890306
24. Thamilarasu, G., Chawla, S.: Towards deep-learning-driven intrusion detection for the internet of things. Sensors **19**, 1977 (2019). https://doi.org/10.3390/s19091977
25. Varanasi, V.R., Razia, S.: Cnn implementation for ids. In: 2021 3rd International Conference on Advances in Computing, Communication Control and Networking (ICAC3N), pp. 970–975 (2021). https://doi.org/10.1109/ICAC3N53548.2021.9725426

26. Vishwakarma, M., Kesswani, N.: A new two-phase intrusion detection system with naïve bayes machine learning for data classification and elliptic envelop method for anomaly detection. Decis. Anal. J. **7**, 100233 (2023). https://doi.org/10.1016/j.dajour.2023.100233
27. Yin, C., Zhu, Y., Fei, J., He, X.: A deep learning approach for intrusion detection using recurrent neural networks. IEEE Access **5**, 21954–21961 (2017). https://doi.org/10.1109/ACCESS.2017.2762418
28. Zeiler, M.D., Fergus, R.: Visualizing and understanding convolutional networks. In: Fleet, D., Pajdla, T., Schiele, B., Tuytelaars, T. (eds.) ECCV 2014. LNCS, vol. 8689, pp. 818–833. Springer, Cham (2014). https://doi.org/10.1007/978-3-319-10590-1_53

SAFARI: A Scalable Air-Gapped Framework for Automated Ransomware Investigation

Tommaso Compagnucci[1], Franco Callegati[1], Saverio Giallorenzo[1,2], Andrea Melis[1(✉)], Simone Melloni[3], and Alessandro Vannini[1]

[1] Alma Mater Studiorum - Università di Bologna,Bologna, Italy
a.melis@unibo.it
[2] Olas Team, INRIA,Sophia Antipolis, France
[3] ARPAE Emilia-Romagna,Bologna, Italy

Abstract. Ransomware poses a significant threat to individuals and organisations, compelling tools to investigate its behaviour and the effectiveness of mitigations. To answer this need, we present SAFARI, an open-source framework designed for safe and efficient ransomware analysis. SAFARI's design emphasises scalability, air-gapped security, and automation, democratising access to safe ransomware investigation tools and fostering collaborative efforts. SAFARI leverages virtualisation, Infrastructure-as-Code, and OS-agnostic task automation to create isolated environments for controlled ransomware execution and analysis. The framework enables researchers to profile ransomware behaviour and evaluate mitigation strategies through automated, reproducible experiments. We demonstrate SAFARI's capabilities by building a proof-of-concept implementation and using it to run two case studies. The first analyses five renowned ransomware strains (including WannaCry and LockBit) to identify their encryption patterns and file targeting strategies. The second evaluates Ranflood, a contrast tool which we use against three dangerous strains. Our results provide insights into ransomware behaviour and the effectiveness of countermeasures, showcasing SAFARI's potential to advance ransomware research and defence development.

Keywords: Analysis Automation · Ransomware · Infrastructure as Code

1 Introduction

Ransomware is malware that seizes users' and organizations' data, demanding payment to restore access to the rightful owners [16]. Ransomware [25,27] is one of the most pressing cybersecurity threats facing organisations and individuals worldwide. In its most general definition, ransomware extorts victims through their data. Economically, ransomware impose sizable costs to society [10,23]. Indeed, ransomware forms a sophisticated, multi-billion dollar industry that continues to adapt and overcome defensive measures [22].

Published by Springer Nature Switzerland AG 2025
L. Nemec Zlatolas et al. (Eds.): SEC 2025, IFIP AICT 745, pp. 210–223, 2025.
https://doi.org/10.1007/978-3-031-92882-6_15

Despite increased awareness and investment in cybersecurity, ransomware attacks continue to proliferate, causing significant financial losses, operational disruptions, and potential harm to human life and safety [5].

The study of the behaviour of ransomware in different contexts and conditions provides fundamental knowledge for its contrast. The scientific and technical literature abounds with solutions to counteract ransomware [1,2,8,20,21,25]. Studying the behaviour of these solutions against real-world malware is important to both evaluate their effectiveness and efficiency and help their evolution.

We respond to such needs with a platform for the *safe* and *efficient* investigation of ransomware and its mitigations. Safety and efficiency of investigation are the main challenges we address in the design of our proposal. To perform an evaluation of ransomware attacks and of contrast strategies, one needs numerous tests in which real ransomware attempts to encrypt users' data. We provide a framework to run these tests *safely*, ensuring that the ransomware infection is fully contained, and *efficiently*, automating the management of the experiment parametrisation, to generate test batteries in a consistent and reproducible manner, and to collect and analyse indicators useful to understand the behaviour and estimate the effectiveness of ransomware and defensive configurations.

SAFARI. We call our proposal Scalable, Air-gapped Framework for Automated Ransomware Investigation (SAFARI), available as an open-source project at https://github.com/Flooding-against-Ransomware/SAFARI.

One of the foundational principles behind SAFARI is the *democratisation of security research*. Indeed, while SAFARI's architecture is general and can encompass the usage of Cloud virtual machines (VM), its design—and the prototype we build to showcase it—targets on-premises deployments where investigators can use local resources to assemble the system. In this way, small research groups, as well as student collectives who can access home-lab-sized hardware can configure their own deployment and run experiments.

Given the dangerous and highly infective nature of ransomware, SAFARI run experiments in *air-gapped* environments. Thanks to the virtualisation of the testing environment, SAFARI isolates malware processes within VMs from those of the hosting environment and the other VMs (to avoid interference).

SAFARI integrates complementary technologies for the definition of experiments and the collection and analysis of attack data. Our proof-of-concept, presented in Sect. 2, illustrates the architecture of SAFARI both in terms of concepts and of software (off-the-shelf and purpose-made by us) that SAFARI integrates to analyse the behaviour of ransomware and their contrast solutions.

While SAFARI's architecture can accommodate the study of malware in general (combined with countermeasures), we focus our proposal on *ransomware* of the crypto kind, since it targets the data of the user, which we use as the metric to measure the effectiveness of both malware and contrast tools. In Sect. 3, we showcase SAFARI through two case studies. The first investigates the behaviour and efficiency of real-world, infamous ransomware such as WannaCry, LockBit, and Phobos. The second analyses the effectiveness and efficiency of a recent tool, Ranflood [3,4], which contrasts ransomware attacks through data flooding—an innovative technique that mixes dynamic honeypots and moving-target defence to contrast ransomware attacks.

Notably, while we provide the experimental data in Sect. 3 as evidence of the potential of SAFARI, the analysis itself constitutes a contribution that adds new knowledge about the analysed malware's behaviour. We position our contribution within the literature in Sect. 4 and discuss final remarks and future development in Sect. 5.

2 Implementing a SAFARI Prototype

In this section, we present our prototypical implementation of SAFARI. We outline its architecture and detail the concepts, technologies, and tools employed for and their respective roles in the implementation.

The fundamental concepts behind SAFARI's efficiency are: *a*) *Infrastructure as Code* (IaC), which is a paradigm where an orchestrator manages the provisioning of infrastructure components, like computing, network, and storage devices, using code rather than manual configuration, *b*) *OS-agnostic Task Automation* (OTA), which offers a uniform interface that allows users to execute processes independently of the underlying operating system, and *c*) *Investigation Tools*, which are the software that provide visibility/metrics on malware's behaviour.

Our prototype reifies IaC with Terraform[1] and OTA with Ansible[2]. Since our application context is crypto-ransomware, we concretise IT with ad-hoc tools that generates a report of the files and checksums of a target VM and compare the reports from before and after running tests to collect the experiments' data.

Before delving into our prototype's architecture, we briefly describe which hypervisor technology we choose. Indeed, while SAFARI's design abstracts away from a specific virtualisation technology, one needs to fix it when considering a specific deployment. We choose Proxmox[3], which is a widely-used and renowned open-source type-2 hypervisor (hosted in Linux/Debian) that supports enterprise-level virtualisation and includes an integrated web-based interface that complements the API-based one for the management of virtual machines, software-defined storage, and networking.

2.1 Software Architecture

We illustrate the architecture and experiments behaviour of our prototype in Fig. 1. The main components of the architecture are the prototype software components (labelled "SAFARI" in the figure, for brevity), test VMs, analysis VMs, and remote persistence. We use borders, in the figure, to represent ephemerality with a dashed line and persistence with a solid one. The VMs that run the experiments (test VM) and the related analysis (analysis VM) correspond to a test run and are ephemeral and discarded within the related test session.

[1] https://www.terraform.io/.
[2] https://www.redhat.com/en/ansible-collaborative.
[3] https://www.proxmox.com/.

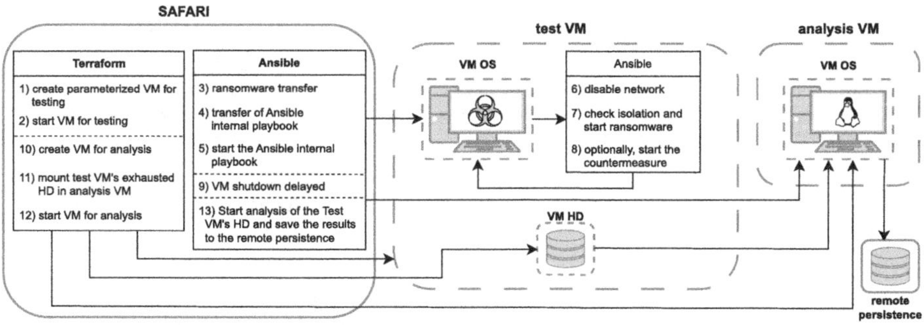

Fig. 1. SAFARI's prototype architecture and functionalities.

The prototype's software and persistence components respectively orchestrate the experiments and store their results (encompassing all the test sessions).

In Fig. 1, from the left, we find the core components of the SAFARI prototype, which orchestrate the operations required to carry out the tests. Terraform and Ansible scripts mainly conduct these operations. The numbered operations shown in the schema correspond to a test session, which one can run multiple times and in parallel to gather statistical experimental data.

We describe the workflow of the prototype following the sequence in Fig. 1.

At the start of an experiment, the system interacts with the hypervisor to create a VM (1) and to start it (2). Then, control passes to OTA, which transfers the malware to the VM (3), along with a list of tasks that the VM must execute (4). This step is peculiar and particularly important for the *air-gapping* principle mentioned in Sect. 1. We require the VMs to run an internal OTA engine. In this way, we avoid the network-based orchestration of the ransomware and rather inject a part of the OTA tasks within the VM. We adopt a multi-tiered approach to enforce isolation, which leads us to divide the logic of OTA orchestration into two parts, one external and one internal. The internal one disables the network connection (6) and makes sure that the VM is isolated before starting the ransomware (7). The in-VM OTA component can also start possible countermeasures present in the VM (8), according to the experiment's design.

All experiments have a set timeout, which triggers (9) the shutdown of the test VM. Then, control passes back to IaC for the creation of the analysis VM (10), which mounts the disk of the test VM for analysis and the remote persistence disk for storing the analysis results (11, 12). OTA orchestrates this step (13), which uses the IT tools to analyse the files and generate the results.

Since SAFARI simplifies managing VMs running different operating systems, our recommendation is, e.g., to use Linux VMs for the analysis of Windows-specific ransomware, to avoid possible accidental activations of the ransomware that would threaten the reliability of the analysis.

2.2 Filechecker and Profiler as IT

We close this section with details of the other software contribution presented in this paper for the implementation of IT tools in SAFARI to study ransomware.

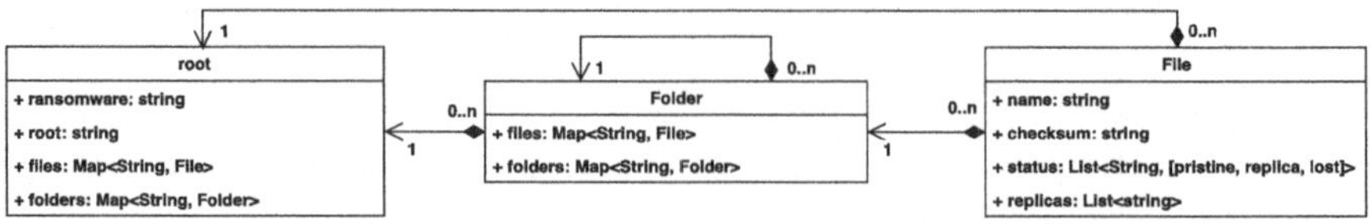

Fig. 2. Schema of the Hierarchical Profile.

To implement the IT part of our SAFARI prototype, we develop a set of open-source tools, available at https://github.com/Flooding-against-Ransomware/profiling. We use these tools to compare the state of VMs before and after a crypto-ransomware attack. Specifically, we use a Filechecker tool to create VM file *reports*. The software generates a JSON-formatted list of the *paths* of all the files (descending within folders) contained within a given *root* location, associated with their *checksum* signature (MD5). We expect investigators to launch the Filechecker manually (one can automate this task with tools like Vagrant[4].) when they assemble a test VM template, so they generate a report of the pristine test VM for later use in the analysis VM. Once obtained the report of the test VM, we run a second tool, called Profiler. The Profiler, given two report files, a reference one and a post-attack one, generates a JSON *profile* file of the difference between the two input files. Specifically, the profile indicates which files are *pristine*, which have been *lost* due to encryption, and possible *replicas* that one can use to restore the original files of the user (i.e., files with a different location but the same content of files of the reference report). Interestingly, while having the pristine-lost ratio would already give us a reading of the effectiveness/efficiency of ransomware and contrast tools, measuring the replicas sheds further light on the modality of execution of ransomware, since many of these create copies of the files to encrypt before deleting them [14]. In addition to a file-to-file comparison, the Profiler generates a *hierarchical* view of the profile, following file locations, i.e., starting from the root, we find a list *files* contained therein, with their related status (pristine/lost/replica) and a list of *folders*, each containing a list of files and subfolders. For reference, we report in Fig. 2 the structure of hierarchical profiles—which also contain contextual information of the experiment/analysis, like the name of the ransomware and the root location (according to the reports). The Profiler can process a hierarchical profile to generate a *summary* profile that indicates measures such as the total numbers of pristine/lost/replica files found in hierarchical order—so that the root reports the overall numbers, then broken down by the folders it contains—and also aggregated by extension (useful to investigate e.g., which file formats a given ransomware mainly targets). Finally, the Profiler can *aggregate* multiple summary profiles of the same kind of experiment to provide statistical data about it. The result of is a JSON profile with the same structure of the summary one but with additional elements that report statistical measures on the files such as

[4] https://github.com/hashicorp/vagrant.

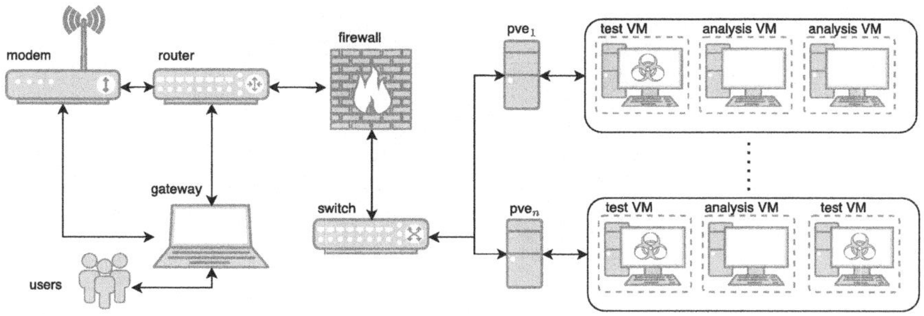

Fig. 3. SAFARI's Prototype Deployment Infrastructure.

averages and standard deviations. By integrating the Filechecker and Profiler in our SAFARI prototype, we obtain the automatic generation of statistics about the execution of ransomware and their countermeasures.

3 Case Studies

To illustrate the usage of SAFARI, we use our prototype to conduct two case studies. The first regards the analysis of the behaviour of a set of known ransomware, to profile their activity. The second showcases the integration within tests of a ransomware countermeasure, Ranflood, to benchmark its effectiveness against attacks. Before describing the case studies and their results, we report on the deployment used to run an instance of our SAFARI prototype.

3.1 SAFARI's Prototype Deployment Infrastructure

The case studies helps us illustrate an on-premises deployment of our prototype. We build the infrastructure shown in Fig. 3 as a companion contribution to SAFARI's definition, designed to let users remotely run safe experiments.

Following Fig. 3, users can authenticate and execute the prototype's functionalities through a gateway connected to the Internet. From the gateway, users can interact with the nodes, named $\text{pve}_1, \ldots, \text{pve}_n$ (where pve stands for Proxmox virtualisation environment), that make up the cluster and host the test and analysis VMs. All these nodes and VMs are behind a firewall that regulates access to the Internet through the router and via the modem.

We detail the main features of the components found in Fig. 3. The *gateway* runs Debian v.12 (although unlikely, we use a Linux machine to further stave off possible infections from Windows ransomware) and represents the only network access point that experimenters use to connect to the nodes. Users connect to the gateway via the ZeroTier VPN and use sshuttle[5] to access directly the nodes, i.e., to run commands as if executed on machines in their local network.

[5] Resp. https://www.zerotier.com/ and https://github.com/sshuttle/sshuttle.

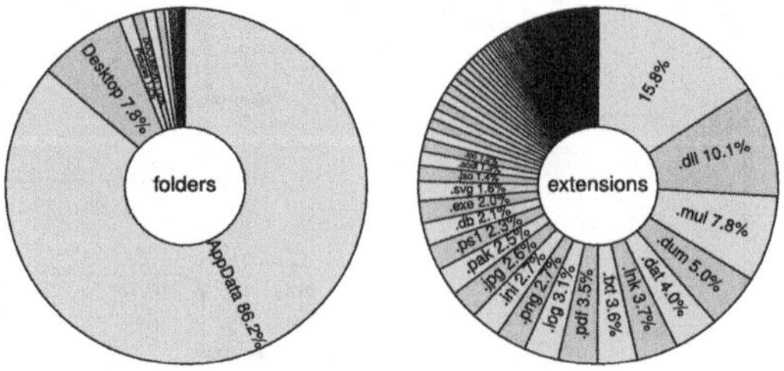

Fig. 4. Visualisation of the user's file profiles.

The *router*, mounting OpenWrt [24], can give Internet connection to the nodes in the cluster, but by default its *firewall* prevents VMs from accessing the Internet to avoid the possible propagation of ransomware.

The hardware of the pve cluster represents typical office/desktop personal computers, and it encompasses eight machines. The nodes run ProxMox 7.0–8 and include two VM templates, Linux Ubuntu 24.04 for the analysis VM and a Windows 10 (x64) 1809 template for the test VM. While each node can run multiple VMs, to have good performance, we run at most two VMs per node.

3.2 Case Study: Ransomware Profiling

To conduct the testing of our prototype, we start by defining a testing protocol, comprising various types of ransomware. We base the selection of these ransomware samples on an analysis of the history of ransomware and its evolution over time [25]. We source the samples used for the tests from repositories previously used and recognised in other academic contexts [18], such as VirusTotal.

In the first case study, we demonstrate our SAFARI prototype's capability to analyse the encryption patterns of five well-known Windows ransomware: Ryuk, Vipasana, WannaCry, LockBit, and Phobos. To simulate a real-world scenario, we configured the test VM with a typical user profile, modelled after Hansley [9], including the primary directories of the Windows 10 file system. The profile features 2 GB of user data, aligned with file type recommendations from Scaife et al. [29] and Kaspersky [13], along with file names commonly targeted by ransomware [15]. Additionally, it incorporates user-interactive programs such as a web browser and an office suite [28]. The profile includes 13 "user" folders, such as "Documents", "Desktop", "Music", and "Pictures" with the breakdown reported in Fig. 4, using the prototype's Filechecker and Profiler tools.

For each ransomware strain, we run 32 experiments with a timeout of 10 min for each experiment. We obtain at least 16 valid experiments for each ransomware—22 for LockBit, 32 for Ryuk and Vipasana, and 16 for Phobos and Wannacy, where we discard the ones where the ransomware did not start.

We visualise the results in Fig. 5, reporting in the rows the data of a given ransomware and divide these (from left to right) respectively between the percentage summary of pristine/lost/replica files and the percentage breakdown of

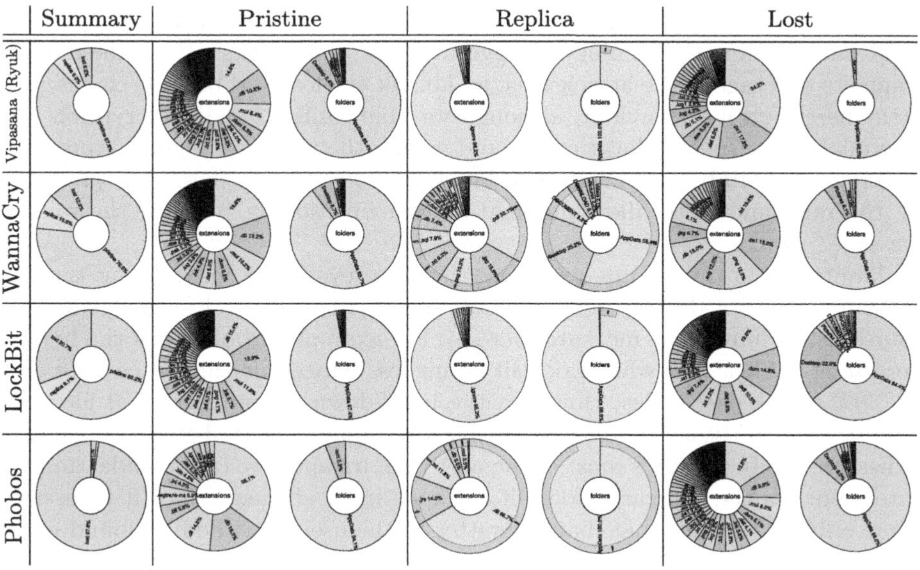

Fig. 5. Attack profiles of Vipasana/Ryuk, WannaCry, LockBit, and Phobos.

pristine, replica, and lost files by extensions and folders. As Ryuk and Vipasana exhibit similar behavior, only Vipasana's results are shown for brevity. Replica file plots include smaller outer segments indicating the percentage of distinct replicas within a partition, e.g., the 3% in Ryuk/Vipasana folder replicas denotes that only 3% are unique, with the remainder having multiple copies.

Before analysing the results, we observe that all ransomware generate replicas, leading to two key insights. First, the samples employ a copy-based strategy, involving a copy phase followed by encryption—the replicas found are temporary files left unencrypted due to the VM shutdown. Second, the presence of replicas is a performance indicator, suggesting that the 10-minute delay was insufficient for the ransomware to encrypt all target files.

We comment on the results in Fig. 5 from top to bottom.

Ryuk and Hiragana exhibit similar behaviour, primarily targeting the "AppData" folder (containing application files restorable through reinstallation). They create ".ignore" files in "AppData", often making multiple copies (3% are distinct). This strategy likely aims to prevent recovery by simple renaming.

WannaCry also focuses on "AppData" but spreads its attack across other directories like "Pictures", "Music", "Desktop", and "Documents". It creates unique copies before encryption and targets common file types such as ".png", ".jpg", ".svg", ".pdf", ".txt", and ".doc" while skipping files without extensions.

LockBit outperforms WannaCry, encrypting 30% of files compared to WannaCry's 12%. It targets user directories like "Desktop" (23%), "Pictures", and "Documents" while still focusing on "AppData". Like Ryuk/Vipasana, LockBit generates ".ignore" copies but also appears to use a three-stage strategy involving direct copying, renaming to ".ignore", and encryption. Phobos seems the most dangerous one, reaching a staggering 98% of lost files. Given the almost-complete coverage of the attack area, looking at the lost and pristine charts gives little insight on its behaviour, although we might infer that its encryption routine might skip specific locations, found within the user profile and "AppData" folders that mainly contain executable and configuration files, e.g., preserved by the ransomware to allow minimal system functioning to show the ransom message.

Summarising the results, we notice that the severity of the different types of ransomware is not directly related to the mere percentage of lost files (which, of course, is an important measure, per se). For example, Phobos has the highest percentage of lost files while LockBit seems less dangerous since it encrypt only ca. 30% of the user's files. However, the breakdown of the encrypted files tells a more nuanced story. Phobos is much more "blunt" in its behaviour, since it indiscriminately encrypts most of the user files, irrespective of the folder and the extension. On the contrary, LockBit, is much more efficient, since it focuses its effort only on the files that mainly matter to the user, i.e., the files found under "Desktop", whose sequester compel the user to pay the ransom.

3.3 Ransomware Mitigation Profiling

The second case study provides an example of how one can use SAFARI to evaluate mitigation tools and techniques in a realistic yet safe scenario.

Concretely, we profile a recent ransomware tool, called Ranflood [4], exponent of a family of solutions, called Data Flooding against Ransomware [3]. Essentially, Ranflood contrasts ransomware attacks by confounding the files of the user with a "flood" of decoy ones, stymieing the attack both file- and resource-wise (by contending IO access with the ransomware).

Ranflood provides two families of flooding strategies: *random* and *copy-based*. The *random* family, implemented by the *Random* strategy, generates files of varying sizes and formats (mimicking those targeted by ransomware) with random content, requiring only a disk location to flood.

The *copy-based* family, implemented by the *On-the-fly* and *Shadow* strategies, require a target location and a preliminary setup under normal conditions: *On-the-fly* collects checksums of pristine files to avoid copying corrupted ones, while *Shadow* creates backups of user files to use as the source for flood copies.

Since Vipasana/Ryuk do not attack the files of the user (cf. Fig. 5), we concentrate on WannaCry, LockBit, and Phobos. We report, in Fig. 6, the results of the experiments after running 12 attack-and-contrast instances on the template VM used in the first case study. For each selected ransomware, we run the different Ranflood strategies with a 30-second delay since starting the ransomware, launching 13 flooding instances in parallel on distinct folders of the user, including "Documents", "Desktop", "Music", and "Pictures", purposefully avoiding flooding the "AppData" folder which contains application files rather than the user's ones and stopping the VM after 10 min.

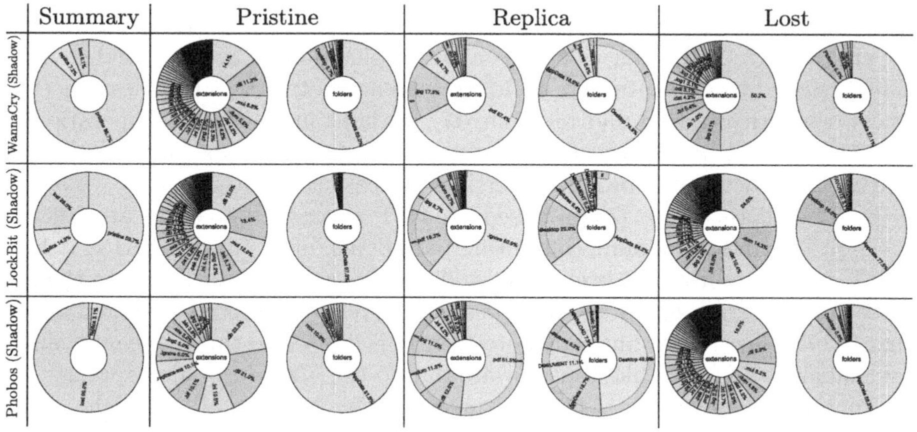

Fig. 6. Ranflood's contrast profiles against WannaCry, LockBit, and Phobos.

For brevity, we show, in Fig. 6, only the best-performing strategy, i.e., the one that minimises the percentage of lost files, which is Shadow. The interested reader can find all data and plots at https://zenodo.org/records/13891513. The data in the plots is the average of 12 runs, amounting to an average standard deviation of 20.66% (across pristine, lost, and replica files).

Considering the specific ransomware, we find that Ranflood reduces the number of lost files in all cases, albeit with different impacts—WannaCry -52%, LockBit -15%, and Phobos -1.6%. As expected, since the Shadow strategy is copy-based, we find an increased number of replicas in most cases—LockBit +46.1% and Phobos +442.8%—except for WannaCry, where we observe a decrease of 32%. While the latter result deserves further investigation, we conjecture it might derive from the high number of replicas used by WannaCry during attacks (the largest among the tested ransomware, cf. Fig. 5), which Ranflood hindered via IO access contention. The breakdown of the WannaCry replicas in Fig. 6 sheds some light on the phenomenon. While, in Fig. 5, we find most (55.4%) replicas under the "AppData" folder and fewer (25.2%) in "Desktop", the scenario with Ranflood reverses the ratios, with most replicas under "Desktop" (74.8%) and fewer under "AppData", which we attribute to the flooding performed by Ranflood that hinders the attacks of the ransomware.

The replica plots of LockBit and Phobos greatly differ from the respective ones in Fig. 5, hinting at the "fight" put up by Ranflood against the ransomware on folders like "Desktop" and "Pictures".

4 Related Work

Since SAFARI simulates real-world scenarios of hosts in an emulated air-gapped network, we can see it as an implementation of a Digital Twin (DT); a transformative technology that predicts system failures and identifies anomalies.

SAFARI fits into such a technological paradigm, particularly Cyber Ranges. A Cyber Range [26], when viewed as a DT application, is a virtualised environment designed to replicate real-world IT systems, networks, and infrastructures for cybersecurity testing and research [17], without impacting live operations.

In the literature, practical technological implementations of this type are scarce, or are developed around a vertical use-case scenario.

De Benedictis et al. [7] proposed an IIoT anomaly detection architecture based on DT and autonomic computing paradigms, utilizing the MAPE-K feedback loop to monitor, analyze, plan, and execute reconfiguration or mitigation strategies based on deviations from prescriptive behavior stored as shared knowledge. While effective for anomaly detection, it is limited to this scope and cannot test malicious software like ransomware due to the absence of air-gapping.

Another related work is the one presented by Masi et al. [19], who derive a cybersecurity DT as part of the security-by-design practice for Industrial Automation and Control Systems used in Critical Infrastructures. Although conceptually similar to SAFARI, this work offers only an architectural overview without detailing the enabling technologies required for implementation. In contrast, our work focuses on technological specifics, providing detailed guidance on implementing SAFARI and its practical applications in experiments.

SCASS [6], although completely Open Source, proposes a DT oriented to the implementation of a specific Industrial Component System Use Case, which is composed by a mix of virtualized components and"Hardware-in-the-loop" physical components. This hybrid testbed is then utilized to test cyber attacks specific to the ICS context. Similar to SCASS, EPICTWIN [12] proposes an Open Source virtualization of a highly specific ICS Use Case and allows for live attack simulations on SCADA systems. Differently from the last two cited works, SAFARI doesn't aim to reproduce a specific Use Case, but allows the user to configure any kind of virtualized network, will it be IT or OT/ICS oriented.

In terms of structure and implementation, one work close to SAFARI is PANDORA [11], which is a safe testing environment that allows users to conduct experiments on automated cyber-attack tools. The differences between the two proposals lie in their focus. PANDORA is designed mainly for testing automated cybersecurity tools, such as scanners or IDS systems. In contrast, SAFARI focuses on creating test scenarios that are as close as possible to real-world ones, prioritising open tools and highly modular networking virtualisation technologies, ensuring greater fidelity and enhancing flexibility in adapting to various testing needs. We report the key points of the comparison in Table 1.

Table 1. Tabular comparison of SAFARI (last row) with related work (one work per row) under the main characteristics of the considered proposals.

Compared solutions	Configurable Virtualized Infrastructure	Sandboxing Capabilities	General Purpose	Hardware Agnostic	Air-gapped by design	Open Source Code
De Benedictis et al. [7]	●	○	◐	◐	○	○
Masi et al. [19]	●	○	◐	●	○	○
PANDORA [11]	●	●	●	◐	○	○
SCASS [6]	●	●	○	○	○	●
EPIC [12]	●	●	○	◐	○	●
SAFARI	●	●	●	●	●	●

5 Conclusion

Studying malware behaviour and testing detection and mitigation tools is challenging, requiring strict safety protocols and reliable statistical data. SAFARI addresses these needs by offering a democratised framework for ransomware investigation, designed for scalability, air-gapped security, and automation, catering to users including small research groups and educational institutions. At its core, SAFARI is an open-source framework that automates ransomware (and countermeasure) testing in realistic environments. Built with modern technologies, it integrates Infrastructure-as-Code and OS-agnostic Task Automation for reproducible and consistent experiment setups across diverse hardware. We present a prototype that demonstrates SAFARI's feasibility and effectiveness.

As an additional contribution, we conduct two case studies on profiling the behaviour of five renowned ransomware strains (Ryuk, Vipasana, WannaCry, LockBit, and Phobos) and evaluating the effectiveness of a ransomware mitigation tool (Ranflood) against three of these strains. Thanks to SAFARI we described the distinct attack strategies of the strains. Briefly, Ryuk and Vipasana primarily target the "AppData" folder, leaving behind many ".ignore" files as part of their encryption approach, while WannaCry shows a broader attack pattern, affecting multiple user directories and targeting common file extensions. LockBit exhibits the most targeted strategy, focusing on user-important files such as those on the "Desktop", "Documents", and "Pictures" folders. Phobos seems the most aggressive ransomware, encrypting nearly all files indiscriminately. Studying the effectiveness of Ranflood, we found that the copy-based strategies are the most effective in preserving user-critical data.

Future work aims to expand SAFARI's capabilities to support a wider range of malware types, such as exfiltration ransomware [20], by incorporating tools to track malicious network activities. Another direction involves enabling hybrid on-premises-cloud deployments, allowing users to scale on-premises capacity with cloud resources. For the prototype, we plan to integrate and automate additional analysis tools, such as those leveraging dynamic ransomware behaviour analysis and automated malware behaviour pattern recognition, to aid in interpreting results. To make SAFARI accessible to non-technical users, we are exploring user-friendly interfaces to help define high-level testing plans, which the framework would automatically translate into corresponding IoC and OTA components.

Acknowledgments. We thank Matteo Cicognani for supporting the collaboration between ARPAE and Università di Bologna. This study was carried out within the "CYBER RANGE FOR INDUSTRIAL SECURITY - CRI4.0 NELL'AMBITO DEL BANDO PER PROGETTI DI RICERCA INDUSTRIALE STRATEGICA" (PR FESR 2021–2027 AZIONE 1.1.2 CUP: E37G22000490007).

References

1. Al-rimy, B., Maarof, M.A., Shaid, S.: Ransomware threat success factors, taxonomy, and countermeasures: a survey and research directions. Comput. Secur. **74**, 144–166 (2018). https://doi.org/10.1016/j.cose.2018.01.001
2. Beaman, C., Barkworth, A., Akande, T.D., Hakak, S., Khan, M.K.: Ransomware: recent advances, analysis, challenges and future research directions. Comput. Secur. **111**, 102490 (2021). https://doi.org/10.1016/j.cose.2021.102490
3. Berardi, D., Giallorenzo, S., Melis, A., Melloni, S., Onori, L., Prandini, M.: Data flooding against ransomware: concepts and implementations. Comput. Secur., 103295 (2023). https://doi.org/10.1016/j.cose.2023.103295
4. Berardi, D., Giallorenzo, S., Melis, A., Melloni, S., Prandini, M.: Ranflood: a mitigation tool based on the principles of data flooding against ransomware. SoftwareX **25**, 101605 (2024). https://doi.org/10.1016/j.softx.2023.101605
5. Connolly, A.Y., Borrion, H.: Reducing ransomware crime: analysis of victims' payment decisions. Comput. Secur. **119**, 102760 (2022). https://doi.org/10.1016/J.COSE.2022.102760
6. d'Ambrosio, N., Capodagli, G., Perrone, G., Romano, S.P.: Scass: breaking into scada systems security. Comput. Secur. **151**, 104315 (2025). https://doi.org/10.1016/j.cose.2025.104315
7. De Benedictis, A., Flammini, F., Mazzocca, N., Somma, A., Vitale, F.: Digital twins for anomaly detection in the industrial internet of things: conceptual architecture and proof-of-concept. IEEE TII **19**(12), 11553–11563 (2023). https://doi.org/10.1109/TII.2023.3246983
8. Dey, A., Totel, E., Costé, B.: Daemon: dynamic auto-encoders for contextualised anomaly detection applied to security monitoring. In: IFIP SEC, pp. 53–69. Springer, Heidelberg (2022). https://doi.org/10.1007/978-3-031-06975-8_4
9. Halsey, M.: Windows 10 file structure in depth. In: Windows 10 Troubleshooting, pp. 449–457. Apress, Berkeley (2016). https://doi.org/10.1007/978-1-4842-0925-7_27
10. Hernandez-Castro, J., Cartwright, A., Cartwright, E.: An economic analysis of ransomware and its welfare consequences. RSOS **7**(3), 190023 (2020). https://doi.org/10.1098/rsos.190023
11. Jiang, H., Choi, T., Ko, R.: Pandora: a cyber range environment for the safe testing and deployment of autonomous cyber attack tools. In: Thampi, S.M., Wang, G., Rawat, D.B., Ko, R., Fan, C.-I. (eds.) SSCC 2020. CCIS, vol. 1364, pp. 1–20. Springer, Singapore (2021). https://doi.org/10.1007/978-981-16-0422-5_1

12. Kandasamy, N.K., Venugopalan, S., Wong, T.K., Leu, N.J.: An electric power digital twin for cyber security testing, research and education. Comput. Electr. Eng. **101**, 108061 (2022). https://doi.org/10.1016/j.compeleceng.2022.108061
13. Kaspersky: Ransomware attacks and types (2021)
14. Kharraz, A., Arshad, S., Mulliner, C., Robertson, W.K., Kirda, E.: UNVEIL: a large-scale, automated approach to detecting ransomware. In: Holz, T., Savage, S. (eds.) USENIX Security Symposium, pp. 757–772. USENIX Association (2016)
15. Kroll: Data exfiltration ransomware attacks (2021)
16. Liska, A., Gallo, T.: Ransomware: Defending Against Digital Extortion, 1st edn. O'Reilly Media, Inc., Newton (2016)
17. Mahmoud, R.V., Anagnostopoulos, M., Pedersen, J.M.: Detecting cyber attacks through measurements: learnings from a cyber range. IEEE IMM **25**(6), 31–36 (2022). https://doi.org/10.1109/MIM.2022.9847127
18. Maigida, A.M., Abdulhamid, S.M., Olalere, M., Alhassan, J.K., Chiroma, H., Dada, E.G.: Systematic literature review and metadata analysis of ransomware attacks and detection mechanisms. J. Reliable Intell. Environ., 1–23 (2019). https://doi.org/10.1007/s40860-019-00080-3
19. Masi, M., Sellitto, G.P., Aranha, H., Pavleska, T.: Securing critical infrastructures with a cybersecurity digital twin. Softw. Syst. Model. **22**(2), 689–707 (2023)
20. McIntosh, T., et al.: Ransomware reloaded: re-examining its trend, research and mitigation in the era of data exfiltration. ACM Comput. Surv. (2024). https://doi.org/10.1145/3691340
21. McIntosh, T., et al.: Ransomware mitigation in the modern era: a comprehensive review, research challenges, and future directions. ACM Comput. Surv. **54**(9) (2021). https://doi.org/10.1145/3479393
22. Meland, P.H., Bayoumy, Y., Sindre, G.: The ransomware-as-a-service economy within the darknet. Comput. Secur. **92**, 101762 (2020). https://doi.org/10.1016/J.COSE.2020.101762
23. Meurs, T., Junger, M., Tews, E., Abhishta, A.: Ransomware: how attacker's effort, victim characteristics and context influence ransom requested, payment and financial loss. In: APWG eCrime, pp. 1–13. IEEE (2022). https://doi.org/10.1109/ECRIME57793.2022.10142138
24. OpenWrt Team: Openwrt. https://openwrt.org/. Accessed Sept 2024
25. Oz, H., Aris, A., Levi, A., Uluagac, A.S.: A survey on ransomware: evolution, taxonomy, and defense solutions. ACM Comput. Surv. **54**(11s) (2022). https://doi.org/10.1145/3514229
26. Pokhrel, A., Katta, V., Colomo-Palacios, R.: Digital twin for cybersecurity incident prediction: a multivocal literature review. In: ICSEW'20, pp. 671–678. ACM, New York (2020). https://doi.org/10.1145/3387940.3392199
27. Richardson, R., North, M.: Ransomware: evolution, mitigation and prevention. Int. Manag. Rev. **13**(1), 10–21,101 (2017). https://www.proquest.com/scholarly-journals/ransomware-evolution-mitigation-prevention/docview/1881414570/se-2
28. Rossow, C., et al.: Prudent practices for designing malware experiments: status quo and outlook. In: IEEE S&P, pp. 65–79. IEEE (2012)
29. Scaife, N., Carter, H., Traynor, P., Butler, K.R.B.: Cryptolock (and drop it): stopping ransomware attacks on user data. In: IEEE ICDCS, pp. 303–312 (2016). https://doi.org/10.1109/ICDCS.2016.46

SAVA Deployment for Spoofed Source Attacks

Wenjie Yang, Yong Tang, and Wenyong Wang(✉)

University of Electronic Science and Technology of China, Chengdu, China
{worldgulit,wangwy}@uestc.edu.cn

Abstract. Distributed Denial of Service (DDoS) attacks are one of the main threats facing the Internet today, and a considerable number of them originate from attacks using spoofed source addresses. The Source Address Verification Architecture (SAVA) technology can effectively mitigate such attacks by verifying the legitimacy of the source address. However, the deployment of SAVA faces some practical challenges, including the complexity of real network topologies, high deployment costs, and the impracticality of full deployment. To address these issues, this paper describes the SAVA deployment model in detail and proposes an incremental deployment approximation algorithm. The algorithm can identify a set of approximately optimal SAVA deployment points in any network topology, aiming to maximize the filtering of attack traffic. Experimental results show that compared with conventional deployment methods, the deployment algorithm shows superior performance in handling spoofed source attacks while maintaining a low false negative probability.

Keywords: DDoS · Spoofed source · SAVA · Deployment

1 Introduction

With the continuous expansion of the network scale and the diversification of attack methods, network security has become a crucial issue for the Internet today. Distributed denial-of-service (DDoS) attacks, in particular, represent one of the main threats to the Internet [8]. Spoofed source attacks are a common form of DDoS attack, which mainly hides the true identity of the attacker by forging the source IP address. This attack method makes it difficult for the victim to track the source of the attack, thus increasing the difficulty of defense.

Spoofed source attacks mainly include two forms: Spoofed source flooding and reflection amplification. Spoofed source flooding attack is an attack method that floods the target server by sending a large number of SYN requests with spoofed source IP addresses. In this attack, the attacker replaces the source IP address in the data packet with a spoofed address, causing the target server to try to send a response to these spoofed IP addresses after receiving the SYN request. Since these spoofed IP addresses may not exist, the resources of the target server will be exhausted, making it unable to process requests from legitimate users. The

Published by Springer Nature Switzerland AG 2025
L. Nemec Zlatolas et al. (Eds.): SEC 2025, IFIP AICT 745, pp. 224–237, 2025.
https://doi.org/10.1007/978-3-031-92882-6_16

typical characteristics of this attack are high concurrent connection requests and a large number of half-open connection states. Reflection amplification attacks amplify initial traffic by exploiting vulnerabilities in network services, causing bandwidth consumption, resource exhaustion, and potentially leading to service interruptions, security risks, reputation loss, and financial losses [11,12]. Reflection amplification attacks in spurious sources pose unique challenges: they generate massive traffic capable of crippling a victim's server in a short time, obscure the source by using spoofed IP addresses, and are difficult to defend against as reflection servers are legitimate Internet services, making simple IP blocking an ineffective measure [9]. Given these characteristics, Spoofed source flooding and reflection amplification attacks pose a serious threat to Internet security today, highlighting the urgent need for effective countermeasures. The Source Address Validation Architecture (SAVA) [15] offers a promising solution to mitigate spoofed source attacks by verifying the legitimacy of source addresses. The next paragraph provides a brief overview of SAVA technology.

SAVA is a multi-layer IP source address validation technology designed to prevent malicious attacks based on spoofed source addresses, thereby enhancing Internet security. It enables source address validation at multiple points-within access networks, inside autonomous systems, and between autonomous systems ensuring the authenticity of source addresses. At the subnet level, SAVA dynamically binds router ports to valid source IP addresses, ensuring that network devices can only use legitimate source IP addresses. Within autonomous systems, SAVA establishes filtering tables in routers that associate each incoming interface with a valid set of source address blocks, thereby filtering out packets with spoofed source addresses. Across autonomous systems, SAVA performs route-based validation to confirm the authenticity of source addresses, ensuring that traffic between systems is traceable and legitimate [15,16]. This layered, multi-level protection mechanism verifies the legitimacy of each packet's source address throughout its transmission, effectively preventing DDoS attacks based on spoofed source address.

Despite its effectiveness in preventing attacks based on spoofed source addresses, deploying SAVA in practical faces several challenges. SAVA requires a certain deployment scale to achieve optimal effectiveness. Given the complexity of real-world Internet topologies and the multitude of potential deployment nodes, full deployment is impractical, and conventional deployment approaches often fail to yield satisfactory results [2]. Based on the above analysis, this paper mainly solves the deployment problem of SAVA. Our contributions are summarized as follows:

- We present a rigorous mathematical model for the SAVA deployment problem and prove that the deployment benefit function is submodular.
- We propose the Submodularity-based Dynamic Greedy (SDG) algorithm, and demonstrate that the SDG algorithm achieves a constant-factor approximation to the optimal solution under resource constraints.
- We analyze of the limitations with conventional deployment approaches, including near-source and near-destination deployment tactics. We compare

the performance of the SDG deployment algorithm against these conventional approaches.

The remainder of this paper is structured as follows. Section 2 of this paper summarizes the relevant background and related literature. Section 3 introduces the system architecture, gives the specific modeling process, describes the algorithmic flow and gives a detailed proof of the approximation ratio of the algorithm. Section 4 presents the SDG deployment results and experimental comparisons. Finally, we conclude this paper in Sect. 5.

2 Related Work

Source Address Validation (SAV) mechanisms are crucial for preventing IP address spoofing, a common tactic in various network attacks. The Source Address Validation Architecture (SAVA) was introduced to ensure that every packet's source address is verifiable throughout its transmission path. Wu et al. [15] proposed SAVA as a multilayer framework capable of enforcing source address validation at access networks, within autonomous systems, and across inter-domain traffic.

Building upon SAVA, the Source Address Validation Improvement (SAVI) framework was developed to provide finer-grained, standardized IP source address validation at the level of individual IP addresses. Bi et al. [14] described the design and motivation behind SAVI methods, which prevent nodes on the same IP link from spoofing each other's IP addresses, thereby complementing ingress filtering.

SAVA and SAVI are effective in theory, their deployment in real-world networks presents challenges. An early framework by Bremler-Barr and Levy [4] discussed incremental deployment strategies for router-assisted services, emphasizing the importance of strategic placement to enhance network performance. Korczyski and Nosyk [6] conducted an Internet-wide active measurement study to assess the deployment of SAV mechanisms, revealing that a significant number of networks remain vulnerable to IP spoofing due to the lack of proper SAV implementation.

In terms of deployment, the integration of submodular optimization in deployment strategies has been investigated. Wilder [13] examined equilibrium computation and robust optimization in zero-sum games with submodular structure, providing insights relevant to security resource allocation in adversarial settings.

Despite these advancements, challenges remain in applying submodular optimization techniques to deployment in real-world network scenarios. This paper address these challenges by developing a submodularity-based deployment algorithm tailored for spoofed source attacks.

3 System Model

3.1 SAVA Deployment Architecture

The SAVA deployment architecture for preventing spoofed source attacks is illustrated in Fig. 1. Attacker can control zombie hosts in botnets to spoof IP addresses of other hosts to attack victims. We can deploy SAVA devices in place of conventional routers to prevent traffic with spoofed source addresses from passing through. Deploying SAVA devices can mitigate the impact of spoofed source attacks on victims, thereby enhancing network security and stability. The main deployment challenge lies in selecting optimal deployment points within a real network topology to maximize attack traffic filtration within resource constraints, achieving a strong defensive effect [10].

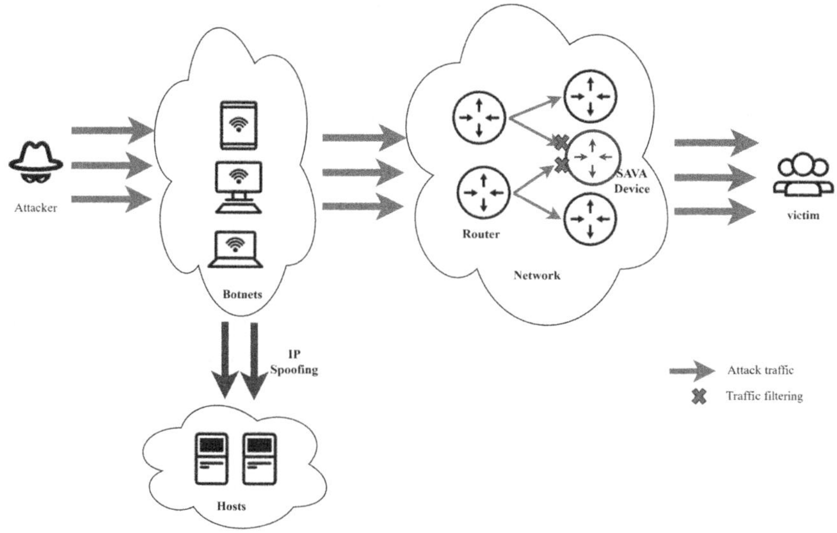

Fig. 1. Deployment Architecture

In real-world network environments, hardware and device costs vary depending on node performance requirements; high-traffic nodes often require higher-performance servers and network devices, leading to different deployment costs across nodes. Geographic location also affects costs, as remote nodes far from central infrastructure may require more resources for connection and maintenance. Additionally, nodes with high bandwidth and traffic demands necessitate more network resources, resulting in higher operational costs. Maintenance and management costs also vary, as complex network environments require more resources for node management, necessitating an effective deployment strategy.

3.2 Problem Modeling

The existing SAVA deployment problem is restated, the corresponding mathematical model is established, a SAVA device balanced deployment strategy based on reliability evaluation is proposed, and relevant indicators are defined and explained. The relevant symbol definitions are shown in Table 1.

Table 1. Symbol Definition

symbol	implication
V	The set of network nodes
E	The set of network edges (adjacencies)
G	The inter-domain topology of the network
S	The set of nodes that have deployed SAVA devices
N	The set of nodes that have not yet deployed SAVA, $N = V - S$
n	Node, $n \in V$
σ_n	Boolean value, 0 or 1, indicating whether node n is a deployment point
T_n	Attack traffic passing through node n
x_n	The cost of deploying at location n
W	Attack traffic dataset

We focus on reducing the amount of attack packets. According to the expected linear property, the expected difference is equal to the expected difference, when the deployed set is S, the number of additional packets that can be filtered by the deployment point n is:

$$reduce(S, n) = \mathrm{E}[benefit_{S \cup \{n\}}] - \mathrm{E}[benefit_S] \tag{1}$$

We use $reduce_S$ to represent the number of attack packets that can be reduced when the deployment set is S. From the definition of deployment benefit above, it can be seen that the benefit of deploying SAVA device is related to the deployed set S, that currently deploy the method and current deployment node n.

After n deploys SAVA, over a period of time, the set of legal packets identified by n is leg_n, the set of illegal packets is $ileg_n$, and the set of packets that are judged as spoofed and discarded by n is dis_n. Then the set of false negative packets is:

$$risk(S, n) = |leg_n \cap ileg_n| \tag{2}$$

An attack packet is defined as follows: $a : (s, d)$, where a is the attacker, i.e., the sender of the packet, s is the source address of the spoofed packet, and d is the target of the attack [7]. The filtering method is based on the principle of path filtering. The path-based method identifies whether an packet is a spoofed packet by verifying the forwarding path of a packet. Although the attacker can write a spoofed source address in the packet, it cannot control the forwarding path of the packet because it cannot control the entire routing system. Specifically, for a packet (s, d), when the packet is sent from different locations on the network, its forwarding path should also be different.

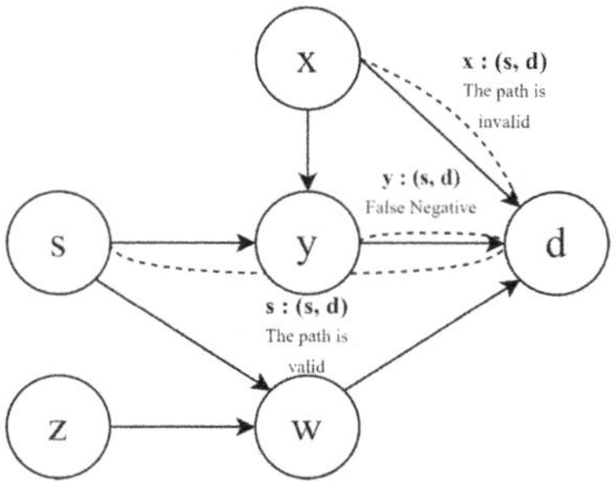

Fig. 2. Filter Method

In Fig. 2, the forwarding paths of $x : (s, d)$ and $s : (s, d)$ are different. From d's point of view, the legitimate packet $s : (s, d)$ should be forwarded from d's upstream node y, not x.

Formally define the filter function after deploying the SAVA devices. A filter function completes the following work: given a topology with routing information, deployment nodes and an packet $a : (s, d)$ as input, given a deployment node n and assuming that n has deployed SAVA devices, if packet $a : (s, d)$ passes through n when forwarding, n can determine whether the data packet is spoofed. Its form is $filter(S, n, a : (s, d))$, and returns 1 if it is spoofed; otherwise, returns 0.

Given the filter function, the calculation method of the discard function is as follows:

$$discard(S, a : (s, d)) = \text{sgn}(\sum_{n \in S} \sum_{a:(s,d) \in W} filter(S, n, a : (s, d))) \tag{3}$$

$sgn()$[1] is a symbolic function. Its form is as follows.

$$\text{sgn}(x) = \begin{cases} 0, & x = 0 \\ 1, & x > 0 \end{cases} \tag{4}$$

[1] Regarding the definition, when x>0, sgn will be –1, but in formula (3), the value in () will only be >=0. If >0, the value of the discard function is 1, indicating that the message is discarded. Similarly, if = 0, the value of the discard function is 0, indicating that the message is retained.

If only consider the number of filtered packets, we need to subtract false negative packets:

$$\begin{aligned}\text{reduce}(S, n) = \sum_{a:(s,d)\in W} \Big(&\text{discard}(S \cup \{n\}, a:(s,d)) \\ &- \text{discard}(S, a:(s,d)) - \text{risk}(S, n)\Big)\end{aligned} \tag{5}$$

We can calculate the ratio of filtered packets to total attack packets. The set of legal packets identified by n is leg_n, the set of illegal packets is $ileg_n$, and the set of packets judged as spoofed and discarded by n is dis_n, we use γ to represent the filtering percentage:

$$\gamma = |dis_n|/|ileg_n| \tag{6}$$

In real-world network deployment, deployable resources are limited. By setting budget constraints, we can ensure that the optimal deployment solution can be achieved under limited resource conditions. The upgrade budget is the total cost of upgrading SAVA devices and does not exceed $M > 0$. We have the following constraints:

$$\sum_{i\in N} x_i * \sigma_i \le M \tag{7}$$

Our goal is to update the deployment set S to SAVA devices to maximize the deployment benefits, so our objective function is as follows:

$$\max benefit(S_G) \tag{8}$$

S_G is the set of SAVA deployments that satisfy condition (7). The target of filtering percentage can be set to $0 < P < 1$. The percentage of traffic to be filtered may not always meet the filtering requirements if the deployment cost M is too small in actual situations. Our goal is to maximize the deployment benefit, i.e., to calculate (8).

The problem of solving (7) under the condition of (8) is NP, which means that in the worst case, the time complexity of finding the best deployment solution will increase rapidly with the increase of network size.

3.3 Proof of Submodular Function

In order to optimize the deployment of SAVA devices, we use the total benefit function to represent the total traffic size that can be filtered by deploying SAVA devices on a set of nodes. Proving that $benefit$ is a submodular function is important because submodular functions have specific mathematical properties that can be used to develop efficient greedy algorithms, thereby ensuring that the algorithm strikes a good balance between computational complexity and defensive effectiveness. Submodularity ensures effectiveness in algorithm design, especially in optimization problems. Specifically, as the set grows, the additional benefit of adding nodes to the set decreases.

We can prove that the function $benefit$ is a submodular function.

For a collection function $benefit : 2^N \rightarrow S$, Assume that $A \subseteq N$ is a set, $B \subseteq N$ is a set, and $A \subseteq B$ is a set, $\exists i \in N \setminus B$

2^Nrepresents the power set of set N, i.e., the set of all subsets of N

$$\text{benefit}(\{n\} \cup B) - \text{benefit}(B) \leq \text{benefit}(\{n\} \cup A) - \text{benefit}(A) \quad (9)$$

The formula points out that as the set becomes larger, the value of n will become smaller, which is the characteristic of diminishing marginal benefits. When $A \subseteq B$, $f(A) \leq f(B)$, this submodular function is monotonic.

Proof. Select any two sets $A \subseteq B \subseteq N$, and any element $n \in N \setminus B$. N is the set of nodes in the network topology; we need to prove that inequality (9) holds

For a smaller set A, the addition of element n will bring more significant marginal benefits, because the traffic T_n carried by n is not shared or filtered by other nodes in the smaller set. For the larger set B, since it already contains more nodes, there may be redundant nodes. The traffic that these nodes can filter cannot be filtered by the nodes in the set A. Compared with the total traffic, it can The incremental number is small, and the incremental effect brought by the addition of element n is relatively small, because the nodes in set B have already taken on more traffic filtering tasks. Therefore, for any $A \subseteq B \subseteq V$ and $n \in V \setminus B$:

$$benefit(\{n\} \cup A) - benefit(A) \geq benefit(\{n\} \cup B) - benefit(B) \quad (10)$$

$$\text{benefit}(\{n\} \cup A) \geq \text{benefit}(\{n\} \cup B) \quad (11)$$

We have thus proved that the function $benefit$ is a submodular function. □

Therefore, we have proved that under the given algorithm steps and benefit function definition, the function $benefit$ is a submodular function. This means that when selecting nodes, the marginal benefit of each new node is decreasing, which is of great significance for solving optimization problems.

3.4 Algorithm Design

The pseudocode of the Algorithm 1. is as follows:

Proof of approximation ratio can provide theoretical guarantee for the performance of the algorithm, ensuring that the gap between the solution and the optimal solution is within an acceptable range. It shows the effectiveness and reliability of the algorithm in practical applications. The proof process of approximation ratio solved by SDG algorithm is as follows:

Proof. S_i is the deployment set after the ith iteration. The deployment cost of the deployment point selected by the algorithm in the ith iteration is $c(x_i)$, and

Algorithm 1. SDG

Step 1:
$S = \emptyset$, $F = 0$
Step 2:
while $N \neq \emptyset$ **do**
  Compute the benefit $benefit(x_i)$ for each node i
  Compute the unit cost-benefit ratio $\frac{benefit(x_i)}{x_i}$ for each node
  Step 3:
  select the node x^* with the highest unit cost-benefit ratio and add it to set S
  Update the state of node x^* to $\sigma = 1$
  if $\gamma < P$ and $\sum_{i \in S} x_i \cdot \sigma_i \leq M$ **then**
    $\mathcal{S} \leftarrow \mathcal{S} \cup \{x^*\}$
    $F = F + benefit(x^*)$
    $\mathcal{N} \leftarrow \mathcal{N} \setminus \{x^*\}$
  else
    Return to Step 2
  end if
end while
Step 4:
Output the deployment set S and total benefit F

S^* is the deployment solution with the largest total deployment benefit. The recursive inequality can be derived from the submodularity:

$$\begin{aligned} benefit(S^*) &\leq benefit(S_{i-1}) + benefit(S^* \backslash S_{i-1}) \\ &\leq benefit(S_{i-1}) + \frac{benefit(S_i) - benefit(S_{i-1})}{c(x_i)} \cdot \sum_{x \in S^* \backslash S_{i-1}} c(x) \\ &\leq benefit(S_{i-1}) + \frac{M}{c(x_i)} \cdot (benefit(S_i) - benefit(S_{i-1})) \end{aligned} \tag{12}$$

The first inequality in Eq. (12) uses Corollary 5 from the middle literature [3], and the second inequality utilizes the greedy nature of the algorithm, i.e., $\frac{benefit(S_i) - benefit(S_{i-1})}{c(x_i)}$ is the highest current profit per unit. The last inequality states that $S^* \backslash S_{i-1}$ the cost of all items never exceeds the total cost space M [1].

Subtracting $\frac{M}{c(x_i)}$ on both sides and reordering the terms:

$$benefit(S_i) \geq benefit(S^*) + \left(1 - \frac{c(x_i)}{M}\right) \cdot (benefit(S_{i-1}) - benefit(S^*)) \tag{13}$$

By recursively applying the inequality and introducing the ratio of the cost of each step to the total cost, we get:

$$benefit(S_i) \geq \left(1 - \prod_{k=1}^{i} \left(1 - \frac{c(x_k)}{M}\right)\right) \cdot benefit(S^*) \tag{14}$$

Use the inequality $1 - x \le e^{-x}$ to replace the accumulated terms:

$$benefit(S_i) \ge \left(1 - \exp\left(-\sum_{k=1}^{i} \frac{c(x_k)}{M}\right)\right) \cdot benefit(S^*) \tag{15}$$

$C(x^*)$ is the current highest unit profit. The last inequality depends on the cost of all items never exceeding the total deployment cost M. When $c(S) + c(x^*) > M$, replace S_i with $S \cup x^*$, we have:

$$benefit(S \cup x^*) \ge (1 - \exp\left(-\frac{c(S) + c(x^*)}{M}\right)) \cdot benefit(S^*) \tag{16}$$

That is to say, $benefit(S \cup x^*) \ge (1 - \frac{1}{e}) \cdot benefit(S^*)$
When the maximum deployment cost is reached, i.e., $c(S) + c(x^*) > M$
$benefit(S \cup x^*) \ge (1 - e^{-1}) \cdot benefit(S^*)$ holds □

The proof shows the approximation guarantee of the greedy selection algorithm for submodular functions under the cost constraints, where the algorithm tries to maximize the ratio of marginal benefit to cost at each iteration. It is proved that the algorithm can maintain a good approximation to the optimal solution when the cumulative cost is close to the cost constraints.

4 Experiments

4.1 Conventional Deployment Approaches

Conventional deployment approaches include near-source deployment and near-destination deployment. When dealing with spoofed source attacks, near-source and near-destination deployment strategies have their own advantages and disadvantages, and are applicable to different network environments and requirements. Near-source deployment deploys defense devices (SAVA devices) close to the source of the attack, with the goal of detecting and filtering malicious traffic as early as possible to mitigate the impact of the attack on the downstream network. The advantage of this approach lies in the ability to detect and filter early and reduce the amount of malicious traffic entering the network core, thereby reducing network bandwidth consumption and reducing the pressure on subsequent nodes. However, this strategy also suffers from high deployment costs, complex management, and difficulty in locating the source of the attack, especially when the source of the attack is constantly changing or dispersed, the effectiveness may be limited.

Near-destination deployment deploys defense appliances close to the target server or network node, i.e. near victims, aiming to protect the target from attacks by intercepting and filtering the attack traffic before it reaches the target. Advantages of near-destination deployment include centralized defense, cost-effectiveness, and relatively simple management. However, this strategy also faces some challenges such as high network bandwidth pressure, concentrated attack pressure and potential latency issues. Malicious traffic can still consume a large amount of network bandwidth before reaching its destination, which may lead to network congestion and performance degradation, and defense devices need to handle large-scale attack traffic, placing higher demands on device performance and stability.

Combining the above, the selected deployment strategy needs to consider the network structure and attack characteristics. If the attack sources are decentralized and change frequently, near-destination deployment may be more effective; whereas, if the attack traffic is centralized and targeted, near-source deployment may be more suitable. In addition, cost and management factors need to be considered. Near-source deployment is suitable for network environments with sufficient resources and strong management capabilities, while near-destination deployment is suitable for scenarios with limited resources and the need for centralized management. In practice, a combination of the two deployment strategies may be the best way to achieve the optimal defense effect in order to strike a balance between cost, management and defense effect.

4.2 Experimental Results and Comparative Analysis

In this paper, we simulated the SAVA device filtering attack traffic using Python3. The network topology was generated randomly using Python's built-in random module with a fixed seed to ensure reproducibility. This approach allowed us to generate topologies that conform to the desired statistical properties. The network consists of 287 routers, 85 hosts, and 1568 links. Among the hosts, 40 were designated as zombie hosts, 5 as victim hosts, and the source addresses of the remaining 40 hosts were spoofed by the zombie hosts. The attack traffic from the 40 zombie hosts to the 5 victim hosts ranged from 100 to 1000 Mbps, and the unit deployment cost of each router node was set to 1. In this paper, we compare the near-source deployment, near-destination deployment, and the SDG deployment algorithm proposed above. The experimental parameters were set with reference to similar studies [5], and care was taken to ensure that every host maintained an active link connection.

The experimental results we obtained are as follows:

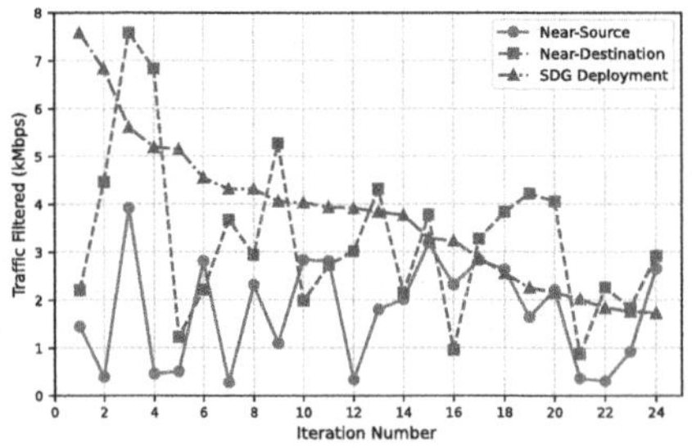

Fig. 3. Iterative Node Traffic Filtering

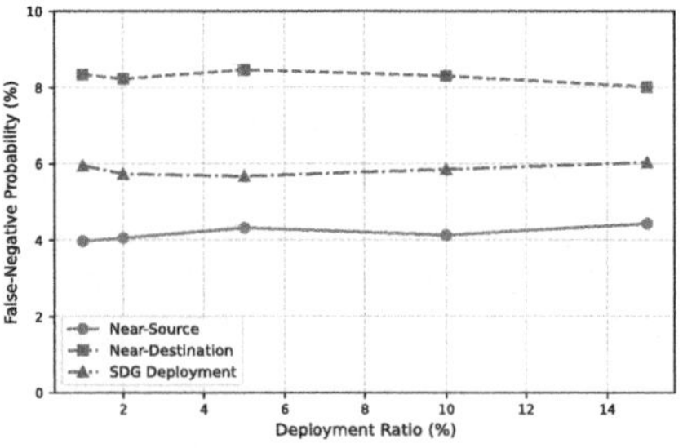

Fig. 4. False negative probability

Figure 3 shows that the nodes selected by the SDG algorithm each time meet the submodular function property, i.e., the marginal benefits of each selected node are decreasing. This means that as nodes are continuously selected, the additional filtered traffic brought by each new node is gradually reduced. The two deployment approaches of near source and near destination show large fluctuations and instability in filtering traffic.

The false negative probability of different deployment approaches is shown in Fig. 4. The near-source deployment shows the lowest false negative probability because attack traffic is intercepted early, reducing the likelihood of same path. In contrast, near-destination deployment shows the highest false negative probability. Because the attack traffic has already spread widely in the network before reaching the filtering node, the possibility that the zombie host and the host whose source address is spoofed by it take the same path increases.

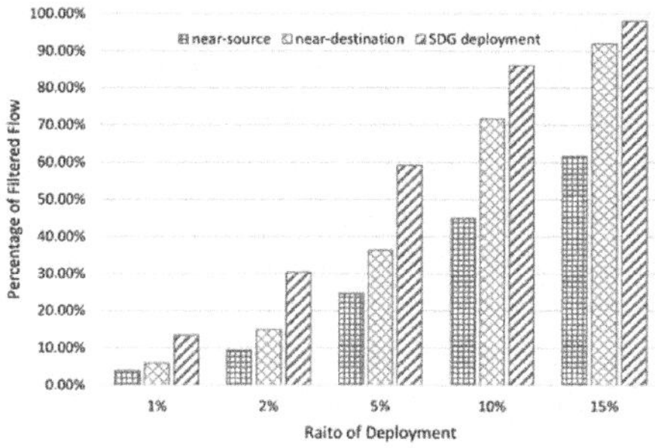

Fig. 5. Traffic Filtering Comparison

Figure 5 shows that the filtering efficiency of the deployment nodes selected by the SDG algorithm is better than that of near source deployment and near destination deployment. Although near source deployment can intercept attack traffic before it enters the network core, reducing network bandwidth occupation and subsequent node pressure, this strategy requires the deployment of defense devices at multiple source locations. But the defense effect is unstable because the attack source may change or disperse continuously. Near destination deployment concentrates defense devices near the target server or key node, but malicious traffic will still occupy a lot of bandwidth before reaching the target, resulting in network congestion and performance degradation. The SDG algorithm selects the optimal deployment node for dynamic adjustment to ensure that each new node can maximize the overall defense benefits. The SDG algorithm can significantly improve filtering efficiency at different deployment ratios[2].

The SDG deployment algorithm, proposed in this paper, strikes a balance between false negative probability and filtering efficiency. This ensures that each

[2] It is worth mentioning that when the deployment costs at different points differ too much, the SDG algorithm is likely to fail. Considering that we deploy the same SAVA devices, the actual deployment costs are similar, which can achieve good results.

selected node maximizes its marginal contribution to overall defense performance. SDG achieves moderate false negative probabilities while significantly outperforming near-source and near-destination approaches in terms of filtering effectiveness. This demonstrates the SDG algorithm's ability to adaptively and incrementally optimize deployment strategies, making it more effective in real-world network environments.

5 Conclusion and Future Work

This paper proposes a SAVA incremental deployment algorithm SDG for spoofed source attacks. The algorithm dynamically selects the optimal deployment node through a submodular optimization strategy, while taking into account false negative, to achieve good defense effects under limited resource conditions, and can more flexibly adapt to changes in the network environment. The article gives detailed proof of the design process and approximation ratio of the algorithm. And through experimental simulation and comparison with near-source deployment and near-destination deployment, the experimental results verify the effectiveness of the algorithm in defending against spoofed source attacks. Subsequent research can further test and optimize this algorithm in a more complex network environment, and explore its potential for application in defense against other types of DDoS network attacks.

Our study focused on the deployment of SAVA and did not make an in-depth discussion on how SAVA devices filtering attack traffic, which is related to false positive and is the focus of our future research.

Acknowledgments. This work was funded by the Science and Technology Department of Sichuan Province (Grant No. 2024ZHCG0044) and the Natural Science Foundation of Sichuan Province (Grant No. M112024NSFSC0473).

References

1. Chen, S., et al.: Collaborative edge caching and dynamic bitrate adaptation for shvc-based vr video streaming. In: Proceedings of the IEEE Conference on Local Computer Networks (LCN), pp. 1–9. IEEE, Daytona Beach (2024). https://doi.org/10.1109/LCN60385.2024.10639785
2. Du, P., Nakao, A.: Ddos defense deployment with network egress and ingress filtering. In: Proceedings of the IEEE International Conference on Communications, pp. 1–6. IEEE, Cape Town (2010). https://doi.org/10.1109/ICC.2010.5502654
3. Fujishige, S.: Submodular Functions and Optimization, 2nd edn. Elsevier, Amsterdam (2005)
4. He, X., Papadopoulos, C., Radoslavov, P.: A framework for incremental deployment strategies for router-assisted services. In: Proceedings of IEEE INFOCOM, pp. 1488–1498. IEEE, San Francisco (2003). https://doi.org/10.1109/INFCOM.2003.1208984
5. Hui, L., et al.: Sav-d: defending ddos with incremental deployment of sav. IEEE Internet Comput. **27**(3), 44–49 (2023). https://doi.org/10.1109/MIC.2023.3264319

6. Korczyński, M., Nosyk, Y.: Source address validation. In: Encyclopedia of Cryptography and Security, pp. 1–8. Springer, Boston (2014). https://doi.org/10.1007/978-3-642-27739-9_1626-1
7. Liu, B.Y., Bi, J.: On the deployability evaluation model of internet inter-domain source address validation. Chin. J. Comput. **38**(3), 500–514 (2015)
8. Mirkovic, J., Reiher, P.: A taxonomy of ddos attack and ddos defense mechanisms. ACM SIGCOMM Comput. Commun. Rev. **34**(2), 39–53 (2004). https://doi.org/10.1145/997150.997156
9. Rossow, C.: Amplification hell: revisiting network protocols for ddos abuse. In: Proceedings of the Network and Distributed System Security Symposium (NDSS), pp. 1–15. Internet Society, San Diego (2014). https://dud.inf.tu-dresden.de/~strufe/rn_lit/rossow14amplification.pdf
10. Ryba, F.J., et al.: Amplification and drdos attack defense - a survey and new perspectives. arXiv preprint (2015). https://arxiv.org/abs/1505.07892
11. Soliman, A.K., Salama, C., Mohamed, H.K.: Detecting dns reflection amplification ddos attack originating from the cloud. In: Proceedings of the 13th International Conference on Computer Engineering and Systems (ICCES), pp. 145–150. IEEE, Cairo (2018). https://doi.org/10.1109/ICCES.2018.8639414
12. Vasques, A.T., Gondim, J.J.: Amplified reflection ddos attacks over iot mirrors: a saturation analysis. In: Proceedings of the Workshop on Communication Networks and Power Systems (WCNPS), pp. 1–6. IEEE, Brasilia (2019). https://doi.org/10.1109/WCNPS.2019.8896290
13. Wilder, B.: Equilibrium computation and robust optimization in zero sum games with submodular structure. In: Proceedings of the AAAI Conference on Artificial Intelligence, pp. 817–824. AAAI Press, New Orleans (2018). https://ojs.aaai.org/index.php/AAAI/article/view/11455
14. Wu, J., Bi, J., Bagnulo, M., Baker, F., Vogt, C.: Source address validation improvement (savi) framework. RFC 7039 (2013). https://www.rfc-editor.org/rfc/rfc7039
15. Wu, J., Bi, J., Li, X., Ren, G., Xu, K., Williams, M.: A source address validation architecture (sava) testbed and deployment experience. RFC 5210 (2008). https://www.rfc-editor.org/rfc/rfc5210
16. Wu, J., Ren, G., Li, X.: Source address validation: architecture and protocol design. In: Proceedings of the IEEE International Conference on Network Protocols, pp. 276–283. IEEE, Beijing (2007). https://doi.org/10.1109/ICNP.2007.4375858

Lightweight and Persistent Remote Attestation: Leveraging a Continuous Chain of Trust in Software Integrity Measurements

Florian Kohnhäuser[1], Nicolas Coppik[1(✉)], Christian Göttel[2], and Sören Finster[1]

[1] ABB Corporate Research, Mannheim, Germany
{florian.kohnhaeuser,nicolas.coppik,soeren.finster}@de.abb.com
[2] ABB Corporate Research, Baden-Dättwil, Switzerland
christian.goettel@ch.abb.com

Abstract. A key challenge in Internet of Things deployments is ensuring that devices run legitimate software, free from malware. Remote attestation addresses this challenge by enabling a third party, the verifier, to check the integrity of a remote device, the prover. Existing solutions typically establish a chain of trust in the prover's software during boot. At its root are security properties provided by the prover's hardware, such as an immutable bootloader and secure key storage. Despite being the de facto standard, this method has drawbacks, like the need for secure hardware and the difficulty in detecting advanced self-erasing malware. We present a novel attestation approach that utilizes a continuous trust chain in software integrity measurements. While existing solutions establish a new trust chain at each boot, we propose maintaining the trust chain over reboots of the prover. This provides two main benefits. First, unlike existing approaches, provers no longer need to provide secure hardware key storage. Second, it enables detection of sophisticated attacks, in which malware attempts to evade detection by erasing itself and triggering a reboot of the prover. We also explore disadvantages of our approach, namely, issues in recovering a compromised trust chain as well as an increased attestation overhead. Finally, we present extensions to address both disadvantages and show the security of our solution.

Keywords: remote attestation · minimal secure HW · IoT

1 Introduction

Internet of Things (IoT) deployments typically comprise resource-constrained devices that lack significant security features due to cost considerations. They commonly share the same software stacks and configurations, making them susceptible to scalable attacks when a vulnerability is found. As a result, IOT deployments become prime targets for malware infections [3,7,19]. Infected

Published by Springer Nature Switzerland AG 2025
L. Nemec Zlatolas et al. (Eds.): SEC 2025, IFIP AICT 745, pp. 238–252, 2025.
https://doi.org/10.1007/978-3-031-92882-6_17

devices can be leveraged for various malicious activities, such as being utilized as bots in Distributed Denial of Service (DDoS) attacks, exemplified by the Mirai botnet [3].

Remote attestation (RA) is a promising technique to detect malware, as it allows a verifier to check the software integrity of a remote device, the prover. To ensure a secure attestation, existing solutions rely on a Root of Trust (RoT) that is either software-based [12] or hardware-based [6,18,21]. Over time, software-based solutions have been shown to provide debatable security guarantees [4,5] and have not been adopted by industry. On the other hand, hardware-based attestation establishes solid security guarantees by relying on some form of secure hardware as part of the prover. The prover measures its software, authenticates the measurements with a hardware-protected attestation key, and sends them to the verifier. The verifier validates and compares the received measurements with expected reference measurements to determine whether the software running on the prover is healthy or compromised. This enables the verifier to remotely establish trust in the prover. However, existing hardware-based RA solutions also have shortcomings, of which two are relevant for this work.

First, hardware-based attestation solutions rely on built-in secure hardware on the prover, *e.g.*, a Trusted Platform Module (TPM). Even the most minimal attestation solutions require at least immutable and uninterruptible boot code with exclusive access to a secure key [6,18,21]. However, legacy or low-end devices frequently lack the necessary secure key storage [9].

Second, RA solutions start with a fresh trust chain at each start of the prover, which is extended by conducting and incorporating software integrity measurements during boot and runtime. Although this approach reestablishes trust at each boot, it can allow an attacker to evade detection. For instance, an attacker may infect the prover with malware, perform malicious actions, remove the malware, and then trigger a reboot. If this sequence of actions occurs between two attestation requests from the verifier, the attack will remain undetected.

Contribution. We propose a novel lightweight and persistent hardware-based attestation solution, which introduces the concept of a continuous chain of trust in the prover's software integrity. While existing RA solutions reset the trust chain at each reboot, we propose maintaining it for the lifetime of the prover. The core of our chain of trust is a hash chain that is continuously extended over all software integrity measurements. The verifier detects any malware installed on the prover as it causes the hash chain to deviate from its expected value.

Our solution provides two main benefits: First, provers only require an immutable and uninterruptible boot code, but no secure key storage. These lightweight hardware properties are available on a broad range of devices, enabling attestation on more resource-constrained devices than today. Second, our solution enables reboot-persistent malware detection. Any self-cleaning malware performing a reboot for evading detection by the verifier is identified as the trust chain, and therefore the entire software integrity, is maintained over restarts. We propose extensions and performance improvements to our solution at various trade-offs between hardware requirements and security. Finally, we show the security of our attestation solution against the typical adversary model for RA.

Structure. Section 2 summarizes related work. In Sect. 3, we explain our system and attacker model. Section 4 describes our attestation solution. In Sect. 5, we introduce extensions to our solution. Section 6 concludes our work.

2 Related Work

Remote Attestation. Recent surveys on RA [2,11,14,16] give an overview on existing solutions and their categorization. In the following paragraphs, we elaborate in more detail on software- and hardware-based solutions in order to motive our desirable objective of lightweight attestation with minimal secure hardware.

Software-based attestation [4,12,20] commonly establishes security on precise time measurements without the need for secure hardware, but relies on assumptions that are hard to achieve in practice [4,5]. The verifier measures the time a prover takes to solve a challenge-response network protocol. If the prover takes longer than expected, due to malicious code interfering with the computation, or the response is incorrect, it is regarded as compromised.

Hardware-based attestation provides stronger security guarantees by building on a RoT accessible through secure hardware, such as a TPM [17], Trusted Execution Environment (TEE) [1,16] or Physically Unclonable Functions (PUFs) [15]. The secure hardware prevents malicious code from accessing a secret attestation key or tampering with software integrity measurements. While such secure hardware is nowadays commonly available in servers, desktops, and mid- to high-end embedded systems, it may not be available in low-end and legacy devices.

Attestation with Minimal Hardware Properties. Embedded and IOT devices have limited resources that make implementation of RA functionalities challenging. Minimal attestation solutions for resource-constrained devices have been extensively researched [18] to identify necessary and sufficient properties [6] of required hardware and software features for minimal RA solutions. For example, the Trusted Computing Group (TCG) proposes the Device Identifier Composition Engine (DICE) [21] – a hardware RoT on devices without TPM. DICE defines a layered architecture with the DICE layer at its base, forming a RoT located in read-only memory (ROM) with exclusive access to a so-called Unique Device Secret (UDS). From the UDS, a Compound Device Identifier (CDI) is derived based on measurements of the next boot stage and provided to the first mutable code. Later stages can derive further keys and compute further CDIs based on additional measurements. The CDI and derived keys are ultimately bound to the UDS as well as the device's software integrity. DICE can be used as a foundation for implementing RA schemes [10]. One such scheme is DICEguard [23], which introduces a technique to detect malware that was injected through remote attacks during firmware updates, leveraging hardware-based hash engines for periodic integrity verification of firmware, reducing attestation overhead and preventing time-of-check-time-of-use (TOCTOU) attacks.

3 Background

System Model. We consider two entities: a verifier and a prover. The verifier aims to ensure that the prover's software is in a healthy state, *i.e.*, free from malware or manipulations. To this end, verifier and prover participate in a RA process, in which the verifier validates the prover's software integrity.

The prover is assumed to be a low-cost IOT device, commonly found in smart home devices or industrial applications. These devices typically use single-purpose microcontroller units (MCU) with minimal memory and computing power. They integrate CPU, memory, peripherals, and communication interfaces on a single System on Chip (SoC). The verifier is typically the owner of the prover device or an operator who manages the prover on behalf of the owner.

Attacker Model. We assume an adversary with full control over the network who can eavesdrop, modify, insert, or delete any messages (Dolev-Yao model).

In addition, we assume that the adversary can compromise a prover with malware, *e.g.*, by exploiting a vulnerability in the prover's software. We expect that the adversary has full control over the prover once infected with malware and can read, write, and execute arbitrary data on the prover. However, we assume the adversary cannot bypass hardware protections, and thus, cannot tamper with code, data, or the execution state of hardware-protected memory regions.

We regard physical attacks to be out of scope. Nevertheless, in Sect. 5, we propose and discuss protection mechanisms to defend against simple physical attacks, such as reading out flash memory via debugging interfaces.

Finally, the goal of our attestation solution against the specified adversary is: The adversary must be unable to forge a healthy system state for a prover that is compromised at the time of its attestation or has been compromised in the past.

4 Lightweight Persistent Remote Attestation

In this section, we present our lightweight persistent RA solution. We describe its building blocks, namely, generation of the software integrity trust chain (Sect. 4.1) and measurement log (Sect. 4.2), followed by a description of the attestation protocol (Sect. 4.3), and a security analysis (Sect. 4.4).

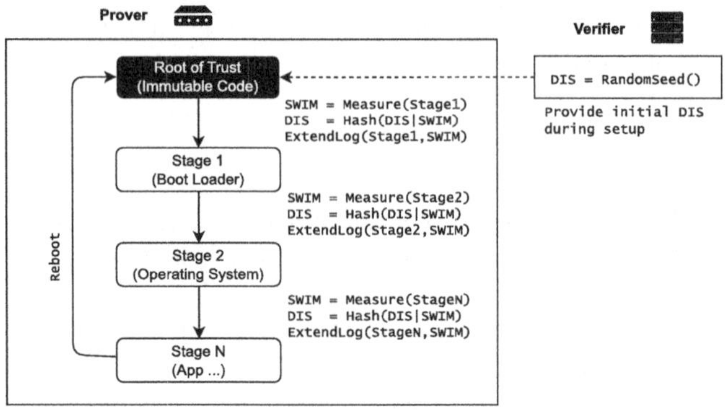

Fig. 1. Our approach for establishing a continuous chain of trust in the prover's integrity.

4.1 Continuous Software Integrity Trust Chain

Core of our novel approach is a continuous chain of trust that gets established in the prover's software integrity measurements. The chain of trust is a hash chain that is computed and extended over all software integrity measurements performed at the prover. Although hash-based chain of trust constructions are *de facto* standard for attestation, our approach introduces two minor, yet significant, changes: (i) the trust chain does not start from zero, but is initialized once with a unique device-dependent value by the verifier, and (ii) the trust chain is continuously maintained, even through reboots of the prover. These extensions enable the advantages provided by our solution. Figure 1 illustrates our approach.

Before a prover can be attested, its chain of trust is initialized once by the verifier. The verifier sets the prover's Device Integrity Secret (DIS) to a cryptographically secure random number $DIS = DIS_{init} = RandomSeed()$. During operation, DIS gets extended through a hash chain incorporating SoftWare Integrity Measurements ($SWIM$) conducted by the prover. Whenever new code is executed, the prover performs a software integrity measurement $SWIM$ for this code and extends DIS by computing $DIS = Hash(DIS|SWIM)$. In this way, a chain of trust is built where one application after the other is measured during boot and runtime of the prover. As opposed to DIS, $SWIMs$ are not secret. They are stored in a measurement log with $ExtendLog(StageN, SWIM)$.

We deliberately abstract from implementation details for computing $SWIMs$ with $Measure()$ to support a wide range of integrity measurement mechanisms. In practice, $Measure()$ is typically implemented as a hash function measuring the binary data of any executable code before it is started, *e.g.*, as implemented in Linux via the Integrity Measurement Architecture (IMA) [17,24].

The trust chain gets extended throughout the entire lifetime of the prover. DIS is stored in non-volatile storage that retains its value during shutdowns of the prover. When extending DIS, it is crucial for security that the previous DIS gets overwritten and cannot leak. An adversary who gets access to a previous DIS that did not (yet) capture the measurement of the adversary's installed malware can break our attestation solution. For this reason, it is crucial that malware cannot evade an integrity measurement $SWIM$, and subsequent extension of DIS with $SWIM$. To ensure this property directly at the prover's start, we utilize the same approach as other hardware-based attestation solutions and protect the initial execution stage by immutable storage, forming our root of trust. For this purpose, the prover must provide ROM for code that is guaranteed to be executed first on every prover reset. This code must be uninterruptible and conducts a $SWIM$ of the first mutable code and extends the trust chain in DIS.

In summary, the described measures ensure that DIS reflects the integrity of all measured software that have ever been executed by the prover, which is a property we leverage for the attestation with the verifier (see Sect. 4.3).

4.2 Measurement Log

The measurement log captures the content and order of all software integrity measurements conducted by the prover. It is required by the verifier during attestation to reconstruct and verify the prover's software integrity trust chain (see Sect. 4.3). Thus, when the prover performs a software integrity measurement $SWIM$, it both extends DIS by $SWIM$ and adds a new entry to the measurement log, exemplified by $ExtendLog(StageN, SWIM)$ in Fig. 1. Figure 2 shows an exemplary measurement log where software gets updated and also compromised over multiple boots of the prover.

An entry in the measurement log may also contain metadata about $SWIM$, such as the software's name, version, or file path. This metadata is not needed

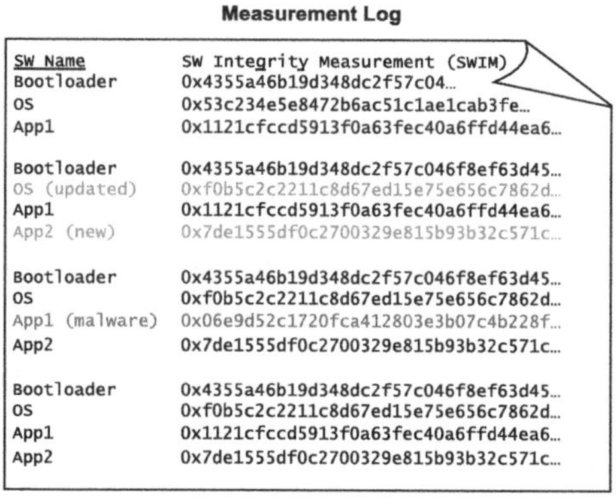

Fig. 2. Illustration of a measurement log. At boot 2, the OS was updated, so its integrity measurement changed, and a new application called App2 was installed (green). At boot 3, App1 was compromised with malware that attempted to evade detection by erasing itself (red). Thus, the original measurement of App1 shows up at boot 4 again. (Color figure online)

for a secure attestation, but it may provide valuable information to the verifier if the attestation fails. For instance, the file path could enable the verifier to track down the location of installed malware at the prover. While malware can potentially tamper with the measurement log and its provided metadata must be treated with caution, this does not pose a security risk for our solution, as the verifier will detect any tampering with the log during attestation (see Sect. 4.4). When extending DIS and the measurement log with a $SWIM$, it is crucial that both steps occur as an atomic operation. Were DIS extended by $SWIM$ but $SWIM$ not captured in the log, or *vice versa,*, the verifier would be unable to reconstruct the trust chain and the attestation would fail. This may happen when both steps are executed sequentially without proper locking and the prover loses power.

4.3 Attestation Protocol

The prover continuously measures its software and extends its trust chain and measurement log. For the actual attestation, prover and verifier execute the challenge-response network protocol shown in Fig. 3. It is similar to existing attestation protocols [22], except it uses the prover's initial DIS and the long-term measurement log to verify the software integrity. The protocol can be executed at any time, in particular also repeatedly at regular time intervals.

To initiate the attestation, the verifier sends the prover a cryptographic nonce N_v (the challenge). The prover derives an attestation key AK from its DIS. To compute its response R to the verifier's challenge, the prover generates a cryptographic nonce N_p, and computes a MAC with the derived AK over the verifier's nonce N_v and the prover's nonce N_p ($R = MAC(AK, N_v|N_p)$). The prover then sends N_p, R, and the measurement log to the verifier.

The verifier uses the received measurement log and its knowledge of the prover's initial device integrity secret DIS_{init} to recompute the prover's expected DIS' by starting with the value $DIS' = DIS_{init}$ and recomputing the hash chain $DIS' = Hash(DIS'|SWIM)$ successively for all entries in the measurement log. The verifier then derives the expected attestation key AK' from DIS' and recomputes the expected response $R' = MAC(AK', N_v|N_p)$. Finally, the verifier compares whether R' matches R and whether the measurement log contains only known-good measurements. To check the latter, the verifier holds a whitelist of

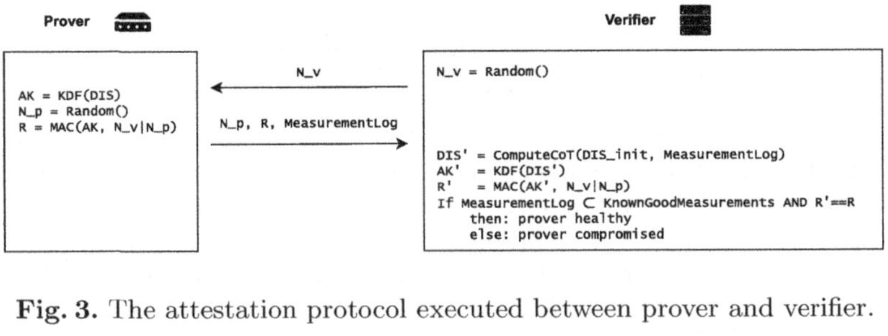

Fig. 3. The attestation protocol executed between prover and verifier.

all known-good software and their corresponding integrity measurements. Only if both response and measurement log are valid, the verifier assumes that the prover is healthy. Otherwise, the verifier assumes that the prover is compromised.

4.4 Security Analysis

Discussion. Since parts of our attestation approach and protocol resemble existing hardware-based attestation solutions, we focus our security analysis on the novel aspects, *i.e.*, the construction of the prover's DIS and the corresponding measurement log. Existing works provide a security analysis of the software integrity trust chain [6,18,21] and attestation challenge-response protocol [22].

As specified in our attacker model (Sect. 3), we consider our solution broken if an adversary passes the attestation with a compromised prover. To achieve this, an adversary requires a DIS that corresponds to a known-good measurement log. During initialization, the DIS_{init} is provided by the verifier. Once it has been extended, the initial or other previous values are not stored on the device anymore. Since extension relies on a cryptographic one-way function, it is impossible to roll back the DIS to a previous state without breaking the security of the one-way function. This leaves an adversary with two ways of obtaining a valid DIS corresponding to a known-good measurement log: Either obtaining DIS_{init} from the verifier or from verifier-prover communication during the initialization phase, or compromising the prover to leak a valid DIS.

We focus on the second of these options as the first is out of scope for this discussion. Per our attacker model (Sect. 3), an adversary may compromise a prover with malware, downloading and executing malicious code. However, since all code gets measured before execution, DIS would be extended with the $SWIM$ of the malicious code prior to execution and no longer correspond to a known-good measurement log. While the measurement log could be modified by the adversary, rolling back DIS is not possible as described above. Therefore, an adversary is not able to exfiltrate a DIS that passes attestation with this approach. Moreover, while the adversary can tamper with all future measurements, the prover will not pass attestation again, including after a reboot (as the trust chain persists across reboots), even if the malicious code is no longer present.

Table 1. Overview which security properties can be realized by built-in secure hardware

Available Secure Hardware Storage	Detect self-erasing malware	Protect simple physical readout	Remotely recover from runtime compromise	Mitigate runtime secret leak
Option 1: ROM Boot Code	✓	✗[a]	✗	✗
Option 2: ROM + SNVS	✓	✓	✗	✗
Option 3: ROM + Read-lockable Key	✓	✓	✓	✗
Option 4: ROM + TPM	✓	✓	✓	✓

[a] Only realizable with strong limitations that renders the protection impractical

Shortcomings. Our solution protects against the commonly defined adversary model for RA, but it also has disadvantages compared to other hardware-based attestation solutions when facing sophisticated runtime attacks, in which the adversary aims to bypass detection. For instance, an adversary may exploit a vulnerability to alter the control flow of benign software and trigger malicious actions, such as exfiltrating the DIS. Other vulnerabilities, like out-of-bound reads, can also allow an adversary to read the DIS. Since such attacks do not involve loading additional code that is subject to integrity measurement, the DIS is not extended, and can still be used to pass attestation. While such attacks are a well-known weak spot for attestation solutions [8], our solution is particularly exposed to them, as it lacks the capability for remote recovery. Hardware-based attestation solutions typically rely on a hardware-protected secret that cannot be leaked, even by sophisticated runtime attacks. This secret can be used to recover trust in the prover if other attestation secrets leak to an adversary. Because our attestation solution does not rely on a hardware-protected key storage, a runtime attack or a physical readout attack (*e.g.*, through a debug interface) may leak all attestation secrets, which makes such attacks unrecoverable from remote. Thus, the verifier can only recover trust in a prover by physically approaching the prover and flashing new secrets to the device, starting a new trust chain.

5 Extensions

This section presents two extensions. We describe how our solution can be extended with secure hardware for enhanced security in Sect. 5.1. We then show how to reduce the performance overhead of attestation in Sect. 5.2.

5.1 Secure Hardware Extensions

In the following, we present four distinct secure hardware configurations, which provide different trade-offs regarding security and required hardware. They range from the basic solution with no secure storage (Option 1) to a fully integrated cryptoprocessor (Option 4). Table 1 provides an overview of the hardware configurations and their entailed security properties.

Option 1: Read-only Memory (ROM) Boot Code

Explanation. Option 1 is the approach described so far, with the prover's boot code stored in ROM and DIS stored in unprotected memory. ROM is available on almost any MCU. Many MCUs provide stronger hardware protection and allow implementing Option 2–4. If such features are available, we recommend using them. In other cases, Option 1 can still be a suitable solution.

Security Analysis. We describe the shortcomings of this option in Sect. 4.4. The main drawback is a weakness against sophisticated runtime attacks. In addition, without secure key storage (see Option 3 and 4), it is impossible to remotely recover our solution, since the verifier would need to set up a new DIS at the prover. Without a shared secret between verifier and prover, *e.g.*, a secret stored in secure key storage, the verifier cannot securely transmit a new DIS to the prover. Thus, to recover from compromise, the verifier needs to physically connect to the prover, erase all memory, flash new software, and initialize a new DIS.

Simple physical readout attacks constitute another security risk. Without secure storage, an adversary may physically access a prover and read out DIS from memory to break our attestation solution.

Option 2: ROM + Secure Non-volatile Storage (SNVS)

Explanation. Option 2 extends our solution by secure non-volatile storage (SNVS) that holds the prover's DIS. The SNVS protects the confidentiality of DIS against simple readout attacks. SNVS is a feature that can be found on a broad range of MCUs, including low-cost devices.

Security Analysis. SNVS prevents an adversary who has physical access to a prover to read DIS (*e.g.*, via SWD) and subsequently break our solution. It does not protect against sophisticated attacks that exfiltrate DIS at runtime, and it does not enable remote recovery of provers whose DIS has leaked.

Option 3: ROM + Read-lockable Key (cf. DICE)

Explanation. Option 3 extends our solution with lockable key storage. This enables the immutable boot code to have exclusive access to a hardware-protected attestation key. Note that these requirements, *i.e.*, ROM and read-lockable key storage, are the minimal secure hardware properties deemed necessary by all existing hardware-based attestation solutions [6,18,21].

Read-lockable key storage is implementable on many MCUs. Existing works propose combining multiple Flash protection mechanisms [13] or leverage memory side effects for an SRAM PUF key storage [18]. However, such workarounds may lead to security pitfalls during implementation as well as features not being available for their original purpose [9]. Dedicated hardware implementations of a read-lockable key storage have been proposed for DICE [9].

We propose combining the approach from DICE [21] with our solution. The prover maintains a UDS that is only known to the verifier and prover, and stored in the prover's lockable key storage. During startup, the immutable boot code accesses and utilizes it to extend DIS with the first software integrity measurement, *i.e.*, $DIS = Hash(UDS|DIS|SWIM)$, incorporating the UDS in the computation of DIS at each boot. To verify the software integrity trust chain, the verifier must also incorporate the UDS when recomputing DIS' during attestation. Further changes to our solution are not necessary.

Security Analysis. The proposed solution provides advantages when facing sophisticated runtime attacks. An adversary who manages to compromise the prover at runtime is no longer able to access the UDS. The adversary may still leak DIS and bypass our attestation solution [8], but we can now easily recover into a trustworthy state by rebooting the prover. The UDS, which is inaccessible to the attacker, is incorporated in the computation of the new DIS. A leaked DIS from a previous boot therefore no longer enables the attacker to compute the new DIS after a reboot. The attacker would need to perform another runtime attack to compromise the prover again, but if the vulnerability is known, a patch can be developed and remotely installed, and, after a reboot, the verifier can remotely ensure that the prover is not running a vulnerable version anymore.

Our hardware-enhanced solution now has the same hardware requirements as DICE, but still provides a distinct advantage: Our solution can detect malware that attempts to hide by erasing itself and rebooting the prover.

Option 4: ROM + Trusted Platform Module

Explanation. Option 4 extends our solution by a TPM that is built-in the prover's device. A TPM provides two valuable features for our solution: (1) It allows a prover to generate and use keys, *e.g.*, for encryption or signing, that never leave the TPM. (2) It allows a prover to extend integrity measurements in a Platform Configuration Registerss (PCRs). PCRs are computed like our DIS, but are additionally protected by secure hardware. An adversary cannot reset PCRs at runtime, only extend them with new measurements. TPMs are common in mid- and high-end embedded systems, but rare in low-end systems.

To utilize the TPM, we propose following a typical TPM-based attestation as presented in [17]. Assuming the TPM can be used exclusively for our solution, we introduce two modifications for reboot-persistent malware detection: (1) We utilize our long-term measurement log (see Sect. 4.2), (2) The TPM PCRs are not reset at reboot or shutdown of the prover device. Typically, the TPM PCRs are reset when the power supply is off or when the system reboots. We propose to supply the TPM with battery power in case the prover is shutdown and not reset the TPM on reboot. Thus, the TPM PCRs are continuously extended, similar to our construction of DIS in Option 1–3.

Security Analysis. Utilizing a TPM mitigates runtime attacks to a certain degree, since the TPM protects the attestation key from being read. An adversary who is capable of reading any memory on the prover at runtime, is no longer able to bypass the attestation solution. However, runtime attacks that modify control flow maliciously can still evade detection by integrity measurements.

Finally, with our modifications, PCRs are never reset. As a result, any malware being captured once in PCRs will eventually be detected by the verifier, ensuring that reboot-persistent malware gets detected.

5.2 Reducing Attestation Overhead

Since IoT devices are usually resource-constrained, keeping attestation overhead low for the prover is crucial. The verifier is not necessarily subject to such constraints, and we do not consider solutions for reducing its overhead here. For the prover, our approach introduces two potential forms of overhead: Network and CPU when the attestation protocol is executed, and storage overhead for the measurement log, which captures the content and order of all software integrity measurements conducted by the prover, throughout the lifetime of the device. To reduce CPU load, the attestation interval can be extended, or execution of the attestation protocol can be scheduled when the system is idle or under low load. The size of the measurement log affects both network and storage overhead. Since it is not reset on reboot of the prover, it continues to grow with each software integrity measurement. For example, a measurement log that only consists of SHA-256 hash sums for the $SWIMs$ can grow to 3 mb after 100 000 $SWIMs$ are added to it. We show two possible solutions to this problem.

Solution 1: Compact Log Entries

This solution focuses on reducing the size of the measurement log as it is stored and transmitted by the prover. The measurement log must at least capture the integrity measurements $SWIMs$, so that the verifier can compute the prover's expected DIS. However, instead of recording the actual value of a $SWIM$, the prover can also only record a compact pointer to each $SWIM$ that allows the verifier to identify and derive its actual value. Compact log entries can consist of unique software identifiers, which are significantly shorter than a $SWIM$. Based on these identifiers, the verifier can retrieve the actual measurements from a database of known-good measurements. This way, an entry in the log can be reduced from 32 bytes (*e.g.*, SHA-256 hash) to only as many bits as are sufficient to uniquely identify all expected $SWIMs$. Depending on the specific use case, it may be sufficient to use 2 bytes for each entry, enough for 65 536 unique measurements. This is a reduction in both storage and network overhead by roughly an order of magnitude.

Moreover, many IOT devices rarely load additional mutable code after completing their boot process and are only rarely rebooted. Even assuming as many as 8 entries for each reboot, this scheme would require just 160 mb after 10 000 reboots, more than would be expected over the lifetime of an IOT device. A further reduction can be achieved by introducing compact pointers to common sequences of $SWIMs$, like those collected during a normal boot process.

Solution 2: Partial Attestation

While the whole measurement log is needed for verification, it is not necessary to keep all of it on the prover. The verifier can store the last received and successfully attested measurement log. Subsequently, the prover only needs to store and transmit the newly added entries for the verifier to have an up to date measurement log for verification. Entries that have been transferred to the verifier can be removed. Note that this prevents attestation by multiple, independent verifiers, unless the removed part of the measurement log can be replaced with a verifiable starting point.

To support such use cases, we propose the following: After attestation, the verifier sends an authenticated command to replace old entries with a specific replacement entry that is verifiable by all verifiers with knowledge of the DIS and includes a starting hash that can be used to verify subsequent entries. This approach limits log size to the delta to the last successful attestation, significantly reducing storage requirements and network overhead and preventing the unbounded growth of the measurement log on the prover.

Note that it is crucial to authenticate the command to replace the measurement log entries. Otherwise, attackers could easily perform a denial of service attack. In addition, the command should be bound to a specific attestation state, so both prover and verifier are synchronized properly. Therefore, the verifier uses the attestation key AK which depends on the current DIS to send the prover an authenticated command: $MAC(AK; N_v|N_p|purgelog|DIS_{ver})$, with $DIS_{ver} = MAC(DIS_{init}; DIS)$. By using DIS_{ver}, the current DIS gets authenticated, such that other verifiers can verify a valid DIS as starting point. Receiving this command, the prover purges the measurement log and saves DIS_{ver}. On subsequent attestations, a verifier either has access to the complete historical measurement log or can use DIS_{ver} to bootstrap verification from the last known-good attestation. In essence, DIS_{ver} can be seen as a placeholder for the measurement log up to the last successful attestation.

6 Conclusion

We presented a novel approach to hardware-based RA in which a continuous chain of trust in software integrity measurements is maintained over the entire lifetime of the prover. Existing works establish a fresh chain of trust in the software integrity at each boot of the prover. This small but significant modification to capture integrity measurements provides two main benefits: 1) self-erasing malware is detected, and 2) hardware requirements have been reduced. In particular, our solution does not rely on a hardware-protected key storage while providing similar security guarantees as existing hardware-based solutions. It can be implemented on resource-constrained embedded devices that lack the secure hardware to implement existing solutions. In addition, we presented lightweight secure hardware extensions to our solution that address shortcomings in mitigating certain kinds of physical and runtime attacks. Furthermore, we proposed a second extension that minimizes the overhead of our solution compared to existing hardware-based solutions.

In future work, analyzing commercial resource-constrained devices regarding their available secure hardware would help to demonstrate the practical relevance of the proposed solution. Additionally, implementing the solution on a target device and making it available as open-source software could further encourage adoption and foster collaboration within both research and industry communities.

References

1. Abera, T., et al.: C-flat: control-flow attestation for embedded systems software. In: Proceedings of the 2016 ACM SIGSAC Conference on Computer and Communications Security, pp. 743–754 (2016)

2. Ambrosin, M., Conti, M., Lazzeretti, R., Rabbani, M.M., Ranise, S.: Collective remote attestation at the internet of things scale: state-of-the-art and future challenges. IEEE Commun. Surv. Tutor. **22**(4), 2447–2461 (2020)
3. Antonakakis, M., et al.: Understanding the mirai botnet. In: 26th USENIX Security Symposium, pp. 1093–1110 (2017)
4. Armknecht, F., Sadeghi, A.R., Schulz, S., Wachsmann, C.: A security framework for the analysis and design of software attestation. In: Proceedings of the 2013 ACM SIGSAC Conference on Computer & Communications Security, pp. 1–12 (2013)
5. Castelluccia, C., Francillon, A., Perito, D., Soriente, C.: On the difficulty of software-based attestation of embedded devices. In: Proceedings of the 16th ACM Conference on Computer and Communications Security, pp. 400–409 (2009)
6. Francillon, A., Nguyen, Q., Rasmussen, K.B., Tsudik, G.: A minimalist approach to remote attestation. In: 2014 Design, Automation & Test in Europe Conference & Exhibition (DATE), pp. 1–6. IEEE (2014)
7. Frustaci, M., Pace, P., Aloi, G., Fortino, G.: Evaluating critical security issues of the iot world: present and future challenges. IEEE Internet Things J. **5**(4), 2483–2495 (2017)
8. Hristozov, S., Wettermann, M., Huber, M.: A toctou attack on dice attestation. In: Proceedings of the Twelfth ACM Conference on Data and Application Security and Privacy, pp. 226–235 (2022)
9. Jäger, L., Petri, R.: Dice harder: a hardware implementation of the device identifier composition engine. In: Proceedings of the 15th International Conference on Availability, Reliability and Security, pp. 1–8 (2020)
10. Jäger, L., Petri, R., Fuchs, A.: Rolling dice: lightweight remote attestation for cots iot hardware. In: Proceedings of the 12th International Conference on Availability, Reliability and Security, pp. 1–8 (2017)
11. Kuang, B., Fu, A., Susilo, W., Yu, S., Gao, Y.: A survey of remote attestation in Internet of Things: attacks, countermeasures, and prospects. Comput. Secur. **112**, 102498 (2022)
12. Li, Y., McCune, J.M., Perrig, A.: Viper: verifying the integrity of peripherals' firmware. In: Proceedings of the 18th ACM Conference on Computer and Communications Security, pp. 3–16 (2011)
13. Lorych, D., Jäger, L.: Design space exploration of dice. In: Proceedings of the 17th International Conference on Availability, Reliability and Security, pp. 1–10 (2022)
14. Makhdoom, I., et al.: Detecting compromised IoT devices: existing techniques, challenges, and a way forward. Comput. Secur. **132**, 103384 (2023)
15. Marastoni, N., Ceccato, M.: Remote attestation of IoT devices using physically unclonable functions: recent advancements and open research challenges. In: Proceedings of the 5th Workshop on CPS&IoT Security and Privacy, CPSIoTSec '23, pp. 25–36. Association for Computing Machinery, New York (2023)
16. Ménétrey, J., et al.: Attestation mechanisms for trusted execution environments demystified. In: Eyers, D., Voulgaris, S. (eds.) Distributed Applications and Interoperable Systems. LNCS, pp. 95–113. Springer, Cham (2022). https://doi.org/10.1007/978-3-031-16092-9_7
17. Sailer, R., Zhang, X., Jaeger, T., Van Doorn, L.: Design and implementation of a tcg-based integrity measurement architecture. In: USENIX Security Symposium, vol. 13, pp. 223–238 (2004)
18. Schulz, S., Schaller, A., Kohnhäuser, F., Katzenbeisser, S.: Boot attestation: secure remote reporting with off-the-shelf IoT sensors. In: Foley, S.N., Gollmann, D.,

Snekkenes, E. (eds.) ESORICS 2017. LNCS, vol. 10493, pp. 437–455. Springer, Cham (2017). https://doi.org/10.1007/978-3-319-66399-9_24
19. Serror, M., Hack, S., Henze, M., Schuba, M., Wehrle, K.: Challenges and opportunities in securing the industrial internet of things. IEEE Trans. Ind. Inf. **17**(5), 2985–2996 (2020)
20. Surminski, S., Niesler, C., Brasser, F., Davi, L., Sadeghi, A.R.: Realswatt: remote software-based attestation for embedded devices under realtime constraints. In: Proceedings of the 2021 ACM SIGSAC Conference on Computer and Communications Security, pp. 2890–2905 (2021)
21. TCG: Specification: Hardware requirements for a device identifier composition engine. Technical Report. Ver 1.0 Rev 0.91, Trusted Computing Group (2018)
22. TCG: Specification: Symmetric identity based device attestation. Technical Report. Ver 1.0 Rev 0.95, Trusted Computing Group (2020)
23. Yamak, Y., Tosun, S., Aydos, M.: Diceguard: enhancing dice security for iot devices with periodic memory forensics. J. Supercomput., 1–21 (2024)
24. Zohar, M., Safford, D.: An overview of the linux integrity subsystem (2010)

Author Index

Published by Springer Nature Switzerland AG 2025
L. Nemec Zlatolas et al. (Eds.): SEC 2025, IFIP AICT 745, pp. 253–254, 2025.
https://doi.org/10.1007/978-3-031-92882-6

The manufacturer's authorised representative in the EU is Springer Nature Customer Service Centre GmbH, Europaplatz 3, 69115 Heidelberg, Germany. If you have any concerns regarding our products, please contact ProductSafety@springernature.com

Printed and bound by CPI Group (UK) Ltd, Croydon, CR0 4YY
30/09/2026
02225589-0010